Philosophy: Adventures on the Frontier of Ignorance

First Edition

Joseph P. White | Santa Barbara City College

HAYDEN
McNEIL

Hayden-McNeil Publishing
14903 Pilot Drive
Plymouth, MI 48170
www.hmpublishing.com

WhiteJ 4825-3 F11

11 AM May 14th Final

Table of Contents

Preface

This short Introduction to Philosophy textbook takes a rather specific philosophical point of view. That philosophical point of view is primarily one of philosophical doubt—uncertainty, but not a commitment to skepticism. Additionally, this textbook recognizes that while a philosophical point of view is deeply personal, its philosophical examination and criticism are not personal. The doubt and uncertainty here is not that of the standard textbook variety of stalemated doubt. So often students are introduced to a number of central philosophical problems, each seeming equally warranted by various pro/con positions presented. In such standard texts, introductory students will confront an extensive array of new-to-them philosophical problems (some hefty texts at 700+ pages full of new-to-them philosophical perplexities), all seemingly stalemated. As a result, students often get bogged down at the very outset of their philosophical studies in ever-subtle conceptual quagmires. In this short textbook, the doubt and uncertainty results from the view that some solutions to some of the central problems of philosophy are rationally preferable to others but remain incomplete, e.g., the abandonment of Cartesian Dualism and the rise of varieties of 20th-century physicalism while recognizing the apparent, nagging role of property dualism.

The point here is that there remains much positive, fascinating, even progressive philosophical work yet to be done. Thus, while apparent incompatibilities persist amongst the various traditional and popular philosophical perspectives, such problems indicate that some *Homo sapiens*, perhaps billions of us, are simply unwarranted in some of our deepest philosophical beliefs. What we believe about the nature and constituents of Reality, the nature and possibility of Knowledge, along with the nature and warrant of Morality, may all be variously riddled with a variety of errors, some real, some only apparent. The point of view in this textbook is that there are no comprehensive philosophical views available in the 21st century that are not without deep, systemic problems, yet some philosophical views do appear rationally preferable, more compelling, than others and some philosophical views should simply be abandoned at this time. These latter views have fossilized into philosophical anachronisms.

As this book develops its point of view, it leaves the student to either work within and further develop that point of view (though tenuous and incomplete it may be) or it encourages the student to react against this developing point of view. In so reacting, the student recognizes and appreciates the burden of proof he or she now bears in formulating an alternative philosophical perspective. The student will examine here some of the traditional, central problems of philosophy through some of its central figures, realizing that Philosophy plays a unique role in attempting to clarify and rationally examine the many incomplete, problematic philosophical perspectives *Homo sapiens* have had and still do have. Thus some of the traditional world religious doctrines will be critically examined and, while fascinating in their conceptual elaborations, will be found to be essentially anachronistic. While knowledge appears possible, it is elusive and hard won. Metaphysical theories such as dualism, as alluded to previously, are highly problematic, and while variously evolving, remain on the defensive at this time in our philosophical history. Morality appears much more complex and rationally compelling in some aspects than popular thinking confusingly would have it as being simply culturally relative and/or essentially a matter of some sort of feeling or emotion. Finally, this textbook, being selective and short, is constructed on the assumption that the student new to Philosophy should embark upon philosophical investigations at a glacial speed guided and enriched in dialogue with a professional philosopher. At such speed, the young mind can take root in the vast historical richness that is our collective philosophical heritage and perhaps more fully appreciate the extensive opportunities available to her or him for further study and philosophical refinement.

In sum, this introductory text operates on the view that it is pedagogically preferable to give the student a somewhat specific point of view, with its own recognized incompleteness and need for further development, to either embrace, at this impressionable period of his or her life, or to rationally react against by clearly articulating its many weaknesses and developing their own, comparably complex, compelling philosophical point of view. Our history would indicate that the complex webs of belief that define our philosophical perspectives contain strands within those webs which intelligent, reasonable people may simply disagree over at this time. By means of questions, philosophers have investigated and tested many of these typically implicit strands. Welcome to *Philosophy: Adventures on the Frontier of Ignorance*.

Introduction

WARNING: If you are a serious, patient thinker, Philosophy can be dangerous. Philosophy courses have been known to change a person's fundamental beliefs pertaining to his or her identity, a variety of typically implicit presuppositions concerning what she or he assumed was knowledge as well as formal affiliations with organized ideologies, faiths, and the like. Please give careful consideration to the potential effects philosophical reflection might have upon you prior to taking this course. If you are disposed toward fanaticism, dogma, or are perversely obstinate, philosophy may not be your best choice. Thank you for your conscientious, mature attention to this serious, existential matter.

While every thinking person has a philosophical perspective relying upon a variety of philosophical assumptions, few people have the philosophical tools for investigating and critiquing their philosophical assumptions. Philosophical reflection is to philosophical systems what nutrition studies are to traditional diets or what modern medicine is to folk medicine. While *Homo sapiens* have evolved with an astounding variety of more or less nutritional diets, it is only in recent history that we have developed the intellectual ability to investigate the subtle strengths and weaknesses of what constitutes nutritional value within traditional diets. As any diet can now be analyzed and critiqued (for example: too much of a particular type of fish and one may consume too much mercury, or a culture's diet may be systemically lacking in a particular vitamin, trace mineral, fiber, etc.), so can traditional philosophical perspectives and their operative assumptions be discovered to lack a degree of intellectual sustenance or epistemic warrant (see Epistemology). Some traditional philosophical perspectives now seem to have had an intellectual viability in bygone eras, when, for example, demons and spirits seemingly roamed a stationary Earth located at the center of an orbiting universe. Now many of the philosophical assumptions of such traditional perspectives no longer prove to be philosophically viable in a 21st century in which demons and spirits have gone apparently philosophically extinct for *Homo sapiens* finding themselves living on a 4.6-billion-year-old planet orbiting a hydrogen-fusing star located in the outer bounds of one of the billions of known galaxies in an expanding 14-billion-year-old universe seemingly permeated with Dark Energy and Dark Matter.

A prominent 20th-century philosopher, W. V. Quine, claimed that *the purpose of philosophy was to make explicit, that which is tacit, to add clarity to vagueness; to discover and resolve paradoxes, to smooth the kinks, to lop-off vestigial growths and to clear ontological slums.* This is what we will be attempting to do this semester. For example, many *Homo sapiens* speak explicitly of a life after death. Presently, scattered about our planet are wars, which involve individuals becoming suicide bombers. Many of these suicide bombers leave behind messages of resolve showing a courageous commitment to political principles and causes they consider noble, even divinely sanctioned. Some of these suicide bombers are considered martyrs for their cause and are assured a special place in a next life often described within their tradition as Paradise. Such views, often with subtle variations, are explicitly stated and widely known throughout the literate world at this time in the early 21st century. Seldom discussed, however, are the central and critical philosophical assumptions which these explicitly stated and acted upon beliefs tacitly or implicitly rest upon. For present purposes, let's briefly discuss the tacit metaphysical assumptions for such actionable and lethal beliefs.

Metaphysics is an area of philosophical study focused upon questions concerning the ultimate nature and constituents of Reality. Science focuses primarily upon reality while Metaphysics focuses upon Reality. For example, Substance Dualism, a metaphysical view with a long, influential history, claims that human beings consist of two quite distinct metaphysical things, typically understood as a physical body and a nonphysical mind/soul/spirit. (Mind/soul/spirit are used interchangeably in this context.) Metaphysical Dualism supports traditional views claiming that the physical body and the nonphysical mind/soul/spirit may have distinct histories. In some versions the mind/soul/spirit exists prior to the existence of the physical body, as in some versions of reincarnation, while in other traditions the mind/soul/spirit lives on past the death of the body with or without having had an existence prior to the physical body. Popularly, the implicit assumption of Substance Dualism allows for a belief that the physical body and the nonphysical mind/soul/spirit have two quite distinct histories with the soul/mind/spirit able to exist without the physical body. Hence, the previously described martyr can go to Paradise after the often-violent destruction of his or her physical body. However, as we shall discover, Substance Dualism, once explicitly examined, is a traditional metaphysical view facing serious challenges and, at this time in our philosophical history, abandoned by many philosophers. Perhaps some other, even incompatible, metaphysical view has greater warrant. Welcome to **Metaphysics**, the philosophical study of the ultimate nature and constituents of Reality.

Adding clarity to vagueness allows the student new to philosophy to discover, for example, that the concept of knowledge requires something more precise than simply believing. The student quickly discovers that having a belief is not the same as possessing knowledge if that belief, even earnestly held, is false. When someone has a false belief and does not know that his or her belief is false, those who do know the belief to be false describe the person holding the false belief as not actually knowing what he or she may think he or she knows. In 2003, President George Bush led the United States into war in the country of Iraq. President Bush and his staff repeatedly warned the American public that Iraqi President Saddam Hussein possessed and was actively seeking weapons of mass destruction to be used either directly against the United States or the weapons were to be provided to international terrorist organizations committed to attacking the United States. It turned out that President Bush and his staff did not know what Saddam Hussein actually possessed in terms of weapons of mass destruction. They thought they knew but they did not actually know. Their ignorance has cost hundreds of thousands of lives and hundreds of billions of dollars. Responsibility for one's ignorance is another complicated conceptual issue also needing implicit or tacit assumptions to be made explicit along with vagueness clarified, but that is not our concern at this moment. It is enough to appreciate at this juncture that no *Homo sapiens* is omniscient or infallible and to believe is not to know. So, if belief alone is not sufficient for having knowledge and something like truth is required, what is truth

and are any other conditions required to possess genuine knowledge? Welcome to **Epistemology**, the philosophical study of knowledge.

In *discovering and attempting to resolve paradoxes*, we find that no philosophical system, including scientific and mathematical systems along with religious systems, are free of paradox and perplexity. While discovering paradoxes and perplexities embedded in our many systems of belief tends to be intellectually exciting for philosophers, some non-philosophers, who tend to fear doubt and uncertainty, tend to find paradoxes threatening. As we shall discover, within the great monotheistic world religions of Judaism, Christianity, and Islam there lurks at the very heart of this shared system a fascinating yet deeply perplexing paradox, traditionally referred to as the Problem of Evil. These three prominent world religions together include billions of *Homo sapiens*. All three traditions trace their lineage to the Old Testament patriarch Abraham. They share a belief in the actual existence of a Supreme Being, variously named but referred to here as God. Their God is supreme in that He, typically regarded as masculine though the implicit assumptions for such masculinity may also be highly problematic, is All Powerful, All Knowing, and All Good. The paradox involved in the Problem of Evil arises in accounting for the possibility of, or more perplexing, the existence of evil, given the existence of this particular Supreme Being. The paradox is that the actual existence of a Being that is All Powerful, All Knowing, and All Good does not seem logically possible given the existence of Evil.

Believers in such a Supreme Being are sometimes tested when confronted with evil. They may ask why so much of our resources, both blood and money, are spent on police, crime prevention, health and medical support, the military, and war when there is a super-surgeon, super-policeman, a super-soldier always on duty. Why does such a God allow the child to be raped or slowly and painfully die of disease as parents and guardians exhaust themselves trying to do the right thing? If a *Homo sapiens* was capable of creating a tsunami that killed hundreds of thousands of children, women, and men and destroyed thousands of homes, wouldn't such an individual be considered a mass murderer? How does such a God escape such a judgment? Many responses have been given for this supremely good God's silence in the face of persistent, deep, and agonizing suffering on the part of His self-described children. Perhaps one of these standard accounts can solve the paradox. Perhaps the paradox can only be solved by abandoning the idea of such a Supreme Being. This will be part of your task this semester as we discover and attempt to resolve such paradoxes.

Some *smoothing of kinks* occurs with **Value Theory**. For example, some *Homo sapiens* seem conceptually confused by an entanglement between morality and ethics. I have listened to animated discussions amongst people perplexed over which of their value judgments are moral and which are ethical. A ready resolution to this perplexing conceptual kink is to adopt the traditional philosophical view that **Ethics** is the philosophical study of morality. Morality is a type of value amongst many other types of values. The claim that, "All value judgments are moral judgments," is false given such different types of evaluation as Law, Aesthetics, Supererogation, Etiquette, perhaps Self-Interest, and others. The question arises in Ethics, "What is morality?" How do we understand the seeming uniqueness of Morality from the Law or Self-Interest, even our enlightened, rational Self-Interest? Morality appears to be such a significant type of value that many disciplines study it, including psychology, sociology, and anthropology. Morality is the value that typically sanctions the taking of life, the going to war. Nonetheless, as you will discover through your philosophical studies, it is the normative focus, the attempt to reasonably or rationally answer the question, "What *ought* I to do?" that distinguishes much of philosophical ethics from the study of morality within the social sciences.

The *lopping-off of vestigial growths* in the contemporary philosophical world may be exemplified by the abandonment of the concept of human nature on the part of a number of contemporary philosophical perspectives. In particular the abandonment of some specific definition of human nature as essential to understanding what The Good Life is for a member of our species. For much of civilized *Homo sapiens'* history a concept of human nature was variously employed to justify or warrant some particular evaluative or metaphysical system either secular or sacred. Thus, one might find, "Humans, by nature, were created to know, love and serve their Creator" or "Humans are by nature seekers of pleasure and avoiders of pain." Such views of human nature then entail, for their adherents, theories as to what the right thing to do is in organizing their individual lives, families, communities, societies and, historically and typically, all of humanity. However, at this time in our collective, philosophical history, it may be the case that these many, often incompatible, views of Human Nature are simply vestigial growths. Perhaps there is nothing of substantial, normative significance that constitutes Human Nature. Shall we simply lop it off?

As we shall discover, the history of philosophy in part began as an attempt to *clear ontological slums.* Ontology is an area of Metaphysics concerned, in part, with understanding what sort of things exist. Slums in this context are dilapidated areas of abandoned, useless ontological junk. Even prior to any philosophical investigation into ontology, *Homo sapiens* with one set of ontological commitments will readily clear the perceived ontological slums of other *Homo sapiens'* ontological commitments by dismissing those other ontological commitments as superstitions. This seems the case many times between monotheists and polytheists. On a grand scale, the debate between atheists and theists, whether the theist is a monotheist or polytheist, is a debate to determine and clear ontological slums. Thales, considered the first philosopher, attempted in the 6th century B.C.E. to clear some ontological slums by laying a new ontological foundation arguing that all things are made of water. Much of pre-Socratic philosophy consisted of various attempts to articulate a defensible ontology.

So, welcome to *Philosophy: Adventures on the Frontier of Ignorance,* where by means of systematic, focused questioning we will delve into what we think we know so *as to make explicit, that which is tacit, to add clarity to vagueness; to discover and resolve paradoxes, to smooth the kinks, to lop-off vestigial growths and to clear ontological slums.* Any questions?

SECTION I

A Love of Wisdom

Paradox and Perplexity: Intellectual Knots in Our Web of Belief

Paradox: When two firmly established beliefs are brought side by side and seen to be contrary or contradictory.

or

An absurd belief that seems to follow from very good reasons.

The basic assumption of philosophical inquiry is that the perplexing paradoxes of life will finally yield to rational resolution.

Paradoxes of Religion

Problem of Evil: How can God, traditionally defined as being all good, all knowing, all powerful, exist given the presence of evil? How could such a Being, also understood as the Creator, create Satan knowing what the seemingly inevitable consequences were?

Problem of Omniscience and Freedom: If God knows everything, thus the future being as "frozen" as the past, how is it possible to choose any action other than that course which is foreordained?

Problem of Omnipotence and Freedom: If we are free to choose our actions then God cannot control our will but if God cannot control our will then God is not omnipotent.

Problem of Omniscience and Omnibenevolence: God cannot be all knowing and all good. If being good includes respecting the rights of others and among these rights is the right to privacy then if I have a right to privacy, there are things about me you have no right to know. If God is all knowing then he violates the right to privacy and hence is not all good. If God is all good then he respects the right to privacy and hence he is not all knowing.

Paradox of Omnipotence: Can God create something so large that he or she or it cannot move it?

Paradoxes of Appearance

Problems of Appearance and Reality: If each of our senses sometimes deceives us and only informs us of how the world appears but not how the world really is, then by what rule or criterion/ criteria do I reasonably distinguish between Appearance and Reality?

Problems of Thought and Object: If thought/ experience is a private, mental act how can it be related to a public, physical world? [As discussed in class—If you believe you dream in images, how are such images (mental, private) to be understood given present scientific descriptions of the brain, e.g., physical, public, neuron function, neural transmitters, etc.? Where are those images? How are such images possible? Where is the self, when we claim to be **SELF**-conscious?]

Paradox of Scepticism: How can it be true that there is no truth? Or how can someone know there is no knowledge?

Paradoxes of Freedom

Problem of Universal Causality: If every event has a cause, as science requires, and my actions constitute events, how can I be said to be free? Is Free Will an illusion to be dispelled by the onset of scientific discovery as was the illusion of the motion of the sun accounted for by the motion of the earth? But then are choice, deliberation, responsibility also illusions or empty concepts?

Paradox of Materialism: If all events are caused and all of my thoughts are events then all of my thoughts are caused. If the relationships between all of my thoughts are causal then there are no logical relationships. If there are no logical relationships among my thoughts then none of my thoughts constitute knowledge, if knowledge is justified (e.g., logically warranted) true belief. Thus if all events are caused, then I cannot know that all events are caused.

Paradoxes of Moral Experience

Problem of Moral Progress: If morality is simply a matter of how a person feels, then how can the elimination of a variety of forms of bigotry, prejudice, racism, etc., constitute moral progress as opposed to simply different moral feelings or practices?

Paradox of Tolerance: If a person claims that morals are relative and thus people should be tolerant of other moral views, then that person has not adopted a morally relative point of view since intolerance is also equally well-warranted on relativistic grounds.

Problem of Moral Evaluation: If it is false that all **value** judgments are moral judgments then what, specifically, is a moral judgment? What distinguishes morality from other types of evaluation?

Paradoxes of Authority

Problem of Obedience to the Law: Sometimes the law conflicts with my self-interest and I know by disobeying the law I will benefit but I know the law is not intended or designed to simply maximize my self-interest, so why is self-interest relevant in disobeying the law?

or

If my self-interest is not the reason for the existence of law then how is my self-interest logically relevant for disobeying the law, when the law conflicts with my self-interest?

Problems of Morality and the Law: If I have a moral duty to obey the law but a law conflicts with morality, what should I do? Is there a moral duty to obey the law?

For your consideration from one of the 20th century's greatest philosophers:

Three great passions, simple but overwhelmingly strong, have governed my life: the longing for love, the search for knowledge, and the unbearable pity for the suffering of mankind...I have sought love because it brings ecstasy... and because it relieves loneliness—that terrible loneliness, in which one shivering consciousness looks over the rim of the world into the cold, unfathomable, lifeless abyss. I have sought knowledge to understand the hearts of man....why the stars shine. And to try and apprehend the Pythagorean power by which number holds sway above the flux.

Love and knowledge, so far as they were possible, led upward toward the heavens. But always pity brought me back to earth. Echoes of cries of pain reverberate in my heart. Children in famine, victims tortured by oppressors, helpless old people a hated burden to their off-spring, and the whole world of loneliness, poverty and pain make a mockery of what human life should be.

This has been my life. I have found it worth living and would gladly live it again, if the chance were offered me.

—Lord Bertrand Russell,
The Autobiography

William K. Clifford

The Ethics of Belief

The danger to society is not merely that it should believe wrong things, though that is great enough; but that it should become credulous, and lose the habit of testing things and inquiring into them; for then it must sink back into savagery.

If a man, holding a belief which he was taught in childhood or persuaded of afterwards, keeps down and pushes away any doubts which arise about it in his mind, purposely avoids the reading of books and the company of men that call into question or discuss it, and regards as impious those questions which cannot easily be asked without disturbing it—the life of that man is one long sin against mankind.

William Kingdon Clifford (1845–1879) was primarily a mathematician making significant contributions in geometry. His primary focus was on non-Euclidean geometry while the primary focus in Cambridge at the time of his studies was on analytic geometry. His article, *On the Space-Theory of Matter* (1870), took the view that energy and matter were intimately related to the curvature of space. As such, Clifford's ideas were significant in the growth of research culminating in *The General Theory of Relativity* (1915) by Albert Einstein.

Having survived a shipwreck on Sicily in 1870, Clifford's opening example in the following reading of a ship owner sending a ship of dubious integrity to sea may account for his stringent principle defended in the article, "It is wrong always, everywhere, and for anyone, to believe anything upon insufficient evidence." Though Clifford writes at length, particularly in chapters following the reading here, providing some precision to the vague idea of "insufficient evidence," it remains the case that virtues such as kindness, justice, and prudence find value not only in pure ignorance but also the possession of false belief, even the instilling and perpetuation of false belief in others.

Considered an insightful and original thinker, Clifford was also respected by friends and colleagues as an eloquent speaker displaying both wit and warmth. In 1876, he suffered a breakdown. He went to the island of Madeira to recover, but died there of tuberculosis, leaving a widow with two children. He died at the age of 33.

From *The Ethics of Belief*. London: Macmillan, 1897, pp. 177–188.

I. The Duty of Inquiry

A shipowner was about to send to sea an emigrant-ship. He knew that she was old, and not overwell built at the first; that she had seen many seas and climes, and often had needed repairs. Doubts had been suggested to him that possibly she was not seaworthy. These doubts preyed upon his mind, and made him unhappy; he thought that perhaps he ought to have her thoroughly overhauled and and refitted, even though this should put him at great expense. Before the ship sailed, however, he succeeded in overcoming these melancholy reflections. He said to himself that she had gone safely through so many voyages and weathered so many storms that it was idle to suppose she would not come safely home from this trip also. He would put his trust in Providence, which could hardly fail to protect all these unhappy families that were leaving their fatherland to seek for better times elsewhere. He would dismiss from his mind all ungenerous suspicions about the honesty of builders and contractors. In such ways he acquired a sincere and comfortable conviction that his vessel was thoroughly safe and seaworthy; he watched her departure with a light heart, and benevolent wishes for the success of the exiles in their strange new home that was to be; and he got his insurance-money when she went down in mid-ocean and told no tales.

What shall we say of him? Surely this, that he was verily guilty of the death of those men. It is admitted that he did sincerely believe in the soundness of his ship; but the sincerity of his conviction can in no wise help him, because he had no right to believe on such evidence as was before him. He had acquired his belief not by honestly earning it in patient investigation, but by stifling his doubts. And although in the end he may have felt so sure about it that he could not think otherwise, yet inasmuch as he had knowingly and willingly worked himself into that frame of mind, he must be held responsible for it.

Let us alter the case a little, and suppose that the ship was not unsound after all; that she made her voyage safely, and many others after it. Will that diminish the guilt of her owner? Not one jot. When an action is once done, it is right or wrong for ever; no accidental failure of its good or evil fruits can possibly alter that. The man would not have been innocent, he would only have been not found out. The question of right or wrong has to do with the origin of his belief, not the matter of it; not what it was, but how he got it; not whether it turned out to be true or false, but whether he had a right to believe on such evidence as was before him.

There was once an island in which some of the inhabitants professed a religion teaching neither the doctrine of original sin nor that of eternal punishment. A suspicion got abroad that the professors of this religion had made use of unfair means to get their doctrines taught to children. They were accused of wresting the laws of their country in such a way as to remove children from the care of their natural and legal guardians; and even of stealing them away and keeping them concealed from their friends and relations. A certain number of men formed themselves into a society for the purpose of agitating the public about this matter. They published grave accusations against individual citizens of the highest position and character, and did all in their power to injure these citizens in their exercise of their professions. So great was the noise they made, that a Commission was appointed to investigate the facts; but after the Commission had carefully inquired into all the evidence that could be got, it appeared that the accused were innocent. Not only had they been accused of insufficient evidence, but the evidence of their innocence was such as the agitators might easily have obtained, if they had attempted a fair inquiry. After these disclosures the inhabitants of that country looked upon the members of the agitating society, not only as persons whose judgment was to be distrusted, but also as no longer to be counted honourable men. For although they had sincerely and conscientiously believed in the charges they had made, yet they had no right to believe on such evidence as was before them. Their sincere

convictions, instead of being honestly earned by patient inquiring, were stolen by listening to the voice of prejudice and passion.

Let us vary this case also, and suppose, other things remaining as before, that a still more accurate investigation proved the accused to have been really guilty. Would this make any difference in the guilt of the accusers? Clearly not; the question is not whether their belief was true or false, but whether they entertained it on wrong grounds. They would no doubt say, "Now you see that we were right after all; next time perhaps you will believe us." And they might be believed, but they would not thereby become honourable men. They would not be innocent, they would only be not found out. Every one of them, if he chose to examine himself in *foro conscientiae*, would know that he had acquired and nourished a belief, when he had no right to believe on such evidence as was before him; and therein he would know that he had done a wrong thing.

It may be said, however, that in both these supposed cases it is not the belief which is judged to be wrong, but the action following upon it. The shipowner might say, "I am perfectly certain that my ship is sound, but still I feel it my duty to have her examined, before trusting the lives of so many people to her." And it might be said to the agitator, "However convinced you were of the justice of your cause and the truth of your convictions, you ought not to have made a public attack upon any man's character until you had examined the evidence on both sides with the utmost patience and care."

In the first place, let us admit that, so far as it goes, this view of the case is right and necessary; right, because even when a man's belief is so fixed that he cannot think otherwise, he still has a choice in the action suggested by it, and so cannot escape the duty of investigating on the ground of the strength of his convictions; and necessary, because those who are not yet capable of controlling their feelings and thoughts must have a plain rule dealing with overt acts.

But this being premised as necessary, it becomes clear that it is not sufficient, and that our previous judgment is required to supplement it. For it is not possible so to sever the belief from the action it suggests as to condemn the one without condemning the other. No man holding a strong belief on one side of a question, or even wishing to hold a belief on one side, can investigate it with such fairness and completeness as if he were really in doubt and unbiased; so that the existence of a belief not founded on fair inquiry unfits a man for the performance of this necessary duty.

Nor is it that truly a belief at all which has not some influence upon the actions of him who holds it. He who truly believes that which prompts him to an action has looked upon the action to lust after it, he has committed it already in his heart. If a belief is not realized immediately in open deeds, it is stored up for the guidance of the future. It goes to make a part of that aggregate of beliefs which is the link between sensation and action at every moment of all our lives, and which is so organized and compacted together that no part of it can be isolated from the rest, but every new addition modifies the structure of the whole. No real belief, however trifling and fragmentary it may seem, is ever truly insignificant; it prepares us to receive more of its like, confirms those which resembled it before, and weakens others; and so gradually it lays a stealthy train in our inmost thoughts, which may someday explode into overt action, and leave its stamp upon our character for ever.

And no one man's belief is in any case a private matter which concerns himself alone. Our lives are guided by that general conception of the course of things which has been created by society for social purposes. Our words, our phrases, our forms and processes and modes of thought, are common property, fashioned and perfected from age to age; an heirloom which every succeeding generation inherits as a precious deposit and a sacred trust to be handled on to the next one, not unchanged but enlarged and purified, with some clear marks of its proper handiwork.

Into this, for good or ill, is woven every belief of every man who has speech of his fellows. An awful privilege, and an awful responsibility, that we should help to create the world in which posterity will live.

In the two supposed cases which have been considered, it has been judged wrong to believe on insufficient evidence, or to nourish belief by suppressing doubts and avoiding investigation. The reason of this judgment is not far to seek: it is that in both these cases the belief held by one man was of great importance to other men. But forasmuch as no belief held by one man, however seemingly trivial the belief, and however obscure the believer, is ever actually insignificant or without its effect on the fate of mankind, we have no choice but to extend our judgment to all cases of belief whatever. Belief, that sacred faculty which prompts the decisions of our will, and knits into harmonious working all the compacted energies of our being, is ours not for ourselves but for humanity. It is rightly used on truths which have been established by long experience and waiting toil, and which have stood in the fierce light of free and fearless questioning. Then it helps to bind men together, and to strengthen and direct their common action. It is desecrated when given to unproved and unquestioned statements, for the solace and private pleasure of the believer; to add a tinsel splendour to the plain straight road of our life and display a bright mirage beyond it; or even to drown the common sorrows of our kind by a self-deception which allows them not only to cast down, but also to degrade us. Whoso would deserve well of his fellows in this matter will guard the purity of his beliefs with a very fanaticism of jealous care, lest at any time it should rest on an unworthy object, and catch a stain which can never be wiped away.

It is not only the leader of men, statesmen, philosopher, or poet, that owes this bounden duty to mankind. Every rustic who delivers in the village alehouse his slow, infrequent sentences, may help to kill or keep alive the fatal superstitions which clog his race. Every hard-worked wife of an artisan may transmit to her children beliefs which shall knit society together, or rend it in pieces. No simplicity of mind, no obscurity of station, can escape the universal duty of questioning all that we believe.

It is true that this duty is a hard one, and the doubt which comes out of it is often a very bitter thing. It leaves us bare and powerless where we thought that we were safe and strong. To know all about anything is to know how to deal with it under all circumstances. We feel much happier and more secure when we think we know precisely what to do, no matter what happens, then when we have lost our way and do not know where to turn. And if we have supposed ourselves to know all about anything, and to be capable of doing what is fit in regard to it, we naturally do not like to find that we are really ignorant and powerless, that we have to begin again at the beginning, and try to learn what the thing is and how it is to be dealt with—if indeed anything can be learnt about it. It is the sense of power attached to a sense of knowledge that makes men desirous of believing, and afraid of doubting.

This sense of power is the highest and best of pleasures when the belief on which it is founded is a true belief, and has been fairly earned by investigation. For then we may justly feel that it is common property, and hold good for others as well as for ourselves. Then we may be glad, not that I have learned secrets by which I am safer and stronger, but that we men have got mastery over more of the world; and we shall be strong, not for ourselves but in the name of Man and his strength. But if the belief has been accepted on insufficient evidence, the pleasure is a stolen one. Not only does it deceive ourselves by giving us a sense of power which we do not really possess, but it is sinful, because it is stolen in defiance of our duty to mankind. That duty is to guard ourselves from such beliefs as from pestilence, which may shortly master our own body and then spread to the rest of the town. What would be thought of one who, for the sake of a sweet fruit, should deliberately run the risk of delivering a plague upon his family and his neighbours?

And, as in other such cases, it is not the risk only which has to be considered; for a bad action is always bad at the time when it is done, no matter what happens afterwards. Every time we let ourselves believe for unworthy reasons, we weaken our powers of self-control, of doubting, of judicially and fairly weighing evidence. We all suffer severely enough from the maintenance and support of false beliefs and the fatally wrong actions which they lead to, and the evil born when one such belief is entertained is great and wide. But a greater and wider evil arises when the credulous character is maintained and supported, when a habit of believing for unworthy reasons is fostered and made permanent. If I steal money from any person, there may be no harm done from the mere transfer of possession; he may not feel the loss, or it may prevent him from using the money badly. But I cannot help doing this great wrong towards Man, that I make myself dishonest. What hurts society is not that it should lose its property, but that it should become a den of thieves, for then it must cease to be society. This is why we ought not to do evil, that good may come; for at any rate this great evil has come, that we have done evil and are made wicked thereby. In like manner, if I let myself believe anything on insufficient evidence, there may be no great harm done by the mere belief; it may be true after all, or I may never have occasion to exhibit it in outward acts. But I cannot help doing this great wrong towards Man, that I make myself credulous. The danger to society is not merely that it should believe wrong things, though that is great enough; but that it should become credulous, and lose the habit of testing things and inquiring into them; for then it must sink back into savagery.

The harm which is done by credulity in a man is not confined to the fostering of a credulous character in others, and consequent support of false beliefs. Habitual want of care about what I believe leads to habitual want of care in others

about the truth of what is told to me. Men speak the truth of one another when each reveres the truth in his own mind and in the other's mind; but how shall my friend revere the truth in my mind when I myself am careless about it, when I believe things because I want to believe them, and because they are comforting and pleasant? Will he not learn to cry, "Peace," to me, when there is no peace? By such a course I shall surround myself with a thick atmosphere of falsehood and fraud, and in that I must live. It may matter little to me, in my cloud-castle of sweet illusions and darling lies; but it matters much to Man that I have made my neighbours ready to deceive. The credulous man is father to the liar and the cheat; he lives in the bosom of this his family, and it is no marvel if he should become even as they are. So closely are our duties knit together, that whoso shall keep the whole law, and yet offend in one point, he is guilty of all.

To sum up: it is wrong always, everywhere, and for anyone, to believe anything upon insufficient evidence.

If a man, holding a belief which he was taught in childhood or persuaded of afterwards, keeps down and pushes away any doubts which arise about it in his mind, purposely avoids the reading of books and the company of men that call into question or discuss it, and regards as impious those questions which cannot easily be asked without disturbing it—the life of that man is one long sin against mankind.

If this judgment seems harsh when applied to those simple souls who have never known better, who have been brought up from the cradle with a horror of doubt, and taught that their eternal welfare depends on what they believe, then it leads to the very serious question, Who hath made Israel to sin?

It may be permitted me to fortify this judgment with the sentence of Milton—

A man may be a heretic in the truth; and if he believe things only because his pastor says so, or the assembly so determine, without knowing other reason, though his belief be true, yet the very truth he holds becomes his heresy.

And with this famous aphorism of Coleridge—

He who begins by loving Christianity better than Truth, will proceed by loving his own sect or Church better than Christianity, and end loving himself better than all.

Inquiry into the evidence of a doctrine is not to be made once for all, and then taken as finally settled. It is never lawful to stifle a doubt; for either it can be honestly answered by means of the inquiry already made, or else it proves that the inquiry was not complete.

"But," says one, "I am a busy man; I have no time for the long course of study which would be necessary to make me in any degree a competent judge of certain questions, or even able to understand the nature of the arguments."

Then he should have no time to believe.

Study Questions

1. What is the story of the ship owner? Why does Clifford find him guilty of the deaths of those at sea on his lost ship?

2. Clifford claims, "If a man, holding a belief which he was taught in childhood or persuaded of afterwards, keeps down and pushes away any doubts which arise about it in his mind, purposely avoids the reading of books and the company of men that call into question or discuss it, and regards as impious those questions which cannot easily be asked without disturbing it—the life of that man is one long sin against mankind." Do you agree or disagree? Can you describe a case in your own life when doubts were raised about a belief of yours and instead of "patient investigation" the doubts were simply stifled?

3. What does Clifford mean when he claims, "The question of right or wrong has to do with the origin of his belief, not the matter of it"?

4. "And no one man's belief is in any case a private matter, which concerns himself alone." What does Clifford mean by this and do you agree? Can you give an example that would support Clifford and one that may count against?

5. "No simplicity of mind, no obscurity of station, can escape the universal duty of questioning all that we believe." Do you agree or disagree with Clifford? Is it actually possible to do what Clifford directs? Could you sit down and make a list of all that you believe? Are there beliefs like your first girlfriend's or boyfriend's hair color that you might overlook or should overlook?

Bertrand Russell

The Value of Philosophy

Bertrand Arthur William Russell, 3rd Earl Russell (1872–1970), British philosopher, historian, and prolific social critic. For contemporary philosopher Colin McGinn (1950–), Russell was both a cultural force and a deeply personal influence. McGinn writes, "Russell had a kind of rock star philosopher's life: Russell made philosophy do for him what music did for, say, John Lennon. They were both romantic public figures, heroes of youth, vocal critics of the establishment, master of the word…Lennon and Russell had eloquence, talent, courage, and style…There was something radical about philosophy—audacious, potent, fundamental…It was Russell who extinguished the last remnants of religiosity from my soul."

A leader of the British revolt against idealism at the turn of the 20th century, Bertrand Russell is considered a founder, along with Gottlob Frege, G.E. Moore, Ludwig Wittgenstein, and others, of what has come to be broadly referred to as analytic philosophy. Analytic philosophy is distinguished in the history of philosophy, and primarily defines contemporary English language philosophy, with its emphasis upon language and conceptual analysis in resolving philosophical problems. Russell and A. N. Whitehead wrote the monumental, three volume *Principia Mathematica* (1910) providing a grounding for mathematics upon logic. Russell's philosophical writings ranged over philosophy of language, epistemology, metaphysics, and logic but his writings also extended to mathematics, set theory, linguistics, education, political theory, religious studies, and history, especially his popular *History of Western Philosophy* (1945), along with the illustrated, coffee table book *Wisdom of the West* (1959).

As a prominent anti-war activist, Russell was briefly imprisoned for six months toward the end of World War I. He did not remain a pacifist during World War II as he opposed Adolf Hitler and supported the Allied effort. He did later oppose the United States' Vietnam War and was an activist in the Ban of the Bomb movement, which focused upon nuclear disarmament. In 1961, Russell spent one week imprisoned for political protests.

By 1940, Russell had married a second time and in that year was appointed professor at the City College of New York, a position he sought but was unable to finally take. After a public outcry concerning his writings relating to sexual morality in his *Marriage and Morals* (1930), an outcry instigated by the mother of a student who would not have been eligible for his graduate-level course in mathematical logic, Russell's appointment was annulled by a court judgment finding him "morally unfit" to teach at the college. As Albert Einstein famously wrote at the time in Russell's support, "Great spirits have always encountered violent opposition from mediocre minds…" In 1949 Russell was awarded the Order of Merit. At that ceremony King George VI was congratulatory but with a respectful reprimand remarked, "You have sometimes

From *The Problems of Philosophy*, New York: Oxford University Press, 1997, pp. 153–161. Reprinted by permission of Oxford University Press, Inc..

behaved in a manner that would not do if generally adopted." Receiving the Nobel Prize in Literature in 1950, the Nobel Committee acknowledged Russell, "in recognition of his varied and significant writings in which he champions humanitarian ideals and freedom of thought."

Married for the fourth time in 1952, after a number of liaisons, Russell died February 2, 1970 at his home in Wales. Cremated in Colwyn Bay, Russell had made it clear there were to be no religious ceremonies and his ashes were to be scattered over the Welsh mountains. The elder Bertrand Russell can be watched on YouTube in a number of interviews. See http://www.youtube.com/watch?v=OziPcicgmbw.

The following reading is from the last chapter of Russell's popular book, *The Problems of Philosophy* (1912). In this paper, Russell initially confronts the "narrowly" practical person who suffers two misconceptions regarding the ends of life and the goods of philosophy. This "narrowly" practical person seems overly focused upon goods of the body and fails to appreciate the goods of the mind. For Russell, the primary good of philosophy is to liberate us from our narrow, instinctive lives. Through philosophy's embrace of questioning, we come to expect uncertainty, thereby increasing what is possible. Through such questioning we are able to philosophically contemplate the universe thereby nurturing a cosmopolitan understanding, an autonomous disposition, so as to become magnanimous beings.

Having now come to the end of our brief and very incomplete review of the problems of philosophy, it will be well to consider, in conclusion, what is the value of philosophy and why it ought to be studied. It is the more necessary to consider this question, in view of the fact that many men, under the influence of science or of practical affairs, are inclined to doubt whether philosophy is anything better than innocent but useless trifling, hair-splitting distinctions, and controversies on matters concerning which knowledge is impossible.

This view of philosophy appears to result, partly from a wrong conception of the ends of life, partly from a wrong conception of the kind of goods which philosophy strives to achieve. Physical science, through the medium of inventions, is useful to innumerable people who are wholly ignorant of it; thus the study of physical science is to be recommended, not only, or primarily, because of the effect on the student, but rather because of the effect on mankind in general. Thus utility does not belong to philosophy. If the study of philosophy has any value at all for others than students of philosophy, it must be only indirectly, through its effects upon the lives of those who study it. It is in these effects, therefore, if anywhere, that the value of philosophy must be primarily sought.

But further, if we are not to fail in our endeavour to determine the value of philosophy, we must first free our minds from the prejudices of what are wrongly called "practical" men. The "practical" man, as this word is often used, is one who recognizes only material needs, who realizes that men must have food for the body, but is oblivious of the necessity of providing food for the mind. If all men were well off, if poverty and disease had been reduced to their lowest possible point, there would still remain much to be done to produce a valuable society; and even in the existing world the goods of the mind are at least as important as the goods of the body. It is exclusively among the goods of the mind that the value of philosophy is to be found; and only those who are not indifferent to these goods can be persuaded that the study of philosophy is not a waste of time.

Philosophy, like all other studies, aims primarily at knowledge. The knowledge it aims at is the kind of knowledge which gives unity and system to the body of the sciences, and the kind which results from a critical examination of the grounds of our convictions, prejudices, and beliefs. But it cannot be maintained that philosophy has had any very great measure of success in its attempts to provide definite answers to its questions. If you ask a mathematician, a mineralogist, a historian, or any other man of learning, what definite body of truths has been ascertained by his science, his answer will last as long as you are willing to listen. But if you put the same question to a philosopher, he will, if he is candid, have to confess that his study has not achieved positive results such as have been achieved by other sciences. It is true that this is partly accounted for by the fact that, as soon as definite knowledge concerning any subject becomes possible, this subject ceases to be called philosophy, and becomes a separate science. The whole study of the heavens, which now belongs to astronomy, was once included in philosophy; Newton's great work was called "the mathematical principles of natural philosophy." Similarly, the study of the human mind, which was a part of philosophy, has now been separated from philosophy and has become the science of psychology. Thus, to a great extent, the uncertainty of philosophy is more apparent than real: those questions which are already capable of definite answers are placed in the sciences, while those only to which, at present, no definite answer can be given, remain to form the residue which is called philosophy.

This is, however, only a part of the truth concerning the uncertainty of philosophy. There are many questions—and among them those that are of the profoundest interest to our spiritual life—which, so far as we can see, must remain insoluble to the human intellect unless its powers become of quite a different order from what they are now. Has the universe any unity of plan or purpose, or is it a fortuitous concourse of atoms? Is consciousness a permanent part of the universe, giving hope of indefinite growth in wisdom, or is it a transitory accident on a small planet on which life must ultimately become impossible? Are good and evil of importance to the universe or only to man? Such questions are asked by philosophy, and variously answered by various philosophers. But it would seem that, whether answers be otherwise discoverable or not, the answers suggested by philosophy are none of them demonstrably true. Yet, however slight may be the hope of discovering an answer, it is part of the business of philosophy to continue the consideration of such questions, to make us aware of their importance, to examine all the approaches to them, and to keep alive that speculative interest in the universe which is apt to be killed by confining ourselves to definitely ascertainable knowledge.

Many philosophers, it is true, have held that philosophy could establish the truth of certain answers to such fundamental questions. They have supposed that what is of most importance in religious beliefs could be proved by strict demonstration to be true. In order to judge of such attempts, it is necessary to take a survey of human knowledge, and to form an opinion as to its methods and its limitations. On such a subject it would be unwise to pronounce dogmatically; but if the investigations of our previous chapters have not led us astray, we shall be compelled to renounce the hope of finding philosophical proofs of religious beliefs. We cannot, therefore, include as part of the value of philosophy any definite set of answers to such questions. Hence, once more, the value of philosophy must not depend upon any supposed body of definitely ascertainable knowledge to be acquired by those who study it.

The value of philosophy is, in fact, to be sought largely in its very uncertainty. The man who has no tincture of philosophy goes through life imprisoned in the prejudices derived from common sense, from the habitual beliefs of his age or his nation, and from convictions which have grown up in his mind without the cooperation or consent of his deliberate reason. To such a man the world tends to become definite, finite, obvious; common objects rouse no questions, and unfamiliar possibilities are contemptuously rejected. As soon as we begin to philosophize, on the contrary, we find, as we saw in our opening chapters, that even the most everyday things lead to problems to which only very incomplete answers can be given. Philosophy, though unable to tell us with certainty what is the true answer to the doubts which it raises, is able to suggest many possibilities which enlarge our thoughts and free them from the tyranny of custom. Thus, while diminishing our feeling of certainty as to what things are, it greatly increases our knowledge as to what they may be; it removes the somewhat arrogant dogmatism of those who have never travelled into the region of liberating doubt, and it keeps alive our sense of wonder by showing familiar things in an unfamiliar aspect.

Apart from its utility in showing unsuspected possibilities, philosophy has a value—perhaps its chief value—through the greatness of the objects which it contemplates, and the freedom from narrow and personal aims resulting from this contemplation. The life of the instinctive man is shut up within the circle of his private interests: family and friends may be included, but the outer world is not regarded except as it may help or hinder what comes within the circle of instinctive wishes. In such a life there is something feverish and confined, in comparison with which the philosophic life is calm and free. The private world of instinctive interests is a small one, set in the midst of a great and powerful world which must, sooner or later, lay our private world in ruins. Unless we can so enlarge our interests as to include the whole outer world, we remain like a garrison in a beleaguered fortress, knowing that the enemy prevents escape and that ultimate surrender is inevitable. In such a life there is no peace, but a constant strife between the insistence of desire and the powerlessness of will. In one way or another, if our life is to be great and free, we must escape this prison and this strife.

One way of escape is by philosophic contemplation. Philosophic contemplation does not, in its widest survey, divide the universe into two hostile camps—friends and foes, helpful and hostile, good and bad—it views the whole impartially. Philosophic contemplation, when it is unalloyed, does not aim at proving that the

rest of the universe is akin to man. All acquisition of knowledge is an enlargement of the Self, but this enlargement is best attained when it is not directly sought. It is obtained when the desire for knowledge is alone operative, by a study which does not wish in advance that its objects should have this or that character, but adapts the Self to the characters which it finds in its objects. This enlargement of Self is not obtained when, taking the Self as it is, we try to show that the world is so similar to this Self that knowledge of it is possible without any admission of what seems alien. The desire to prove this is a form of self-assertion and, like all self-assertion, it is an obstacle to the growth of Self which it desires, and of which the Self knows that it is capable. Self-assertion, in philosophic speculation as elsewhere, views the world as a means to its own ends; thus it makes the world of less account than Self, and the Self sets bounds to the greatness of its goods. In contemplation, on the contrary, we start from the not-Self, and through its greatness the boundaries of Self are enlarged; through the infinity of the universe the mind which contemplates it achieves some share in infinity.

For this reason greatness of soul is not fostered by those philosophies which assimilate the universe to Man. Knowledge is a form of union of Self and not-Self; like all union, it is impaired by dominion, and therefore by any attempt to force the universe into conformity with what we find in ourselves. There is a widespread philosophical tendency towards the view which tells us that Man is the measure of all things, that truth is manmade, that space and time and the world of universals are properties of the mind, and that, if there be anything not created by the mind, it is unknowable and of no account for us. This view, if our previous discussions were correct, is untrue; but in addition to being untrue, it has the effect of robbing philosophic contemplation of all that gives it value, since it fetters contemplation to Self. What it calls knowledge is not a union with the not-Self, but a set of prejudices, habits, and desires, making an impenetrable veil between us and the world beyond. The man who finds

pleasure in such a theory of knowledge is like the man who never leaves the domestic circle for fear his word might not be law.

The true philosophic contemplation, on the contrary, finds its satisfaction in every enlargement of the not-Self, in everything that magnifies the objects contemplated, and thereby the subject contemplating. Everything, in contemplation, that is personal or private, everything that depends upon habit, self-interest, or desire, distorts the object, and hence impairs the union which the intellect seeks. By thus making a barrier between subject and object, such personal and private things become a prison to the intellect. The free intellect will see as God might see, without a *here* and *now*, without hopes and fears, without the trammels of customary beliefs and traditional prejudices, calmly, dispassionately, in the sole and exclusive desire of knowledge—knowledge as impersonal, as purely contemplative, as it is possible for man to attain. Hence also the free intellect will value more the abstract and universal knowledge into which the accidents of private history do not enter, than the knowledge brought by the senses, and dependent, as such knowledge must be, upon an exclusive and personal point of view and a body whose sense-organs distort as much as they reveal.

The mind which has become accustomed to the freedom and impartiality of philosophic contemplation will preserve something of the same freedom and impartiality in the world of action and emotion. It will view its purposes and desires as parts of the whole, with the absence of insistence that results from seeing them as infinitesimal fragments in a world of which all the rest is unaffected by any one man's deeds. The impartiality which, in contemplation, is the unalloyed desire for truth, is the very same quality of mind which, in action, is justice, and in emotion is that universal love which can be given to all, and not only to those who are judged useful or admirable. Thus contemplation enlarges not only the objects of our thoughts, but also the objects of our actions and our affections: it makes us citizens of the universe, not only of one walled city at war with all the rest. In this citizenship of the universe consists man's true freedom, and his liberation from the thraldom of narrow hopes and fears.

Thus, to sum up our discussion of the value of philosophy; Philosophy is to be studied, not for the sake of any definite answers to its questions, since no definite answers can, as a rule, be known to be true, but rather for the sake of the questions themselves; because these questions enlarge our conception of what is possible, enrich our intellectual imagination and diminish the dogmatic assurance which closes the mind against speculation; but above all because, through the greatness of the universe which philosophy contemplates, the mind also is rendered great, and becomes capable of that union with the universe which constitutes its highest good.

Study Questions

1. What would be your parents' reaction if you announced you had decided to major in Philosophy?

2. Who is the "practical" man according to Russell? Can you name and describe anyone you know who would fit Russell's description?

3. Does Russell find a sharp demarcation between Philosophy and Science?

4. Russell claims, "But it cannot be maintained that philosophy has had any very great measure of success in its attempts to provide definite answers to its questions." Then, on the following page, he writes, "...but if the investigations of our previous chapters have not led us astray, we shall be compelled to renounce the hope of finding philosophical proofs of religious beliefs." Is there a conflict between these two claims?

5. Who is the instinctive person according to Russell?

6. What is philosophic contemplation and what affect does it have upon us?

From *The Republic*

Plato's The Myth of the Cave

Plato (427–347 BCE) wrote approximately 36 dialogues in which Socrates (470–399 BCE) is the featured speaker in nearly all of them. While other writers at the time wrote of Socrates, it is Plato's Socrates that is primarily known.

Apparently, Plato traveled throughout the Mediterranean visiting Italy, Sicily, and Egypt. At around the age of forty, Plato returned to Athens and founded his school, The Academy. The Academy lasted for nearly 900 years until 529 CE when it was closed by Pope Justinian I, who considered it a threat to the evangelical mission of Christianity. Among many prominent alumni, Aristotle is perhaps its most illustrious.

Throughout his later life, Plato was entangled in politics. At one time, he visited the city of Syracuse in an attempt to apply his philosophical model. According to an ancient account, during Plato's first trip, Dionysus, the tyrant of Syracuse, turned against Plato and sold him into slavery. In Cyrene, a city at war with Athens, Plato faced death prior to an admirer who bought his freedom. After Dionysius's death, Plato was invited to return to Syracuse to tutor Dionysus II into becoming a philosopher king. Plato this time found himself under house arrest and held against his will. Eventually, Plato left Syracuse, never to return.

According to the 20th-century philosopher A.N. Whitehead, "The safest general characterization of the European philosophical tradition is that it consists of a series of footnotes to Plato. I do not mean the systematic scheme of thought which scholars have doubtfully extracted from his writings. I allude to the wealth of general ideas scattered through them."

The following classic work of Western literature is from Plato's major philosophical work *The Republic*. The selection here, "The Allegory of the Cave," is included as a fascinating characterization of the human experience of moving out of ignorance. Following Russell's *The Value of Philosophy*, Plato's description of the disorienting social process of reluctantly ascending from the bottom of the cave of ignorance can be likened to Russell's description regarding the instinctive person's natural bias toward imposing his own prejudices upon reality prior to a transition toward philosophical contemplation which no longer imposes but invites the universe in by means of questioning.

From "Epistemology and Metaphysics." *The Dialogues of Plato*, Benjamin Jowett, trans. London: The Clarendon Press, 1892, with emendations by the author.

And now, I said, let me show in a figure how far our nature is enlightened or unenlightened:

Behold! Human beings living in an underground cave, which has a mouth open towards the light and reaching all along the cave; here they have been from their childhood, and have their legs and necks chained so that they cannot move, and can only see before them, being prevented by the chains from turning round their heads. Above and behind them a fire is blazing at a distance, and between the fire and the prisoners there is a raised way; and you will see, if you look, a low wall built along the way, like the screen which marionette players have in front of them, over which they show the puppets.

I see.

And do you see, I said, men passing along the wall carrying all sorts of vessels, and statues and figure of animals made of wood and stone and various materials, which appear over the wall? Some of them are talking, others silent.

You have shown me a strange image, and they are strange prisoners.

Like ourselves, I replied; and they see only their own shadows, or the shadows of one another, which the fire throws on the opposite wall of the cave?

True, he said; how could they see anything but the shadows if they were never allowed to move their heads?

And of the objects which are being carried in like manner they would only see the shadows?

Yes, he said.

And if they were able to converse with one another, would they not suppose that they were naming what was actually before them?

Very true.

And suppose further that the prison had an echo which came from the other side, would they not be sure to fancy when one of the passers-by spoke that the voice which they heard came from the passing shadow?

No question, he replied.

To them, I said, the truth would be literally nothing but the shadows of the images.

That is certain.

And now look again, and see what will naturally follow if the prisoners are released and disabused of their error. At first, when any of them is liberated and compelled suddenly to stand up and turn his neck round and walk and look towards the light, he will suffer sharp pains; the glare will distress him, and he will be unable to see the realities of which in his former state he had seen the shadows; and then conceive someone saying to him, that what he saw before was an illusion, but that now, when he is approaching nearer to being and his eye is turned towards more real existence, he has a clearer vision—what will be his reply? And you may further imagine that his instructor is pointing to the objects as they pass and requiring him to name them—will he not be perplexed? Will he not fancy that the shadows which he formerly saw are truer than the objects which are now shown to him?

Far truer.

And if he is compelled to look straight at the light, will he not have a pain in his eyes which will make him turn away to take refuge in the objects of vision which he can see, and which he will conceive to be in reality clearer than the things which are now being shown to him?

True, he said.

And suppose once more, that he is reluctantly dragged up a steep and rugged ascent, and held fast until he is forced into the presence of the sun himself, is he not likely to be pained and irritated? When he approaches the light his eyes will be dazzled, and he will not be able to see anything at all of what are now called realities.

Not all in a moment, he said.

He will require to grow accustomed to the sight of the upper world. And first he will see the shadows best, next the reflections of men and other objects in the water, and then the objects themselves; then he will gaze upon the light of the moon and the stars and the spangled heaven; and he will see the sky and the stars by night better than the sun or the light of the sun by day?

Certainly.

Last of all he will be able to see the sun, and not mere reflections of him in the water, but he will see him in his own proper place, and not in another; and he will contemplate him as he is.

Certainly.

He will then proceed to argue that this is he who gives the season and the years, and is the guardian of all that is in the visible world, and in a certain way the cause of all things which he and his fellows have been accustomed to behold?

Clearly, he said, he would first see the sun and then reason about him.

And when he remembered his old habitation, and the wisdom of the den and his fellow prisoners, do you not suppose that he would felicitate himself on the change, and pity them?

Certainly, he would.

And if they were in the habit of conferring honors among themselves on those who were quickest to observe the passing shadows and to remark which of them went before, and which followed after, and which were together; and who were therefore best able to draw conclusions as to the future, do you think that he would care for such honors and glories, or envy the possessors of them? Would he not say with Homer, "Better to be the poor servant of a poor master," and to endure anything, rather than think as they do and live after their manner?

Yes, he said, I think that he would rather suffer anything than entertain these false notions and live in this miserable manner.

Imagine once more, I said, this person coming suddenly out of the sun to be replaced in his old situation; would he not be certain to have his eyes full of darkness?

To be sure, he said.

And if there were a contest, and he had to compete in measuring the shadows with the prisoners who had never moved out of the cave, while his sight was still weak, and before his eyes had become steady (and the time which would be needed to acquire this new habit of sight might be very considerable), would he not be ridiculous? Men would say of him that up he went and down he came without his eyes; and that it was better not even to think of ascending; and if anyone tried to loose another and lead him up to the light, let them only catch the offender, and they would put him to death.

No question, he said.

This entire allegory, I said, you may now attach, dear Glaucon, to the previous argument; the cave is the world of sight, the light of the fire is the sun, and you will not misapprehend me if you interpret the journey upwards to be the ascent of the soul into the intellectual world according to my poor belief, which, at your desire, I have expressed—whether rightly or wrongly God knows. But, whether true or false, my opinion is that in the world of knowledge the idea of good appears last of all, and is seen only with an effort; and, when seen, is also inferred to be the universal author of all things beautiful and right, parent of light and of the lord of light in this visible world, and the immediate source, of reason and truth in the intellectual; and that this is the power upon which he who would act rationally either in public or private life must have his eye fixed.

I agree, he said, as far as I am able to understand you.

Moreover, I said, you must not wonder that those who attain to this beatific vision are unwilling to descend to human affairs; for their souls are ever hastening into the upper world where they desire to dwell; which desire of theirs is very natural, if our allegory may be trusted.

Yes, very natural.

And is there anything surprising in one who passes from divine contemplations to the evil state of man, misbehaving himself in a ridiculous manner; if, while his eyes are blinking and before he has become accustomed to the surrounding darkness, he is compelled to fight in courts of law, or in other places, about the images or the shadows of images of justice, and is endeavouring to meet the conceptions of those who have never yet seen absolute justice?

Anything but surprising, he replied.

Anyone who has common sense will remember that the bewilderments of the eyes are of two kinds, and arise from two causes, either from coming out of the light or from going into the light, which is true of the mind's eye, quite as much as of the bodily eye; and he who remembers this when he sees anyone whose vision is perplexed and weak, will not be too ready to laugh; he will first ask whether that soul of man has come out of the brighter life, and is unable to see because unaccustomed to the dark, or having turned from darkness to the day is dazzled by excess of light. And he will count the one happy in his condition and state of being, and he will pity the other; or, if he have a mind to laugh at the soul which comes from below into the light, there will be more reason in this than in the laugh which greets him who returns from above out of the light into the den.

That, he said, is a very just distinction.

But then, if I am right, certain professors of education must be wrong when they say that they can put a knowledge into the soul which was not there before, like sight into blind eyes.

They undoubtedly say this, he replied.

Whereas, our argument shows that the power and capacity of learning exists in the soul already; and that just as the eye was unable to turn from darkness to light without the whole body, so too the instrument of knowledge can only by the movement of the whole soul be turned from the world of becoming into that of being, and learn by degrees to endure the sight of being, and of the brightest and best of being, or in other words, of the good.

Very true.

And must there not be some art which will effect conversion in the easiest and quickest manner; not implanting the faculty of sight, for that exists already, but has been turned in the wrong direction, and is looking away from the truth?

Yes, he said, such an art may be presumed.

And whereas the other so-called virtues of the soul seem to be akin to bodily qualities, for even when they are not originally innate they can be implanted later by habit and exercise, the virtue of wisdom more than anything else contains a divine element which always remains, and by this conversion is rendered useful and profitable; or, on the other hand, hurtful and useless.

Notice what happens when the philosopher leaves the cave. He becomes, literally, enlightened. But he has lived so long in the darkness, among the shadows, that his eyes have grown accustomed to the dark and so now he cannot see the truth, the real sun; reality blinds rather than illuminates him. At first. But then if he does not give in to fear but remains in the blinding light that obliterates everything—if he can stand being surrounded by an apparent nothingness until he, literally, comes to his senses a new and brilliant world of absolute truth and ultimate being reveals itself. What then?

The philosopher, if he is a true lover of wisdom, is unselfish and does not remain outside the cave. He must go back into the cave and try to enlighten the others. So he stumbles back into the dark. He tries to tell the others but they think he is a fool; they want him to prove that he has attained true wisdom and enlightenment by, for instance, predicting the patterns of the shadows on the cave wall. He cannot even see them! He clumsily knocks into things; the philosopher is blind in the darkness they call light.

Study Questions

1. What is the story in the "Allegory of the Cave"?

2. What is the difference between allegorical truth and historical truth? In our time, how should the Bible be understood? As allegory or history?

3. According to Plato, are humans curious by nature?

4. Does Plato see the transition from ignorance as primarily an isolated undertaking or a social process?

5. Would you conclude from this allegory that Plato is an optimist or pessimist?

6. Since you have been involved in the educational process for as many as 12 years, write your Allegory. Don't write about people locked in a theatre, glued to their seats and only able to watch one show—that would be a cheap, derivative rip-off. Be creative so that people for hundreds of generations will want to read and share your writing.

SECTION II

What's Going On?

Introduction

In this section, you will study how different groups of *Homo sapiens* conceive of what they considered to be the ultimate nature of reality. How reality, or at least this world, came about and what the meaning of this life came to be for them. These constitute metaphysical views but do not involve metaphysical analysis as philosophers today research metaphysics. At this juncture, issues of knowledge are also not primary but rather the attempt, as Aristotle remarked, of an educated person being able to entertain another person's thought without having to believe it. As you already know, *Homo sapiens* have believed many different and mutually conflicting narratives regarding this world and their role in it. Throughout history and up to the present, these comprehensive narratives at times collide, often with ensuing violence culminating in war. Usually the violence results from these narratives being ethnocentrically protected.

From the selections provided here, ask if the story told involves supernatural elements or beings, or is it simply natural? If it is a supernatural story, is it monotheistic or polytheistic? Are the gods or the God male, female, both, neither? Is the conception of reality embodied in the narrative static or dynamic? By static it is meant that the story told is one set in a rather familiar world and that what is foremost in the narrative is the story of the human drama and not the world that drama occurs in. Thus in the case of the story of Genesis in the Bible, that conception of reality is essentially static in that the Garden of Eden is located in a familiar, to this day, geographical area, between rivers still so named and the animals created are all familiar as well. Hence, what is significant to the Genesis narrative is the human drama as it unfolds in a basically static reality. On the other hand, when you read the scientific account of reality it is quite dynamic. *Homo sapiens* are one episode in a highly changing environment, which at one time appeared nothing as it does today and at a future time will appear nothing as it does today. Once you have studied these many narratives, you will want to check your epistemic sense to understand if one seems to you at this early stage more warranted or justified than the others.

Egyptian Book of the Dead

The dead will say:

Homage to you, Great God, the Lord of the double Ma'at (Truth)!

I have come to you, my Lord,

I have brought myself here to behold your beauties.

I know you, and I know your name,

And I know the names of the two and forty gods,

Who live with you in the Hall of the Two Truths,

Who imprison the sinners, and feed upon their blood,

On the day when the lives of men are judged in the presence of Osiris.

In truth, you are "The Twin Sisters with Two Eyes," and "The Daughters of the Two Truths."

In truth, I now come to you, and I have brought Ma'at to you,

And I have destroyed wickedness for you.

I have committed no evil upon men.

I have not oppressed the members of my family.

I have not wrought evil in the place of right and truth.

I have had no knowledge of useless men.

I have brought about no evil.

I did not rise in the morning and expect more than was due to me.

I have not brought my name forward to be praised.

I have not oppressed servants.

I have not scorned any god.

I have not defrauded the poor of their property.

I have not done what the gods abominate.

I have not caused harm to be done to a servant by his master.

I have not caused pain.

I have caused no man to hunger.

I have made no one weep.

I have not killed.

I have not given the order to kill.

I have not inflicted pain on anyone.

I have not stolen the drink left for the gods in the temples.

I have not stolen the cakes left for the gods in the temples.

I have not stolen the cakes left for the dead in the temples.

I have not fornicated.

I have not polluted myself.

I have not diminished the bushel when I've sold it.

I have not added to or stolen land.

Chapter 125, The Judgment of the Dead. *Introduction.* From: http://www.wsu.edu/~dee/EGYPT/BOD125. HTM. Reprinted with permission.

I have not encroached on the land of others.

I have not added weights to the scales to cheat buyers.

I have not misread the scales to cheat buyers.

I have not stolen milk from the mouths of children.

I have not driven cattle from their pastures.

I have not captured the birds of the preserves of the gods.

I have not caught fish with bait made of like fish.

I have not held back the water when it should flow.

I have not diverted the running water in a canal.

I have not put out a fire when it should burn.

I have not violated the times when meat should be offered to the gods.

I have not driven off the cattle from the property of the gods.

I have not stopped a god in his procession through the temple,

I am pure.

I am pure.

I am pure.

I am pure.

My purity is the purity of the great Bennu (heron) in Heracleopolis.

Behold, I am the nose of the God of Breath, who gives life to the people,

On the day of completing the Eye of Ra in Heliopolis,

On the last day of the second month of winter,

In the presence of the pharaoh of this land.

I have seen the the Eye of Horus when it was full in Heliopolis!

Therefore, let no evil befall me in this land

In this Hall of the Two Truths,

Because I know the names of all the gods within it,

And all the followers of the great God.

The Creation and the Fall

In the beginning God created the heaven and the earth. And the earth was without form, and void; and darkness was upon the face of the deep. And the Spirit of God moved upon the face of the waters. And God said, Let there be light: and there was light. And God saw the light, that it was good: and God divided the light from the darkness. And God called the light Day, and the darkness he called Night. And the evening and the morning were the first day.

And God said, Let there be a firmament in the midst of the waters, and let it divide the waters from the waters. And God made the firmament, and divided the waters which were under the firmament from the waters which were above the firmament: and it was so. And God called the firmament Heaven. And the evening and the morning were the second day.

And God said, Let the waters under the heaven be gathered together unto one place, and let the dry land appear: and it was so. And God called the dry land Earth; and the gathering together of the waters called he Seas: and God saw that it was good. And God said, Let the earth bring forth grass, the herb yielding seed, and the fruit tree yielding fruit after his kind, whose seed is in itself, upon the earth: and it was so. And the earth brought forth grass, and herb yielding seed after his kind, and the tree yielding fruit, whose seed was in itself, after his kind: and God saw that it was good. And the evening and the morning were the third day.

And God said, Let there be lights in the firmament of the heaven to divide the day from the night; and let them be for signs, and for seasons, and for days, and years: And let them be for lights in the firmament of the heaven to give light upon the earth: and it was so. And God made two great lights; the greater light to rule the day, and the lesser light to rule the night: he made the stars also. And God set them in the firmament of the heaven to give light upon the earth. And to rule over the day and over the night, and to divide the light from the darkness: and God saw that it was good. And the evening and the morning were the fourth day.

And God said, Let the waters bring forth abundantly the moving creature that hath life, and fowl that may fly above the earth in the open firmament of heaven. And God created great whales, and every living creature that moveth, which the waters brought forth abundantly, after their kind, and every winged fowl after his kind: and God saw that it was good. And God blessed them, saying, Be fruitful, and multiply, and fill the waters in the seas, and let fowl multiply in the earth. And the evening and the morning were the fifth day.

And God said, Let the earth bring forth the living creature after his kind, cattle, and creeping thing, and beast of the earth after his kind: and it was so. And God made the beast of the earth after his kind, and cattle after their kind, and every thing that creepeth upon the earth after his kind: and God saw that

From the book of Genesis, The Bible. Source: http://www.gutenberg.org/cache/epub/10/pg10.txt

it was good. And God said, Let us make man in our image, after our likeness: and let them have dominion over the fish of the sea, and over the fowl of the air, and over the cattle, and over all the earth, and over every creeping thing that creepeth upon the earth. So God created man in his own image, in the image of God created he him; male and female created he them. And God blessed them, and God said unto them, Be fruitful, and multiply, and replenish the earth, and subdue it: and have dominion over the fish of the sea, and over the fowl of the air, and over every living thing that moveth upon the earth. And God said, Behold, I have given you every herb bearing seed, which is upon the face of all the earth, and every tree, in the which is the fruit of a tree yielding seed; to you it shall be for meat. And to every beast of the earth, and to every fowl of the air, and to every thing that creepeth upon the earth, wherein there is life, I have given every green herb for meat: and it was so. And God saw every thing that he had made, and, behold, it was very good. And the evening and the morning were the sixth day.

Thus the heavens and the earth were finished, and all the host of them.

And on the seventh day God ended his work which he had made; and he rested on the seventh day from all his work which he had made. And God blessed the seventh day, and sanctified it: because that in it he had rested from all his work which God created and made. These are the generations of the heavens and of the earth when they were created, in the day that the LORD God made the earth and the heavens, And every plant of the field before it was in the earth, and every herb of the field before it grew: for the LORD God had not caused it to rain upon the earth, and there was not a man to till the ground. But there went up a mist from the earth, and watered the whole face of the ground. And the LORD God formed man of the dust of the ground, and breathed into his nostrils the breath of life; and man became a living soul. And the LORD God planted a garden eastward in Eden; and there he put the man whom he had formed. And out of the ground made the LORD God to grow every tree that is pleasant to the sight, and good for food; the tree of life also in the midst of the garden, and the tree of knowledge of good and evil.

And a river went out of Eden to water the garden; and from thence it was parted, and became into four heads. The name of the first is Pison: that is it which compasseth the whole land of Havilah, where there is gold; And the gold of that land is good: there is bdellium and the onyx stone. And the name of the second river is Gihon: the same is it that compasseth the whole land of Ethiopia. And the name of the third river is Hiddekel: that is it which goeth toward the east of Assyria. And the fourth river is Euphrates.

And the LORD God took the man, and put him into the garden of Eden to dress it and to keep it. And the LORD God commanded the man, saying, Of every tree of the garden thou mayest freely eat: But of the tree of the knowledge of good and evil, thou shalt not eat of it: for in the day that thou eatest thereof thou shalt surely die. And the LORD God said, It is not good that the man should be alone; I will make him an help meet for him. And out of the ground the LORD God formed every beast of the field, and every fowl of the air; and brought them unto Adam to see what he would call them: and whatsoever Adam called every living creature, that was the name thereof. And Adam gave names to all cattle, and to the fowl of the air, and to every beast of the field; but for Adam there was not found an help meet for him. And the LORD God caused a deep sleep to fall upon Adam, and he slept: and he took one of his ribs, and closed up the flesh instead thereof; And the rib, which the LORD God had taken from man, made he a woman, and brought her unto the man. And Adam said,

This is now bone of my bones, and flesh of my flesh: she shall be called Woman, because she was taken out of Man.

Therefore shall a man leave his father and his mother, and shall cleave unto his wife: and they shall be one flesh. And they were both naked, the man and his wife, and were not ashamed.

Now the serpent was more subtil than any beast of the field which the LORD God had made. And he said unto the woman, Yea, hath God said, Ye shall not eat of every tree of the garden? And the woman said unto the serpent, We may eat of the fruit of the trees of the garden: But of the fruit of the tree which is in the midst of the garden, God hath said, Ye shall not eat of it, neither shall ye touch it, lest ye die. And the serpent said unto the woman, Ye shall not surely die: For God doth know that in the day ye eat thereof, then your eyes shall be opened, and ye shall be as gods, knowing good and evil. And when the woman saw that the tree was good for food, and that it was pleasant to the eyes, and a tree to be desired to make one wise, she took of the fruit thereof, and did eat, and gave also unto her husband with her; and he did eat. And the eyes of them both were opened, and they knew that they were naked; and they sewed fig leaves together, and made themselves aprons.

And they heard the voice of the LORD God walking in the garden in the cool of the day: and Adam and his wife hid themselves from the presence of the LORD God amongst the trees of the garden. And the LORD God called unto Adam, and said unto him, Where art thou? And he said, I heard thy voice in the garden, and I was afraid, because I was naked; and I hid myself. And he said, Who told thee that thou wast naked? Hast thou eaten of the tree, whereof I commanded thee that thou shouldest not eat? And the man said, The woman whom thou gavest to be with me, she gave me of the tree, and I did eat. And the LORD God said unto the woman, What is this that thou hast done? And the woman said, The serpent beguiled me, and I did eat. And the LORD God said unto the serpent,

> Because thou hast done this, thou art cursed above all cattle, and above every beast of the field; upon thy belly shalt thou go, and dust shalt thou eat all the days of thy life: And I will put enmity between thee and the woman, and between thy seed and her seed; it shall bruise thy head, and thou shalt bruise his heel.

Unto the woman he said,

> I will greatly multiply thy sorrow and thy conception; in sorrow thou shalt bring forth children; and thy desire shall be to thy husband, and he shall rule over thee.

And unto Adam he said,

> Because thou hast hearkened unto the voice of thy wife, and hast eaten of the tree, of which I commanded thee, saying, Thou shalt not eat of it: cursed is the ground for thy sake; in sorrow shalt thou eat of it all the days of thy life; Thorns also and thistles shall it bring forth to thee; and thou shalt eat the herb of the field; In the sweat of thy face shalt thou eat bread, till thou return unto the ground; for out of it wast thou taken: for dust thou art, and unto dust shalt thou return.

And Adam called his wife's name Eve; because she was the mother of all living. Unto Adam also and to his wife did the LORD God make coats of skins, and clothed them. And the LORD God said, Behold, the man is become as one of us, to know good and evil: and now, lest he put forth his hand, and take also of the tree of life, and eat, and live for ever: Therefore the LORD God sent him forth from the garden of Eden, to till the ground from whence he was taken. So he drove out the man; and he placed at the east of the garden of Eden Cherubims, and a flaming sword which turned every way, to keep the way of the tree of life.

Robert Baum

Indigenous Religions: Africa

If archaeologists are correct in believing that the first human beings came from Africa, then it stands to reason that the first religions also originated there. For decades, a succession of archaeological finds in East Africa, between Ethiopia and Tanzania, has been pushing back the date for the earliest human presence in the region. But evidence regarding religion is scanty at best. Excavations of Paleolithic burial sites, dating back as far as 100,000 years, have revealed that bodies were placed in the ground with faces turned towards the setting sun, and were often painted with ochre. These practices suggest that early humans valued their dead and may have linked their passage out of life to the setting of the sun, while the personal items (such as hunting weapons, tools, or food) often placed in the grave with the body suggest a belief in some form of afterlife. Graves from the end of the Paleolithic Age, approximately 10,000 years ago, sometimes contain animal bones that appear to have been heated until they cracked—perhaps so that a diviner could study the patterns and use them to foresee the future or understand the causes of current problems. Discoveries such as these suggest that the earliest humans were concerned with making an uncertain world more predictable and controllable.

As early as 10,000 years ago, Saharan and southern African rock paintings depicted people hunting various types of animals. Some of these scenes include images of figures with rays coming out of their heads. Commentators have suggested that the latter represent a freely circulating spiritual power that some powerful individuals were able to tap. But we cannot know what these images meant for the people who painted them. Even if the culture in question has an oral tradition explaining the origins of the world, for example, it may provide little information on religious practices or the nature of the deities, spirits, or powers that were active in the formative period. It is also possible that, as the earliest humans slowly migrated to other areas of Africa and other continents of the world, they carried with them religious ideas and practices that originated in quite different places.

Africa is the world's second largest continent, stretching from the Mediterranean Sea in the north to the southern reaches of the Atlantic Ocean. Through most of its history, the area north of the Sahara Desert had close connections with the Mediterranean and Middle Eastern cultural regions, and most of its peoples were converted to either Christianity or Islam during the first eight centuries of the Common Era. The Saharan and sub-Saharan regions, however, had relatively little contact with the Mediterranean world. Today the sub-Saharan region is home to the world's largest concentrations of indigenous practitioners—perhaps as many as 200 million.

The first Europeans to visit sub-Saharan Africa were Portuguese navigators who explored the western coastline in their

From *A Concise Introduction to World Religions*, Willard G. Oxtoby & Alan F. Segal, eds., Oxford University Press, 2007, pp. 15–22. Reprinted by permission of Oxford University Press, Inc.

search for a sea route to India and the Spice Islands during the Age of Discovery. Some explorers recorded vivid descriptions of African rituals, though their lack of a shared language and the brevity of their visits made their interpretations questionable. With the beginning of the Atlantic slave trade in the late fifteenth century, European accounts of Africa became increasingly lurid, describing "brutal" rituals that made the idea of slavery more palatable to Europeans. Some claimed that Africans had no religion at all and maintained that the rituals described by early travellers were only "superstitions." The German philosopher Georg Friedrich Hegel (1770–1831) described Africa as a land without history, a place of sorcery and superstition.

By the late 1800s European scholars were developing evolutionary theories that traced the origins of religion to Africa. Such theories typically saw humanity as progressing in stages from "primitive" African beliefs in multiple gods and spirits to the final flowering of Western monotheism. Thus Edward Tylor saw Africans as animists, believing that there were souls in all things. Charles de Brosses and James Frazer thought that Africans worshipped objects endowed with special powers; these objects they called fetishes. Others suggested that Africans were polytheists, worshippers of many gods who were often represented by statues and masks. These images filtered into Western popular culture. The ballet *Petrouchka* (1911) includes a character called the Blackamoor who worships a coconut, and more recent notions of African religions have been shaped by Hollywood movies, from the Tarzan series to Jim Carrey's *When Nature Calls*. The anthropologist E.E. Evans-Prichard described the standard "recipe":

> A reference to cannibalism, a description of Pygmies (by preference with a passing reference to Herodotus), a denunciation of the inequities of the slave trade, the need for the civilizing influence of commerce, something about rain-makers and other superstitions, some sex

(suggestive though discreet), add snakes and elephants to taste; bring slowly to the boil and serve (Evans-Prichard cited in Ray 1976:3)

These were my first images of African religions as well. They reflected the long history of slave trading, colonization, and Western ethnocentrism, which tended to minimize the creative genius of African peoples.

African Religious Thought

So what are African religions really like? First, it is important to recognize that the continent is home to more than a thousand distinct religious traditions. Their diversity reflects the diversity of the communities in which they developed, each of which has its own history, patterns of contact with other cultures, ecological environment, and economic system. One thing they have in common, however, is a focus on life in this world, on human communities and their immediate environments. Reflecting that focus, they are strongly instrumental in emphasis, seeking direct assistance from deities, spirits, or ancestors who might be able to ease the difficulties of daily life.

African religions also share a focus on a supreme being, what English-speakers would call God, who is seen as the source of all life. Individual traditions differ on whether the supreme being actually created the world or delegated that task to subordinates. The Yoruba of Nigeria and Benin maintain that Olodumare, the lord of the heavens, delegated the creation to lesser gods called *orisha*, while the Dogon of Mali believe that their supreme being, Amma, began the task of creating the world but left it to be completed by spirits known as Nummo, also created by Amma. The Nuer and Dinka of the southern Sudan, the BaMbuti of Congo, and the Khoisan of South Africa, for their part, all emphasize that the supreme being alone was responsible for creation. The fact that almost every African ethnic group already had a term for the supreme being made it relatively easy for nineteenth-century missionaries to translate the Christian idea of 'God.'

Different traditions also differ in their views of the role that the supreme being plays in the daily affairs of their communities. The Yoruba tradition suggests that Olodumare reigns but does not rule—just as the Yoruba kings are sacred symbols of the townships that they oversee but do not rule their city-states. Similarly, the Igbo of southeastern Nigeria have a saying—'God is like a rich man, you approach him through his servants'—that suggests their supreme being is far removed from human beings and has created lesser spirits, divine servants, to handle specific types of problems. In both cases, the implication is that humans should avoid appealing to the supreme being except in matters of great importance or when appeals to lesser spirits have repeatedly failed. To ask the supreme being for help with minor concerns like getting a job or winning a football game would be to show an arrogance bordering on blasphemy.

Most African religious communities do not have specific shrines for the worship of the supreme being, though they have many shrines dedicated to the lesser spirits or deities whose job it is to assist humans in daily life. This pattern has created the false impression in the West that the supreme being is not central to African religious life. On the contrary, it shows both the people's reverence for the supreme being, who has no need of sacrificial offerings, and their recognition of how insignificant their concerns are in the context of the universe. (Sometimes the supreme being is male, sometimes female, sometimes both, but there are no gendered pronouns in West African languages.)

The matters that are controlled by the supreme being are the most critical ones: the life transitions of birth and death, and the precious, life-sustaining resource that is water. Many traditions maintain that the supreme being is the source of the vital force that enters into a woman's womb to create life. For the Dogon of Mali and Burkina Faso, that force—nyama—originates with the supreme being, Amma, and flows throughout the universe. For the Yoruba, conception occurs when the supreme being Olodumare allows the spirit of an ancestor seeking rebirth to enter a woman and assigns the unborn infant a fate that determines the broad outlines of his or her life. Particularly in regions where rainfall is scarce, the supreme being also gives or withholds rain depending on the community's ethical conduct and fulfillment of ritual obligations. In most African religions, the supreme being judges people after death and assigns them to an afterlife of either punishment or reward, depending on their conduct in life. Most people, however, are eventually reincarnated and return to the living community in a never-ending cycle of life and death.

The precise nature of the lesser gods and spirits varies. The Nuer people of Sudan regard them as emanations of the supreme being and use the same term for both: the supreme being is called Kwoth Nhial, while lesser spirits are known simply as "kwoth." Among the Yoruba, lesser spirits have distinct personalities, extraordinary independence, and rich bodies of sacred traditions or myths describing their activities. By contrast, the Bantu-speaking peoples of Equatorial, East, and southern Africa tend to emphasize the importance of ancestors, people who, having led basically good lives, have passed into the realm of the dead but continue to influence the lives of their living descendants. Eventually, they may be reborn within their own lineages or extended families. In societies with traditions of kingship, like the Buganda of Uganda and the BaKongo of Angola and Congo, royal ancestors have major shrines dedicated to their memory.

In much of West Africa the lesser deities have their own elaborate mythologies. The Yoruba recognize 401 orisha, each of which has a unique personality and history, a distinct set of duties, and special preferences for ritual offerings and behaviour by followers. Oduduwa, for example, is an orisha who completed the creation of the world after his brother Obatala got drunk and fell asleep. Oduduwa eventually became the king of Ile-Ife, the place where the world was created and the oldest of the Yoruba cities. His sister Oshun is associated with women's fertility, sexuality, and beauty, and has acquired the additional powers of her male husbands or lovers. The *orisha* can possess their devotees, mounting them as if they were horses and using their bodies to make themselves present and communicate necessary information. The *orisha* continue to develop new functions in community life. Thus Ogun, the god of iron and war, has come to be associated with the protection of metal workers, car mechanics, and chauffeurs. Shopona, a goddess traditionally associated with smallpox, became linked with HIV-AIDS when smallpox was eradicated and AIDS became a grave threat. At the same time Yoruba religion reserves a vital role for ancestors, people who have crossed over into the realm of the spirit and who continue to assist their living descendants. Throughout most of Yorubaland, the ancestors can become physically present in masked dances.

Trickster deities are particularly important in West Africa. The trickster is not a force for evil, but one who loves chaos and disorder. He encourages impulsive behavior in humans and often acts impulsively himself, disrupting any kind of social order. For instance, tricksters often serve as messengers for the other gods and purposely make minor changes in their messages so that they can enjoy the resulting confusion. In Dogon religion the Pale Fox or Jackal, a sibling of the Nummo, not only disrupts earthly existence but also possesses the power to see into the future and discern the causes of disorder in the distant past.

The Yoruba trickster, Eshu, is the messenger god who summons the other *orisha* to attend all major rituals in Yoruba religion. Eshu delights in forgetting parts of messages or changing them in small ways, just to see what will happen. He loves to play tricks on human beings, whose greed, laziness, or desire makes them easy to fool. He is also described as a kind of perpetual adolescent, over-sexed and promiscuous.

Christian missionaries, who saw good and evil as locked in eternal conflict, often associated tricksters like Eshu with Satan, but for the Yoruba the forces that enhance life and detract from it are commingled. These radically different worldviews are often described as 'conflict' and 'complementary' dualism. African religions (like most indigenous religions) generally tend towards the 'complementary' model.

Ritual

The purpose of rituals such as prayer, animal sacrifice, offerings of grain and libations of palm wine, water, or milk is to communicate with gods or spirits. Such ceremonies release life forces that nourish the gods and spirits, who then return those life forces to those seeking assistance. In turn, the participants in the ritual commit themselves to the purpose of the ceremony by consuming the food and libations after they have been offered to the gods. In this way the ritual nourishes all the participants, divine and human. Sacrifices may be offered for fertility (of crops, livestock, or humans), for adequate rain, for healing, for protection against dangerous tasks or witchcraft, or to ensure a successful transition from one life stage to another.

The rituals associated with life transitions—events such as puberty, marriage, birth, and death—are often referred to as rites of passage. Many of these rituals have a three-stage structure. In the first stage the initiates are separated from their familiar world; for example, boys entering puberty may eat a last meal with their mothers before attending a ceremony in which they prepare to separate from the community for a time. The second stage is often described as one of liminality (from the Latin for 'threshold'). It is during this marginal stage, when initiates are between life phases, that much of the work of the transition or passage takes place. Initiates are instructed in their new religious and social responsibilities, and develop a feeling of solidarity with other initiates that the anthropologist

Victor Turner has called 'communitas.' Finally they are reintegrated into their communities, with the added powers and responsibilities of their new status.

Throughout Africa, special containers are used to hold ritual libations, and special spears and knives are used for animal sacrifices and preparation of the ritual meals that follow. Of all the material objects used in rituals, however, the ones that have attracted the most attention are images of gods and ancestors in the form of statues and masks. Non-Africans have dismissed such images as idols—objects of worship in themselves—based on the erroneous assumption that the image contains the god. In some cases statues of gods are ritually prepared with special medicines to summon the presence of the god, but the god can be present in many places at once and is never contained by an object.

There has been a similar confusion about the masks used in ritual dances. Activation of the dancers' spiritual power may allow them to receive the presence of the gods, spirits, or ancestors represented by the masks they wear, but the dancer's body is merely a temporary dwelling place. The masks bring the god, spirit, or ancestor into the community, sometimes symbolically, sometimes by displacing the conscious mind of the dancer so that the deity or ancestor may speak through him or her, but the mask is only a vehicle that allows the spiritual power to manifest itself.

The design of masks and statues is highly symbolic. Thus spirits associated with women's fertility tend to be depicted with faces that represent idealized forms of beauty, and their bodies have large hips and breasts that evoke the ability to bear and nourish children. Masks of spirits that protect against malevolent forces, such as witches, often emphasize their power to terrorize spirits and humans alike.

Witchcraft

In many African traditions witchcraft serves to explain the presence of evil and suffering in the world. Witches are believed to be people whose souls travel outside their bodies to attack and consume other people's souls or objects that are considered valuable. There is no material evidence for witchcraft. It takes place entirely in the realm of the soul. For evidence, witch-finders typically look to dreams, visions, or divination, though sometimes suspects will be forced to drink special witch-finding beverages believed to be capable of making the guilty fall ill or die. Witchcraft is also used to explain chance misfortune—the sort of thing that Westerners call 'bad luck.' For example, Azande elders told the anthropologist Evans-Pritchard of a man who took a nap under a corn crib and was crushed to death when the crib collapsed. While the immediate cause of death did not need explaining, the fact that the crib collapsed while the victim was sleeping under it was attributed to witchcraft.

In many instances the society of witches is envisioned as the exact opposite of ordinary existence. Diola witches, for instance, organize in hierarchical and authoritarian groups, in stark contrast to ordinary Diola society, which emphasizes egalitarianism and opposes any concentration of authority in a single person or group. Similarly among the Yoruba, in ordinary society women are subordinate, but female witches can wield extraordinary power over men. Although most societies recognize witches of both sexes, some believe that witchcraft is restricted to either women or men. These variations may reflect tensions between the sexes, or competition between various social groups.

Richard Hooker

The Historical Siddhartha

The other major challenge to orthodox Vedism was founded by the son of a chief of a region called the Shakyas. This region lay among the foothills of the Himalayas in the farthest northern regions of the plains of India in Nepal. This founder, Siddhartha Gautama, the Buddha, has many legends and stories that have accreted around his life. While we can't be certain which of these stories and legends are true and which of the thousands of sayings attributed to him were actually said by him, we do know that the basic historical outlines of his life are accurate.

He was the chief's son of a tribal group, the Shakyas, so he was born a Kshatriya around 566 BC. At the age of twenty-nine, he left his family in order to lead an ascetic life. A few years later he reappears with a number of followers; he and his followers devote their lives to "The Middle Way," a lifestyle that is midway between a completely ascetic lifestyle and one that is world-devoted. At some point he gained "enlightenment" and began to preach this new philosophy in the region of Bihar and Uttar Kadesh. His teaching lasted for several decades and he perished at a very old age, somewhere in his eighties. Following his death, only a small group of followers continued in his footsteps.

Calling themselves bhikkus, or "disciples," they wandered the countryside in yellow robes (in order to indicate their bhakti, or "devotion" to the master). For almost two hundred years, these followers of Buddha were a small, relatively inconsequential group among an infinite variety of Hindu sects. But when the great Mauryan emperor, Asoka, converted to Buddhism in the third century BC, the young, inconsequential religion spread like wildfire throughout India and beyond. Most significantly, the religion was carried across the Indian Ocean (a short distance, actually) to Sri Lanka. The Buddhists of Sri Lanka maintained the original form of Siddhartha's teachings, or at least, they maintained a form that was most similar to the original.

While in the rest of India, and later the world, Buddhism fragmented into a million sects, the original form, called Theravada Buddhism, held its ground in Sri Lanka.

That's all we know about the historical life of Siddhartha, his mission, and the fate of his teachings. When we move into the Buddhist histories, the record becomes much more uncertain, particularly since the events of the Buddha's life vary from sect to sect.

What follows, however, is the most common outline of the nature of Siddhartha's life and philosophy. When Siddhartha Gautama was born, a seer predicted that he would either become a great king or he would save humanity. Fearing that his son would not follow in his footsteps, his father raised Siddhartha in a wealthy and pleasure-filled palace in order to shield his son from any experience of human misery or suffering. This, however, was a futile project, and when Siddhartha saw four sights: a sick man, a poor man,

The Historical Siddhartha. From: http://www.wsu.edu/~dee/BUDDHISM/BUDDHISM.HTM. Reprinted with permission.

a beggar, and a corpse, he was filled with infinite sorrow for the suffering that humanity has to undergo.

After seeing these four things, Siddhartha then dedicated himself to finding a way to end human suffering. He abandoned his former way of life, including extreme asceticism. So harsh was this way of life that he grew thin enough that he could feel his hands if he placed one on the small of his back and the other on his stomach. In this state of wretched concentration, in heroic but futile self-denial, he overheard a teacher speaking of music. If the strings on the instrument are set too tight, then the instrument will not play harmoniously. If the strings are set too loose, the instrument will not produce music. Only the middle way, not too tight and not too loose, will produce harmonious music. This chance conversation changed his life overnight. The goal was not to live a completely worldly life, nor was it to live a life in complete denial of the physical body, but to live in a Middle Way. The way out of suffering was through concentration, and since the mind was connected to the body, denying the body would hamper concentration, just as overindulgence would distract one from concentration.

With this insight, Siddhartha began a program of intense yogic meditation beneath a pipal tree in Benares. At the end of this program, in a single night, Siddhartha came to understand all his previous lives and the entirety of the cycle of birth and rebirth, or samsara, and most importantly, figured out how to end the cycle of infinite sorrow. At this point, Siddhartha became the Buddha, or "Awakened One." Instead, however, of passing out of this cycle himself, he returned to the world of humanity in order to teach his new insights and help free humanity of their suffering.

His first teaching took place at the Deer Park in Benares. It was there that he expounded his "Four Noble Truths," which are the foundation of all Buddhist belief:

1. All human life is suffering (dhukka).

2. All suffering is caused by human desire, particularly the desire that impermanent things be permanent.

3. Human suffering can be ended by ending human desire.

4. Desire can be ended by following the "Eightfold Noble Path": right understanding, right thought, right speech, right action, right livelihood, right effort, right mindfulness, and right concentration.

From a metaphysical standpoint, these Noble Truths make up and derive from a single fundamental Truth (in Sanskrit, Dharma, and in Pali, Dhamma). The Buddhist Dharma is based on the idea that everything in the universe is causally linked. All things are composite things, that is, they are composed of several elements. Because all things are composite, they are all transitory, for the elements come together and then fall apart. It is this transience that causes human beings to sorrow and to suffer. We live in a body, which is a composite thing, but that body decays, sickens, and eventually dies, though we wish it to do otherwise. Since everything is transient, that means that there can be no eternal soul either in the self or in the universe. This, then, is the eternal truth of the world: everything is transitory, sorrowful, and soulless—the three-fold character of the world.

As pessimistic as this sounds, the philosophy of Siddhartha Gautama is a kind of therapy. In fact, classifying it in Western terms is impossible. We think of Buddhism as a religion, which it unquestionably became, but Siddhartha was less concerned with theology or ritual or prayer as he was with providing a tool for individuals to use to escape suffering. The goal of this method, the Eightfold Noble Path, is the elimination of one's desires and one's attachment to one's self. Once one has understood correctly the nature of the universe (Right Understanding) and devoted one's life to selfless and altruistic actions (Right

Action) and, finally, by losing all sense of one's self and by losing all one's desires, one then passes into a state called Nirvana (in Pali, Nibbana). The word means "snuffed out" in the way a fire is snuffed out or extinguished. At this point, the self no longer exists.

It is not folded into a higher reality nor is it transported to a land of bliss, it simply ceased at his death.

Like Jainism, then, Buddhism centrally concerns the problem of the eternal birth and rebirth of the human soul. Unlike Jainism, Buddhism in its original form does not posit some transcendent alternative as a goal. In fact, Buddhism in its original form held that the soul actually died when the body died. How, then, could a soul pass from body to body?

What passed from body to body was a chain of causes set in motion by each soul; the Buddhist philosopher Nagsena said it was like a flame passing from candle to candle. The individual, in snuffing out the self, brings those chain of causes to an end.

A large part of the program prescribed by Buddha involved selflessness in the world. Buddhism represents one of the most humane and advanced moral systems in the ancient world. The first steps on the road to Nirvana were to focus one's actions on doing good to others. In this way one could lose the illusion that one is a unique self. The Buddhist scriptures disapprove of violence, meat-eating, animal sacrifice, and war. Buddha enjoined on his followers four moral imperatives: friendliness, compassion, joy, and equanimity, the "Four Cardinal Virtues."

This is the philosophy that Buddha left the world. In the years following his death, the teachings began to slowly develop into various sects. Buddhism became so fragmented that barely one hundred years after the death of Siddhartha, a council of Buddhists was called to straighten out the differences. The earliest forms of Buddhism, which are now only practiced by a small minority, are called Theravada, or "The Teachings of the Elders."

From the Upanishads

Creation of the World from the Self

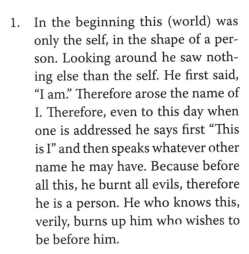

1. In the beginning this (world) was only the self, in the shape of a person. Looking around he saw nothing else than the self. He first said, "I am." Therefore arose the name of I. Therefore, even to this day when one is addressed he says first "This is I" and then speaks whatever other name he may have. Because before all this, he burnt all evils, therefore he is a person. He who knows this, verily, burns up him who wishes to be before him.

2. He was afraid. Therefore one who is alone is afraid. This one then thought to himself, "Since there is nothing else than myself, of what am I afraid?" Thereupon his fear, verily, passed away, for of what should he have been afraid? Assuredly it is from a second that fear arises.

3. He, verily, had no delight. Therefore he who is alone has no delight. He desired a second. He became as large as a woman and a man in close embrace. He caused that self to fall into two parts. From that arose husband and wife. Therefore, as Yājñavalkya used to say, this (body) is one half of oneself, like one of the two halves of a split pea. Therefore this space is filled by a wife. He became united with her. From that human beings were produced.

4. She thought, "How can he unite with me after having produced me from himself?" Well, let me hide myself. She became a cow, the other became a bull and was united with her and from that cows were born. The one became a mare, the other a stallion. The one became a she-ass, the other a he-ass and was united with her; and from that one-hoofed animals were born. The one became a she-goat, the other a he-goat, the one became a ewe, the other became a ram and was united with her and from that goats and sheep were born. Thus, indeed, he produced everything whatever exists in pairs, down to the ants.

5. He knew, I indeed am this creation for I produced all this. Therefore he became the creation. He who knows this as such comes to be in that creation of his.

6. Then he rubbed back and forth and produced fire from its source, the mouth and the hands. Both these (mouth and the hands) are hairless on the inside for the source is hairless on the inside. When they (the people) say "sacrifice to him," "sacrifice to the other one," all this is his creation indeed and he himself is all the gods. And now whatever is moist, that he produced from semen, and that is Soma. This whole (world) is just food and the eater of food. Soma is food and fire is the eater of food. This is the highest creation of *Brahma*, namely, that he created the gods who are superior to him. He, although mortal himself,

"Creation of the World from the Self: The Fourth Brahman," from *The Principal Upanishads*, S. Radhakrishnan, trans. London: George Allen & Unwin, 1953, pp. 163–173.

created the immortals. Therefore it is the highest creation. Verily, he who knows this becomes (a creator) in this highest creation.

7. At that time this (universe) was undifferentiated. It became differentiated by name and form (so that it is said) he has such a name, such a shape. Therefore even today this (universe) is differentiated by name and shape (so that it is said) he has such a name, such a shape. He (the self) entered in here even to the tips of the nails, as a razor is (hidden) in the razor-case, or as fire in the fire-source. Him they see not for (as seen) he is incomplete, when breathing he is called the vital force, when speaking voice, when seeing the eye, when hearing the ear, when thinking the mind. These are merely the names of his acts. He who meditates on one or another of them (aspects) does not know, for he is incomplete, with one or another of these (characteristics). The self is to be meditated upon for in it all these become one. This self is the foot-trace of all this, for by it one knows all this, just as one can find again by footprints (what was lost). He who knows this finds fame and praise.

8. That self is dearer than a son, is dearer than wealth, is dearer than everything else and is innermost. If one were to say to a person who speaks of anything else than the Self as dear that he will lose what he holds dear, he would very likely do so. One should meditate on the Self alone as dear. He who meditates on the Self alone as dear, what he holds dear, verily, will not perish.

9. They say, since men think that, by the knowledge of *Brahman*, they become all, what, pray, was it that *Brahman* knew by which he became all?

10. *Brahman*, indeed, was this in the beginning. It knew itself only as "I am *Brahman*." Therefore it became all. Whoever among the gods became awakened to this, he, indeed, became that. It is the same in the case of seers, the same in the case of men. Seeing this, indeed, the seer Vāma-deva knew, "I was Manu and the Sun, too." This is so even now. Whoever knows thus, "I am *Brahman*," becomes this all. Even the gods cannot prevent his becoming thus, for he becomes their self. So whoever worships another divinity (than his self) thinking that he is one and (*Brahman*) another, he knows not. He is like an animal to the gods. As many animals serve a man so does each man serve the gods. Even if one animal is taken away, it causes displeasure, what should one say of many (animals)? Therefore it is not pleasing to those (gods) that man should know this.

Richard Hooker

On the Aztec

The term, Aztec, is a startlingly imprecise term to describe the culture that dominated the Valley of Mexico in the fifteenth and sixteenth centuries. Properly speaking, all the Nahua-speaking peoples in the Valley of Mexico were Aztecs, while the culture that dominated the area was a tribe of the Mexica (pronounced "me-shee-ka") called the Tenochca ("te-noch-ka"). At the time of the European conquest, they called themselves either "Tenochca" or "Toltec," which was the name assumed by the bearers of the Classic Mesoamerican culture. The earliest we know about the Mexica is that they migrated from the north into the Valley of Mexico as early as the twelfth century AD, well after the close of the Classic Period in Mesoamerica. They were a subject and abject people, forced to live on the worst lands in the valley. They adopted the cultural patterns (called Mixteca-Pueblo) that originated in the culture of Teotihuacán, so the urban culture they built in the fifteenth and sixteenth centuries is essentially a continuation of Teotihuacán culture.

As stated in the section on the Toltecs, the peoples of Mesoamerica distinguished between two types of people: the Toltec (which means "craftsman"), who continued Classic urban culture, and the Chichimec, or wild people, who settled Mesoamerica from the north. The Mexica were, then, originally Chichimec when they migrated into Mexico, but eventually became Toltecs proper.

The history of the Tenochca is among the best preserved of the Mesoamericans. They date the beginning of their history to 1168 and their origins to an island in the middle of a lake north of the Valley of Mexico. Their god, Huitzilopochtli, commanded them on a journey to the south and they arrived in the Valley of Mexico in 1248. According to their history, the Tenochca were originally peaceful, but their Chichimec ways, especially their practice of human sacrifice, revolted other peoples who banded together and crushed their tribe. In 1300, the Tenochcas became vassals of the town of Culhuacan; some escaped to settle on an island in the middle of the lake. The town they founded was Tenochtitlan, or "place of the Tenochcas."

Tenochtitlan Ruins, Mexico City

Relations between the Tenochcas and Culhuacan became bitter after the Tenochcas sacrificed a daughter of the king of Culhuacan; so enraged were the Culhuacans that they drove all the Tenochcas from the mainland to the island. There, the Tenochcas who had lived in Culhuacan taught urban culture and architecture to the peoples on the island and the Tenochcas began to build a city. The city of Tenochtitlan was founded, then, sometime between 1300 and 1375.

The Tenochcas slowly became more powerful and militarily more skilled, so much so that they became allies of choice in the constant conflicts between

The Mexica/Aztecs. From: http://www.wsu.edu/~dee/CIVAMRCA/CIVAMRCA.HTM. Reprinted with permission.

the various peoples of the area. The Tenoch-cas finally won their freedom under Itzacoatl (1428–1440), and they began to build their city, Tenochtitlan, with great fervor. Under Itzacoatl, they built temples, roads, a causeway linking the city to the mainland, and they established their government and religious hierarchy. Itzacoatl and the chief who followed him, Mocteuzma I (1440–1469), undertook wars of conquest throughout the Valley of Mexico and the southern regions of Vera Cruz, Guerrero, and Puebla. As a result, Tenochtitlan grew dramatically: not only did the city increase in size, precipitating the need for an aqueduct system to bring water from the mainland, it grew culturally as well as the Tenochcas assimilated the gods of the region into their religion.

A succession of kings followed Mocteuzma I until the accession of Mocteuzma II in 1502; despite a half century of successful growth and conquest, Tenochca culture and society began to suffer disasters under Mocteuzma II. First, tribute peoples conquered territories and it is highly likely that Tenochca influence would eventually have declined by the middle of the sixteenth century. Most importantly, the reign of Mocteuzma II was interrupted by the invasion of the Spaniards under Cortez in 1519–1522. The Spaniards kidnapped Mocteuzma and eventually killed him in 1524. When the city of Tenochtitlan fell, the remainder of Mexico fell very rapidly. The Spaniards managed this conquest for several reasons. First, Aztec conquest was not concerned with political or territorial influence; the conqests only had to do with the payment of tribute. There was, then, a large group of subject peoples with no loyalty to Tenochtitlan and a lot of hostility. Cortez conquered Tenochtitlan largely by using these enmities. Second, the Aztecs had nothing like formal military strategy; wars were largely fought as large-scale individual combats. Finally, Cortez and his men were desperate; they had entered Mexico against orders and knew that, unless they conquered Mexico, that they would be severely punished when they returned.

Economy and Society

The economy of Tenochtitlan was built off of one overwhelming fact: the urban population on the island required high levels of economic support from surrounding areas. In its earliest history, Tenochtitlan was self-supporting; the village was small and agriculture was managed through the chinampa method of architecture, practiced widely throughout Mesoamerica. In the chinampa, flat reeds were placed in the shallow areas of the lake, covered with soil, and then cultivated. In this way, the Aztecs reclaimed much of the lake for agriculture. A large part of the city's population were farmers; at its height (100,000–300,000), at least half the population would leave the city in the morning to go farm and return in the evening.

The city itself consisted of a large number of priests and craftspeople; the bulk of the economy rested on extensive trade of both necessary and luxury items. Tenochtitlan was a true urban center. It had a permanent population, it had a large and bustling market (the Spanish estimated that at least 60,000 people crowded the market), and it had the beginnings of economic class for the kinship groups of the city were divided up into calpulli, many of which practiced a specific craft or trade, such as rope-making or pot-making. While there is a great deal of controversy over the precise nature of the capulli, it seems to be a transition point between kinship organization (the calpulli were kinship groups) and economic class (the calpulli specialized in particular crafts). In addition, the calpulli seemed to be arranged in ranks: there was the highest calpulli, another five calpulli that had schools for nobility, and then all the rest.

The Aztecs did have two clearly differentiated social classes. At the bottom were the macehualles, or "commoners," and at the top the pilli, or nobility. These were not clearly differentiated by birth, for one could rise into the pilli by virtue of great skill and bravery in war.

All male children went to school. At the age of 15, each male child went to telpuchcalli ("house of youth"), where he learned the history and religion of the Aztecs, the art of war and fighting, the trade or craft specific to his calpulli, and the religious and civic duties of everyday citizenship. The children of nobility also attended another school, a school of nobility or calmecac, if he was a member of one of the top six calpulli. There the child learned the religious duties of priests and its secret knowledge; for the distinction between government and religious duties was practically non-existent. This public education was only limited to boys.

In Aztec society, women were regarded as the subordinate of men. Above everything else, they were required to behave with chastity and high moral standards. For the most part, all government and religious functions were closed off to women. In fact, one of the religious offices, the Snake Woman, was always filled by men. There were some temples and gods that had priestesses, who had their own schools, but their exact position in the hierarchy is unknown.

Aztec laws were simple and harsh. Almost every crime, from adultery to stealing, was punished by death and other offenses usually involved severe corporal punishment or mutilation (the penalty for slander, for instance, was the loss of one's lips). This was not a totalitarian state, however; there was a strong sense of community among the Aztecs and these laws, harsh as they seem, were supported by the community rather than an autocratic judiciary.

Slavery was common among the Aztecs; it was not, however, racial or permanent. One became a slave by being captured in war, by committing certain crimes, such as theft, by voluntarily entering into slavery, or by being sold by one's parents. If one was captured in war, slavery was a pleasant option, for the purpose of Aztec warfare was primarily the capture of live human sacrifices. If, however, one had a useful trade, the Tenochca would forego the sacrifice and employ the captive in that trade.

There was little distinction between the religious and the secular hierarchy, although historians and anthropologists argue that the Aztecs developed farther than any other Mesoamerican group a secular aspect of society. At the very top of the hierarchy was the tlacatecuhtli, or "chief of men." He dominated all the religious ceremonies and served as a military leader. Below the tlacatecuhtli were a series of religious offices and some secular functions, such as military generals.

Religion

The religion of the Aztecs was incredibly complicated, partly due to the fact that they inherited much of it from conquered peoples. Their religion was dominated by three gods: Huitzilopochtli ("hummingbird wizard," the native and chief god of the Tenochca, Huitzilopochtli was the war and sun god), Tezcatlipoca ("Smoking Mirror," chief god of the Aztecs in general), and Quetzalcoatl ("Sovereign Plumed Serpent," widely worshipped throughout Mesoamerica and the god of civilization, the priesthood, and learning). Below these three gods were four creating gods who were remote and aloof from the human world. Below these were an infinity of other gods, of which the most important were Tlaloc, the Rain God, Chalchihuitlicue, the god of growth, and Xipe, the "Flayed One," a god associated with spring.

The Wall of Skulls, Tenochtitlan

The overwhelming aspect of Aztec religious life in the imaginations of non-Aztecs was the predominance of human sacrifice. This had been practiced all throughout the Mesoamerican world, but the Tenochca practiced it at a scale never seen before or since. We don't know a great deal about the details, but we have a fairly good idea of its general character and justification. Throughout Mesoamerica, the theology involved the concept that the gods gave things to human beings only if they were nourished by human beings. Among the Maya, for instance, the priests would nourish the gods by drawing their own blood by piercing their tongues, ears, extremities, or genitals. Other sacrifices involved prayer, offerings of food, sports, and even dramas. The Aztecs practiced all of these sacrifices, including blood-letting. But the Aztec theologians also developed the notion that the gods are best nourished by the living hearts of sacrificed captives; the braver the captive, the more nourishing the sacrifice. This theology led to widespread wars of conquest in search of sacrificial victims both captured in war and paid as tribute by a conquered people.

Great Temple Stairs, Mexico City

We can successfully reconstruct Aztec human sacrifice with a high level of accuracy. Some sacrifices were very minimal, involving the sacrifice of a slave to a minor god, and some were very spectacular, involving hundreds or thousands of captives. Aztec history claims that Ahuitzotl (1468–1502), who preceded Mocteuzma II as king, sacrificed 20,000 people after a campaign in Oaxaca ("O-a-sha-ka"). No matter what the size of the sacrifice, it was always performed the same way. The victim was held down by four priests on an altar at the top of a pyramid or raised temple while the officiant made an incision below the rib cage and pulled out the living heart. The heart was then burned and the corpse was pushed down the steep steps; a very brave or noble victim was carried down the steps. The most brutal of human sacrifices were those dedicated to the god Huehueteotl. Sacrificial victims were drugged and then thrown into a fire at the top of the ceremonial platform. Before they were killed by the fire, they were dragged out with hooks and their living hearts were pulled out and thrown back into the fire.

While human sacrifice was the most dramatic element of Aztec sacrifice, the most common form of sacrifice was voluntary blood-letting which occurred at every religious function. Such blood-letting was tied to rank: the higher one was in social or priestly rank, the more blood one had to sacrifice.

There was an urgency to all this sacrifice. The Aztec believed that the world was controlled by divine forces that were in constant conflict and opposition to one another. The universe was poised between conflicting forces of creation and destruction; human beings could, in part, influence this balance through the practice of sacrifice.

In addition to sacrifice, the Aztec religion, like the Mayan religion, was dominated by calculations of time. The Aztecs had several calendars; each day was controlled by two gods, each of which had a benificient and a malevolent aspect. In a complex series of astronomical calculations, one could precisely determine how to behave and what to do in order to achieve the best results.

It is not unfair to say that Aztec culture was overwhelmingly eschatological in a way that can only be rivalled by early Christianity. The Aztecs, like the Mayans, believed that the universe had been created five times and destroyed four times; each of these five eras was called a Sun. The first age was called Four Ocelot (for it began on the date called Four Ocelot). Tezcatlipoca (Smoking Mirror) dominated the universe and eventually became the sun disk. The world was destroyed by jaguars. The second age was Four Wind, dominated by Quetzalcoatl (Sovereign Plumed Serpent); men were turned to monkeys and the world was destroyed by hurricanes and tempests. The third age was Four Rain, dominated by Tlaloc (the rain god); the world was destroyed by a rain of fire. The fourth era was Four Water and was dominated by Chalchihuitlicue (Woman with the Turquoise Skirt); the world was destroyed by a flood. The fifth era, the one we live in now, is Four Earthquake, and is dominated by Tonatiuh, the Sun-God. This age will end in earthquakes.

The Aztecs had two calendars: the ritual year and the solar year. The ritual year lasted for 260 days and the solar year lasted for 365 days. Every fifty-two years these two calendars would resynchronize; the Aztecs, then, lived in 52-year cycles. In Aztec religion, the destruction of every era always occurred on the last day of each 52-year

cycle (although each era lasted for several of these cycles). Every 52 years, then, the Aztecs believed that the world was about to end and the close of the 52-year cycle was the most important religious event in Aztec life for this period was the most dangerous period in human life. This was the time when the gods could decide to destroy humanity. Every cycle ended with the New Fire Ceremony. For five days before the end of the cycle, all religious altar fires were extinguished and people all over the Aztec world destroyed furniture and possessions and went into mourning for the world. On the last day, the priests went to the Hill of the Star, a crater in the Valley of Mexico, and waited for the constellation of the Pleiades to appear. If it appeared, that meant that the world would continue for fifty-two more years. The priests would light a fire in an animal carcass, and Mexico would be lit from this single fire. The day after saw sacrifices, blood-letting, feasting, and renovation of possessions and houses.

Writing

We can barely read Mayan writing, but we do know how to read Aztec writing. Like the Mayans, the Aztecs developed a true system of writing. Aztec writing isn't phonetic but rather a loose system of rebus writing. Still, if the testimony of the Spanish is reliable, this writing system was seen as an aid to oral traditions rather than as a replacement. Aztec writing was used for many purposes: calculation, calendrical counts, chronicles, diaries, and even history. This is why we know far more about Aztec history before 1500—and in far greater chronological detail—than any other American peoples. Many theories have been presented for the development of a widespread literate tradition among the Aztecs, while the same didn't occur for the Mayas. Perhaps the most convincing is the fact that Aztec society was far more complex than any other preceding culture. The persistent need for accurate record-keeping which is introduced with social complexity led to the development of the most literate society on the American continents.

Sean Carroll

Cosmology Primer

Professor Sean Carroll is a theoretical physicist. Presently on the faculty at Caltech, he has worked at the Institute for Theoretical Physics at the University of California, Santa Barbara, MIT, and University of Chicago. His research focuses on a number of areas in theoretical physics, including cosmology, particle physics, and General Relativity, with special emphasis on dark matter, dark energy, and the origin of the universe. He is the author of *From Eternity to Here*, *Space-time and Geometry*, and a co-founder of Cosmic Variance, http://blogs.discovermagazine.<wbr>com/cosmicvariance/.

The universe is a big place, filled with surprises, and including realms far beyond everyday experience. To be honest, it's a lot to contemplate in one sitting. On this page of the *Primer*, we give a quick overview of the basic features of our universe, as understood by contemporary cosmologists. The pages to follow go into more detail about the specific ideas mentioned here.

The most important features of the universe on very large scales can be summarized quite concisely: it's big, it's smooth, and it's getting bigger. When we look into the sky on a clear night, the first things we notice (besides the Moon and possibly the planets) are the stars. Each star is an object comparable to our Sun, although there is quite a range of star types. We live in a collection of stars bound together by their mutual gravitational attraction: the Milky Way galaxy.

But the Milky Way is just one of billions of galaxies in our observable universe; the basic characteristics of this collection are described in the page on the luminous universe. Fortunately, on the largest scales the distribution of galaxies is very similar throughout the universe;

this is what is meant by the smoothness of the universe. Most remarkably, distant galaxies are all moving away from each other, as discovered by Edwin Hubble in 1929. This mutual moving-away is described in the page on the expanding universe.

The universe was a different place early in its history. Since the universe is expanding today, in the past it was much more hot and dense, as its constituents were packed more tightly. Traced back sufficiently far, it should be too hot for atoms to exist, as electrons are continually jostled away from atomic nuclei; even earlier, nuclei themselves would be torn into individual protons and neutrons, and the universe should be an incredibly hot plasma of subnuclear particles. If we try to go all the way to the beginning, we would reach a singular point called the Big Bang. A timeline of important events in the history of the universe is provided in the page on the evolving universe.

Winding the picture forward from the Big Bang, we evolve from a hot and dense plasma to the cooled-off universe we observe today. Along the way, there is a

Cosmology Primer: Overview. From http://preposterousuniverse.com/writings/cosmologyprimer/measured.html. Reprinted with permission from Sean Carroll.

brief period when the universe is about one minute old in which protons and neutrons are being synthesized into light nuclei (helium, deuterium, and lithium, along with individual protons comprising hydrogen nuclei). Later, electrons combine with these nuclei into atoms when the universe is about 370,000 years old. It is at this point that the universe becomes transparent, and the ambient radiation streams freely to us today. Light waves get stretched to longer wavelengths as the universe expands, so this radiation has cooled to approximately 3 degrees Kelvin, forming the cosmic microwave background (CMB). This basic framework is verified to high precision by observations today, as described on the page about the early universe.

There is much more to the universe than what is immediately visible. Fortunately, everything gives rise to a gravitational field, so we can detect additional sources of matter and energy by probing for their gravitational effects. It turns out that only about 5% of the universe is "ordinary matter" (the atoms of which stars, gas, dust, and planets are made). About 25% of the universe is "dark matter," a new kind of particle never yet detected in any laboratory here on Earth. A full 70% of the universe is "dark energy," a smoothly-distributed and persistent kind of energy which remains a fundamental mystery of science. The dark energy might be a vacuum energy inherent in spacetime itself, or it might be something even more exotic. The pieces of evidence we have accumulated for dark matter and dark energy, as well as theories proposed to account for them and experiments ongoing to constrain them, are discussed in the page on the dark universe.

The conventional Big Bang model provides an excellent fit to observations, as long as we impose very specific initial conditions at early times: an expanding universe with almost the same density at all points in space, but with small perturbations that eventually grow into galaxies today. Why did the universe start like that? A possible answer is provided by "inflation," which posits a brief period of accelerated expansion at very early

times. A related problem concerns the imbalance of matter and antimatter in the universe: why are there more particles than antiparticles? The page on the really early universe discusses the idea of inflation as well as mechanisms to explain the matter/antimatter asymmetry.

It goes without saying that we still have a lot to learn about the universe, but scientists are planning an exciting array of new experiments to push the frontiers of our understanding forward. The page on the measured universe describes the different kinds of experiments under development, as well as some of the most important ones already in operation. We have every reason to believe that new discoveries about the universe will continue to surprise and delight us.

Cosmology Primer: The Expanding Universe

In thinking about the expanding universe, it is tempting to appeal to some sort of simile: distant galaxies are like raisins in a baking loaf of bread, or dots drawn on the surface of a balloon. But the universe is a unique place, and similes tend not to do it justice (or worse, to suggest something misleading). It's actually best just to think about the universe itself, and what it looks like.

So imagine standing outside on a clear night and looking into the sky. Imagine further that you have perfect vision, including not only ordinary light but all other kinds of radiation (radio waves, infrared and ultraviolet light, X-rays and gamma-rays). The first thing you notice are stars; each star is much like our Sun, but further away and correspondingly fainter. But the stars aren't distributed equally throughout the sky; they are arranged into a disk, and our solar system is near one edge of the disk. This disk of stars, orbiting slowly under their mutual gravitational attraction, is our galaxy, the Milky Way. There are almost one trillion stars in the Milky Way; in the night sky it shows up as a faint band stretching from one horizon to the other.

But stars aren't the only thing we see; there are tiny patches of fuzzy light, which stand out in contrast to the pointlike stars. The patches are "nebulae," and were a source of controversy earlier in the twentieth century—were they clouds of gas and dust within our galaxy, or separate galaxies in their own right? Eventually Edwin Hubble showed that many (although not all) of the nebulae were in fact distant systems of stars, comparable in size to our own Milky Way galaxy. In our observable universe, there are approximately one hundred billion such galaxies. For more discussion, see the page on the luminous universe.

Cosmology, as the study of the entire universe, would be a completely intractable subject if it weren't for one crucially simplifying feature: if we look over large enough distances, the distribution of galaxies is basically the same everywhere. In technical terms, we say that the universe is both "homogeneous" (the same at every point) and "isotropic" (the same in every direction). Of course these statements are not strictly true; the center of a galaxy has a higher average density than the space in between galaxies. But as we look over larger and larger distances, the deviations from place to place become smaller and smaller; once we are considering distances of hundreds of millions of light years and more, the universe looks extremely uniform.

However, although galaxies are spread evenly throughout space, they are not static as a function of time; Hubble's second great discovery is that the universe is expanding. The concept of an expanding universe can be a tricky one, so it is worth being careful about what we mean. It is best to think of space itself stretching, so that the amount of space between any two distant galaxies is increasing. The observable phenomenon that leads us to this conclusion is the redshift: as light travels from one galaxy to another, its wavelength is stretched as the universe expands, reaching the second galaxy having been shifted to the red (longer wavelengths). We therefore see relatively nearby galaxies slightly redshifted,

and very distant galaxies extremely redshifted. The cosmological redshift is similar in result (although different in underlying cause) to the well-known Doppler shift that results when an object is moving away from you. It is therefore convenient to assign a "velocity" to this redshift; Hubble's Law states that this apparent velocity is directly proportional to the distance to the galaxy, with the constant of proportionality being the Hubble constant. (At a deep level, the expansion of space is different than the motion of objects through a static space; however, the differences are negligible when the apparent velocities are much less than the speed of light, so the abuse of language is acceptable.)

Since we see distant galaxies moving away from us, it is tempting to think that we are in the center of something big. But that's an incorrect impression; if we were living on any one of the other galaxies, we would still see all the galaxies moving directly away from us, as a consequence of the general expansion. There is no center to the universe, nor any preferred location; it's basically the same everywhere. Likewise, the universe is not (so far as we know) expanding "into" anything; it's just that the amount of space in our single universe is growing with time.

Einstein's general theory of relativity, which states that spacetime is curved and that curvature is what we perceive as "gravity," provides a dynamical framework for understanding the expansion of the universe. In cosmology, the curvature of spacetime comes from two contributions: the curvature of space by itself, and the expansion rate of the universe. The curvature of space is the same throughout space, and can be positive, negative, or zero; recent observations of the Cosmic Microwave Background indicate that it is close to zero. General relativity then relates the expansion rate and spatial curvature to the energy density of the universe—the amount of energy in each volume of space. If we know the spatial curvature, and we know the energy density, and we know how the energy density changes

as the universe expands, we can reconstruct the entire expansion history of the universe.

In particular, we can extrapolate backwards from our current situation to describe the very early universe. Since it is expanding now, it was smaller in the past; galaxies were closer together, and the universe was both hotter and more dense. Going back sufficiently far, the universe was so hot that galaxies and stars could not exist; further back, individual atoms could not exist; further still, it was too hot for atomic nuclei themselves to exist. If we extend ourselves fearlessly all the way back, the universe was of essentially zero size about 13.7 billion years ago—the Big Bang. Of course there is a lot we don't know about this period, although there is some that we do; see the pages on the early universe and the really early universe for details.

If we can extrapolate into the past, we can also extrapolate into the future. The problem there, of course, is that we have no observational data to check our speculations. Strictly speaking, therefore, we really don't know what the far future history of the universe will bring. Our best current models, in which the universe is dominated by dark matter and dark energy, predict that it is likely for the universe to continue expanding forever, becoming increasingly cold and dark as time goes by. See the page on the dark universe for more specifics. However, our current ideas are still speculative, so it pays to keep an open mind.

Cosmology Primer:
The Dark Universe

Our knowledge of the universe comes from looking at it in various ways—different wavelengths of light, neutrinos, cosmic rays, and hopefully some day gravitational radiation. But how do we know that we are seeing everything there is? How could we determine whether there were substances in the universe not directly visible in our telescopes?

The answer lies with gravity. Long ago, Galileo determined that every object falls the same way in a gravitational field. Later, Einstein extended

this idea: every substance with any kind of energy will create a gravitational field. (Note that mass is a kind of energy, since $E=mc^2$.) So we can, in principle, detect everything in the universe, by mapping out the gravitational field throughout spacetime. To our surprise, there is much more out there than we can see directly. The invisible stuff comes in two forms: dark matter and dark energy.

Dark matter is some kind of particle that we have not yet detected in experiments here on Earth, but nevertheless comprises most of the matter in the universe. The first evidence for its existence came from studying the dynamics of galaxies and clusters of galaxies. The basic point is that something in orbit around a massive object moves more rapidly, the more mass the object has. Fritz Zwicky was the first to put this idea into action, studying the motion of galaxies in the Coma cluster; their motions were too rapid to be accounted for by the visible matter in the galaxies. Later, Vera Rubin looked at matter orbiting at the edges of individual galaxies, and noticed a similar effect—the rotation speeds of the galaxies did not fall off with distance as they should if the gravitational fields were being caused by the visible matter alone.

These discrepant motions, and more modern methods confirming this behavior with greater precision, are strong evidence for unseen matter in galaxies and clusters. Of course, it is natural to imagine that the extra matter is quite ordinary, but simply invisible and transparent (much like air on a clear day). And indeed, observations in different wavelengths have provided evidence for previously unseen gas in galaxies and clusters. However, we have very good evidence that the substantial majority of dark matter is something exotic, rather than ordinary matter that we can't see. This evidence comes from two independent sources—the abundance of light elements from primordial nucleosynthesis, and temperature anisotropies in the cosmic microwave background. Both phenomena are described in the page on the early universe. The result is that the abundance of exotic dark matter, some kind of particle that has never been directly observed here on Earth, is about five times the abundance of ordinary matter in the universe.

What we know about dark matter, then, is that it is a new kind of unseen particle that falls readily into galaxies and clusters. The fact that it is dark means that it is neutral, rather than electrically charged; in general, charged particles interact readily with light, and would not be dark. The fact that the dark matter is concentrated in galaxies and clusters indicates that it is slowly moving; particles of this form are referred to as "cold." What could the cold dark matter be made of? We are not at all sure, although numerous theories have been proposed. Two ideas are especially popular: neutralinos and axions. "Neutralinos" are a kind of particle predicted by supersymmetry, a popular (but as yet purely conjectural) theory in particle physics. According to supersymmetry, each kind of known particle has a "superpartner" with a different intrinsic spin; the neutralino is simply a massive, neutral, stable superpartner of one of the known particles, and is a natural dark matter candidate. (Such a particle would interact predominantly through the weak nuclear force, and is therefore an example of a Weakly Interacting Massive Particle, or WIMP.) Axions, on the other hand, are another kind of hypothetical particle, originally postulated to explain certain symmetries of the strong nuclear force. In the case of both neutralinos and axions, active experimental programs are underway to detect these dark matter candidates in the laboratory, either by producing them directly or by observing the effects of ambient particles floating through the Solar System. Finally, it may be possible to detect dark matter particles indirectly, if they annihilate into photons in high-density regions of the universe; the resulting radiation would have a characteristic form that would signal the existence of a new kind of particle.

Of course, there is a kind of known particle which is neutral, stable, and (as we now know) massive—the neutrino. Neutrinos are abundant in the universe, approximately as abundant as photons. However, they are not good dark matter candidates, because they are not very cold. Even if neutrinos today are moving relatively slowly, in the early universe they were moving near the speed of light. As a result, they would stream freely away from galaxies and clusters, rather than settling into them as dark matter is observed to do. Indeed, a useful way to put an upper limit on the mass of the neutrino is to insist that it not comprise such a significant fraction of the mass of the universe that it would interfere with the evolution of large-scale structure.

As if dark matter weren't exotic enough, dark energy is even more mysterious. We know very little about dark energy, other than two characteristic features: it is spread uniformly throughout space, and maintains an approximately constant density as the universe expands. It must be (nearly) uniform throughout space, since otherwise it would clump into galaxies and clusters and affect local motions just as dark matter does. Instead, the dark energy only affects the overall curvature of spacetime. How, then, do we know that dark energy exists? Its affects on spacetime curvature show up in two ways—it makes the universe accelerate, and it contributes (along with matter) to the curvature of space alone.

According to Einstein, the rate of expansion depends on the average energy density of the universe. To measure the expansion rate, we use standard candles, objects whose intrinsic brightness is known. The further away a standard candle is, the dimmer it will appear, allowing us to accurately determine its distance. We want standard candles that are very bright, so they can be observed at cosmological distances; good candidates are provided by supernova explosions, which can rival the entire light output of the galaxy they are in. It turns out that supernovae come in various forms, of different brightness; but a certain kind, the Type Ia supernovae, have a brightness which depends directly on how fast they explode and fade away. Observations of Type Ia supernovae at high redshifts by two

groups (the Supernova Cosmology Project and the High-Redshift Supernova Team) in 1998 provided the first direct evidence that the universe is accelerating rather than slowing down.

Why does dark energy make the universe accelerate? Because, unlike matter and radiation, it does not dilute away as the universe expands—the density of dark energy remains close to constant. Therefore, according to Einstein, the Hubble parameter remains close to constant. But remember that the apparent velocity of a galaxy is given by the Hubble parameter times the distance, as explained in the page on the expanding universe. Since the distance to any given galaxy is increasing, a nearly-constant Hubble parameter implies that the apparent velocity will also be increasing—in other words, the galaxies are accelerating away from us.

The other piece of evidence for dark energy comes from the curvature of space, as measured through temperature fluctuations of the Cosmic Microwave Background. As described in the page on the expanding universe, the curvature of spacetime can be thought of as a combination of the curvature of space, and the expansion of space through time. Through observations of temperature fluctuations in the CMB (described in the page on the early universe), we can measure the overall curvature of space, and find that it is close to zero. Meanwhile, the total amount of matter in the universe (both ordinary and dark) falls well short of what is needed to explain the flatness of space. It turns out that the amount of dark energy required to explain the acceleration of the universe is just right to explain the fact that space is flat. We therefore seem to have a complete inventory of the constituents of our contemporary universe:

> five percent ordinary matter,
> twenty-five percent dark matter,
> seventy percent dark energy.

The completion of this inventory is one of the most impressive successes of modern cosmology.

We don't know what the dark energy is. Since observations constrain its density to be close to uniform throughout space and approximately constant in time, the simplest candidate would be something that is exactly constant in space and time. Such a substance is called vacuum energy—an energy density that is inherent in empty space itself, unchanging from point to point in the universe. But once we admit the possibility of vacuum energy, we can go back and estimate how large such energy should be. The result, according to our best understanding of quantum field theory, is 10^{120} times the observed amount—a fantastically large factor, and a sure sign that there is something we don't understand about vacuum energy. This discrepancy is known as the "cosmological constant problem," since the vacuum energy turns out to be equivalent to Einstein's old idea of a cosmological constant. In addition to this problem, there is the puzzle of why the dark energy and the matter density are relatively close to each other (only differing by a factor of two or three. After all, matter dilutes away as the universe expands, while dark energy remains essentially constant, so their relative abundance changes dramatically; we seem to be born lucky, in an era when both matter and dark energy play an important role in the universe.

In an effort to address these puzzles, cosmologists are trying to learn all they can about dark energy. In particular, they would like to know whether it really is absolutely constant, or merely changing very slowly. If dark energy is dynamical, rather than a strictly-constant vacuum energy, its origin in fundamental physics would be completely different. It is even conceivable that the acceleration and flatness of the universe are not due to dark energy at all, but rather to a breakdown of Einstein's theory of general relativity on cosmological scales. All of these possibilities are in play, and future observations will help us decide between them once and for all.

SECTION III

Western Monotheism: The Problem of Evil

Mark Twain

Letters from the Earth

Samuel Langhorne Clemens (1835–1910), *nom de plume*, Mark Twain. Mark Twain is most noted for his novel, *The Adventures of Tom Sawyer* and its sequel, *The Adventures of Huckleberry Finn*.

Twain grew up in Hannibal, Missouri, which would later provide the setting for Huckleberry Finn and Tom Sawyer, apparently modeling the character of Huckleberry Finn after a childhood friend. Early in life, Twain thought the closest a man could be to God on Earth was to be a riverboat captain. After apprenticing with a printer, he worked as a typesetter before becoming a master riverboat pilot on the Mississippi River. With the Civil War beginning and his brief, distasteful, noncombatant military experience, he headed west to join his older brother, Orion. Failing at gold mining, he turned to journalism. Moving to San Francisco, he ended up broke and nearly suicidal before finally writing the humorous, *The Celebrated Jumping Frog of Calaveras County*, and writing his travelogues from Hawaii. It was initially through his satirical story telling at public speaking engagements in theatres that Twain's popularity spread.

Born during an appearance of Halley's Comet, Mark Twain died on its return in 1910. He is considered one of America's greatest humorists William Faulkner called Mark Twain "the father of American literature."

The Creator sat upon the throne, thinking. Behind him stretched the illimitable continent of heaven, steeped in a glory of light and color; before him rose the black night of Space, like a wall. His mighty bulk towered rugged and mountain-like into the zenith, and His divine head blazed there like a distant sun. At His feet stood three colossal figures, diminished to extinction, almost, by contrast—archangels—their heads level with His ankle-bone.

When the Creator had finished thinking, He said, "I have thought. Behold!"

He lifted His hand, and from it burst a fountain-spray of fire, a million stupendous suns, which clove the blackness and soared, away and away and away, diminishing in magnitude and intensity as they pierced the far frontiers of Space, until at last they were but as diamond nailheads sparkling under the domed vast roof of the universe.

At the end of an hour the Grand Council was dismissed.

They left the Presence impressed and thoughtful, and retired to a private place, where they might talk with freedom. None of the three seemed to want to begin, though all wanted somebody to do it. Each was burning to discuss the great event, but would prefer not to commit himself till he should know how the others regarded it. So there was some aimless and halting conversation about matters of no consequence, and this dragged tediously along, arriving nowhere, until at last the archangel Satan gathered his courage together—of which he had a very good supply—and broke ground. He said: "We know what we are here to talk about, my lords, and we may as well put pretense aside, and begin. If this is the opinion of the Council—"

"It is, it is!" said Gabriel and Michael, gratefully interrupting.

"Very well, then, let us proceed. We have witnessed a wonderful thing; as to that, we are necessarily agreed. As to the value of it—if it has any—that is a matter which does not personally concern us. We can have as many opinions about it as we like, and that is our limit. We have no vote. I think Space was well enough, just as it was, and useful, too. Cold and dark—a restful place, now and then, after a season of the over-delicate climate and trying splendors of heaven. But these are details of no considerable moment; the new feature, the immense feature, is—what, gentlemen?"

"The invention and introduction of automatic, unsupervised, self-regulating *law* for the government of those myriads of whirling and racing suns and worlds!"

"That is it!" said Satan. "You perceive that it is a stupendous idea. Nothing approaching it has been evolved from the Master Intellect before. Law—*Automatic* Law—exact and unvarying Law—requiring no watching, no correcting, no readjusting while the eternities endure! He said those countless vast bodies would plunge through the wastes of Space ages and ages, at unimaginable speed, around stupendous orbits, yet never collide, and never lengthen nor shorten their orbital periods by so much as the hundredth part of a second in two thousand years! That is the new miracle, and the greatest of all—*Automatic Law*! And He gave it a name—the LAW OF NATURE—and said Natural Law is the LAW OF GOD—interchangeable names for one and the same thing."

"Yes," said Michael, "and He said He would establish Natural Law—the Law of God—throughout His dominions, and its authority should be supreme and inviolable."

"Also," said Gabriel, "He said He would by and by create animals, and place them, likewise, under the authority of that Law."

"Yes," said Satan, "I heard Him, but did not understand. What *is* animals, Gabriel?"

"Ah, how should I know? How should any of us know? It is a new word."

[*Interval of three centuries, celestial time—the equivalent of a hundred million years, earthly time. Enter a Messenger-Angel.*]

"My lords, He is making animals. Will it please you to come and see?"

They went, they saw, and were perplexed. Deeply perplexed—and the Creator noticed it, and said, "Ask. I will answer."

"Divine One," said Satan, making obeisance, "what are they for?"

"They are an experiment in Morals and Conduct. Observe them, and be instructed."

There were thousands of them. They were full of activities. Busy, all busy—mainly in persecuting each other. Satan remarked—after examining one of them through a powerful microscope: "This large beast is killing weaker animals, Divine One."

"The tiger—yes. The law of his nature is ferocity. The law of his nature is the Law of God. He cannot disobey it."

"Then in obeying it he commits no offense, Divine One?"

"No, he is blameless."

"This other creature, here, is timid, Divine One, and suffers death without resisting."

"The rabbit—yes. He is without courage. It is the law of his nature—the Law of God. He must obey it."

"Then he cannot honorably be required to go counter to his nature and resist, Divine One?"

"No. No creature can be honorably required to go counter to the law of his nature—the Law of God."

After a long time and many questions, Satan said, "The spider kills the fly, and eats it; the bird kills the spider and eats it; the wildcat kills the goose; the—well, they all kill each other. It is murder all along the line. Here are countless multitudes of creatures, and they all kill, kill, kill, they are all

murderers. And they are not to blame, Divine One?"

"They are not to blame. It is the law of their nature. And always the law of nature is the Law of God. Now—observe—behold! A new creature—and the masterpiece—*Man*!"

Men, women, children, they came swarming in flocks, in droves, in millions.

"What shall you do with them, Divine One?"

"Put into each individual, in differing shades and degrees, all the various Moral Qualities, in mass, that have been distributed, a single distinguishing characteristic at a time, among the nonspeaking animal world—courage, cowardice, ferocity, gentleness, fairness, justice, cunning, treachery, magnanimity, cruelty, malice, malignity, lust, mercy, pity, purity, selfishness, sweetness, honor, love, hate, baseness, nobility, loyalty, falsity, veracity, untruthfulness—each human being shall have *all* of these in him, and they will constitute his nature. In some, there will be high and fine characteristics which will submerge the evil ones, and those will be called good men; in others the evil characteristics will have dominion, and those will be called bad men. Observe—behold—they vanish!"

"Whither are they gone, Divine One?"

"To the earth—they and all their fellow animals."

"What is the earth?"

"A small globe I made, a time, two times and a half ago. You saw it, but did not notice it in the explosion of worlds and suns that sprayed from my hand. Man is an experiment, the other animals are another experiment. Time will show whether they were worth the trouble. The exhibition is over; you may take your leave, my lords."

Several days passed by.

This stands for a long stretch of (our) time, since in heaven a day is as a thousand years.

Satan had been making admiring remarks about certain of the Creator's sparkling industries—remarks which, being read between the lines, were sarcasms. He had made them confidentially to his safe friends the other archangels, but they had been overheard by some ordinary angels and reported at Headquarters.

He was ordered into banishment for a day—the celestial day. It was a punishment he was used to, on account of his too flexible tongue. Formerly he had been deported into Space, there being nowhither else to send him, and had flapped tediously around there in the eternal night and the Arctic chill; but now it occurred to him to push on and hunt up the earth and see how the Human-Race experiment was coming along.

By and by he wrote home—very privately—to St. Michael and St. Gabriel about it.

Satan's Letter

This is a strange place, an extraordinary place, and interesting. There is nothing resembling it at home. The people are all insane, the other animals are all insane, the earth is insane, Nature itself is insane. Man is a marvelous curiosity. When he is at his very very best he is a sort of low grade nickel-plated angel; at his worst he is unspeakable, unimaginable; and first and last and all the time he is a sarcasm. Yet he blandly and in all sincerity calls himself the "noblest work of God." This is the truth I am telling you. And this is not a new idea with him, he has talked it through all the ages, and believed it. Believed it, and found nobody among all his race to laugh at it.

Moreover—if I may put another strain upon you—he thinks he is the Creator's pet. He believes the Creator is proud of him; he even believes the Creator loves him; has a passion for him; sits up nights to admire him; yes, and watch over him and keep him out of trouble. He prays to Him, and thinks He listens. Isn't it a quaint idea? Fills his prayers with crude and bald and florid flatteries of Him, and thinks He sits and purrs over these extravagancies and enjoys them. He prays for help, and favor, and protection, every day; and does it with hopefulness and confidence, too, although no prayer of his has ever been answered. The daily affront, the daily defeat, do not discourage him, he goes on praying just the same. There is something almost fine about this perseverance. I must put one more strain upon you: he thinks he is going to heaven!

He has salaried teachers who tell him that. They also tell him there is a hell, of everlasting fire, and that he will go to it if he doesn't keep the Commandments. What are Commandments? They are a curiosity. I will tell you about them by and by.

Letter II

1. First of all, I recall to your attention the extraordinary fact with which I began. To wit, that the human being, like the immortals, naturally places sexual intercourse far and away above all other joys—yet he has left it out of his heaven! The very thought of it excites him; opportunity sets him wild; in this state he will risk life, reputation, everything—even his queer heaven itself—to make good that opportunity and ride it to the overwhelming climax. From youth to middle age all men and all women prize copulation above all other pleasures combined, yet it is actually as I have said: it is not in their heaven; prayer takes its place.

They prize it thus highly; yet, like all their so-called "boons," it is a poor thing. At its very best and longest the act is brief beyond imagination—the imagination of an immortal, I mean. In the matter of repetition the man is limited—oh, quite beyond immortal conception. We who continue the act and its supremest ecstasies unbroken and without withdrawal for centuries, will never be able to understand or adequately pity the awful poverty of these people in that rich gift which, possessed as we possess it, makes all other possessions trivial and not worth the trouble of invoicing.

2. In man's heaven *everybody sings*! The man who did not sing on earth sings there; the man who could not sing on earth is able to do it there. The universal singing is not casual, not occasional, not relieved by intervals of quiet; it goes on, all day long, and every day, during a stretch of twelve hours. And *everybody stays*; whereas in the earth the place would be empty in two hours. The singing is of hymns alone. Nay, it is of *one* hymn alone. The words are always the same, in number they are only about a dozen, there is no rhyme, there is no poetry: "Hosannah, hosannah, hosannah, Lord God of Sabaoth, 'rah! 'rah! 'rah! siss!—boom!…a-a-ah!"

3. Meantime, every person is playing on a harp—those millions and millions!—whereas not more than twenty in the thousand of them could play an instrument in the earth, or ever wanted to.

   Consider the deafening hurricane of sound— millions and millions of voices screaming at once and millions and millions of harps gritting their teeth at the same time! I ask you: is it hideous, is it odious, is it horrible?

   Consider further: it is a *praise* service; a service of compliment, of flattery, of adulation! Do you ask who it is that is willing to endure this strange compliment, this insane compliment; and who not only endures it, but likes it, enjoys it, requires if, *commands* it? Hold your breath!

   It is God! This race's god, I mean. He sits on his throne, attended by his four and twenty elders and some other dignitaries pertaining to his court, and looks out over his miles and miles of tempestuous worshipers, and smiles, and purrs, and nods his satisfaction northward, eastward, southward; as quaint and naive a spectacle as has yet been imagined in this universe, I take it.

It is easy to see that the inventor of the heavens did not originate the idea, but copied it from the show-ceremonies of some sorry little sovereign State up in the back settlements of the Orient somewhere.

All sane white people hate noise; yet they have tranquilly accepted this kind of heaven—without thinking, without reflection, without examination—and they actually want to go to it! Profoundly devout old gray-headed men put in a large part of their time dreaming of the happy day when they will lay down the cares of this life and enter into the joys of that place. Yet you can see how unreal it is to them, and how little it takes a grip upon them as being fact, for they make no practical preparation for the great change: you never see one of them with a harp, you never hear one of them sing.

As you have seen, that singular show is a service of praise: praise by hymn, praise by prostration. It takes the place of "church." Now then, in the earth these people cannot stand much church—an hour and a quarter is the limit, and they draw the line at once a week. That is to say, Sunday. One day in seven; and even then they do not look forward to it with longing. And so—consider what their heaven provides for them: "church" that lasts forever, and a Sabbath that has no end! They quickly weary of this brief hebdomadal Sabbath here, yet they long for that eternal one; they dream of it, they talk about it, they *think* they think they are going to enjoy it—with all their simple hearts they think they think they are going to be happy in it!

It is because they do not think at all; they only think they think. Whereas they can't think; not two human beings in ten thousand have anything to think with. And as to imagination—oh, well, look at their heaven! They accept it, they approve it, they admire it. That gives you their intellectual measure.

Letter III

You have noticed that the human being is a curiosity. In times past he has had (and worn out and flung away) hundreds and hundreds of religions; today he has hundreds and hundreds of religions, and launches not fewer than three new ones every year. I could enlarge that number and still be within the facts.

One of his principle religions is called the Christian. A sketch of it will interest you. It sets forth in detail in a book containing two million words, called the Old and New Testaments. Also it has another name—The Word of God. For the Christian thinks every word of it was dictated by God—the one I have been speaking of.

It is full of interest. It has noble poetry in it; and some clever fables; and some blood-drenched history; and some good morals; and a wealth of obscenity; and upwards of a thousand lies.

This Bible is built mainly out of the fragments of older Bibles that had their day and crumbled to ruin. So it noticeably lacks in originality, necessarily. Its three or four most imposing and impressive events all happened in earlier Bibles; all its best precepts and rules of conduct came also from those Bibles; there are only two new things in it: hell, for one, and that singular heaven I have told you about.

What shall we do? If we believe, with these people, that their God invented these cruel things, we slander him; if we believe that these people invented them themselves, we slander them. It is an unpleasant dilemma in either case, for neither of these parties has done us any harm.

For the sake of tranquility, let us take a side. Let us join forces with the people and put the whole ungracious burden upon *him*—heaven, hell, Bible and all. It does not seem right, it does not seem fair; and yet when you consider that heaven, and how crushingly charged it is with everything that is repulsive to a human being, how can we believe a human being invented it? And when I come to tell you about hell, the stain will be greater still,

and you will be likely to say, No, a man would not provide that place, for either himself or anybody else; he simply couldn't.

That innocent Bible tells about the Creation. Of what—the universe? Yes, the universe. In six days!

God did it. He did not call it the universe—that name is modern. His whole attention was upon this world. He constructed it in five days—and then? It took him only one day to make twenty million suns and eighty million planets!

What were they for—according to this idea? To furnish light for this little toy-world. That was his whole purpose; he had no other. One of the twenty million suns (the smallest one) was to light it in the daytime, the rest were to help one of the universe's countless moons modify the darkness of its nights.

It is quite manifest that he believed his fresh-made skies were diamond-sown with those myriads of twinkling stars the moment his first-day's sun sank below the horizon; whereas, in fact, not a single star winked in that black vault until three years and a half after that memorable week's formidable industries had been completed.[1] Then one star appeared, all solitary and alone, and began to blink. Three years later another one appeared. The two blinked together for more than four years before a third joined them. At the end of the first hundred years there were not yet twenty-five stars twinkling in the wide wastes of those gloomy skies. At the end of a thousand years not enough stars were yet visible to make a show. At the end of a million years only half of the present array had sent their light over the telescopic frontiers, and it took another million for the rest to follow suit, as the vulgar phrase goes. There being at that time no telescope, their advent was not observed.

---

1 It takes the light of the nearest star (61 Cygni) three and a half years to come to the earth, traveling at the rate of 186,000 miles per second. Arcturus had been shining 200 years before it was visible from the earth. Remoter stars gradually became visible after thousands and thousands of years.—The Editor (M.T.)

For three hundred years, now, the Christian astronomer has known that his Deity didn't make the stars in those tremendous six days; but the Christian astronomer does not enlarge upon that detail. Neither does the priest.

In his Book, God is eloquent in his praises of his mighty works, and calls them by the largest names he can find—thus indicating that he has a strong and just admiration of magnitudes; yet he made those millions of prodigious suns to light this wee little orb, instead of appointing this orb's little sun to dance attendance upon them. He mentions Arcturus in his book—you remember Arcturus; we went there once. It is one of the earth's night lamps!—that giant globe which is fifty thousand times as large as the earth's sun, and compares with it as a melon compares with a cathedral.

However, the Sunday school still teaches the child that Arcturus was created to help light this earth, and the child grows up and continues to believe it long after he has found out that the probabilities are against it being so.

According to the Book and its servants the universe is only six thousand years old. It is only within the last hundred years that studious, inquiring minds have found out that it is nearer a hundred million.

During the Six Days, God created man and the other animals.

He made a man and a woman and placed them in a pleasant garden, along with the other creatures. They all lived together there in harmony and contentment and blooming youth for some time; then trouble came. God had warned the man and the woman that they must not eat of the fruit of a certain tree. And he added a most strange remark: he said that if they ate of it they should surely die. Strange, for the reason that inasmuch as they had never seen a sample death they could not possibly know what he meant. Neither would he nor any other god have been able to make those ignorant children understand what was meant, without furnishing a sample. The mere word could have no meaning for them, any more than it would have for an infant of days.

Presently a serpent sought them out privately, and came to them walking upright, which was the way of serpents in those days. The serpent said the forbidden fruit would store their vacant minds with knowledge. So they ate it, which was quite natural, for man is so made that he eagerly wants to know; whereas the priest, like God, whose imitator and representative he is, has made it his business from the beginning to keep him from knowing any useful thing.

Adam and Eve ate the forbidden fruit, and at once a great light streamed into their dim heads. They had acquired knowledge. What knowledge—useful knowledge? No—merely knowledge that there was such a thing as good, and such a thing as evil, and how to do evil. They couldn't do it before. Therefore all their acts up to this time had been without stain, without blame, without offense.

But now they could do evil—and suffer for it; now they had acquired what the Church calls an invaluable possession, the Moral Sense; that sense which differentiates man from the beast and sets him above the beast. Instead of below the beast—where one would suppose his proper place would be, since he is always foul-minded and guilty and the beast always clean-minded and innocent. It is like valuing a watch that must go wrong, above a watch that can't.

The Church still prizes the Moral Sense as man's noblest asset today, although the Church knows God had a distinctly poor opinion of it and did what he could in his clumsy way to keep his happy Children of the Garden from acquiring it.

Very well, Adam and Eve now knew what evil was, and how to do it. They knew how to do various kinds of wrong things, and among them one principal one—the one God had his mind on principally. That one was the art and mystery of sexual intercourse. To them it was a magnificent discovery, and they stopped idling around and turned their entire attention to it, poor exultant young things!

In the midst of one of these celebrations they heard God walking among the bushes, which was an afternoon custom of his, and they were smitten with fright. Why? Because they were naked. They had not known it before. They had not minded it before; neither had God.

In that memorable moment immodesty was born; and some people have valued it ever since, though it would certainly puzzle them to explain why.

Adam and Eve entered the world naked and unashamed—naked and pure-minded; and no descendant of theirs has ever entered it otherwise. All have entered it naked, unashamed, and clean in mind. They have entered it modest. They had to acquire immodesty and the soiled mind; there was no other way to get it. A Christian mother's first duty is to soil her child's mind, and she does not neglect it. Her lad grows up to be a missionary, and goes to the innocent savage and to the civilized Japanese, and soils their minds. Whereupon they adopt immodesty, they conceal their bodies, they stop bathing naked together.

The convention miscalled modesty has no standard, and cannot have one, because it is opposed to nature and reason, and is therefore an artificiality and subject to anybody's whim, anybody's diseased caprice. And so, in India the refined lady covers her face and breasts and leaves her legs naked from the hips down, while the refined European lady covers her legs and exposes her face and her breasts. In lands inhabited by the innocent savage the refined European lady soon gets used to full-grown native stark-nakedness, and ceases to be offended by it. A highly cultivated French count and countess—unrelated to each other—who were marooned in their nightclothes, by shipwreck, upon an uninhabited island in the eighteenth century, were soon naked. Also ashamed—for a week. After that their nakedness did not trouble them, and they soon ceased to think about it.

You have never seen a person with clothes on. Oh, well, you haven't lost anything.

To proceed with the Biblical curiosities. Naturally you will think the threat to punish Adam and Eve for disobeying was of course not carried out, since they did not create themselves, nor their natures nor their impulses nor their weaknesses, and hence were not properly subject to anyone's commands, and not responsible to anybody for their acts. It will surprise you to know that the threat was carried out. Adam and Eve were punished, and that crime finds apologists unto this day. The sentence of death was executed.

As you perceive, the only person responsible for the couple's offense escaped; and not only escaped but became the executioner of the innocent.

In your country and mine we should have the privilege of making fun of this kind of morality, but it would be unkind to do it here. Many of these people have the reasoning faculty, but no one uses it in religious matters.

The best minds will tell you that when a man has begotten a child he is morally bound to tenderly care for it, protect it from hurt, shield it from disease, clothe it, feed it, bear with its waywardness, lay no hand upon it save in kindness and for its own good, and never in any case inflict upon it a wanton cruelty. God's treatment of his earthly children, every day and every night, is the exact opposite of all that, yet those best minds warmly justify these crimes, condone them, excuse them, and indignantly refuse to regard them as crimes at all, when he commits them. Your country and mine is an interesting one, but there is nothing there that is half so interesting as the human mind.

Very well, God banished Adam and Eve from the Garden, and eventually assassinated them. All for disobeying a command which he had no right to utter. But he did not stop there, as you will see. He has one code of morals for himself, and quite another for his children. He requires his children to deal justly—and gently—with offenders, and forgive them seventy-and-seven times; whereas he deals neither justly nor gently with anyone, and he did not forgive the ignorant and thoughtless first pair of juveniles even their first small offense and say, "You may go free this time, and I will give you another chance."

On the contrary! He elected to punish *their* children, all through the ages to the end of time, for a trifling offense committed by others before they were born. He is punishing them yet. In mild ways? No, in atrocious ones.

You would not suppose that this kind of Being gets many compliments. Undeceive yourself: the world calls him the All-Just, the All-Righteous, the All-Good, the All-Merciful, the All-Forgiving, the All-Truthful, the All-Loving, the Source of All Morality. These sarcasms are uttered daily, all over the world. But not as conscious sarcasms. No, they are meant seriously: they are uttered without a smile.

Letter IV

So the First Pair went forth from the Garden under a curse—a permanent one. They had lost every pleasure they had possessed before "The Fall"; and yet they were rich, for they had gained one worth all the rest: they knew the Supreme Art.

They practiced it diligently and were filled with contentment. The Deity ordered them to practice it. They obeyed, this time. But it was just as well it was not forbidden, for they would have practiced it anyhow, if a thousand Deities had forbidden it.

Results followed. By the name of Cain and Abel. And these had some sisters; and knew what to do with them. And so there were some more results: Cain and Abel begot some nephews and nieces. These, in their turn, begot some second cousins. At this point classification of relationships began to get difficult, and the attempt to keep it up was abandoned.

The pleasant labor of populating the world went on from age to age, and with prime efficiency; for in those happy days the sexes were still competent for the Supreme Art when by rights they ought to have been dead eight hundred years. The sweeter sex, the dearer sex, the lovelier sex was manifestly at its very best, then, for it was even able to attract gods. Real gods. They came down out of heaven and had wonderful times with those hot young blossoms. The Bible tells about it.

By help of those visiting foreigners the population grew and grew until it numbered several millions. But it was a disappointment to the Deity. He was dissatisfied with its morals; which in some respects were not any better than his own. Indeed they were an unflatteringly close imitation of his own. They were a very bad people, and as he knew of no way to reform them, he wisely concluded to abolish them. This is the only really enlightened and superior idea his Bible has credited him with, and it would have made his reputation for all time if he could only have kept to it and carried it out. But he was always unstable—except in his advertisements—and his good resolution broke down. He took a pride in man; man was his finest invention; man was his pet, after the housefly, and he could not bear to lose him wholly; so he finally decided to save a sample of him and drown the rest.

Nothing could be more characteristic of him. He created all those infamous people, and he alone was responsible for their conduct. Not one of them deserved death, yet it was certainly good policy to extinguish them; especially since in creating them the master crime had already been committed, and to allow them to go on procreating would be a distinct addition to the crime. But at the same time there could be no justice, no fairness, in any favoritism—all should be drowned or none.

No, he would not have it so; he would save half a dozen and try the race over again. He was not able to foresee that it would go rotten again, for he is only the Far-Sighted One in his advertisements.

He saved out Noah and his family, and arranged to exterminate the rest. He planned an Ark, and Noah built it. Neither of them had ever built an Ark before, nor knew anything about Arks; and so something out of the common was to be expected. It happened. Noah was a farmer, and although he knew what was required of the Ark he was quite incompetent to say whether this one would be large enough to meet the requirements or not (which it wasn't), so he ventured no advice. The Deity did not know it wasn't large enough, but took the chances and made no adequate measurements. In the end the ship fell far short of the necessities, and to this day the world still suffers for it.

Noah built the Ark. He built it the best he could, but left out most of the essentials. It had no rudder, it had no sails, it had no compass, it had no pumps, it had no charts, no lead-lines, no anchors, no log, no light, no ventilation, and as for cargo room—which was the main thing—the less said about that the better. It was to be at sea eleven months, and would need fresh water enough to fill two Arks of its size—yet the additional Ark was not provided. Water from outside could not be utilized: half of it would be salt water, and men and land animals could not drink it.

For not only was a sample of man to be saved, but business samples of the other animals, too. You must understand that when Adam ate the apple in the Garden and learned how to multiply and replenish, the other animals learned the Art, too, by watching Adam. It was cunning of them, it was neat; for they got all that was worth having out of the apple without tasting it and afflicting themselves with the disastrous Moral Sense, the parent of all immoralities.

Letter V

Noah began to collect animals. There was to be one couple of each and every sort of creature that walked or crawled, or swam or flew, in the world of animated nature. We have to guess at how long it took to collect the creatures and how much it cost, for there is no record of these details. When

Symmachus made preparation to introduce his young son to grown-up life in imperial Rome, he sent men to Asia, Africa and everywhere to collect wild animals for the arena-fights. It took the men three years to accumulate the animals and fetch them to Rome. Merely quadrupeds and alligators, you understand—no birds, no snakes, no frogs, no worms, no lice, no rats, no fleas, no ticks, no caterpillars, no spiders, no houseflies, no mosquitoes—nothing but just plain simple quadrupeds and alligators: and no quadrupeds except fighting ones. Yet it was as I have said: it took three years to collect them, and the cost of animals and transportation and the men's wages footed up $4,500,000.

How many animals? We do not know. But it was under five thousand, for that was the largest number ever gathered for those Roman shows, and it was Titus, not Symmachus, who made that collection. Those were mere baby museums, compared to Noah's contract. Of birds and beasts and fresh-water creatures he had to collect 146,000 kinds; and of insects upwards of two million species.

Thousands and thousands of those things are very difficult to catch, and if Noah had not given up and resigned, he would be on the job yet, as Leviticus used to say. However, I do not mean that he withdrew. No, he did not do that. He gathered as many creatures as he had room for, and then stopped.

If he had known all the requirements in the beginning, he would have been aware that what was needed was a fleet of Arks. But he did not know how many kinds of creatures there were, neither did his Chief. So he had no Kangaroo, and no 'possom, and no Gila monster, and no ornithorhynchus, and lacked a multitude of other indispensable blessings which a loving Creator had provided for man and forgotten about, they having long ago wandered to a side of this world which he had never seen and with whose affairs he was not acquainted. And so everyone of them came within a hair of getting drowned.

They only escaped by an accident. There was not water enough to go around. Only enough was provided to flood one small corner of the globe—the rest of the globe was not then known, and was supposed to be nonexistent.

However, the thing that really and finally and definitely determined Noah to stop with enough species for purely business purposes and let the rest become extinct, was an incident of the last days: an excited stranger arrived with some most alarming news. He said he had been camping among some mountains and valleys about six hundred miles away, and he had seen a wonderful thing there: he stood upon a precipice overlooking a wide valley, and up the valley he saw a billowy black sea of strange animal life coming. Presently the creatures passed by, struggling, fighting, scrambling, screeching, snorting—horrible vast masses of tumultuous flesh! Sloths as big as an elephant; frogs as big as a cow; a megatherium and his harem huge beyond belief; saurians and saurians and saurians, group after group, family after family, species after species—a hundred feet long, thirty feet high, and twice as quarrelsome; one of them hit a perfectly blameless Durham bull a thump with its tail and sent it whizzing three hundred feet into the air and it fell at the man's feet with a sigh and was no more. The man said that these prodigious animals had heard about the Ark and were coming. Coming to get saved from the flood. And not coming in pairs, they were all coming: they did not know the passengers were restricted to pairs, the man said, and wouldn't care a rap for the regulations, anyway—they would sail in that Ark or know the reason why. The man said the Ark would not hold the half of them; and moreover they were coming hungry, and would eat up everything there was, including the menagerie and the family.

All these facts were suppressed, in the Biblical account. You find not a hint of them there. The whole thing is hushed up. Not even the names of those vast creatures are mentioned. It shows you that when people have left a reproachful vacancy in a contract they can be as shady about it in Bibles as elsewhere. Those powerful animals would be of inestimable value to man now, when transportation is so hard pressed and expensive, but they are all lost to him. All lost, and by Noah's fault. They all got drowned. Some of them as much as eight million years ago.

Very well, the stranger told his tale, and Noah saw that he must get away before the monsters arrived. He would have sailed at once, but the upholsterers and decorators of the housefly's drawing room still had some finishing touches to put on, and that lost him a day. Another day was lost in getting the flies aboard, there being sixty-eight billions of them and the Deity still afraid there might not be enough. Another day was lost in stowing forty tons of selected filth for the flies' sustenance.

Then at last, Noah sailed; and none too soon, for the Ark was only just sinking out of sight on the horizon when the monsters arrived, and added their lamentations to those of the multitude of weeping fathers and mothers and frightened little children who were clinging to the wave-washed rocks in the pouring rain and lifting imploring prayers to an All-Just and All-Forgiving and All-Pitying Being who had never answered a prayer since those crags were builded, grain by grain, out of the sands, and would still not have answered one when the ages should have crumbled them to sand again.

Study Questions

1. How does Twain's version of Satan's expulsion from Heaven compare to what you have traditionally heard of the fall of Satan?

2. Does Twain believe a close reading of the Bible portrays an image of the Creator as a Glorious Father or a Gruesome Fiend?

3. Why does Twain find the Story of the Fall of Adam and Eve so disturbing?

4. What is the purpose or need of there being a double standard of morality operating in these Biblical stories, according to Twain?

5. Would Twain find it ironic that Christians today have variously claimed and celebrated the finding of what they believe to be remnants of Noah's Ark?

Richard Swinburne

Why God Allows Evil

Richard Swinburne (1934–), Emeritus Professor of Philosophy at the University of Oxford. Prof. Swinburne is a defender of natural theology, advancing philosophical arguments for the existence of God. His works in philosophy of religion include: *The Coherence of Theism, The Existence of God, Faith and Reason, The Evolution of the Soul, Miracles, Is There a God?, Providence and the Problem of Evil*, and *The Resurrection of God Incarnate*.

Swinburne, like St. Thomas Aquinas, takes a systematic approach to theology, starting with fundamental philosophical claims then building to specific Christian beliefs. For example, through Jesus, God the Father has communicated propositionally to humanity. Swinburne is a natural theologian. Swinburne has defended traditional Christian beliefs as being compatible with contemporary science. For an interview in 2010 with Prof. Swinburne on consciousness, the soul, and freedom of the will see: http://hardproblem.ru/interview/richardgswinburne/lang-pref/en/. For a list of online publications see: http://users.ox.ac.uk/~orie0087/framesetpdfs.shtml.

The world...contains much evil. An omnipotent God could have prevented this evil, and surely a perfectly good and omnipotent God would have done so. So why is there this evil? Is not its existence strong evidence against the existence of God? It would be unless we can construct what is known as a theodicy, an explanation of why God would allow such evil to occur. I believe that that can be done, and I shall outline a theodicy...I emphasize that...in writing that God would do this or that, I am not taking for granted the existence of God, but merely claiming that, if there is a God, it is to be expected that he would do certain things, including allowing the occurrence of certain evils; and so, I am claiming, their occurrence is not evidence against his existence.

It is inevitable that any attempt by myself or anyone else to construct a theodicy will sound callous, indeed totally insensitive to human suffering. Many theists, as well as atheists, have felt that any attempt to construct a theodicy evinces an immoral approach to suffering. I can only ask the reader to believe that I am not totally insensitive to human suffering, and that I do mind about the agony of poisoning, child abuse, bereavement, solitary imprisonment, and marital infidelity as much as anyone else. True, I would not in most cases recommend that a pastor give this chapter to victims of sudden distress at their worst moment to read for consolation. But this is not because its arguments are unsound; it is simply that most people in deep distress need comfort, not argument. Yet there is a problem about why God allows evil, and, if the theist does not have (in a

From *Is There a God?* Oxford University Press, 1996, pp. 95–113. Reprinted by permission of Oxford University Press, Inc.

cool moment) a satisfactory answer to it, then his belief in God is less than rational, and there is no reason why the atheist should share it. To appreciate the argument of this chapter, each of us needs to stand back a bit from the particular situation of his or her own life and that of close relatives and friends (which can so easily seem the only important thing in the world), and ask very generally what good things would a generous and everlasting God give to human beings in the course of a short earthly life. Of course thrills of pleasure and periods of contentment are good things, and—other things being equal—God would certainly seek to provide plenty of those. But a generous God will seek to give deeper good things than these. He will seek to give us great responsibility for ourselves, each other, and the world, and thus a share in his own creative activity of determining what sort of world it is to be. And he will seek to make our lives valuable, of great use to ourselves and each other. The problem is that God cannot give us these goods in full measure without allowing much evil on the way...

[T]here are plenty of evils, positive bad states, which God could if he chose remove. I divide these into moral evils and natural evils. I understand by "natural evil" all evil which is not deliberately produced by human beings and which is not allowed by human beings to occur as a result of their negligence. Natural evil includes both physical suffering and mental suffering, of animals as well as humans; all the trial of suffering which disease, natural disasters, and accidents unpredictable by humans bring in their train. "Moral evil" I understand as including all evil caused deliberately by humans doing what they ought not to do (or allowed to occur by humans negligently failing to do what they ought to do) *and* also the evil constituted by such deliberate actions or negligent failure. It includes the sensory pain of the blow inflicted by the bad parent on his child, the mental pain of the parent depriving the child of love, the starvation allowed to occur in Africa because of negligence by members of foreign governments who could have prevented it, and also the evil of the parent

or politician deliberately bringing about the pain or not trying to prevent the starvation.

Moral Evil

The central core of any theodicy must, I believe, be the "free-will defence," which deals—to start with—with moral evil, but can be extended to deal with much natural evil as well. The free-will defence claims that it is a great good that humans have a certain sort of free will which I shall call free and responsible choice, but that, if they do, then necessarily there will be the natural possibility of moral evil. (By the "natural possibility" I mean that it will not be determined in advance whether or not the evil will occur.) A God who gives humans such free will necessarily brings about the possibility, and puts outside his own control whether or not that evil occurs. It is not logically possible—that is, it would be self-contradictory to suppose—that God could give us such free will and yet ensure that we always use it in the right way.

Free and responsible choice is not just free will in the narrow sense of being able to choose between alternative actions, without our choice being causally necessitated by some prior cause... [H]umans could have that kind of free will merely in virtue of being able to choose freely between two equally good and unimportant alternatives. Free and responsible choice is rather free will (of the kind discussed) to make significant choices between good and evil, which make a big difference to the agent, to others, and to the world.

Given that we have free will, we certainly have free and responsible choice. Let us remind ourselves of the difference that humans can make to themselves, others, and the world. Humans have opportunities to give themselves and others pleasurable sensations, and to pursue worthwhile activities—to play tennis or the piano, to acquire knowledge of history and science and philosophy, and to help others to do so, and thereby to build deep personal relations founded upon such sensations and activities. And humans are so made that they can form their characters. Aristotle famously remarked: "we become just by doing just acts, prudent by doing prudent acts, brave by doing brave acts." That is, by doing a just act when it is difficult—when it goes against our natural inclinations (which is what I understand by desires)—we make it easier to do a just act next time. We can gradually change our desires, so that—for example—doing just acts becomes natural. Thereby we can free ourselves from the power of the less good desires to which we are subject. And, by choosing to acquire knowledge and to use it to build machines of various sorts, humans can extend the range of the differences they can make to the world—they can build universities to last for centuries, or save energy for the next generation; and by cooperative effort over many decades they can eliminate poverty. The possibilities for free and responsible choice are enormous.

It is good that the free choices of humans should include *genuine* responsibility for other humans, and that involves the opportunity to benefit *or* harm them. God has the power to benefit or to harm humans. If other agents are to be given a share in his creative work, it is good that they have that power too (although perhaps to a lesser degree). A world in which agents can benefit each other but not do each other harm is one where they have only very limited responsibility for each other. If my responsibility for you is limited to whether or not to give you a camcorder, but I cannot cause you pain, stunt your growth, or limit your education, then I do not have a great deal of responsibility for you. A God who gave agents only such limited responsibilities for their fellows would not have given much. God would have reserved for himself the all-important choice of the kind of world it was to be, while simply allowing humans the minor choice of filling in the details. He would be like a father asking his elder son to look after the younger son, and adding that he would be watching the elder son's every move and would intervene the moment the elder son did a thing wrong. The elder son might justly retort that, while he would be happy to share his father's work, he could really do so only if he were left to make his own judgements as to what to do within a significant range of the options available to the father. A good God, like a good father, will delegate responsibility. In order to allow creatures a share in creation, he will allow them the choice of hurting and maiming, of frustrating the divine plan. Our world is one where creatures have just such deep responsibility for each other. I cannot only benefit my children, but harm them. One way in which I can harm them is that I can inflict physical pain on them. But there are much more damaging things which I can do to them. Above all I can stop them growing into creatures with significant knowledge, power, and freedom; I can determine whether they come to have the kind of free and responsible choice which I have. The possibility of humans bringing about significant evil is a logical consequence of their having this free and responsible choice. Not even God could give us this choice without the possibility of resulting evil.

Now...an action would not be intentional unless it was done for a reason—that is, seen as in some way a good thing (either in itself or because of its consequences). And, if reasons alone influence actions, that regarded by the subject as most important will determine what is done; an agent under the influence of reason alone will inevitably do the action which he regards as overall the best. If an agent does not do the action which he regards as overall the best, he must have allowed factors other than reason to exert an influence on him. In other words, he must have allowed desires for what he regards as good only in a certain respect, but not overall, to influence his conduct. So, in order to have a choice between good and evil, agents need already a certain depravity, in the sense of a system of desires for what they correctly believe to be evil. I need to *want* to overeat, get more than my fair share of money or power, indulge my sexual appetites even by deceiving my spouse or partner, want to see you hurt, if I am to have choice between good and evil. This depravity is itself an evil which is a necessary condition of a greater good. It makes possible a choice made seriously and deliberately, because made in the face of a genuine alternative. I stress that, according to the free-will defence, it is the natural possibility of moral evil which is the necessary condition of the great good, not the actual evil itself. Whether that occurs is (through God's choice) outside God's control and up to us.

Note further and crucially that, if I suffer in consequence of your freely chosen bad action, that is not by any means pure loss for me. In a certain respect it is a good for *me*. My suffering would be pure loss for me if the only good thing in life was sensory pleasure, and the only bad thing sensory pain; and it is because the modern world tends to think in those terms that the problem of evil seems so acute. If these were the only good and bad things, the occurrence of suffering would indeed be a conclusive objection to the existence of God. But we have already noted the great good of freely choosing and influencing our future, that of our fellows, and that of the world. And now note another great good—the good of our life serving a purpose, of being of use to ourselves and others. Recall the words of Christ, "it is more blessed to give than to receive" (as quoted by St. Paul (Acts 20:35)). We tend to think, when the beggar appears on our doorstep and we feel obliged to give and do give, that that was lucky for him but not for us who happened to be at home. That is not what Christ's words say. They say that *we* are the lucky ones, not just because we have a lot, out of which we can give a little, but because we are privileged to contribute to the beggar's happiness—and that privilege is worth a lot more than money. And, just as it is a great good freely to choose to do good, so it is also a good to be used by someone else for a worthy purpose (so long, that is, that he or she has the right, the authority, to use us in this way). Being allowed to suffer to make possible a great good is a privilege, even if the privilege is forced upon you. Those who are allowed to die for their country and thereby save their country from foreign oppression are privileged. Cultures less obsessed than our own by the evil of purely physical pain have always recognized that. And

they have recognized that it is still a blessing, even if the one who died had been conscripted to fight.

And even twentieth-century man can begin to see that—sometimes—when he seeks to help prisoners, not by giving them more comfortable quarters, but by letting them help the handicapped; or when he pities rather than envies the "poor little rich girl" who has everything and does nothing for anyone else. And one phenomenon prevalent in end-of-century Britain draws this especially to our attention—the evil of unemployment. Because of our system of Social Security, the unemployed on the whole have enough money to live without too much discomfort; certainly they are a lot better off than are many employed in Africa or Asia or Victorian Britain. What is evil about unemployment is not so much any resulting poverty but the uselessness of the unemployed. They often report feeling unvalued by society, of no use, "on the scrap heap." They rightly think it would be a good for them to contribute; but they cannot. Many of them would welcome a system where they were obliged to do useful work in preference to one where society has no use for them.

It follows from that fact that being of use is a benefit for him who is of use, and that those who suffer at the hands of others, and thereby make possible the good of those others who have free and responsible choice, are themselves benefited in this respect. I am fortunate if the natural possibility of my suffering if you choose to hurt me is the vehicle which makes your choice really matter. My vulnerability, my openness to suffering (which necessarily involves my actually suffering if you make the wrong choice), means that you are not just like a pilot in a simulator, where it does not matter if mistakes are made. That our choices matter tremendously, that we can make great differences to things for good or ill, is one of the greatest gifts a creator can give us. And if my suffering is the means by which he can give you that choice, I too am in this respect fortunate. Though of course suffering is in itself a bad thing, my good fortune is that the suffering is not random, pointless suffering. It is suffering which is a consequence of my vulnerability which makes me of such use.

Someone may object that the only good thing is not *being* of use (dying for one's country or being vulnerable to suffering at your hands), but *believing* that one is of use—believing that one is dying for one's country and that this is of use; the "feel-good" experience. But that cannot be correct. Having comforting beliefs is only a good thing if they are true beliefs. It is not a good thing to believe that things are going well when they are not, or that your life is of use when it is not. Getting pleasure out of a comforting falsehood is a cheat. But if I get pleasure out of a true belief, it must be that I regard the state of things which I believe to hold to be a good thing. If I get pleasure out of the true belief that my daughter is doing well at school, it must be that I regard it as a good thing that my daughter does well at school (whether or not I believe that she is doing well). If I did not think the latter, I would not get any pleasure out of believing that she is doing well. Likewise, the belief that I am vulnerable to suffering at your hands, and that that is a good thing, can only be a good thing if being vulnerable to suffering at your hands is itself a good thing (independently of whether I believe it or not). Certainly, when my life is of use and that is a good for me, it is even better if I believe it and get comfort therefrom; but it can only be even better if it is already a good for me whether I believe it or not.

But though suffering may in these ways serve good purposes, does God have the right to allow me to suffer for your benefit, without asking my permission? For surely, an objector will say, no one has the right to allow one person A to suffer for the benefit of another one B without A's consent. We judge that doctors who use patients as involuntary objects of experimentation in medical experiments which they hope will produce results which can be used to benefit others are doing something wrong. After all, if my arguments about the utility of suffering are

sound, ought we not all to be causing suffering to others in order that those others may have the opportunity to react in the right way?

There are, however, crucial differences between God and the doctors. The first is that God as the author of our being has certain rights, a certain authority over us, which we do not have over our fellow humans. He is the cause of our existence at each moment of our existence and sustains the laws of nature which give us everything we are and have. To allow someone to suffer for his own good or that of others, one has to stand in some kind of parental relationship towards him. I do not have the right to let some stranger suffer for the sake of some good, when I could easily prevent this, but I do have *some* right of this kind in respect of my own children. I may let the younger son suffer *somewhat* for his own good or that of his brother. I have this right because in small part I am responsible for the younger son's existence, his beginning and continuance. If I have begotten him, nourished, and educated him, I have some limited rights over him in return; to a *very limited* extent I can use him for some worthy purpose. If this is correct, then a God who is so much more the author of our being than are our parents has so much more right in this respect. Doctors do have over us even the rights of parents.

But secondly and all-importantly, the doctors *could* have asked the patients for permission; and the patients, being free agents of some power and knowledge, could have made an informed choice of whether or not to allow themselves to be used. By contrast, God's choice is not about how to use already existing agents, but about the sort of agents to make and the sort of world into which to put them. In God's situation there are no agents to be asked. I am arguing that it is good that one agent A should have deep responsibility for another B (who in turn could have deep responsibility for another C). It is not logically possible for God to have asked B if he wanted things thus, for, if A is to be responsible for B's growth in freedom, knowledge, and power, there will not be a B with enough freedom and knowledge to make any choice, before God has to choose whether or not to give A responsibility for him. One cannot ask a baby into which sort of world he or she wishes to be born. The creator has to make the choice independently of his creatures. He will seek on balance to benefit them—all of them. And, in giving them the gift of life—whatever suffering goes with it—that is a substantial benefit. But when one suffers at the hands of another, often perhaps it is not enough of a benefit to outweigh the suffering. Here is the point to recall that it is an additional benefit to the sufferer that his suffering is the means whereby the one who hurt him had the opportunity to make a significant choice between good and evil which otherwise he would not have had.

Although for these reasons, as I have been urging, God has the right to allow humans to cause each other to suffer, there must be a limit to the amount of suffering which he has the right to allow a human being to suffer for the sake of a great good. A parent may allow an elder child to have the power to do some harm to a younger child for the sake of the responsibility given to the elder child; but there are limits. And there are limits even to the moral right of God, our creator and sustainer, to use free sentient beings as pawns in a greater game. Yet, if these limits were too narrow, God would be unable to give humans much real responsibility; he would be able to allow them only to play a toy game. Still, limits there must be to God's rights to allow humans to hurt each other; and limits there are in the world to the extent to which they can hurt each other, provided above all by the short finite life enjoyed by humans and other creatures—one human can hurt another for no more than eighty years or so. And there are a number of other safety-devices in-built into our physiology and psychology, limiting the amount of pain we can suffer. But the primary safety limit is that provided by the shortness of our finite life. Unending, unchosen suffering would indeed to my mind provide a very strong argument against the existence of God. But that is not the human situation.

So then God, without asking humans, has to choose for them between the kinds of world in which they can live—basically either a world in which there is very little opportunity for humans to benefit or harm each other, or a world in which there is considerable opportunity. How shall he choose? There are clearly reasons for both choices. But it seems to me (just, on balance) that his choosing to create the world in which we have considerable opportunity to benefit or harm each other is to bring about a good at least as great as the evil which he thereby allows to occur. *Of course* the suffering he allows is a bad thing; and, other things being equal, to be avoided. But having the natural possibility of causing suffering makes possible a greater good. God, in creating humans who (of logical necessity) cannot choose for themselves the kind of world into which they are to come, plausibly exhibits his goodness in making for them the heroic choice that they come into a risky world where they may have to suffer for the good of others.

Natural Evil

Natural evil is not to be accounted for along the same lines as moral evil. Its main role rather, I suggest, is to make it possible for humans to have the kind of choice which the free-will defence extols, and to make available to humans specially worthwhile kinds of choice.

There are two ways in which natural evil operates to give humans those choices. First, the operation of natural laws producing evils gives humans knowledge (if they choose to seek it) of how to bring about such evils themselves. Observing you catch some disease by the operation of natural processes gives me the power either to use those processes to give that disease to other people, or through negligence to allow others to catch it, or to take measures to prevent others from catching the disease. Study of the mechanisms of nature producing various evils (and goods) opens up for humans a wide range of choice. This is the way in which in fact we learn how to bring about (good and) evil. But could not God give us the requisite knowledge (of how to bring about good or evil) which we need in order to have free and responsible choice by a less costly means? Could he not just whisper in our ears from time to time what are the different consequences of different actions of ours? Yes. But anyone who believed that an action of his would have some effect because he believed that God had told him so would see all his actions as done under the all-watchful eye of God. He would not merely believe strongly that there was a God, but would know it with real certainty. That knowledge would greatly inhibit his freedom of choice, would make it very difficult for him to choose to do evil. This is because we all have a natural inclination to wish to be thought well of by everyone, and above all by an all-good God; that we have such an inclination is a very good feature of humans, without which we would be less than human. Also, if we were directly informed of the consequences of our actions, we would be deprived of the choice whether to seek to discover what the consequences were through experiment and hard cooperative work. Knowledge would be available on tap. Natural processes alone give humans knowledge of the effects of their actions without inhibiting their freedom, and if evil is to be a possibility for them they must know how to allow it to occur.

The other way in which natural evil operates to give humans their freedom is that it makes possible certain kinds of action towards it between which agents can choose. It increases the range of significant choice. A particular natural evil, such as physical pain, gives to the sufferer a choice—whether to endure it with patience, or to bemoan his lot. His friend can choose whether to show compassion towards the sufferer, or to be callous. The pain makes possible these choices, which would not otherwise exist. There is no guarantee that our actions in response to the pain will be good ones, but the pain gives us the opportunity to perform good actions. The good or bad actions which we perform in the face of natural evil themselves provide opportunities for further choice—of good or evil stances towards the former actions. If I am patient with my suffering, you can choose whether to encourage or laugh at my patience; if I bemoan my lot, you can teach me by word and example what a good thing patience is. If you are sympathetic, I have then the opportunity to show gratitude for the sympathy; or to be so self-involved that I ignore it. If you are callous, I can choose whether to ignore this or to resent it for life. And so on. I do not think that there can be much doubt that natural evil, such as physical pain, makes available these sorts of choice. The actions which natural evil makes possible are ones which allow us to perform at our best and interact with our fellows at the deepest level.

It may, however, be suggested that adequate opportunity for these great good actions would be provided by the occurrence of moral evil without any need for suffering to be caused by natural processes. You can show courage when threatened by a gunman, as well as when threatened by cancer; and show sympathy to those likely to be killed by gunmen as well as to those likely to die of cancer. But just imagine all the suffering of mind and body caused by disease, earthquake, and accident unpreventable by humans removed at a stroke from our society. No sickness, no bereavement in consequence of the untimely death of the young. Many of us would then have such an easy life that we simply would not have much opportunity to show courage or, indeed, manifest much in the way of great goodness at all. We need those insidious processes of decay and dissolution which money and strength cannot ward off for long to give us the opportunities, so easy otherwise to avoid, to become heroes.

God has the right to allow natural evils to occur (for the same reason as he has the right to allow moral evils to occur)—up to a limit. It would, of course, be crazy for God to multiply evils more and more in order to give endless opportunity for heroism, but to have *some* significant opportunity for real heroism and consequent character formation is a benefit for the person to whom it is given. Natural evils give to us the knowledge to make a range of choices between good and evil, and the opportunity to perform actions of especially valuable kinds.

There is, however, no reason to suppose that animals have free will. So what about their suffering? Animals had been suffering for a long time before humans appeared on this planet—just how long depends on which animals are conscious beings. The first thing to take into account here is that, while the higher animals, at any rate the vertebrates, suffer. it is most unlikely that they suffer nearly as much as humans do. Given that suffering depends directly on brain events (in turn caused by events in other parts of the body), then, since the lower animals do not suffer at all and humans suffer a lot, animals of intermediate complexity (it is reasonable to suppose) suffer only a moderate amount. So, while one does need a theodicy to account for why God allows animals to suffer, one does not need as powerful a theodicy as one does in respect of humans. One only needs reasons adequate to account for God allowing an amount of suffering much less than that of humans. That said, there is, I believe, available for animals parts of the theodicy which I have outlined above for humans.

The good of animals, like that of humans, does not consist solely in thrills of pleasure. For animals, too, there are more worthwhile things, and in particular intentional actions, and among them serious significant intentional actions. The life of animals involves many serious significant intentional actions. Animals look for a mate, despite being tired and failing to find one. They take great trouble to build nests and feed their young, to decoy predators and explore. But all this inevitably involves pain (going on despite being tired) and danger. An animal cannot intentionally avoid forest fires, or take trouble to rescue its offspring from forest fires, unless there exists a serious danger of getting caught in a forest fire. The action of rescuing despite danger simply cannot be done unless the danger exists—and the danger will not exist unless there is a significant natural probability of being caught

in the fire. Animals do not choose freely to do such actions, but the actions are nevertheless worthwhile. It is great that animals feed their young, not just themselves; that animals explore when they know it to be dangerous; that animals save each other from predators, and so on. These are the things that give the lives of animals their value. But they do often involve some suffering to some creature.

To return to the central case of humans—the reader will agree with me to the extent to which he or she values responsibility, free choice, and being of use very much more than thrills of pleasure or absence of pain. There is no other way to get the evils of this world into the right perspective, except to reflect at length on innumerable very detailed thought experiments (in addition to actual experiences of life) in which we postulate very different sorts of worlds from our own, and then ask ourselves whether the perfect goodness of God would require him to create one of these (or no world at all) rather than our own. But I conclude with a very small thought experiment, which may help to begin this process. Suppose that you exist in another world before your birth in this one, and are given a choice as to the sort of life you are to have in this one. You are told that you are to have only a short life, maybe of only a few minutes, although it will be an adult life in the sense that you will have the richness of sensation and belief characteristic of adults. You have a choice as to the sort of life you will have. You can have either a few minutes of very considerable pleasure, of the kind produced by some drug such as heroin, which you will experience by yourself and which will have no effects at all in the world (for example, no one else will know about it); or you can have a few minutes of considerable pain, such as the pain of childbirth, which will have (unknown to you at the time of pain) considerable good effects on others over a few years. You are told that, if you do not make the second choice, those others will never exist—and so you are under no moral obligation to make the second choice. But you seek to make the choice which will make *your* own life the best

life for *you* to have led. How will you choose? The choice is, I hope, obvious. You should choose the second alternative.

For someone who remains unconvinced by my claims about the relative strengths of the good and evils involved—holding that, great though the goods are, they do not justify the evils which they involve—there is a fallback position. My arguments may have convinced you of the greatness of the goods involved sufficiently for you to allow that a perfectly good God would be justified in bringing about the evils for the sake of the good which they make possible, if and only if God also provided compensation in the form of happiness after death to the victims whose sufferings make possible the goods…. While believing that God does provide at any rate for many humans such life after death, I have expounded a theodicy without relying on this assumption. But I can understand someone thinking that the assumption is needed, especially when we are considering the worst evils. (This compensatory afterlife need not necessarily be the everlasting life of Heaven.)

It remains the case, however, that evil is evil, and there is a substantial price to pay for the goods of our world which it makes possible. God would not be less than perfectly good if he created instead a world without pain and suffering, and so without the particular goods which those evils make possible. Christian, Islamic, and much Jewish tradition claims that God has created worlds of both kinds—our world, and the Heaven of the blessed. The latter is a marvelous world with a vast range of possible deep goods, but it lacks a few goods which our world contains, including the good of being able to reject the good. A generous God might well choose to give some of us the choice of rejecting the good in a world like ours before giving to those who embrace it a wonderful world in which the former possibility no longer exists.

Study Questions

1. What is the Problem of Evil, according to Swinburne?

2. What is the significance in distinguishing different types of evil?

3. Are you persuaded by Swinburne's discussion of the value of free will as a solution to some evil? Would Mark Twain find such a solution on the part of God the Father consistent with ordinary expectations for typical fathers?

4. Which do you find more compassionate and loving—a God who tests in a single, brief lifetime then passes judgment for an eternity of damnation or salvation, or a process of reincarnation in which a soul continuously returns until it learns its lessons to warrant eternal salvation? Which does Swinburne advocate?

J.L. Mackie

Evil and Omnipotence

J.L. Mackie (1917–1981) was an Australian philosopher who spent much of his teaching career at Oxford University. He wrote six books and published numerous articles on Ethics, Philosophy of Religion, Metaphysics, and Philosophy of Language. One of his more well-known positions was that of moral skepticism. In *Ethics: Inventing Right and Wrong*, he argued that values are not to be discovered in the sense that they are independent and objective. Rather, as the title of his book claims, values are invented. In the following popularly anthologized paper, *Evil and Omnipotence*, Mackie defends the view that "by way of the traditional problem of evil…it can be shown that…religious beliefs…are positively irrational…" Lurking in the theologian's position is what Mackie calls the Paradox of Omnipotence. Can God create something He cannot control? This question should not be confused with the question, Can God create something He chooses not to control?

The traditional arguments for the existence of God have been fairly thoroughly criticized by philosophers. But the theologian can, if he wishes, accept this criticism. He can admit that no rational proof of God's existence is possible. And he can still retain all that is essential to his position, by holding that God's existence is known in some other, non-rational way. I think, however, that a more telling criticism can be made by way of the traditional problem of evil. Here it can be shown, not that religious beliefs lack rational support, but that they are positively irrational, that the several parts of the essential theological doctrine are inconsistent with one another, so that the theologian can maintain his position as a whole only by a much more extreme rejection of reason than in the former case. He must now be prepared to believe, not merely what cannot be proved, but what can be *disproved* from other beliefs that he also holds.

The problem of evil, in the sense in which I shall be using the phrase, is a problem only for someone who believes that there is a God who is both omnipotent and wholly good. And it is a logical problem, the problem of clarifying and reconciling a number of beliefs: it is not a scientific problem that might be solved by further observations, or a practical problem that might be solved by a decision or an action. These points are obvious; I mention them only because they are sometimes ignored by theologians, who sometimes parry a statement of the problem with such remarks as "Well, can you solve the problem yourself?" or "This is a mystery which may be revealed to us later" or "Evil is something to be faced and overcome, not to be merely discussed."

In its simplest form the problem is this: God is omnipotent; God is wholly good; and yet evil exists. There seems to be some contradiction between these three propositions, so that if any two of them

From *Mind*, Vol. LXIV, No. 254, 1955. Oxford University Press, pp. 200–212. Reprinted with permission obtained via RightsLink.

were true the third would be false. But at the same time all three are essential parts of most theological positions: the theologian, it seems, at once must adhere and *cannot consistently* adhere to all three. (The problem does not arise only for theists, but I shall discuss it in the form in which it presents itself for ordinary theism.)

However, the contradiction does not arise immediately; to show it we need some additional premises, or perhaps some quasi-logical rules connecting the terms "good," "evil," and "omnipotent." These additional principles are that good is opposed to evil, in such a way that a good thing always eliminates evil as far as it can, and that there are no limits to what an omnipotent thing can do. From these it follows that a good omnipotent thing eliminates evil completely, and then the propositions that a good omnipotent thing exists, and that evil exists, are incompatible.

Adequate Solutions

Now once the problem is fully stated it is clear that it can be solved, in the sense that the problem will not arise if one gives up at least one of the propositions that constitute it. If you are prepared to say that God is not wholly good, or not quite omnipotent, or that evil does not exist, or that good is not opposed to the kind of evil that exists, or that there are limits to what an omnipotent thing can do, then the problem of evil will not arise for you.

There are, then, quite a number of adequate solutions of the problem of evil, and some of these have been adopted, or almost adopted, by various thinkers. For example, a few have been prepared to deny God's omnipotence, and rather more have been prepared to keep the term "omnipotence" but severely to restrict its meaning, recording quite a number of things that an omnipotent being cannot do. Some have said that evil is an illusion, perhaps because they held that the whole world of temporal, changing things is an illusion, and that what we call evil belongs only to this world, or perhaps because they held that although temporal things *are* much as we see

them, those that we call evil are not really evil. Some have said that what we call evil is merely the privation of good, that evil in a positive sense, evil that would really be opposed to good, does not exist. Many have agreed with Pope that disorder is harmony not understood, and that partial evil is universal good. Whether any of these views is *true* is, of course, another question. But each of them gives an adequate solution of the problem of evil in the sense that if you accept it this problem does not arise for you, though you may, of course, have *other* problems to face.

But often enough these adequate solutions are only *almost* adopted. The thinkers who restrict God's power, but keep the term "omnipotence," may reasonably be suspected of thinking, in other contexts, that his power is really unlimited. Those who say that evil is an illusion may also be thinking, inconsistently, that this illusion is itself an evil. Those who say that "evil" is merely privation of good may also be thinking, inconsistently, that privation of good is an evil. (The fallacy here is akin to some forms of the "naturalistic fallacy" in ethics, where some think, for example, that "good" is just what contributes to evolutionary progress, and that evolutionary progress is itself good.) If Pope meant what he said in the first line of his couplet, that "disorder" is only harmony not understood, the "partial evil" of the second line must, for consistency, mean "that which, taken in isolation, falsely appears to be evil", but it would more naturally mean "that which, in isolation, really is evil." The second line, in fact, hesitates between two views, that "partial evil" isn't really evil, since only the universal quality is real, and that "partial evil" is really an evil, but only a little one.

In addition, therefore, to adequate solutions, we must recognize unsatisfactory inconsistent solutions, in which there is only a half-hearted or temporary rejection of one of the propositions which together constitute the problem. In these, one of the constituent propositions is explicitly rejected, but it is covertly re-asserted or assumed elsewhere in the system.

Fallacious Solutions

Besides these half-hearted solutions, which explicitly reject but implicitly assert one of the constituent propositions, there are definitely fallacious solutions which explicitly maintain all the constituent propositions, but implicitly reject at least one of them in the course of the argument that explains away the problem of evil.

There are, in fact, many so-called solutions which purport to remove the contradiction without abandoning any of its constituent propositions. These must be fallacious, as we can see from the very statement of the problem, but it is not so easy to see in each case precisely where the fallacy lies. I suggest that in all cases the fallacy has the general form suggested above: in order to solve the problem one (or perhaps more) of its constituent propositions is given up, but in such a way that it appears to have been retained, and can therefore be asserted without qualification in other contexts. Sometimes there is a further complication: the supposed solution moves to and fro between, say, two of the constituent propositions, at one point asserting the first of these but covertly abandoning the second, at another point asserting the second but covertly abandoning the first. These fallacious solutions often turn upon some equivocation with the words "good" and "evil," or upon some vagueness about the way in which good and evil are opposed to one another, or about how much is meant by "omnipotence." I propose to examine some of these so-called solutions, and to exhibit their fallacies in detail. Incidentally, I shall also be considering whether an adequate solution could be reached by a minor modification of one or more of the constituent propositions, which would, however, still satisfy all the essential requirements of ordinary theism.

1. "Good cannot exist without evil" or "Evil is necessary as a counterpart to good."

It is sometimes suggested that evil is necessary as a counterpart to good, that if there were no evil there could be no good either, and that this solves the problem of evil. It is true that it points to an answer to the question "Why should there be evil?" But it does so only by qualifying some of the propositions that constitute the problem.

First, it sets a limit to what God can do, saying that God *cannot* create good without simultaneously creating evil, and this means either that God is not omnipotent or that there are *some* limits to what an omnipotent thing can do. It may be replied that these limits are always presupposed, that omnipotence has never meant the power to do what is logically impossible, and on the present view the existence of good without evil would be a logical impossibility. This interpretation of omnipotence may, indeed, be accepted as a modification of our original account which does not reject anything that is essential to theism, and I shall in general assume it in the subsequent discussion. It is, perhaps, the most common theistic view, but I think that some theists at least have maintained that God can do what is logically impossible. Many theists, at any rate, have held that logic itself is created or laid down by God, that logic is the way in which God arbitrarily chooses to think. (This is, of course, parallel to the ethical view that morally right actions are those which God arbitrarily chooses to command, and the two views encounter similar difficulties.) And *this* account of logic is clearly inconsistent with the view that God is bound by logical necessities—unless it is possible for an omnipotent being to bind himself, an issue which we shall consider later, when we come to the Paradox of Omnipotence. This solution of the problem of evil cannot, therefore, be consistently adopted along with the view that logic is itself created by God.

But, secondly, this solution denies that evil is opposed to good in our original sense. If good and evil are counterparts, a good thing will not "eliminate evil as far as it can." Indeed, this view suggests that good and evil are not strictly qualities of things at all. Perhaps the suggestion is that good and evil are related in much the same way as great and small. Certainly, when the term "great" is used relatively as a condensation of "greater" than so-and-so," and "small" is used correspondingly, greatness and smallness are counterparts and cannot exist without each other. But in this sense greatness is not a quality, not an intrinsic feature of anything; and it would be absurd to think of a movement in favor of greatness and against smallness in this sense. Such a movement would be self-defeating, since relative greatness can be promoted only by a simultaneous promotion of relative smallness. I feel sure that no theists would be content to regard God's goodness as analogous to this—as if what he supports were not the *good* but the *better*, and as if he had the paradoxical aim that all things should be better than other things.

This point is obscured by the fact that "great" and "small" seem to have an absolute as well as a relative sense. I cannot discuss here whether there is absolute magnitude or not, but if there is, there could be an absolute sense for "great," it could mean of at least a certain size, and it would make sense to speak of all things getting bigger, of a universe that was expanding all over, and therefore it would make sense to speak of promoting greatness. But in *this* sense great and small are not logically necessary counterparts: either quality could exist without the other. There would be no logical impossibility in everything's being small or in everything's being great.

Neither in the absolute nor in the relative sense, then, of "great" and "small" do these terms provide an analogy of the sort that would be needed to support this solution of the problem of evil. In neither case are greatness and smallness *both* necessary counterparts *and* mutually opposed forces or possible objects for support and attack.

It may be replied that good and evil are necessary counterparts in the same way as any quality and its logical opposite: redness can occur, it is suggested, only if non-redness also occurs. But unless evil is merely the privation of good, they are not logical opposites, and some farther argument would be needed to show that they are counterparts in the same way as genuine logical opposites. Let us assume that this could

be given. There is still doubt of the correctness of the metaphysical principle that a quality must have a real opposite: I suggest that it is not really impossible that everything should be, say, red, that the truth is merely that if everything were red we should not notice redness, and so we should have no word "red"; we observe and give names to qualities only if they have real opposites. If so, the principle that a term must have an opposite would belong only to our language or to our thought, and would not be an ontological principle, and, correspondingly, the rule that good cannot exist without evil would not state a logical necessity of a sort that God would just have to put up with. God might have made everything good, though *we* should not have noticed it if he had.

But, finally, even if we concede that this *is* an ontological principle, it will provide a solution for the problem of evil only if one is prepared to say, "Evil exists, but only just enough evil to serve as the counterpart of good." I doubt whether any theist will accept this. After all, the *ontological* requirement that non-redness should occur would be satisfied even if all the universe, except for a minute speck, were red, and, if there were a corresponding requirement for evil as a counterpart to good, a minute dose of evil would presumably do. But theists are not usually willing to say, in all contexts, that all the evil that occurs is a minute and necessary dose.

2. "Evil is necessary as a means to good."

It is sometimes suggested that evil is necessary for good not as a counterpart but as a means. In its simple form this has little plausibility as a solution of the problem of evil, since it obviously implies a severe restriction of God's power. It would be a *causal* law that you cannot have a certain end without a certain means, so that if God has to introduce evil as a means to good, he must be subject to at least some causal laws. This certainly conflicts with what a theist normally means by omnipotence. This view of God as limited by causal laws also conflicts with the view that causal laws are themselves made by God, which is more widely held than the corresponding view about the laws of logic. This conflict would, indeed, be resolved if it were possible for an omnipotent being to bind himself, and this possibility has still to be considered. Unless a favorable answer can be given to this question, the suggestion that evil is necessary as a means to good solves the problem of evil only by denying one of its constituent propositions, either that God is omnipotent or that "omnipotent" means what it says.

3.   "The universe is better with some evil in it than it could be if there were no evil."

Much more important is a solution which at first seems to be a mere variant of the previous one, that evil may contribute to the goodness of a whole in which it is found, so that the universe as a whole is better as it is, with some evil in it, than it would be if there were no evil. This solution may be developed in either of two ways. It may be supported by an aesthetic analogy, by the fact that contrasts heighten beauty, that in a musical work, for example, there may occur discords which somehow add to the beauty of the work as a whole. Alternatively, it may be worked out in connection with the notion of progress, that the best possible organization of the universe will not be static, but progressive, that the gradual overcoming of evil by good is really a finer thing than would be the eternal unchallenged supremacy of good.

In either case, this solution usually starts from the assumption that the evil whose existence gives rise to the problem of evil is primarily what is called physical evil, that is to say, pain. In Hume's rather half-hearted presentation of the problem of evil, the evils that he stresses are pain and disease, and those who reply to him argue that the existence of pain and disease makes possible the existence of sympathy, benevolence, heroism, and the gradually successful struggle of doctors and reformers to overcome these evils. In fact, theists often seize the opportunity to accuse those who stress the problem of evil of taking a low, materialistic view of good and evil, equating these with pleasure and pain, and of ignoring the more spiritual goods which can arise in the struggle against evils.

But let us see exactly what is being done here. Let us call pain and misery "first order evil" or "evil (1)." What contrasts with this, namely, pleasure and happiness, will be called "first order good" or "good (1)." Distinct from this is "second order good" or "good (2)" which somehow emerges in a complex situation in which evil (1) is a necessary component—logically, not merely causally, necessary. (Exactly *how* it emerges does not matter: in the crudest version of this solution good (2) is simply the heightening of happiness by the contrast with misery, in other versions it includes sympathy with suffering, heroism in facing danger, and the gradual decrease of first order evil and increase of first order good.) It is also being assumed that second order good is more important than first order good or evil, in particular that it more than outweighs the first order evil it involves.

Now this is a particularly subtle attempt to solve the problem of evil. It defends God's goodness and omnipotence on the ground that (on a sufficiently long view) this is the best of all logically possible worlds, because it includes the important second order goods, and yet it admits that real evils, namely first order evils, exist. But does it still hold that good and evil are opposed? Not, clearly, in the sense that we set out originally: good does not tend to eliminate evil in general. Instead, we have a modified, a more complex pattern. First order good (e.g., happiness) *contrasts with* first order evil (e.g., misery): these two are opposed in a fairly mechanical way; some second order goods (e.g., benevolence) try to maximize first order good and minimize first order evil; but God's goodness is not this, it is rather the will to maximize *second* order good. We might, therefore, call God's goodness an example of a third order goodness, or good (3). While this account is different from our original one, it might well be held to be an improvement on it, to give a more accurate description of the way in which good is opposed to evil, and to be consistent with the essential theist position.

There might, however, be several objections to this solution.

First, some might argue that such qualities as benevolence—and *a fortiori* the third order goodness which promotes benevolence—have a merely derivative value, that they are not higher sorts of good, but merely means to good (1), that is, to happiness, so that it would be absurd for God to keep misery in existence in order to make possible the virtues of benevolence, heroism, etc. The theist who adopts the present solution must, of course, deny this, but he can do so with some plausibility, so I should not press this objection.

Secondly, it follows from this solution that God is not in our sense benevolent or sympathetic: he is not concerned to minimize evil (1), but only to promote good (2); and this might be a disturbing conclusion for some theists.

But, thirdly, the fatal objection is this. Our analysis shows clearly the possibility of the existence of a *second* order evil, an evil (2) contrasting with good (2) as evil (1) contrasts with good (1). This would include malevolence, cruelty, callousness, cowardice, and states in which good (1) is decreasing and evil (1) increasing. And just as good (2) is held to be the important kind of good, the kind that God is concerned to promote, so evil (2) will, by analogy, be the important kind of evil, the kind which God, if he were wholly good and omnipotent, would eliminate. And yet evil (2) plainly exists, and indeed most theists (in other contexts) stress its existence more than that of evil (1). We should, therefore, state the problem of evil in terms of second order evil, and against this form of the problem the present solution is useless.

An attempt might be made to use this solution again, at a higher level, to explain the occurrence of evil (2): indeed the next main solution that we shall examine does just this, with the help of some new notions. Without any fresh notions,

such a solution would have little plausibility: for example, we could hardly say that the really important good was a good (3), such as the increase of benevolence in proportion to cruelty, which logically required for its occurrence the occurrence of some second order evil. But even if evil (2) could be explained in this way, it is fairly clear that there would be third order evils contrasting with this third order good: and we should be well on the way to an infinite regress, where the solution of a problem of evil, stated in terms of evil (n), indicated the existence of an evil ($n + 1$), and a farther problem to be solved.

4. "Evil is due to human free will."

Perhaps the most important proposed solution of the problem of evil is that evil is not to be ascribed to God at all, but to the independent actions of human beings, supposed to have been endowed by God with freedom of the will. This solution may be combined with the preceding one: first order evil (e.g., pain) may be justified as a logically necessary component in second order good (e.g., sympathy) while second order evil (e.g., cruelty) is not *justified*, but is so ascribed to human beings that God cannot be held responsible for it. This combination evades my third criticism of the preceding solution.

The free-will solution also involves the preceding solution at a higher level. To explain why a wholly good God gave men free will although it would lead to some important evils, it must be argued that it is better on the whole that men should act freely, and sometimes err, than that they should be innocent automata, acting rightly in a wholly determined way. Freedom, that is to say, is now treated as a third order good, and as being more valuable than second order goods (such as sympathy and heroism) would be if they were deterministically produced, and it is being assumed that second order evils, such as cruelty, are logically necessary accompaniments of freedom, just as pain is a logically necessary pre-condition of sympathy.

I think that this solution is unsatisfactory primarily because of the incoherence of the notion of freedom of the will: but I cannot discuss this topic adequately here, although some of my criticisms will touch upon it.

First I should query the assumption that second order evils are logically necessary accompaniments of freedom. I should ask this: if God has made men such that in their free choices they sometimes prefer what is good and sometimes what is evil, why could he not have made men such that they always freely choose the good? If there is no logical impossibility in a man's freely choosing the good on one, or on several, occasions, there cannot be a logical impossibility in his freely choosing the good on every occasion. God was not, then, faced with a choice between making innocent automata and making beings who, in acting freely, would sometimes go wrong: there was open to him the obviously better possibility of making beings who would act freely but always go right. Clearly, his failure to avail himself of this possibility is inconsistent with his being both omnipotent and wholly good.

If it is replied that this objection is absurd, that the making of some wrong choices is logically necessary for freedom, it would seem that "freedom" must here mean complete randomness or indeterminacy, including randomness with regard to the alternatives good and evil, in other words that men's choices and consequent actions can be "free" only if they are not determined by their characters. Only on this assumption can God escape the responsibility for men's actions; for if he made them as they are, but did not determine their wrong choices, this can only be because the wrong choices are not determined by men as they are. But then if freedom is randomness, how can it be a characteristic of *will*? And, still more, how can it be the most important good? What value or merit would there be in free choices if these were random actions which were not determined by the nature of the agent?

I conclude that to make this solution plausible two different senses of "freedom" must be confused, one sense which will justify the view that freedom is a third order good, more valuable than other goods would be without it, and another sense, sheer randomness, to prevent us from ascribing to God a decision to make men such that they sometimes go wrong when he might have made them such that they would always freely go right.

This criticism is sufficient to dispose of this solution. But besides this there is a fundamental difficulty in the notion of an omnipotent God creating men with free will, for if men's wills are really free this must mean that even God cannot control them, that is, that God is no longer omnipotent. It may be objected that God's gift of freedom to men does not mean that he *cannot* control their wills, but that he always *refrains* from controlling their wills. But why, we may ask, should God refrain from controlling evil wills? Why should he not leave men free to will rightly, but intervene when he sees them beginning to will wrongly? If God could do this, but does not, and if he is wholly good, the only explanation could be that even a wrong free act of will is not really evil, that its freedom is a value which outweighs its wrongness, so that there would be a loss of value if God took away the wrongness and the freedom together. But this is utterly opposed to what theists say about sin in other contexts. The present solution of the problem of evil, then, can be maintained only in the form that God has made men so free that he *cannot* control their wills.

This leads us to what I call the Paradox of Omnipotence: can an omnipotent being make things which he cannot subsequently control? Or, what is practically equivalent to this, can an omnipotent being make rules which then bind himself? (These are practically equivalent because any such rules could be regarded as setting certain things beyond his control, and *vice versa*.) The second of these formulations is relevant to the suggestions that we have already met, that an omnipotent God creates the rules of logic or causal laws, and is then bound by them.

It is clear that this is a paradox: the questions cannot be answered satisfactorily either in the affirmative or in the negative. If we answer "Yes," it follows that if God actually makes things which he cannot control, or makes rules which bind himself, he is not omnipotent once he has made them: there are *then* things which he cannot do. But if we answer "No," we are immediately asserting that there are things which he cannot do, that is to say that he is already not omnipotent.

It cannot be replied that the question which sets this paradox is not a proper question. It would make perfectly good sense to say that a human mechanic has made a machine which he cannot control: if there is any difficulty about the question it lies in the notion of omnipotence itself.

This, incidentally, shows that although we have approached this paradox from the free-will theory, it is equally a problem for a theological determinist. No one thinks that machines have free will, yet they may well be beyond the control of their makers. The determinist might reply that anyone who makes anything determines its ways of acting, and so determines its subsequent behavior: even the human mechanic does this by his *choice* of materials and structure for his machine, though he does not know all about either of these: the mechanic thus determines, though he may not foresee, his machine's actions. And since God is omniscient, and since his creation of things is total, he both determines and foresees the ways in which his creatures will act. We may grant this, but it is beside the point. The question is not whether God *originally* determined the future actions of his creatures, but whether he can *subsequently* control their actions, or whether he was able in his original creation to put things beyond his subsequent control. Even on determinist principles the answers "Yes" and "No" are equally irreconcilable with God's omnipotence.

Before suggesting a solution of this paradox, I would point out that there is a parallel Paradox of Sovereignty. Can a legal sovereign make a law restricting its own future legislative power? For example, could the British parliament make a law forbidding any future parliament to socialize banking, and also forbidding the future repeal of this law itself? Or could the British parliament, which was legally sovereign in Australia in, say, 1899, pass a valid law, or series of laws, which made it no longer sovereign in 1933? Again, neither the affirmative nor the negative answer is really satisfactory. If we were to answer "Yes," we should be admitting the validity of a law which, if it were actually made, would mean that parliament was no longer sovereign. If we were to answer "No," we should be admitting that there is a law, not logically absurd, which parliament cannot validly make, that is, that parliament is not now a legal sovereign. This paradox can be solved in the following way. We should distinguish between first order laws, that is, laws governing the actions of individuals and bodies other than the legislature, and second order laws, that is, laws about laws, laws governing the actions of the legislature itself. Correspondingly, we should distinguish two orders of sovereignty, first order sovereignty (sovereignty [1]) which is unlimited authority to make first order laws, and second order sovereignty (sovereignty [2]) which is unlimited authority to make second order laws. If we say that parliament is sovereign we might mean that any parliament at any time has sovereignty (1), or we might mean that parliament has both sovereignty (1) and sovereignty (2) at present, but we cannot without contradiction mean both that the present parliament has sovereignty (2) and that every parliament at every time has sovereignty (1), for if the present parliament has sovereignty (2) it may use it to take away the sovereignty (1) of later parliaments. What the paradox shows is that we cannot ascribe to any continuing institution legal sovereignty in an inclusive sense.

The analogy between omnipotence and sovereignty shows that the paradox of omnipotence can be solved in a similar way. We must distinguish between first order omnipotence (omnipotence [1]), that is unlimited power to act, and second order omnipotence (omnipotence

[2]), that is unlimited power to determine what powers to act things shall have. Then we could consistently say that God all the time has omnipotence (1), but if so no beings at any time have powers to act independently of God. Or we could say that God at one time had omnipotence (2), and used it to assign independent powers to act to certain things, so that God thereafter did not have omnipotence (1). But what the paradox shows is that we cannot consistently ascribe to any continuing being omnipotence in an inclusive sense. An alternative solution of this paradox would be simply to deny that God is a continuing being, that any times can be assigned to his actions at all. But on this assumption (which also has difficulties of its own) no meaning can be given to the assertion that God made men with wills so free that he could not control them. The paradox of omnipotence can be avoided by putting God outside time, but the free-will solution of the problem of evil cannot be saved in this way, and equally it remains impossible to hold that an omnipotent God *binds himself* by causal or logical laws.

Conclusion

Of the proposed solutions of the problem of evil which we have examined, none has stood up to criticism. There may be other solutions which require examination, but this study strongly suggests that there is no valid solution of the problem which does not modify at least one of the constituent propositions in a way which would seriously affect the essential core of the theistic position.

Quite apart from the problem of evil, the paradox of omnipotence has shown that God's omnipotence must in any case be restricted in one way or another, that unqualified omnipotence cannot be ascribed to any being that continues through time. And if God and his actions are not in time, can omnipotence, or power of any sort, be meaningfully ascribed to him?

Study Questions

1. What is the difference, according to Mackie, between adequate solutions, half-hearted solutions, and fallacious solutions? Are these exhaustive of the possible solutions to the Problem of Evil?

2. Among the Theocratic solutions offered: Good cannot exist without evil, evil is necessary as a means to good, the universe is better with some evil in it than it would be if there were no evil and evil is due to human free will, in which do you find Mackie's criticisms weakest and which strongest?

3. Can God create something He cannot control? Do you agree or disagree and why? How does this question differ from "Can God create something so heavy, He cannot move it?"

4. Do you agree or disagree with Mackie that "by way of the traditional problem of evil…it can be shown that…religious beliefs…are positively irrational…"? Why or why not?

5. Have an open, respectful discussion with fellow students over the Problem of Evil, as it can be succinctly stated and most students tend to have an intellectual curiosity about it.

Steven M. Cahn

The Moriarty Hypothesis

Why does an all-powerful, all-knowing, all-good God allow evil? Theists who seek to answer this question may take comfort in firmly embracing a justification that accommodates all past, present, and future evils, however horrific. But this approach leads to a philosophical pitfall.

To see why, consider the fictional example of Sherlock Holmes and his archfiend, Professor Moriarty. Holmes believed that Moriarty was the "great malignant brain" behind crime in London, the "deep organizing power" that unified "every deviltry" into "one connected whole," the "foul spider which lurks in the centre," "never caught—never so much as suspected."[1] Now suppose Moriarty's power extended throughout the universe, so that all events (perhaps excluding acts of human freedom) were the work of one omnipotent, omniscient, omnimalevolent demon. Let us call this theory "the Moriarty hypothesis."

Does the presence of various goods refute the Moriarty hypothesis? No, for just as theism can be shown to be logically consistent with the world's most horrendous evils, so the Moriarty hypothesis can be shown to be logically consistent with the world's most wonderful goods. While evils can be viewed as logically necessary for the greater good, goods can be viewed as logically necessary for the greater evil.[2]

Assuming, then, that the Moriarty hypothesis is not obviously false and leaving aside speculation about whether a next life may bring greater goods or greater evils, do theists have any different expectations about the events of this life than do those who accept the Moriarty hypothesis?

Consider the following two assessments of the human condition:

1. "[I]s not all life pathetic and futile?... We reach. We grasp. And what is left in our hands at the end? A shadow. Or worse than a shadow—misery."

2. "The first entrance into life gives anguish to the new-born infant and to its wretched parent; weakness, impotence, distress attend each stage of that life, and it is at last finished in agony and horror."

Which is the viewpoint of a theist and which that of a believer in the Moriarty hypothesis? As it happens, 1 is uttered by Sherlock Holmes,[3] and 2 by the orthodox believer Demea in Part X of Hume's *Dialogues Concerning Natural Religion*. The positions appear interchangeable.

Both the theist and the believer in the Moriarty hypothesis recognize that life contains happiness as well as misery. No matter how terrible the misery, the theist may regard it as unsurprising; after all, aren't all evils, in principle, explicable?

From *Philosophy for the 21st Century: A Comprehensive Reader*, Steven M. Cahn, ed. 2003, pp. 80–81. Reprinted with permission of Oxford University Press, Inc..

To believers in the Moriarty hypothesis, happiness may be regarded as unsurprising; after all, aren't all goods, in principle, explicable? Supporters of both positions are apt to view events that appear to conflict with their fundamental principles merely as tests of fortitude, opportunities to display strength of commitment.

If defenders of either view modified their beliefs in the light of changing circumstances, then their expectations would differ. But believers are loath to admit doubt. They admire those who stand fast in their faith, regardless of appearances.

Any seemingly contrary evidence can be considered ambiguous. St. Paul says, "we see in a mirror, dimly,"[4] and Sherlock Holmes speaks of seeking the truth "through the veil which shrouded it."[5] If events are so difficult to interpret, they provide little reason for believers to abandon deep-seated tenets. Those who vacillate are typically viewed by other members of their communities as weakhearted and faithless.

One other attempt to differentiate the expectations of the theist and the believer in the Moriarty hypothesis is to suppose that theists have reason to be more optimistic than their counterpart. But this presumption is unwarranted. Recall the words from the Book of Ecclesiastes: "I accounted those who died long since more fortunate than those who are still living; and happier than either are those who have not yet come into being and have never witnessed the miseries that go on under the sun."[6] A more pessimistic view is hard to imagine.

We may be living, as the theist supposes, in the best of all possible worlds, but, if so, the best of all possible worlds contains immense torments. On the other hand, we may be living, as the believer in the Moriarty hypothesis supposes, in the worst of all possible worlds, but, if so, the worst of all possible worlds contains enormous delights. Both scenarios offer us reason to be cheerful and reason to be gloomy. Our outlook depends on our personalities, not our theology or demonology.

So, as we seek to understand life's vicissitudes, does it make any difference whether we believe in God or in the Moriarty hypothesis? Not if we hold either of these beliefs unshakeably. For the more tenaciously we cling to one of them, the less it matters which one.

Notes

1. The *Complete Sherlock Holmes* (Garden City, NY: Doubleday & Company, n.d.), pp. 471, 496, 769. The works cited are "The Final Problem", "The Adventure of the Norwood Builder," and "The Valley of Fear."

2. See my "Cacodaemony," *Analysis* 37 (1977), pp. 69–73.

3. See "The Adventure of the Retired Colourman," p. 1113.

4. I Corinthians 13:12.

5. See "The Final Problem," p. 471.

6. Ecclesiastes 4:2,3. The translation is from *Tanakh: The Holy Scriptures* (Philadelphia: Jewish Publication Society, 1988).

SECTION IV

Does God Exist?

Saint Thomas Aquinas

The Five Ways

Saint Thomas Aquinas (1225–1274) was an Italian Dominican priest in the Catholic Church, known as Doctor Angelicus, Doctor Communis, or Doctor Universalis. "Aquinas" is not Thomas' surname, but rather a Latin adjective meaning "of Aquino," his place of birth, in the Kingdom of Sicily, in present-day Lazio. He was a proponent of natural theology and the father of what is today described as the Catholic theological system of Thomism. His contributions to philosophy and theology range over the areas of metaphysics, epistemology, ethics, natural law, social and political philosophy.

Thomas is still considered by the Catholic Church to be one of the greatest theologians amongst the 33 Doctors of the Church. In his *Fausto appetente*, Pope Benedict XV stated in 1921, "The (Catholic) Church has declared Thomas' doctrines to be her own." In the following selection from his massive *Summa Theologica*, Saint Thomas offers five proofs for the existence of the traditional Judeo-Christian Supreme Being, God. These arguments are traditionally considered *a posteriori* proofs; that is, proofs dependent upon sensory experience unlike *The Ontological Argument of Saint Anselm*, which is considered an *a priori* proof of God's existence since that proof does not depend upon sensory experience.

From *Basic Writings of Saint Thomas Aquinas*, Vol. 1, Anton C. Pegis, ed., 1997, Hackett Publishing, a reprint of the Random House edition of 1945, pp. 22–23. Reprinted by permission of Hackett Publishing Company, Inc. All rights reserved.

The existence of God can be proved in five ways.

The first and more manifest way is the argument from motion. It is certain, and evident to our senses, that in the world some things are in motion. Now whatever is in motion is put in motion by another, for nothing can be in motion except it is in potentiality to that towards which it is in motion; whereas a thing moves inasmuch as it is in act. For motion is nothing else than the reduction of something from potentiality to actuality. But nothing can be reduced from potentiality to actuality, except by something in a state of actuality. Thus that which is actually hot, as fire, makes wood, which is potentially hot, to be actually hot, and thereby moves and changes it. Now it is not possible that the same thing should be at once in actuality and potentiality in the same respect, but only in different respects. For what is actually hot cannot simultaneously be potentially hot; but it is simultaneously potentially cold. It is therefore impossible that in the same respect and in the same way a thing should be both mover and moved, *i.e.*, that it should move itself. Therefore, whatever is in motion must be put in motion by another. If that by which it is put in motion be itself put in motion, then this also must needs be put in motion by another, and that by another again. But this cannot go on to infinity, because then there would be no first mover, and, consequently, no other mover; seeing that subsequent movers move only inasmuch as they are put in motion by the first mover; as the staff moves only because it is put in motion by the hand. Therefore it is necessary to arrive at a first mover, put in motion by no other; and this everyone understands to be God.

The second way is from the nature of efficient cause. In the world of sense we find there is an order of efficient causes. There is no case known (neither is it, indeed, possible) in which a thing is found to be the efficient cause of itself; for so it would be prior to itself, which is impossible. Now in efficient causes it is not possible to go on to infinity, because in all efficient causes following in order, the first is the cause of the intermediate cause, and the intermediate is the cause of the ultimate cause, whether the intermediate cause be several, or only one. Now to take away the cause is to take away the effect. Therefore, if there be no first cause among efficient causes, there will be no ultimate, nor any intermediate cause. But if in efficient causes it is possible to go on to infinity, there will be no first efficient cause, neither will there be an ultimate effect, nor any intermediate efficient causes; all of which is plainly false. Therefore it is necessary to admit a first efficient cause, to which everyone gives the name of God.

The third way is taken from possibility and necessity, and runs thus. We find in nature things that are possible to be and not to be, since they are found to be generated, and to corrupt, and consequently, they are possible to be and not to be. But it is impossible for these always to exist, for that which is possible not to be at some time is not. Therefore, if everything is possible not to be, then at one time there could have been nothing in existence. Now if this were true, even now there would be nothing in existence, because that which does not exist only begins to exist by something already existing. Therefore, if at one time nothing was in existence, it would have been impossible for anything to have begun to exist; and thus even now nothing would be in existence—which is absurd. Therefore, not all beings are merely possible, but there must exist something the existence of which is necessary. But every necessary thing either has its necessity caused by another, or not. Now it is impossible to go on to infinity in necessary things which have their necessity caused by another, as has been already proved in regard to efficient causes. Therefore we cannot but postulate the existence of some being having of itself its own necessity, and not receiving it from another, but rather causing in others their necessity. This all men speak of as God.

The fourth way is taken from the gradation to be found in things. Among beings there are some more and some less good, true, noble and the like. But *more* and *less* are predicated of different things, according as they resemble in their

different ways something which is the maximum, as a thing is said to be hotter according as it more nearly resembles that which is hottest; so that there is something which is truest, something best, something noblest and, consequently, something which is most being, for those things that are greatest in truth are greatest in being, as it is written in *Metaph.* ii.[1] Now the maximum in any genus is the cause of all in that genus, as fire, which is the maximum heat, is the cause of all hot things, as is said in the same book.[2] Therefore there must also be something which is to all beings the cause of their being, goodness, and every other perfection; and this we call God.

The fifth way is taken from the governance of the world. We see that things which lack intelligence, such as natural bodies, act for an end, and this is evident from their acting always, or nearly always, in the same way, so as to obtain the best result. Hence it is plain that not fortuitously, but designedly, do they achieve their end. Now whatever lacks intelligence cannot move towards an end, unless it be directed by some being endowed with knowledge and intelligence; as the arrow is directed by the archer. Therefore some intelligent being exists by whom all natural things are directed to their end; and this being we call God.

Study Questions

1. Why does Saint Thomas draw a distinction between motion and causality in his first two ways? Has the understanding of the domain of causality expanded in modern times compared to Medieval times?

2. If Saint Thomas' First Way from motion depends upon Aristotle's physics, does that render his First Way superfluous given the abandonment of Aristotle's physics?

3. Does Saint Thomas' Second Way dwindle into a historical curiosity given the extensive and deep developments across the many natural sciences?

4. In his Third Way Saint Thomas claims that you cannot get something from nothing. Is this true? If one argues for the truth of this claim on grounds of conceivability, what has that to do with the nature of reality? Does contemporary quantum mechanics allow for creation *ex nihilo*?

5. Is St. Thomas' Fifth Way, From the Governance of the World, a precursor to contemporary Intelligent Design arguments? Do such views logically entail monotheism or polytheism? If one draws analogies to artifacts, as William Paley did with a watch, doesn't inductive reasoning lead to polytheism?

6. Napolean Bonaparte is said to have remarked to Pierre Laplace, one of France's most prominent physicists, "They tell me you have written this large book on the system of the universe, and have never even mentioned its Creator." Laplace is described as simply responding, "Sire, I had no need of that hypothesis." Has the modern world of Laplace and science simply moved beyond the theological arguments of the past?

Notes

1. Aquinas refers here to Aristotle's *Metaphysics*, Ia 1 (993b30).

2. *Metaphysics*, Ia 1 (993b25).

Saint Anselm

The Existence and Nature of God
The Ontological Argument

Anselm of Canterbury, aka St. Anselm (1033–1109 CE), was a Benedictine monk, a philosopher, and Archbishop of Canterbury from 1093 to 1109. Sometimes regarded as the founder of Scholasticism, St. Anselm is best known, perhaps, for his Ontological Argument justifying, even for the fool (atheist), the existence of God.

At birth, Anselm was given the name Anselmus Candiae Genavae. He was born into a noble family in the Aosta Valley region in Northern Italy. His parents were from a noble lineage and holders of fiefdoms within the Burgundian region. When he was fifteen, Anselm informed his family that he wanted to enter a monastery but, without his father's permission, the monastery's abbot refused to accept him. This disappointment apparently left Anselm deeply distraught. Giving up on his studies, Anselm finally left home, crossed the Alps, and traveled through France. At about the age of 26, Anselm had made his way to present-day northern France, Normandy. At about this time, he entered the abbey at Avranches. William II of England first elevated Anselm to Archbishop of Canterbury. Though Anselm was later exiled, he was finally reinstated at Canterbury. In 1720, Pope Clement XI proclaimed Anselm a Doctor of the Church.

Chapter II

Truly there is a God, although the fool hath said in his heart, There is no God.

And so, Lord, do thou, who dost give understanding to faith, give me, so far as thou knowest it to be profitable, to understand that thou art as we believe; and that thou art that which we believe. And, indeed, we believe that thou art a being than which nothing greater can be conceived. Or is there no such nature, since the fool hath said in his heart, there is no God? (Psalms XIV. 1). But, at any rate, this very fool, when he hears of this being of which I speak—a being than which nothing greater can be conceived—understands what he hears, and what he understands is in his understanding; although he does not understand it to exist.

For, it is one thing for an object to be in the understanding, and another to understand that the object exists. When a painter first conceives of what he will afterwards perform, he has it in his understanding, but he does not yet understand it to be, because he has not yet performed it. But after he has made the painting, he both has it in his understanding, and he understands that it exists, because he has made it.

Hence, even the fool is convinced that something exists in the understanding, at least, than which nothing greater can be conceived. For, when he hears of this, he understands it. And whatever is understood, exists in the understanding. And assuredly that, than which nothing greater can be conceived, cannot exist in the understanding alone. For, suppose it exists in the understanding alone: then it can be conceived to exist in reality; which is greater.

Therefore, if that, than which nothing greater can be conceived, exists in the understanding alone, the very being, than which nothing greater can be conceived, is one, than which a greater can be conceived. But obviously this is impossible. Hence, there is no doubt that there exists a being, than which nothing greater can be conceived, and it exists both in the understanding and in reality.

Chapter III

God cannot be conceived not to exist.—God is that, than which nothing greater can be conceived.—That which can be conceived not to exist is not God.

And it assuredly exists so truly, that it cannot be conceived not to exist. For, it is possible to conceive of a being which cannot be conceived not to exist; and this is greater than one which can be conceived not to exist. Hence, if that, than which nothing greater can be conceived, can be conceived not to exist, it is not that, than which nothing greater can be conceived. But this is an irreconcilable contradiction. There is, then, so truly a being than which nothing greater can be conceived to exist, that it cannot even be conceived not to exist; and this being thou art, O Lord, our God.

So truly, therefore, dost thou exist, O Lord, my God, that thou canst not be conceived not to exist; and rightly. For, if a mind could conceive of a being better than thee, the creature would rise above the Creator; and this is most absurd. And, indeed, whatever else there is, except thee alone, can be conceived not to exist. To thee alone, therefore, it belongs to exist more truly than all other beings, and hence in a higher degree than

all others. For, whatever else exists does not exist so truly, and hence in a less degree it belongs to it to exist. Why, then, has the fool said in his heart, there is no God (Psalms XIV. 1), since it is so evident, to a rational mind, that thou dost exist in the highest degree of all? Why, except that he is dull and a fool?

Chapter IV

How the fool has said in his heart what cannot be conceived.—A thing may be conceived in two ways: (1) when the word signifying it is conceived; (2) when the thing itself is understood. As far as the word goes, God can be conceived not to exist; in reality he cannot.

But how has the fool said in his heart what he could not conceive; or how is it that he could not conceive what he said in his heart? since it is the same to say in the heart, and to conceive.

But, if really, nay, since really, he both conceived, because he said in his heart; and did not say in his heart, because he could not conceive; there is more than one way in which a thing is said in the heart or conceived. For, in one sense, an object is conceived, when the word signifying it is conceived; and in another, when the very entity, which the object is, is understood.

In the former sense, then, God can be conceived not to exist; but in the latter, not at all. For no one who understands what fire and water are can conceive fire to be water, in accordance with the nature of the facts themselves, although this is possible according to the words. So, then, no one who understands what God is can conceive that God does not exist; although he says these words in his heart, either without any, or with some foreign, signification. For, God is that than which a greater cannot be conceived. And he who thoroughly understands this, assuredly understands that this being so truly exists, that not even in concept can it be non-existent. Therefore, he who understands that God so exists, cannot conceive that he does not exist.

I thank thee, gracious Lord, I thank thee; because what I formerly believed by thy bounty, I now so understand by thine illumination, that if I were unwilling to believe that thou dost exist, I should not be able not to understand this to be true.

Chapter V

God is whatever it is better to be than not to be; and he, as the only self-existent being, creates all things from nothing.

What are thou, then, Lord God, than whom nothing greater can be conceived? But what art thou, except that which, as the highest of all beings, alone exists through itself, and creates all other things from nothing? For, whatever is not this is less than a thing which can be conceived off. But this cannot be conceived of thee. What good, therefore, does the supreme Good lack, through which every good is? Therefore, thou art just, truthful, blessed, and whatever it is better to be than not to be. For it is better to be just than not just; better to be blessed than not blessed.

Study Questions

1. Sort through Anselm's writing and pick out just those claims specific to the Ontological Argument. Which do you find to be the strongest and which the weakest?

2. How does Anselm move from "exists in the understanding" to "exists in reality"?

3. Do you find it difficult to infer the existence in reality of something whose existence is first in the understanding? If so, what might you infer if a friend told you, "I really want one of those cool bicycles that has only one wheel"?

4. The Ontological Argument has been described as an *a priori* argument, whereas Aquinas' Five Ways have been described as being *a posteriori*. Which type of argument in this context do you find most fascinating, persuasive, or problematic and why?

Bertrand Russell

Why I Am Not a Christian

The subject about which I am going to speak to you tonight is "Why I Am Not a Christian." Perhaps it would be as well, first of all, to try to make out what one means by the word "Christian." It is used these days in a very loose sense by a great many people. Some people mean no more by it than a person who attempts to live a good life. In that sense I suppose there would be Christians in all sects and creeds; but I do not think that that is the proper sense of the word, if only because it would imply that all the people who are not Christians—all the Buddhists, Confucians, Mohammedans, and so on—are not trying to live a good life. I do not mean by a Christian any person who tries to live decently according to his lights. I think that you must have a certain amount of definite belief before you have a right to call yourself a Christian. The word does not have quite such a full-blooded meaning now as it had in the times of St. Augustine and St. Thomas Aquinas. In those days, if a man said that he was a Christian it was known what he meant. You accepted a whole collection of creeds which were set out with great precision, and every single syllable of those creeds you believed with the whole strength of your convictions.

What Is a Christian?

Nowadays it is not quite that. We have to be a little more vague in our meaning of Christianity. I think, however, that there are two different items which are quite essential to anybody calling himself a Christian. The first is one of a dogmatic nature—namely, that you must believe in God and immortality. If you do not believe in those two things, I do not think that you can properly call yourself a Christian. Then, further than that, as the name implies, you must have some kind of belief about Christ. The Mohammedans, for instance, also believe in God and in immortality, and yet they would not call themselves Christians. I think you must have at the very lowest the belief that Christ was, if not divine, at least the best and wisest of men. If you are not going to believe that much about Christ, I do not think you have any right to call yourself a Christian. Of course, there is another sense, which you find in *Whitaker's Almanack* and in geography books, where the population of the world is said to be divided into Christians, Mohammedans, Buddhists, fetish worshipers, and so on; and in that sense we are all Christians. The geography books count us all in, but that is a purely geographical sense, which I suppose we can ignore. Therefore I take it that when I tell you why I am not a Christian I have to tell you two different things: first, why I do not believe in God and in immortality; and, secondly, why I do not think that Christ was the best and wisest of men, although I grant him a very high degree of moral goodness.

But for the successful efforts of unbelievers in the past, I could not take so elastic a definition of Christianity as that. As I

From *Why I am Not a Christian, and Other Essays on Religion and Related Subjects*, 1957, New York: Touchstone, pp. 3–24. Reprinted with permission of Simon & Schuster, Inc. from *Why I am Not a Christian, and Other Essays on Religion and Related Subjects*, by Bertrand Russell. Copyright © 1957 George Allen & Unwin, Ltd.

said before, in olden days it had a much more full-blooded sense. For instance, it included the belief in hell. Belief in eternal hell fire was an essential item of Christian belief until pretty recent times. In this country, as you know, it ceased to be an essential item because of a decision of the Privy Council, and from that decision the Archbishop of Canterbury and the Archbishop of York dissented; but in this country our religion is settled by Act of Parliament, and therefore the Privy Council was able to override their Graces and hell was no longer necessary to a Christian. Consequently I shall not insist that a Christian must believe in hell.

The Existence of God

To come to this question of the existence of God: it is a large and serious question, and if I were to attempt to deal with it in any adequate manner I should have to keep you here until Kingdom Come, so that you will have to excuse me if I deal with it in a somewhat summary fashion. You know, of course, that the Catholic Church has laid it down as a dogma that the existence of God can be proved by the unaided reason. That is a somewhat curious dogma, but it is one of their dogmas. They had to introduce it because at one time the freethinkers adopted the habit of saying that there were such and such arguments which mere reason might urge against the existence of God, but of course they knew as a matter of faith that God did exist. The arguments and the reasons were set out at great length, and the Catholic Church felt that they must stop it. Therefore they laid it down that the existence of God can be proved by the unaided reason and they had to set up what they considered were arguments to prove it. There are, of course, a number of them, but I shall take only a few.

The First Cause Argument

Perhaps the simplest and easiest to understand is the argument of the First Cause. (It is maintained that everything we see in this world has a cause, and as you go back in the chain of causes further

and further you must come to a First Cause, and to that First Cause you give the name of God.) That argument, I suppose, does not carry very much weight nowadays, because, in the first place, cause is not quite what it used to be. The philosophers and the men of science have got going on cause, and it has not anything like the vitality it used to have; but, apart from that, you can see that the argument that there must be a First Cause is one that cannot have any validity. I may say that when I was a young man and was debating these questions very seriously in my mind, I for a long time accepted the argument of the First Cause, until one day, at the age of eighteen, I read John Stuart Mill's Autobiography, and I there found this sentence: "My father taught me that the question 'Who made me?' cannot be answered, since it immediately suggests the further question 'Who made god?'" That very simple sentence showed me, as I still think, the fallacy in the argument of the First Cause. If everything must have a cause, then God must have a cause. If there can be anything without a cause, it may just as well be the world as God, so that there cannot be any validity in that argument. It is exactly of the same nature as the Hindu's view, that the world rested upon an elephant and the elephant rested upon a tortoise; and when they said, "How about the tortoise?" the Indian said, "Suppose we change the subject." The argument is really no better than that. There is no reason why the world could not have come into being without a cause; nor, on the other hand, is there any reason why it should not have always existed. There is no reason to suppose that the world had a beginning at all. The idea that things must have a beginning is really due to the poverty of our imagination. Therefore, perhaps, I need not waste any more time upon the argument about the First Cause.

The Natural Law Argument

Then there is a very common argument from natural law. That was a favorite argument all through the eighteenth century, especially under the influence of Sir Isaac Newton and his cosmogony. People observed the planets going around the sun according to the law of gravitation, and they thought that God had given a behest to these planets to move in that particular fashion, and that was why they did so. That was, of course, a convenient and simple explanation that saved them the trouble of looking any further for explanations of the law of gravitation. Nowadays we explain the law of gravitation in a somewhat complicated fashion that Einstein has introduced. I do not propose to give you a lecture on the law of gravitation, as interpreted by Einstein, because that again would take some time; at any rate, you no longer have the sort of natural law that you had in the Newtonian system, where, for some reason that nobody could understand, nature behaved in a uniform fashion. We now find that a great many things we thought were natural laws are really human conventions. You know that even in the remotest depths of stellar space there are still three feet to a yard. That is, no doubt, a very remarkable fact, but you would hardly call it a law of nature. And a great many things that have been regarded as laws of nature are of that kind. On the other hand, where you can get down to any knowledge of what atoms actually do, you will find they are much less subject to law than people thought, and that the laws at which you arrive are statistical averages of just the sort that would emerge from chance. There is, as we all know, a law that if you throw dice you will get double sixes only about once in thirty-six times, and we do not regard that as evidence that the fall of the dice is regulated by design; on the contrary, if the double sixes came every time we should think that there was design. The laws of nature are of that sort as regards a great many of them. They are statistical averages such as would emerge from the laws of chance; and that makes this whole business of natural law much less impressive than it formerly was. Quite apart from that, which represents the momentary state of science that may change tomorrow, the whole idea that natural laws imply a lawgiver is due to a confusion between natural and human laws. Human laws are behests commanding you to behave a certain way, in which you may choose to behave, or you may choose not to behave; but natural laws are a description of how things do in fact behave, and being a mere description of what they in fact do, you cannot argue that there must be somebody who told them to do that, because even supposing that there were, you are then faced with the question "Why did God issue just those natural laws and no others?" If you say that he did it simply from his own good pleasure, and without any reason, you then find that there is something which is not subject to law, and so your train of natural law is interrupted. If you say, as more orthodox theologians do, that in all the laws which God issues he had a reason for giving those laws rather than others—the reason, of course, being to create the best universe, although you would never think it to look at it—if there were a reason for the laws which God gave, then God himself was subject to law, and therefore you do not get any advantage by introducing God as an intermediary. You really have a law outside and anterior to the divine edicts, and God does not serve your purpose, because he is not the ultimate lawgiver. In short, this whole argument about natural law no longer has anything like the strength that it used to have. I am traveling on in time in my review of the arguments. The arguments that are used for the existence of God change their character as time goes on. They were at first hard intellectual arguments embodying certain quite definite fallacies. As we come to modern times they become less respectable intellectually and more and more affected by a kind of moralizing vagueness.

The Argument from Design

The next step in the process brings us to the argument from design. You all know the argument from design: everything in the world is made just so that we can manage to live in the world, and if the world was ever so little different, we could not manage to live in it. That is the argument from design. It sometimes takes a rather curious form; for instance, it is argued that rabbits have white tails in order to be easy to shoot. I do not know how rabbits would view that application. It is an easy argument to parody. You all know Voltaire's remark, that obviously the nose was designed to be such as to fit spectacles. That sort of parody has turned out to be not nearly so wide of the mark as it might have seemed in the eighteenth century, because since the time of Darwin we understand much better why living creatures are adapted to their environment. It is not that their environment was made to be suitable to them but that they grew to be suitable to it, and that is the basis of adaptation. There is no evidence of design about it.

When you come to look into this argument from design, it is a most astonishing thing that people can believe that this world, with all the things that are in it, with all its defects, should be the best that omnipotence and omniscience have been able to produce in millions of years. I really cannot believe it. Do you think that, if you were granted omnipotence and omniscience and millions of years in which to perfect your world, you could produce nothing better than the Ku Klux Klan or the Fascists? Moreover, if you accept the ordinary laws of science, you have to suppose that human life and life in general on this planet will die out in due course: it is a stage in the decay of the solar system; at a certain stage of decay you get the sort of conditions of temperature and so forth which are suitable to protoplasm, and there is life for a short time in the life of the whole solar system. You see in the moon the sort of thing to which the earth is tending—something dead, cold, and lifeless.

I am told that that sort of view is depressing, and people will sometimes tell you that if they believed that, they would not be able to go on living. Do not believe it; it is all nonsense. Nobody really worries much about what is going to happen millions of years hence. Even if they think they are worrying much about that, they are really deceiving themselves. They are worried about something much more mundane, or it may merely be a bad digestion; but nobody is really seriously rendered unhappy by the thought of something that is going to happen to this world millions and millions of years hence. Therefore, although it is of course a gloomy view to suppose that life will die out—at least I suppose we may say so, although sometimes when I contemplate the things that people do with their lives I think it is almost a consolation—it is not such as to render life miserable. It merely makes you turn your attention to other things.

The Moral Arguments for Deity

Now we reach one stage further in what I shall call the intellectual descent that the theists have made in their argumentations, and we come to what are called the moral arguments for the existence of God. You all know, of course, that there used to be in the old days three intellectual arguments for the existence of God, all of which were disposed of by Immanuel Kant in the *Critique of Pure Reason*; but no sooner had he disposed of those arguments than he invented a new one, a moral argument, and that quite convinced him. He was like many people: in intellectual matters he was skeptical, but in moral matters he believed implicitly in the maxims that he had imbibed at his mother's knee. That illustrates what the psychoanalysts so much emphasize—the immensely stronger hold upon us that our very early associations have than those of later times.

Kant, as I say, invented a new moral argument for the existence of God, and that in varying forms was extremely popular during the nineteenth century. It has all sorts of forms. One form is to say there would be no right or wrong unless God existed. I am not for the moment concerned with whether there is a difference between right and wrong, or whether there is not: that is another question. The point I am concerned with is that, if you are quite sure there is a difference between right and wrong, then you are in this situation: Is that difference due to God's fiat or is it not? If it is due to God's fiat, then for God himself there is no difference between right and wrong, and it is no longer a significant statement to say that God is good. If you are going to say, as theologians do, that God is good, you must then say that right and wrong have some meaning which is independent of God's fiat, because God's fiats are good and not bad independently of the mere fact that he made them. If you are going to say that, you will then have to say that it is not only through God that right and wrong came into being, but that they are in their essence logically anterior to God. You could, of course, if you liked, say that there was a superior deity who gave orders to the God that made this world, or could take up the line that some of the gnostics took up—a line which I often thought was a very plausible one—that as a matter of fact this world that we know was made by the devil at a moment when God was not looking. There is a good deal to be said for that, and I am not concerned to refute it.

The Argument for the Remedying of Injustice

Then there is another very curious form of moral argument, which is this: they say that the existence of God is required in order to bring justice into the world. In the part of this universe that we know there is great injustice, and often the good suffer, and often the wicked prosper, and one hardly knows which of those is the more annoying; but if you are going to have justice in the universe as a whole you have to suppose a future life to redress the balance of life here on earth. So they say that there must be a God, and there must be Heaven and Hell in order that in the long run there may be justice. That is a very curious argument. If you looked at the matter from a scientific point of view, you would say, "After all, I only know this world. I do not know about the rest of the universe, but so far as one can argue at all on probabilities one would say that probably this world is a fair sample, and if there is injustice here the odds are that there is injustice elsewhere also." Supposing you got a crate of oranges that you opened, and you found all the top layer of oranges bad, you would not argue, "The underneath ones must be good, so as to redress the balance." You would say, "Probably the whole lot is a bad consignment"; and that is

really what a scientific person would argue about the universe. He would say, "Here we find in this world a great deal of injustice, and so far as that goes that is a reason for supposing that justice does not rule in the world; and therefore so far as it goes it affords a moral argument against deity and not in favor of one." Of course I know that the sort of intellectual arguments that I have been talking to you about are not what really moves people. What really moves people to believe in God is not any intellectual argument at all. Most people believe in God because they have been taught from early infancy to do it, and that is the main reason.

Then I think that the next most powerful reason is the wish for safety, a sort of feeling that there is a big brother who will look after you. That plays a very profound part in influencing people's desire for a belief in God.

The Character of Christ

I now want to say a few words upon a topic which I often think is not quite sufficiently dealt with by Rationalists, and that is the question whether Christ was the best and the wisest of men. It is generally taken for granted that we should all agree that that was so. I do not myself. I think that there are a good many points upon which I agree with Christ a great deal more than the professing Christians do. I do not know that I could go with Him all the way, but I could go with Him much further than most professing Christians can. You will remember that He said, "Resist not evil: but whosoever shall smite thee on thy right cheek, turn to him the other also." That is not a new precept or a new principle. It was used by Lao-tse and Buddha some 500 or 600 years before Christ, but it is not a principle which as a matter of fact Christians accept. I have no doubt that the present prime minister [Stanley Baldwin], for instance, is a most sincere Christian, but I should not advise any of you to go and smite him on one cheek. I think you might find that he thought this text was intended in a figurative sense.

Then there is another point which I consider excellent. You will remember that Christ said, "Judge not lest ye be judged." That principle I do not think you would find was popular in the law courts of Christian countries. I have known in my time quite a number of judges who were very earnest Christians, and none of them felt that they were acting contrary to Christian principles in what they did. Then Christ says, "Give to him that asketh of thee, and from him that would borrow of thee turn not thou away." That is a very good principle. Your Chairman has reminded you that we are not here to talk politics, but I cannot help observing that the last general election was fought on the question of how desirable it was to turn away from him that would borrow of thee, so that one must assume that the Liberals and Conservatives of this country are composed of people who do not agree with the teaching of Christ, because they certainly did very emphatically turn away on that occasion.

Then there is one other maxim of Christ which I think has a great deal in it, but I do not find that it is very popular among some of our Christian friends. He says, "If thou wilt be perfect, go and sell that which thou hast, and give to the poor." That is a very excellent maxim, but, as I say, it is not much practised. All these, I think, are good maxims, although they are a little difficult to live up to. I do not profess to live up to them myself; but then, after all, it is not quite the same thing as for a Christian.

Defects in Christ's Teaching

Having granted the excellence of these maxims, I come to certain points in which I do not believe that one can grant either the superlative wisdom or the superlative goodness of Christ as depicted in the Gospels; and here I may say that one is not concerned with the historical question. Historically it is quite doubtful whether Christ ever existed at all, and if He did we do not know anything about him, so that I am not concerned with the historical question, which is a very difficult one. I am concerned with Christ as He appears in the Gospels, taking the Gospel narrative as it stands, and there one does find some things that do not seem to be very wise. For one thing, he certainly thought that His second coming would occur in clouds of glory before the death of all the people who were living at that time. There are a great many texts that prove that. He says, for instance, "Ye shall not have gone over the cities of Israel till the Son of Man be come." Then he says, "There are some standing here which shall not taste death till the Son of Man comes into His kingdom"; and there are a lot of places where it is quite clear that He believed that His second coming would happen during the lifetime of many then living. That was the belief of His earlier followers, and it was the basis of a good deal of His moral teaching. When He said, "Take no thought for the morrow," and things of that sort, it was very largely because He thought that the second coming was going to be very soon, and that all ordinary mundane affairs did not count. I have, as a matter of fact, known some Christians who did believe that the second coming was imminent. I knew a parson who frightened his congregation terribly by telling them that the second coming was very imminent indeed, but they were much consoled when they found that he was planting trees in his garden. The early Christians did really believe it, and they did abstain from such things as planting trees in their gardens, because they did accept from Christ the belief that the second coming was imminent. In that respect, clearly He was not so wise as some other people have been, and He was certainly not superlatively wise.

The Moral Problem

Then you come to moral questions. There is one very serious defect to my mind in Christ's moral character, and that is that He believed in hell. I do not myself feel that any person who is really profoundly humane can believe in everlasting punishment. Christ certainly as depicted in the Gospels did believe in everlasting punishment, and one does find repeatedly a vindictive fury against those people who would not listen to His preaching—an attitude which is not uncommon with preachers, but which does somewhat detract from superlative excellence. You do not, for instance find that attitude in Socrates. You find him quite bland and urbane toward the people who would not listen to him; and it is, to my mind, far more worthy of a sage to take that line than to take the line of indignation. You probably all remember the sorts of things that Socrates was saying when he was dying, and the sort of things that he generally did say to people who did not agree with him.

You will find that in the Gospels Christ said, "Ye serpents, ye generation of vipers, how can ye escape the damnation of hell?" That was said to people who did not like His preaching. It is not really to my mind quite the best tone, and there are a great many of these things about hell. There is, of course, the familiar text about the sin against the Holy Ghost: "Whosoever speaketh against the Holy Ghost it shall not be forgiven him neither in this world nor in the world to come." That text has caused an unspeakable amount of misery in the world, for all sorts of people have imagined that they have committed the sin against the Holy Ghost, and thought that it would not be forgiven them either in this world or in the world to come. I really do not think that a person with a proper degree of kindliness in his nature would have put fears and terrors of that sort into the world.

Then Christ says, "The Son of Man shall send forth His angels, and they shall gather out of His kingdom all things that offend, and them which do iniquity, and shall cast them into a furnace of fire; there shall be wailing and gnashing of teeth"; and He goes on about the wailing and gnashing of teeth. It comes in one verse after another, and it is quite manifest to the reader that there is a certain pleasure in contemplating wailing and gnashing of teeth, or else it would not occur so often. Then you all, of course, remember about the sheep and the goats; how at the second coming He is going to divide the sheep from the goats, and He is going to say to the goats, "Depart from me, ye cursed, into everlasting fire." He continues, "And these shall go away into everlasting fire."

Then He says again, "If thy hand offend thee, cut it off; it is better for thee to enter into life maimed, than having two hands to go into hell, into the fire that never shall be quenched; where the worm dieth not and the fire is not quenched." He repeats that again and again also. I must say that I think all this doctrine, that hell-fire is a punishment for sin, is a doctrine of cruelty. It is a doctrine that put cruelty into the world and gave the world generations of cruel torture; and the Christ of the Gospels, if you could take Him as His chroniclers represent Him, would certainly have to be considered partly responsible for that.

There are other things of less importance. There is the instance of the Gadarene swine, where it certainly was not very kind to the pigs to put the devils into them and make them rush down the hill into the sea. You must remember that He was omnipotent, and He could have made the devils simply go away; but He chose to send them into the pigs. Then there is the curious story of the fig tree, which always rather puzzled me. You remember what happened about the fig tree. "He was hungry; and seeing a fig tree afar off having leaves, He came if haply He might find anything thereon; and when He came to it He found nothing but leaves, for the time of figs was not yet. And Jesus answered and said unto it: 'No man eat fruit of thee hereafter for ever'…and Peter…saith unto Him: 'Master, behold the fig tree which thou cursedst is withered away.'" This is a very curious story, because it was not the right time of year for figs, and you really could not blame the tree. I cannot myself feel that either in the matter of wisdom or in the matter of virtue Christ stands quite as high as some other people known to history. I think I should put Buddha and Socrates above Him in those respects.

The Emotional Factor

As I said before, I do not think that the real reason why people accept religion has anything to do with argumentation. They accept religion on emotional grounds. One is often told that it is a very wrong thing to attack religion, because religion makes men virtuous. So I am told; I have not noticed it. You know, of course, the parody of that argument in Samuel Butler's book, *Erewhon Revisited*. You will remember that in Erewhon there is a certain Higgs who arrives in a remote country, and after spending some time there he escapes from that country in a balloon. Twenty years later he comes back to that country and finds a new religion in which he is worshipped under the name of the "Sun Child," and it is said that he ascended into heaven. He finds that the Feast of the Ascension is about to be celebrated, and he hears Professors Hanky and Panky say to each other that they never set eyes on the man Higgs, and they hope they never will; but they are the high priests of the religion of the Sun Child. He is very indignant, and he comes up to them, and he says, "I am going to expose all this humbug and tell the people of Erewhon that it was only I, the man Higgs, and I went up in a balloon." He was told, "You must not do that, because all the morals of this country are bound round this myth, and if they once know that you did not ascend into Heaven they will all become wicked"; and so he is persuaded of that and he goes quietly away.

That is the idea—that we should all be wicked if we did not hold to the Christian religion. It seems to me that the people who have held to it have been for the most part extremely wicked. You find this curious fact, that the more intense has been the religion of any period and the more profound has been the dogmatic belief, the greater has been the cruelty and the worse has been the state of affairs. In the so-called ages of faith, when men really did believe the Christian religion in all its completeness, there was the Inquisition, with all its tortures; there were millions of unfortunate women burned as witches; and there was every kind of cruelty practiced upon all sorts of people in the name of religion.

You find as you look around the world that every single bit of progress in humane feeling, every improvement in the criminal law, every step toward the diminution of war, every step toward

better treatment of the colored races, or every mitigation of slavery, every moral progress that there has been in the world, has been consistently opposed by the organized churches of the world. I say quite deliberately that the Christian religion, as organized in its churches, has been and still is the principal enemy of moral progress in the world.

How the Churches Have Retarded Progress

You may think that I am going too far when I say that that is still so. I do not think that I am. Take one fact. You will bear with me if I mention it. It is not a pleasant fact, but the churches compel one to mention facts that are not pleasant. Supposing that in this world that we live in today an inexperienced girl is married to a syphilitic man; in that case the Catholic Church says, "This is an indissoluble sacrament. You must endure celibacy or stay together. And if you stay together, you must not use birth control to prevent the birth of syphilitic children." Nobody whose natural sympathies have not been warped by dogma, or whose moral nature was not absolutely dead to all sense of suffering, could maintain that it is right and proper that that state of things should continue.

That is only an example. There are a great many ways in which, at the present moment, the church, by its insistence upon what it chooses to call morality, inflicts upon all sorts of people undeserved and unnecessary suffering. And of course, as we know, it is in its major part an opponent still of progress and improvement in all the ways that diminish suffering in the world, because it has chosen to label as morality a certain narrow set of rules of conduct which have nothing to do with human happiness; and when you say that this or that ought to be done because it would make for human happiness, they think that has nothing to do with the matter at all. "What has human happiness to do with morals? The object of morals is not to make people happy."

Fear, the Foundation of Religion

Religion is based, I think, primarily and mainly upon fear. It is partly the terror of the unknown and partly, as I have said, the wish to feel that you have a kind of elder brother who will stand by you in all your troubles and disputes. Fear is the basis of the whole thing—fear of the mysterious, fear of defeat, fear of death. Fear is the parent of cruelty, and therefore it is no wonder if cruelty and religion have gone hand in hand. It is because fear is at the basis of those two things. In this world we can now begin a little to understand things, and a little to master them by help of science, which has forced its way step by step against the Christian religion, against the churches, and against the opposition of all the old precepts. Science can help us to get over this craven fear in which mankind has lived for so many generations. Science can teach us, and I think our own hearts can teach us, no longer to look around for imaginary supports, no longer to invent allies in the sky, but rather to look to our own efforts here below to make this world a better place to live in, instead of the sort of place that the churches in all these centuries have made it.

What We Must Do

We want to stand upon our own feet and look fair and square at the world—its good facts, its bad facts, its beauties, and its ugliness; see the world as it is and be not afraid of it. Conquer the world by intelligence and not merely by being slavishly subdued by the terror that comes from it. The whole conception of God is a conception derived from the ancient Oriental despotisms. It is a conception quite unworthy of free men. When you hear people in church debasing themselves and saying that they are miserable sinners, and all the rest of it, it seems contemptible and not worthy of self-respecting human beings. We ought to stand up and look the world frankly in the face. We ought to make the best we can of the world, and if it is not so good as we wish, after all it will still be better than what these others have made of it in all these ages. A good world needs knowledge, kindliness, and courage; it does not need a regretful hankering after the past or a fettering of the free intelligence by the words uttered long ago by ignorant men. It needs a fearless outlook and a free intelligence. It needs hope for the future, not looking back all the time toward a past that is dead, which we trust will be far surpassed by the future that our intelligence can create.

Study Questions

1. In ancient times, theology was an attempt to explain many natural phenomena in the best way people then knew how to explain them. But, since the advent of modern science, it is no longer acceptable to appeal to God as a source of explanations of things we do not yet know how to explain. It is more typical, if we don't know how to explain something, to admit that we don't know how to explain it. Do you agree? Why?

2. Do you agree with Russell concerning the real grounds of religious belief? Why or why not?

3. What is the primary defect in Christ's moral character according to Russell? Do you agree or disagree?

Section IV

SECTION V

Knowledge and Skepticism

René Descartes

Our Knowledge of the External World
Meditations on First Philosophy

René Descartes (1596–1650), considered the Father of Modern Philosophy, was one of a number of surviving children, two siblings and two half-siblings. Descartes' mother died a year after he was born, leaving him and his full brother and sister to be raised by their grandmother in La Haye. In 1606, Descartes was sent to the Jesuit college of La Fleche. In 1615, he entered the University of Poitiers. In 1618, he joined the army of Prince Maurice of Nassau in the Dutch Republic. It appears that Descartes' military duties were primarily directed toward engineering or education.

On the night of 10–11 November 1619, while stationed in Germany, Descartes reports having three profound dreams. In the first dream, Descartes was walking near a college when he was struck down by a powerful wind. During the second, he was awakened by a thunderous explosion in his head. Upon awaking, he saw sparks flying from the stove in his room. In the third dream, he finds a great dictionary and an anthology of ancient Latin poets on his bedside table. In the anthology, he reads, "What path shall I follow in life?" Descartes claimed that from these dreams he now envisaged the unity of science and he would articulate a new method for scientific inquiry. Around 1622, in France, some property he had inherited was sold. This money would provide a simple income for many years. There is some speculation that between 1623 and 1625 he visited Italy.

In 1630 Descartes moved to Amsterdam where he worked on *The Optics* and *The Meteorology*, which were likely intended to be a part of *The World*. When in 1633, *The World* was ready for publication, Descartes heard of the Church's condemnation of Galileo and decided against publication. *The World*, like Galileo's work, accepted the Copernican heliocentric system. In a letter in November 1633, Descartes expressed his fear that were *The World* to be published, Galileo's condemnation would also befall him.

From *Meditations on First Philosophy*, Elizabeth Haldane and G.R.T. Ross, trans., London: Cambridge University Press, 1931.

Around 1635, a domestic servant, Helene, gave birth to a baby girl, Francine, fathered by Descartes. In 1637 *The Discourse on Method* was published and that same year Descartes brought Francine and Helene to his new home at Santpoort. In 1639 Descartes began writing *The Meditations*. In 1640, he returned to Leiden to help work out its publication when Francine died from a fever. Descartes, at the time, had also been making arrangements for Francine to live with relatives in France so as to ensure her education. It has been reported that Francine's death left Descartes grief-stricken. It was also in 1640 that Descartes' father and sister both died. Queen Christina of Sweden convinced a reluctant Descartes in 1650 to move to Sweden and serve as her personal tutor. He died in Sweden shortly after his arrival. *The Meditations* are presently Descartes' most popular work—though this would not have been the case when he was alive.

Synopsis of the Six Following Meditations

In the first Meditation I set forth the reasons for which we may, generally speaking, doubt about all things and especially about material things, at least so long as we have no other foundations for the sciences than those which we have hitherto possessed. But although the utility of a Doubt which is so general does not at first appear, it is at the same time very great, inasmuch as it delivers us from every kind of prejudice, and sets out for us a very simple way by which the mind may detach itself from the senses; and finally it makes it impossible for us ever to doubt those things which we have once discovered to be true.

In the second Meditation, mind, which making use of the liberty which pertains to it, takes for granted that all those things of whose existence it has the least doubt, are non-existent, recognises that it is however absolutely impossible that it does not itself exist. This point is likewise of the greatest moment, inasmuch as by this means a distinction is easily drawn between the things which pertain to mind—that is to say to the intellectual nature—and those which pertain to body.

But because it may be that some expect from me in this place a statement of the reasons establishing the immortality of the soul, I feel that I should here make known to them that having aimed at writing nothing in all this Treatise of which I do not possess very exact demonstrations, I am obliged to follow a similar order to that made use of by the geometers, which is to begin by putting forward as premises all those things upon which the proposition that we seek depends, before coming to any conclusion regarding it. Now the first and principal matter which is requisite for thoroughly understanding the immortality of the soul is to form the clearest possible conception of it, and one which will be entirely distinct from all the conceptions which we may have of body; and in this Meditation this has been done. In addition to this it is requisite that we may be assured that all the things which we conceive clearly and distinctly are true in the very way in which we think them; and this could not be proved previously to the Fourth Mediation. Further we must have a distinct conception of corporeal nature, which is given partly in this Second, and partly in the Fifth and Sixth Meditations. And finally we should conclude from all this, that those things which we conceive clearly and distinctly as being diverse substances, as we regard mind and body to be, are really substances essentially distinct one from the other; and this is the conclusion of the Sixth Meditation. This is further confirmed in this same Meditation by the fact that we cannot conceive of body excepting in so far as it is divisible, while the mind cannot be conceived of excepting as indivisible. For we are not able to conceive of the half of a mind as we can do of the smallest of all bodies; so that we see that not only are their natures different but even in some respects contrary to one another. I have not however dealt further with this matter in this treatise, both because what I have said is sufficient to show clearly enough that the extinction of the mind does not follow from the corruption of the body, and also to give men the hope of another life after death, as also because the premises from which the immortality of the soul may be deduced depend on an elucidation of a complete system of Physics. This would mean to establish in the first place that all substances generally—that is to say all things which cannot exist without being created by God—are in their nature incorruptible, and that they can never cease to exist unless God, in denying to them his concurrence, reduce them to nought; and secondly that body, regarded generally, is a substance, which is the reason why it also cannot perish, but that the human body, inasmuch as it differs from other bodies, is composed only of a certain configuration of members and of other similar accidents, while the human mind is not similarly composed of any accidents, but is a pure substance. For although all the accidents of mind be changed, although, for instance, it think certain things, will others, perceive others, etc., despite all this it does not emerge from these changes another mind: the human body on the other hand becomes a different thing from the sole fact that the figure or form of any of its portions is found to be changed. From this it follows that the human body may indeed easily enough perish, but the mind [or soul of man (I make no distinction between them)] is owing to its nature immortal.

In the third Meditation it seems to me that I have explained at sufficient length the principal argument of which I make use in order to prove the existence of God. But none the less, because I did not wish in that place to make use of any comparisons derived from corporeal things, so as to withdraw as much as I could the minds of readers from the senses, there may perhaps have remained many obscurities which, however, will, I hope, be entirely removed by the Replies which I have made to the Objections which have been set before me. Amongst others there is, for example, this one, "How the idea in us of a being supremely perfect possesses so much objective reality [that is to say participates by representation in so many degrees of being and perfection]

that it necessarily proceeds from a cause which is absolutely perfect." This is illustrated in these Replies by the comparison of a very perfect machine, the idea of which is found in the mind of some workman. For as the objective contrivance of this idea must have some cause, i.e. either the science of the workman or that of some other from whom he has received the idea, it is similarly impossible that the idea of God which is in us should not have God himself as its cause.

In the fourth Meditation it is shown that all these things which we very clearly and distinctly perceive are true, and at the same time it is explained in what the nature of error or falsity consists. This must of necessity be known both for the confirmation of the preceding truths and for the better comprehension of those that follow. (But it must meanwhile be remarked that I do not in any way there treat of sin—that is to say of the error which is committed in the pursuit of good and evil, but only of that which arises in the deciding between the true and the false. And I do not intend to speak of matters pertaining to the Faith or the conduct of life, but only of those which concern speculative truths, and which may be known by the sole aid of the light of nature.)

In the fifth Meditation corporeal nature generally is explained, and in addition to this the existence of God is demonstrated by a new proof in which there may possibly be certain difficulties also, but the solution of these will be seen in the Replies to the Objections. And further I show in what sense it is true to say that the certainty of geometrical demonstrations is itself dependent on the knowledge of God.

Finally in the Sixth I distinguish the action of the understanding [intellectio] from that of the imagination [imaginatio]; the marks by which this distinction is made are described. I here show that the mind of man is really distinct from the body, and at the same time that the two are so closely joined together that they form, so to speak, a single thing. All the errors which proceed from the senses are then surveyed, while the means of avoiding them are demonstrated, and finally all the reasons from which we may deduce the existence of material things are set forth. Not that I judge them to be very useful in establishing that which they prove, to wit, that there is in truth a world, that men possess bodies, and other such things which never have been doubted by anyone of sense; but because in considering these closely we come to see that they are neither so strong nor so evident as those arguments which lead us to the knowledge of our mind and of God; so that these last must be the most certain and most evident facts which can fall within the cognizance of the human mind. And this is the whole matter that I have tried to prove in these Meditations, for which reason I here omit to speak of many other questions with which I dealt incidentally in this discussion.

Meditation I

Of the things which may be brought within the sphere of the doubtful.

It is now some years since I detected how many were the false beliefs that I had from my earliest youth admitted as true, and how doubtful was everything I had since constructed on this basis; and from that time I was convinced that I must once for all seriously undertake to rid myself of all the opinions which I had formerly accepted, and commence to build anew from the foundation, if I wanted to establish any firm and permanent structure in the sciences. But as this enterprise appeared to be a very great one, I waited until I had attained an age so mature that I could not hope that at any later date I should be better fitted to execute my design. This reason caused me to delay so long that I should feel that I was doing wrong were I to occupy in deliberation the time that yet remains to me for action. To-day, then, since very opportunely for the plan I have in view I have delivered my mind from every care [and am happily agitated by no passions] and since I have procured for myself an assured leisure in a peaceable retirement, I shall at last seriously and freely address myself to the general upheaval of all my former opinions.

Now for this object it is not necessary that I should show that all of these are false—I shall perhaps never arrive at this end. But inasmuch as reason already persuades me that I ought no less carefully to withhold my assent from matters which are not entirely certain and indubitable than from those which appear to me manifestly to be false, if I am able to find in each one some reason to doubt, this will suffice to justify my rejecting the whole. And for that end it will not be requisite that I should examine each in particular, which would be an endless undertaking; for owing to the fact that the destruction of the foundations of necessity brings with it the downfall of the rest of the edifice, I shall only in the first place attack those principles upon which all my former opinions rested.

All that up to the present time I have accepted as most true and certain I have learned either from the senses or through the senses; but it is sometimes proved to me that these senses are deceptive, and it is wiser not to trust entirely to anything by which we have once been deceived.

But it may be that although the senses sometimes deceive us concerning things which are hardly perceptible, or very far away, there are yet many others to be met with as to which we cannot reasonably have any doubt, although we recognise them by their means. For example, there is the fact that I am here, seated by the fire, attired in a dressing gown, having this paper in my hands and other similar matters. And how could I deny that these hands and this body are mine, were it not perhaps that I compare myself to certain persons, devoid of sense, whose cerebella are so troubled and clouded by the violent vapors of black bile, that they constantly assure us that they think they are kings when they are really quite poor, or that they are clothed in purple when they are really without covering, or who imagine that they have an earthenware head or are nothing but pumpkins or are made of glass. But they are mad, and I should not be any the less insane were I to follow examples so extravagant.

At the same time I must remember that I am a man, and that consequently I am in the habit of sleeping, and in my dreams representing to myself the same things or sometimes even less probable things, than do those who are insane in their waking moments. How often has it happened to me that in the night I dreamt that I found myself in this particular place, that I was dressed and seated near the fire, whilst in reality I was lying undressed in bed! At this moment it does indeed seem to me that it is with eyes awake that I am looking at this paper; that this head which I move is not asleep, that it is deliberately and of set purpose that I extend my hand and perceive it; what happens in sleep does not appear so clear nor so distinct as does all this. But in thinking over this I remind myself that on many occasions I have in sleep been deceived by similar illusions, and in dwelling carefully on this reflection I see so manifestly that there are no certain indications by which we may clearly distinguish wakefulness from sleep that I am lost in astonishment. And my astonishment is such that it is almost capable of persuading me that I now dream.

Now let us assume that we are asleep and that all these particulars, e.g., that we open our eyes, shake our head, extend our hands, and so on, are but false delusions; and let us reflect that possibly neither our hands nor our whole body are such as they appear to us to be. At the same time we must at least confess that the things which are represented to us in sleep are like painted representations which can only have been formed as the counterparts of something real and true, and that in this way those general things at least, i.e., eyes, a head, hands, and a whole body, are not imaginary things, but things really existent. For, as a matter of fact, painters, even when they study with the greatest skill to represent sirens and satyrs by forms the most strange and extraordinary, cannot give them natures which are entirely new, but merely make a certain medley of the members of different animals; or if their imagination is extravagant enough to invent something so novel that nothing similar has ever before been seen, and that then their work represents a thing purely fictitious and absolutely false, it is certain all the same that the colours of which this is composed are necessarily real. And for the same reason, although these general things, to wit, [a body], eyes, a head, hands, and such like, may be imaginary, we are bound at the same time to confess that there are at least some other objects yet more simple and more universal, which are real and true; and of these just in the same way as with certain real colours, all these images of things which dwell in our thoughts, whether true and real or false and fantastic, are formed.

To such a class of things pertains corporeal nature in general, and its extension, the figure of extended things, their quantity or magnitude and number, as also the place in which they are, the time which measures their duration, and so on.

That is possibly why our reasoning is not unjust when we conclude from this that Physics, Astronomy, Medicine and all other sciences which have as their end the consideration of composite things, are very dubious and uncertain; but that Arithmetic, Geometry and other sciences of that kind which only treat of things that are very simple and very general, without taking great trouble to ascertain whether they are actually existent or not, contain some measure of certainty and an element of the indubitable. For whether I am awake or asleep, two and three together always form five, and the square can never have more than four sides, and it does not seem possible that truths so clear and apparent can be suspected of any falsity [or uncertainty].

Nevertheless I have long had fixed in my mind the belief that an all-powerful God existed by whom I have been created such as I am. But how do I know that He has not brought it to pass that there is no earth, no heaven, no extended body, no magnitude, no place, and that nevertheless [I possess the perceptions of all these things and that] they seem to me to exist just exactly as I now see them? And, besides, as I sometimes imagine that others deceive themselves in the things which they think they know best, how do I know that I am not deceived every time that I add two and three, or count the sides of a square, or judge of things yet simpler, if anything simpler can be imagined? But possibly God has not desired that I should be thus deceived, for He is said to be supremely good. If, however, it is contrary to His goodness to have made me such that I constantly deceive myself, it would also appear to be contrary to His goodness to permit me to be sometimes deceived, and nevertheless I cannot doubt that He does permit this.

There may indeed be those who would prefer to deny the existence of a God so powerful, rather than believe that all other things are uncertain. But let us not oppose them for the present, and grant that all that is here said of a God is a fable; nevertheless in whatever way they suppose that I have arrived at the state of being that I have reached—whether they attribute it to fate or to accident, or make out that it is by a continual succession of antecedents, or by some other method—since to err and deceive oneself is a defect, it is clear that the greater will be the probability of my being so imperfect as to deceive myself ever, as is the Author to whom they assign my origin the less powerful. To these reasons I have certainly nothing to reply, but at the end I feel constrained to confess that there is nothing in all that I formerly believed to be true, of which I cannot in some measure doubt, and that not merely through want of thought or through levity, but for reasons which are very powerful and maturely considered; so that henceforth I ought not the less carefully to refrain from giving credence to these opinions than to that which is manifestly false, if I desire to arrive at any certainty [in the sciences].

But it is not sufficient to have made these remarks, we must also be careful to keep them in mind. For these ancient and commonly held opinions still revert frequently to my mind, long and familiar custom having given them the right to occupy my mind against my inclination and rendered them almost masters of my belief; nor will I ever lose the habit of deferring to them or

of placing my confidence in them, so long as I consider them as they really are, i.e., opinions in some measure doubtful, as I have just shown, and at the same time highly probable, so that there is much more reason to believe in than to deny them. That is why I consider that I shall not be acting amiss, if, taking of set purpose a contrary belief, I allow myself to be deceived, and for a certain time pretend that all these opinions are entirely false and imaginary, until at last, having thus balanced my former prejudices with my latter [so that they cannot divert my opinions more to one side than to the other], my judgment will no longer be dominated by bad usage or turned away from the right knowledge of the truth. For I am assured that there can be neither peril nor error in this course, and that I cannot at present yield too much to distrust, since I am not considering the question of action, but only of knowledge.

I shall then suppose, not that God who is supremely good and the fountain of truth, but some evil genius not less powerful than deceitful, has employed his whole energies in deceiving me; I shall consider that the heavens, the earth, colours, figures, sound, and all other external things are nought but the illusions and dreams of which this genius has availed himself in order to lay traps for my credulity; I shall consider myself as having no hands, no eyes, no flesh, no blood, nor any senses, yet falsely believing myself to possess all these things; I shall remain obstinately attached to this idea, and if by this means it is not in my power to arrive at the knowledge of any truth, I may at least do what is in my power [i.e., suspend my judgment], and with firm purpose avoid giving credence to any false thing, or being imposed upon by this arch deceiver, however powerful and deceptive he may be. But this task is a laborious one, and insensibly a certain lassitude leads me into the course of my ordinary life. And just as a captive who in sleep enjoys an imaginary liberty, when he begins to suspect that his liberty is but a dream, fears to awaken, and conspires with these agreeable illusions that the deception may be prolonged, so insensibly of my own accord I fall back into my former opinions, and I dread awakening from this slumber, lest the laborious wakefulness which would follow the tranquility of this repose should have to be spent not in daylight, but in the excessive darkness of the difficulties which have just been discussed.

Meditation II

Of the Nature of the Human Mind; and that it is more easily known than the Body.

The Meditation of yesterday filled my mind with so many doubts that it is no longer in my power to forget them. And yet I do not see in what manner I can resolve them; and, just as if I had all of a sudden fallen into very deep water, I am so disconcerted that I can neither make certain of setting my feet on the bottom, nor can I swim and so support myself on the surface. I shall nevertheless make an effort and follow anew the same path as that on which I yesterday entered, i.e., I shall proceed by setting aside all that in which the least doubt could be supposed to exist, just as if I had discovered that it was absolutely false; and I shall ever follow in this road until I have met with something which is certain, or at least, if I can do nothing else, until I have learned for certain that there is nothing in the world that is certain. Archimedes, in order that he might draw the terrestrial globe out of its place, and transport it elsewhere, demanded only that one point should be fixed and immoveable; in the same way I shall have the right to conceive high hopes if I am happy enough to discover one thing only which is certain and indubitable.

I suppose, then, that all the things that I see are false; I persuade myself that nothing has ever existed of all that my fallacious memory represents to me. I consider that I possess no senses; I imagine that body, figure, extension, movement and place are but the fictions of my mind. What, then, can be esteemed as true? Perhaps nothing at all, unless that there is nothing in the world that is certain.

But how can I know there is not something different from those things that I have just considered, of which one cannot have the slightest doubt? Is there not some God, or some other being by whatever name we call it, who puts these reflections into my mind? That is not necessary, for is it not possible that I am capable of producing them myself? I myself, am I not at least something? But I have already denied that I had senses and body. Yet I hesitate, for what follows from that? Am I so dependent on body and senses that I cannot exist without these? But I was persuaded that there was nothing in all the world, that there was no heaven, no earth, that there were no minds, nor any bodies: was I not then likewise persuaded that I did not exist? Not at all; of a surety I myself did exist since I persuaded myself of something [or merely because I thought of something]. But there is some deceiver or other, very powerful and very cunning, who ever employs his ingenuity in deceiving me. Then without doubt I exist also if he deceives me, and let him deceive me as much as he will, he can never cause me to be nothing so long as I think that I am something. So that after having reflected well and carefully examined all things, we must come to the definite conclusion that this proposition: I am, I exist, is necessarily true each time that I pronounce it, or that I mentally conceive it.

But I do not yet know clearly enough what I am, I who am certain that I am; and hence I must be careful to see that I do not imprudently take some other object in place of myself, and thus that I do not go astray in respect of this knowledge that I hold to be the most certain and most evident of all that I have formerly learned. That is why I shall now consider anew what I believed myself to be before I embarked upon these last reflections; and of my former opinions I shall withdraw all that might even in a small degree be invalidated by the reasons which I have just brought forward, in order that there may be nothing at all left beyond what is absolutely certain and indubitable.

What then did I formerly believe myself to be? Undoubtedly I believed myself to be a man. But what is a man? Shall I say a reasonable animal? Certainly not; for then I should have to inquire what an animal is, and what is reasonable; and thus from a single question I should insensibly fall into an infinitude of others more difficult; and I should not wish to waste the little time and leisure remaining to me in trying to unravel subtleties like these. But I shall rather stop here to consider the thoughts which of themselves spring up in my mind, and which were not inspired by anything beyond my own nature alone when I applied myself to the consideration of my being. In the first place, then, I considered myself as having a face, hands, arms, and all that system of members composed on bones and flesh as seen in a corpse which I designated by the name of body. In addition to this I considered that I was nourished, that I walked, that I felt, and that I thought, and I referred all these actions to the soul: but I did not stop to consider what the soul was, or if I did stop, I imagined that it was something extremely rare and subtle like a wind, a flame, or an ether, which was spread throughout my grosser parts. As to body I had no manner of doubt about its nature, but thought I had a very clear knowledge of it; and if I had desired to explain it according to the notions that I had then formed of it, I should have described it thus: By the body I understand all that which can be defined by a certain figure: something which can be confined in a certain place, and which can fill a given space in such a way that every other body will be excluded from it; which can be perceived either by touch, or by sight, or by hearing, or by taste, or by smell: which can be moved in many ways not, in truth, by itself, but by something which is foreign to it, by which it is touched [and from which it receives impressions]: for to have the power of self-movement, as also of feeling or of thinking, I did not consider to appertain to the nature of body: on the contrary, I was rather astonished to find that faculties similar to them existed in some bodies.

But what am I, now that I suppose that there is a certain genius which is extremely powerful, and, if I may say so, malicious, who employs all his powers in deceiving me? Can I affirm that I possess the least of all those things which I have just said pertain to the nature of body? I pause to consider, I revolve all these things in my mind, and I find none of which I can say that it pertains to me. It would be tedious to stop to enumerate them. Let us pass to the attributes of soul and see if there is any one which is in me? What of nutrition or walking [the first mentioned]? But if it is so that I have no body it is also true that I can neither walk nor take nourishment. Another attribute is sensation. But one cannot feel without body, and besides I have thought I perceived many things during sleep that I recognised in my waking moments as not having been experienced at all. What of thinking? I find here that thought is an attribute that belongs to me; it alone cannot be separated from me. I am, I exist, that is certain. But how often? Just when I think; for it might possibly be the case if I ceased entirely to think, that I should likewise cease altogether to exist. I do not now admit anything which is not necessarily true: to speak accurately I am not more than a thing which thinks, that is to say a mind or a soul, or an understanding, or a reason, which are terms whose significance was formerly unknown to me. I am, however, a real thing and really exist; but what thing? I have answered: a thing which thinks.

And what more? I shall exercise my imagination [in order to see if I am not something more]. I am not a collection of members which we call the human body: I am not a subtle air distributed through these members, I am not a wind, a fire, a vapour, a breath, nor anything at all which I can imagine or conceive; because I have assumed that all these were nothing. Without changing that supposition I find that I only leave myself certain of the fact that I am somewhat. But perhaps it is true that these same things which I supposed were non-existent because they are unknown to me, are really not different from the self which I know. I am not sure about this, I shall not dispute about it now; I can only give judgment on things that are known to me. I know that I exist, and I inquire what I am, I whom I know to exist. But it is very certain that the knowledge of my existence taken in its precise significance does not depend on things whose existence is not yet known to me; consequently it does not depend on those which I can feign in imagination. And indeed the very term *feign* in imagination proves to me my error, for I really do this if I image myself a something, since to imagine is nothing else than to contemplate the figure or image of a corporeal thing. But I already know for certain that I am, and that it may be that all these images, and, speaking generally, all things that relate to the nature of body are nothing but dreams [and chimeras]. For this reason I see clearly that I have as little reason to say, I shall stimulate my imagination in order to know more distinctly what I am, than if I were to say, I am now awake, and I perceive somewhat that is real and true: but because I do not yet perceive it distinctly enough, I shall go to sleep of express purpose, so that my dreams may represent the perception with greatest truth and evidence. And, thus, I know for certain that nothing of all that I can understand by means of my imagination belongs to this knowledge which I have of myself, and that it is necessary to recall the mind from this mode of thought with the utmost diligence in order that it may be able to know its own nature with perfect distinctness.

But what then am I? A thing which thinks. What is a thing which thinks? It is a thing which doubts, understands, [conceives], affirms, denies, wills, refuses, which also imagines and feels.

Certainly it is no small matter if all these things pertain to my nature. But why should they not so pertain? Am I not that being who now doubts nearly everything, who nevertheless understands certain things, who affirms that one only is true, who denies all the others, who desires to know more, is averse from being deceived, who imagines many things, sometimes indeed despite his will, and who perceives many likewise, as by the intervention of the bodily organs? Is there

nothing in all this which is as true as it is certain that I exist, even though I should always sleep and though he who has given me being employed all his ingenuity in deceiving me? Is there likewise any one of these attributes which can be distinguished from my thought, or which might be said to be separated from myself? For it is so evident of itself that it is I who doubts, who understands, and who desires, that there is no reason here to add anything to explain it. And I have certainly the power of imagining likewise; for although it may happen (as I formerly supposed) that none of the things which I imagine are true, nevertheless this power of imagining does not cease to be really in use, and it forms part of my thought. Finally, I am the same who feels, that is to say, who perceives certain things, as by the organs of sense, since in truth I see light, I hear noise, I feel heat. But it will be said that these phenomena are false and that I am dreaming. Let it be so; still it is at least quite certain that it seems to me that I see light, that I hear noise and that I feel heat. That cannot be false; properly speaking it is what is in me called feeling; and used in this precise sense that is no other thing than thinking.

From this time I begin to know what I am with a little more clearness and distinction than before; but nevertheless it still seems to me, and I cannot prevent myself from thinking, that corporeal things, whose images are framed by thought, which are tested by the senses, are much more distinctly known than that obscure part of me which does not come under the imagination. Although really it is very strange to say that I know and understand more distinctly these things whose existence seems to me dubious, which are unknown to me, and which do not belong to me, than others of the truth of which I am convinced, which are known to me and which pertain to my real nature, in a word, than myself. But I see clearly how the case stands: my mind loves to wander, and cannot yet suffer itself to be retained within the just limits of truth. Very good, let us once more give it the freest rein, so that, when afterwards we seize the proper occasion for pulling up, it may the more easily be regulated and controlled.

Let us begin by considering the commonest matters, those which we believe to be the most distinctly comprehended, to wit, the bodies which we touch and see; not indeed bodies in general, for these general ideas are usually a little more confused, but let us consider one body in particular. Let us take, for example, this piece of wax: it has been taken quite freshly from the hive, and it has not yet lost the sweetness of the honey which it contains; it still retains somewhat of the odour of the flowers from which it has been culled; its colour, its figure, its size are apparent; it is hard, cold, easily handled, and if you strike it with the finger, it will emit a sound. Finally all the things which are requisite to cause us distinctly to recognise a body, are met with in it. But notice that while I speak and approach the fire what remained of the taste is exhaled, the smell evaporates, the colour alters, the figure is destroyed, the size increases, it becomes liquid, it heats, scarcely can one handle it, and when one strikes it, now no sound is emitted. Does the same wax remain after this change? We must confess that it remains; none would judge otherwise. What then did I know so distinctly in this piece of wax? It could certainly be nothing of all that the senses brought to my notice, since all these things which fall under taste, smell, sight, touch, and hearing, are found to be changed, and yet the same wax remains.

And these passages seem to me clearly fallacious: That apparently real things have changeable qualities makes them neither more nor less real.

Perhaps it was what I now think, viz. that this wax was not that sweetness of honey, nor that agreeable scent of flowers, nor that particular whiteness, nor that figure, nor that sound, but simply a body which a little while before appeared to me as perceptible under these forms, and which is now perceptible under others. But what, precisely, is it that I imagine when I form such conceptions? Let us attentively consider this, and, abstracting from all that does not belong to the

wax, let us see what remains. Certainly nothing remains excepting a certain extended thing which is flexible and movable. But what is the meaning of flexible and movable? Is it not that I imagine that this piece of wax being round is capable of becoming square and of passing from a square to a triangular figure? No, certainly it is not that, since I imagine it admits of an infinitude of similar changes, and I nevertheless do not know how to compass the infinitude by my imagination, and consequently this conception which I have of the wax is not brought about by the faculty of imagination. What now is this extension? Is it not also unknown? For it becomes greater when the wax is melted, greater when it is boiled, and greater still when the heat increases; and I should not conceive [clearly] according to truth what wax is, if I did not think that even this piece that we are considering is capable of receiving more variations in extension than I have ever imagined. We must then grant that I could not even understand through the imagination what this piece of wax is, and that it is my mind alone which perceives it. I say this piece of wax in particular, for as to wax in general it is yet clearer. But what is this piece of wax which cannot be understood excepting by the [understanding or] mind? It is certainly the same that I see, touch, imagine, and finally it is the same which I have always believed it to be from the beginning. But what must particularly be observed is that its perception is neither an act of vision, nor of touch, nor of imagination, and has never been such although it may have appeared formerly to be so, but only an intuition of the mind, which may be imperfect and confused as it was formerly, or clear and distinct as it is at present, according as my attention is more or less directed to the elements which are found in it, and of which it is composed.

Yet in the meantime I am greatly astonished when I consider [the great feebleness of mind] and its proneness to fall [insensibly] into error; for although without giving expression to my thought I consider all this in my own mind, words often impede me and I am almost deceived by the terms of ordinary language. For we say that we see the same wax, if it is present, and not that we simply judge that it is the same from its having the same colour and figure. From this I should conclude that I knew the wax by means of vision and not simply by the intuition of the mind; unless by chance I remember that, when looking from a window and saying I see men who pass in the street, I really do not see them, but infer that what I see is men, just as I say that I see wax. And yet what do I see from the window but hats and coats which may cover automatic machines? Yet I judge these to be men. And similarly solely by the faculty of judgment which rests in my mind, I comprehend that which I believed I saw with my eyes.

A man who makes it his aim to raise his knowledge above the common should be ashamed to derive the occasion for doubting from the forms of speech invented by the vulgar; I prefer to pass on and consider whether I had a more evident and perfect conception of what the wax was when I first perceived it, and when I believed I knew it by means of the external senses or at least by the common sense as it is called, that is to say by the imaginative faculty, or whether my present conception is clearer now that I have most carefully examined what it is, and in what way it can be known. It would certainly be absurd to doubt as to this. For what was there in this first perception which was distinct? What was there which might not as well have been perceived by any of the animals? But when I distinguish the wax from its external forms, and when, just as if I had taken from it its vestments, I consider it quite naked, it is certain that although some error may still be found in my judgment, I can nevertheless not perceive it thus without a human mind.

But finally what shall I say of this mind, that is, of myself, for up to this point I do not admit in myself anything but mind? What then, I who seem to perceive this piece of wax so distinctly, do I not know myself, not only with much more truth and certainty, but also with much more distinctness and clearness? For if I judge that the wax is or exists from the fact that I see it, it certainly follows much more clearly that I am or that I exist myself from the fact that I see it. For it may be that what I see is not really wax, it may also be that I do not possess eyes with which to see anything; but it cannot be that when I see, or (for I no longer take account of the distinction) when I think I see, that I myself who think am nought. So if I judge that the wax exists from the fact that I touch it, the same thing will follow, to wit, that I am; and if I judge that my imagination, or some other cause, whatever it is, persuades me that the wax exists, I shall still conclude the same. And what I have here remarked of wax may be applied to all other things which are external to me [and which are met with outside of me]. And further, if the [notion or] perception of wax has seemed to me clearer and more distinct, not only after the sight or the touch, but also after many other causes have rendered it quite manifest to me, with how much more [evidence] and distinctness must it be said that I now know myself, since all the reasons which contribute to the knowledge of wax, or any other body whatever, are yet better proofs of the nature of my mind! And there are so many other things in the mind itself which may contribute to the elucidation of its nature, that those which depend on body such as these just mentioned, hardly merit being taken into account.

But finally here I am, having insensibly reverted to the point I desired, for, since it is now manifest to me that even bodies are not properly speaking known by the senses or by the faculty of imagination, but by the understanding only, and since they are not known from the fact that they are seen or touched, but only because they are understood, I see clearly that there is nothing which is easier for me to know than my mind. But because it is difficult to rid oneself so promptly of an opinion to which one was accustomed for so long, it will be well that I should halt a little at this point, so that by the length of my meditation I may more deeply imprint on my memory this new knowledge.

Meditation VI

The existence of material things, and the real distinction between mind and body.

The remaining task is to consider whether material things exist. Insofar as they are the subject matter of pure mathematics, I perceive [here = "conceive"] them vividly and clearly; so I at least know that they *could* exist, because anything that I perceive in that way could be created by God. (The only reason I have ever accepted for thinking that something could *not* be made by him is that there would be a contradiction in my perceiving it distinctly.) My faculty of imagination, which I am aware of using when I turn my mind to material things, also suggests that they really exist. For when I think harder about what imagination is, it seems to be simply an application of the faculty of *knowing* to a body that is intimately present to it—and that has to be a body that exists.

To make this clear, I will first examine how imagination differs from pure understanding. When I imagine a triangle, for example, I don't merely understand that it is a three-sided figure, but I also see the three lines with my mind's eye as if they were present to me; that is what imagining is. But if I think of a chiliagon [= "thousand-sided figure," pronounced *kill*-ee-a-gon], although I understand quite well that it is a figure with a thousand sides, I don't imagine the thousand sides or see them as if they were present to me. When I think of a body, I usually form some kind of image; so in thinking of a chiliagon I may construct in my mind—strictly speaking, in my imagination—a confused representation of some figure. But obviously it won't be a chiliagon, for it is the very same image that I would form if I were thinking of, say, a figure with ten thousand sides. So it wouldn't help me to recognize the properties that distinguish a chiliagon from other many-sided figures. In the case of a pentagon, the situation is different. I can, of course, *understand* this figure without the help of the imagination (just as I can understand a chiliagon); but I can also *imagine* a pentagon, by applying my mind's eye to its five sides and the area they enclose.

This imagining, I find, takes more mental effort than understanding does; and that is enough to show clearly that imagination is different from pure understanding.

Being able to imagine isn't essential to me, as being able to understand is; for even if I had no power of imagination I would still be the same individual that I am. This seems to imply that my power of imagining depends on something other than myself; and I can easily understand that if there is such a thing as *my body*—that is, if my mind is joined to a certain body in such a way that it can contemplate that body whenever it wants to—then it *might* be this very body that enables me to imagine corporeal things. So it may be that imagining differs from pure understanding purely like this: when the mind understands, it somehow turns in on itself and inspects one of its own ideas; but when it imagines, it turns away from itself and looks at something in the body (something that conforms to an idea—either one understood by the mind or one perceived by the senses). I can, I repeat, easily see that this might be how imagination comes about if the body exists; and since I can think of no other equally good way of explaining what imagination is, I can conjecture that the body exists. But this is only a probability. Even after all my careful enquiry I still can't see how, on the basis of the idea of corporeal nature that I find in my imagination, to prove for sure that some body exists.

As well as the corporeal nature that is the subject matter of pure mathematics, I am also accustomed to imagining colours, sounds, tastes, pain, and so on—though not so distinctly. Now, I perceive these much better by means of the senses, which is how (helped by memory) they appear to have reached the imagination. So in order to deal with them more fully, I must attend to the senses—that is, to the kind of thinking [here = "mental activity"] that I call "sensory perception." I want to know whether the things that are perceived through the senses provide me with any sure argument for the existence of bodies.

To begin with, I will (1) go back over everything that I *originally* took to be perceived by the senses, and reckoned to be true; and I will go over my reasons for thinking this. Next, I will (2) set out my reasons for *later* doubting these things. Finally, I will (3) consider what I should *now* believe about them.

(1) First of all, then, I perceived by my senses that I had a head, hands, feet, and other limbs making up the body that I regarded as part of myself, or perhaps even as my whole self. I also perceived by my senses that this body was situated among many other bodies that could harm or help it; and I detected the favourable effects by a sensation of pleasure and the unfavourable ones by pain. As well as pain and pleasure. I also had sensations of hunger, thirst, and other such appetites, and also of bodily states tending towards cheerfulness, sadness, anger, and similar emotions. Outside myself, besides the extension, shapes, and movements of bodies, I also had sensations of their hardness and heat, and of the other qualities that can be known by touch. In addition, I had sensations of light, colours, smells, tastes, and sounds, and differences amongst these enabled me to sort out the sky, the earth, the seas, and other bodies from one another. All I was *immediately* aware of in each case were my ideas, but it was reasonable for me to think that what I was perceiving through the senses were external bodies that caused the ideas. For I found that these ideas came to me quite without my consent: I couldn't have *that* kind of idea of any object, even if I wanted to, if the object was not present to my sense organs; and I couldn't avoid having the idea when the object *was* present. Also, since the ideas that came through the senses were much more lively and vivid and sharp than ones that I formed voluntarily when thinking about things, and than ones that I found impressed on my memory, it seemed impossible that sensory ideas were coming from within me; so I had to conclude that they came from external things. My only way of knowing about these things was through the ideas themselves, so it was bound to occur to me that the things might

resemble the ideas. In addition, I remembered that I had the use of my senses before I ever had the use of reason; and I saw that the ideas that I formed were, for the most part, made up of elements of sensory ideas. This convinced me that I had nothing at all in my intellect that I had not previously had in sensation. As for the body that by some special right I called "mine": I had reason to think that it belonged to me in a way that no other body did. There were three reasons for this. I could never be separated from it, as I could from other bodies; I felt all my appetites and emotions *in* it and *on account of* it; and I was aware of pain and pleasurable ticklings in parts of this body but not in any other body. But why should that curious sensation of pain give rise to a particular distress of mind; and why should a certain kind of delight follow on a tickling sensation? Again, why should that curious tugging in the stomach that I call "hunger" tell me that I should eat, or a dryness of the throat tell me to drink, and so on? I couldn't explain any of this, except to say that nature taught me so. For there is no connection (or none that I understand) between the tugging sensation and the decision to eat, or between the sensation of something causing pain and the mental distress that arises from it. It seems that *nature* taught me to make these judgments about objects of the senses, for I was making them before I had any arguments to support them.

(2) Later on, however, my experiences gradually undermined all my faith in the senses. A tower that had looked round from a distance appeared square from close up; an enormous statue standing on a high column didn't look large from the ground. In countless such cases I found that the judgments of the external senses were mistaken, and the same was true of the internal senses. What can be more internal than pain? Yet I heard that an amputee might occasionally seem to feel pain in the missing limb. So even in my own case, I had to conclude, it was not quite certain that a particular limb was hurting, even if I felt pain in it. To these reasons for doubting, I recently added two very general ones. The first was that every

sensory experience I ever thought I was having while awake I can also think of myself as having while asleep; and since I don't believe that what I seem to perceive in sleep comes from things outside me, I didn't see why I should be any more inclined to believe this of what I think I perceive while awake. The second reason for doubt was that for all I knew to the contrary I might be so constituted that I am liable to error even in matters that seem to me most true. (I couldn't rule this out, because I did not know—or at least was pretending not to know—who made me.) And it was easy to refute the reasons for my earlier confidence about the truth of what I perceived by the senses. Since I seemed to be naturally drawn towards many things that reason told me to avoid, I reckoned that I should not place much confidence in what I was taught by nature. Also, I decided, the mere fact that the perceptions of the senses didn't depend on my will was not enough to show that they came from outside me; for they might have been produced by some faculty of mine that I didn't yet know.

(3) But now, when I am beginning to know myself and my maker better, although I don't think I should recklessly accept everything I seem to have acquired from the senses, neither do I think it should all be called into doubt.

First, I know that if I have a vivid and clear thought of something, God could have created it in a way that exactly corresponds to my thought. So the fact that I can vividly and clearly think of one thing apart from another assures me that the two things are distinct from one another—that is, that they are *two*—since they can be separated by God. Never mind *how* they could be separated; that does not affect the judgment that they are distinct. So my mind is a distinct thing from my body. Furthermore, my mind is *me*, for the following reason. I know that I exist and that nothing else belongs to my nature or essence except that I am a thinking thing; from this it follows that my essence consists solely in my being a thinking thing, even though there may be a body that is very closely joined to me. I have a vivid and clear idea of myself as something that thinks and isn't

extended, and one of body as something that is extended and does not think. So it is certain that I am really distinct from my body and can exist without it.

Besides this, I find that I am capable of certain special kinds of thinking [= "mental activity"], namely imagination and sensory perception. Now, I can vividly and clearly understand myself as a whole without these faculties; but I can't understand them without me, that is, without an intellectual substance for them to belong to. A faculty or ability essentially involves *acts*, so it involves some *thing* that acts; so I see that I differ from my faculties as a thing differs from its properties. Of course there are other faculties—such as those of moving around, changing shape, and so on—which also need a substance to belong to; but it must be a bodily or extended substance and not a thinking one, because a vivid and clear conception of those faculties includes extension but not thought. Now, I have a *passive* faculty of sensory perception, that is, an ability to *receive* and recognize ideas of perceptible objects; but I would have no use for this unless something—myself or something else—had an *active* faculty for *producing* those ideas in the first place. But this faculty can't be in me, since clearly it does not presuppose any thought on my part, and sensory ideas are produced without my cooperation and often even against my will. So sensory ideas must be produced by some substance other than me—a substance that actually *has* (either in a straightforward way or in a higher form) all the reality that is *represented* in the ideas that it produces. Either (a) this substance is a body, in which case it will straightforwardly contain everything that is represented in the ideas; or else (b) it is God, or some creature more noble than a body, in which case it will contain in a higher form whatever is to be found in the ideas. I can reject (b), and be confident that God does not transmit sensory ideas to me either directly from himself or through some creature that does not straightforwardly contain what is represented in the ideas. God has given me no way of recognizing any such "higher form" source for these ideas; on the contrary, he has strongly inclined me to believe that bodies produce them. So if the ideas were transmitted from a source other than corporeal things, God would be a deceiver; and he is not. So bodies exist. They may not all correspond exactly with my sensory intake of them, for much of what comes in through the senses is obscure and confused. But at least bodies have all the properties that I vividly and clearly understand, that is, all that fall within the province of pure mathematics.

Those are the clearly understood properties of bodies in general. What about less clearly understood properties (for example light or sound or pain), and properties of particular bodies (for example the size or shape of the sun)? Although there is much doubt and uncertainty about them, I have a sure hope that I can reach the truth even in these matters. That is because God isn't a deceiver, which implies that he has given me the ability to correct any falsity there may be in my opinions. Indeed, everything that I am "taught by nature" certainly contains some truth. For the term "nature," understood in the most general way, refers to God himself or to the ordered system of created things established by him. And my own nature is simply the totality of things bestowed on me by God.

As vividly as it teaches me anything, my own nature teaches me that I have a body, that when I feel pain there is something wrong with this body, that when I am hungry or thirsty it needs food and drink, and so on. So I shouldn't doubt that there is some truth in this.

Nature also teaches me, through these sensations of pain, hunger, thirst, and so on, that I (a thinking thing) am not merely *in* my body as a sailor is in a ship. Rather, I am *closely joined to it*—intermingled with it, so to speak—so that it and I form a unit. If this were not so, I wouldn't *feel* pain when the body was hurt but would *perceive* the damage in an intellectual way, like a sailor seeing that his ship needs repairs. And when the body needed food or drink I would intellectually understand this fact instead of (as I do) having

confused sensations of hunger and thirst. These sensations are confused mental events that arise from the union—the intermingling, as it were—of the mind with the body.

Nature also teaches me that various other bodies exist in the vicinity of my body, and that I should seek out some of these and avoid others. Also, I perceive by my senses a great variety of colours, sounds, smells, and tastes, as well as differences in heat, hardness, and so on; from which I infer that the bodies that cause these sensory perceptions differ from one another in ways that *correspond* to the sensory differences, though perhaps they don't *resemble* them. Furthermore, some perceptions are pleasant while others are nasty, which shows that my body—or rather my whole self insofar as I am a combination of body and mind—can be affected by the various helpful or harmful bodies that surround it.

However, some of what I thought I had learned from nature really came not from nature but from a habit of rushing to conclusions; and those beliefs could be false. Here are a few examples:

- that if a region contains nothing that stimulates my senses, then it must be empty;

- that the heat in a body resembles my idea of heat;

- that the colour I perceive through my senses is also present in the body that I perceive;

- that in a body that is bitter or sweet there is the same taste that I experience, and so on;

- that stars and towers and other distant bodies have the same size and shape that they present to my senses.

To think clearly about this matter, I need to define exactly what I mean when I say that "nature teaches me" something. I am not at this point taking "nature" to refer to the totality of what God has given me. From that totality I am excluding things that belong to the mind alone, such as my knowledge that *what has been done can't be undone* (I know this through the natural light, without help from the body). I am also excluding things that relate to the body alone, such as the tendency bodies have to fall downwards. My sole concern here is with what God has given to me as a combination of mind and body. My "nature," avoid what hurts and to seek out what gives pleasure, and so on. But it doesn't appear to teach us to rush to conclusions about things located outside us without pausing to think about the question; for knowledge of the truth about such things seems to belong to the mind alone, not to the combination of mind and body. So, although a star has no more effect on my eye than a candle's flame, my thinking of the star as no bigger than the flame does not come from any positive "natural" inclination to believe this; it's just a habit of thought that I have had ever since childhood, with no rational basis for it. Similarly, although I feel heat when I approach a fire and feel pain when I go too near, there is no good reason to think that something in the fire resembles the heat, or resembles the pain. There is merely reason to suppose that something or other in the fire causes feelings of heat or pain in us. Again, even when a region contains nothing that stimulates my senses, it does not follow that it contains no bodies. I now realize that in these cases and many others I have been in the habit of misusing the order of nature. The right way to use the sensory perceptions that nature gives me is as a guide to what is beneficial or harmful for my mind-body complex; and they are vivid and clear enough for *that*. But it is a misuse of them to treat them as reliable guides to the essential nature of the bodies located outside me, for on that topic they give only very obscure and confused information.

I have already looked closely enough at how I may come to make false judgments, even though God is good. Now it occurs to me that there is a problem about mistakes I make regarding the things that nature tells me to seek out or avoid, and also regarding some of my internal sensations. Some cases of this are unproblematic. Someone may be tricked into eating pleasant-tasting food that has poison concealed in it; but here nature urges the person towards the pleasant food, not towards the poison, which it doesn't know about. All this shows is that the person's nature doesn't know everything, and that is no surprise.

Other cases, however, raise problems. They are ones where nature urges us towards something that harms us and this can't be explained through nature's not knowing something. Sick people, for example, may want food or drink that is bad for them. "They go wrong because they are ill"—true, but the difficulty remains. A sick man is one of God's creatures just as a healthy one is, and in each case it seems a contradiction to suppose that God has given him a nature that deceives him. A badly made clock conforms to the laws of its nature in telling the wrong time, just as a well made and accurate clock does; and we might look at the human body in the same way. We could see it as a kind of machine made up of bones, nerves, muscles, veins, blood, and skin in such a way that, even if there were no mind in it, it would still move exactly as it now does in all the cases where movement isn't under the control of the will or, therefore, of the mind. If such a body suffers from dropsy [a disease in which abnormal quantities of water accumulate in the body], for example, and is affected by the dryness of the throat that normally produces in the mind a sensation of thirst, that will affect the nerves and other bodily parts in such a way as to dispose the body to take a drink, which will make the disease worse. Yet this is as *natural* as a healthy body's being stimulated by a similar dryness of the throat to take a drink that is good for it. In a way, we might say, it is *not* natural. Just as we could say that a clock that works badly is "departing from its nature," we might say that the dropsical body that takes a harmful drink is "departing from its nature," that is, from the pattern of movements that usually occur in human bodies. But that involves using "nature" as a way of comparing one thing with another—a sick man with a healthy one, a badly made clock with an accurate one—whereas I have been using "nature" not to make comparisons but to speak of what can be found in the things themselves; and this usage is legitimate.

When we describe a dropsical body as having "a disordered nature," therefore, we are using the term "nature" merely to compare sick with healthy. What has gone wrong in the mind-body complex that suffers from dropsy, however, is not a mere matter of comparison with something else. There is here a real, intrinsic error of nature, namely that the body is thirsty at a time when drink will cause it harm. We have to enquire how it is that the goodness of God does not prevent nature from deceiving us in this way. This enquiry will fall into four main parts.

There is a great difference between the mind and the body. Every body is by its nature divisible, but the mind can't be divided. When I consider the mind—i.e., consider myself purely as a thinking thing—I can't detect any parts within myself; I understand myself to be something single and complete. The whole mind seems to be united to the whole body, but not by a uniting of parts to parts, because: If a foot or arm or any other part of the body is cut off, nothing is thereby taken away from the mind. As for the faculties of willing, of understanding, of sensory perception and so on, these are not *parts* of the mind, since it is one and the same mind that wills, understands and perceives. They are (I repeat) not *parts* of the mind, because they are *properties* or *powers* of it. By contrast, any corporeal thing can easily be divided into parts in my thought; and this shows me that it is really divisible. This one argument would be enough to show me that the mind is completely different from the body, even if I did not already know as much from other considerations presented in the second meditation.

The mind isn't immediately affected by all parts of the body but only by the brain—or perhaps just by the small part of it which is said to contain the "common sense." [Descartes is referring to the pineal gland. The "common sense" was a supposed faculty, postulated by Aristotle, whose role was to integrate the data from the five specialized senses.] The signals that reach the mind depend upon what state this part of the brain is in, irrespective of the condition of the other parts of the body. There is abundant experimental evidence for this, which I needn't review here.

Whenever any part of the body is moved by another part that is some distance away, it can be moved in the same fashion by any of the parts that lie in between, without the more distant part doing anything. For example, in a cord ABCD, if one end D is pulled so that the other end A moves, A could have been moved in just the same way if B or C had been pulled and D had not moved at all. Similarly, when I feel a pain in my foot, this happens by means of nerves that run from the foot up to the brain. When the nerves are pulled in the foot, they pull on inner parts of the brain and make them move; and nature has laid it down that this motion should produce in the mind a sensation of *pain as though occurring in the foot*. But since these nerves stretch from the foot to the brain through the calf, the thigh, the lumbar region, the back and the neck, that same sensation of "pain in the foot" can come about when one of the intermediate parts is pulled, even if nothing happens in the foot. This presumably holds for any other sensation.

One kind of movement in the part of the brain that immediately affects the mind always produces just one kind of sensation; and it would be best for us if it were always the kind that would contribute the most to keeping us alive and well. Experience shows that the sensations that nature has given us are all of just such kinds; so everything about them bears witness to the power and goodness of God. For example, when the nerves in the foot are set in motion in a violent and unusual manner, this motion reaches the inner parts of the brain via the spinal cord, and gives the mind its signal for having a sensation of a pain as occurring in the foot. This stimulates the mind to do its best to remove the cause of the pain, which it takes to be harmful to the foot. God could have made our nature such that this motion in the brain indicated something else to the mind—for example, making the mind aware of the actual motion occurring in the brain, or in the foot, or in any of the intermediate regions. [Descartes is here contrasting the foot with other parts of the body, *and* contrasting a feeling of pain with a merely intellectual awareness that a movement is occurring.] But nothing else would have been so conducive to the continued well-being of the body. In the same way, when we need drink a certain dryness arises in the throat; this moves the nerves of the throat, which in turn move the inner parts of the brain. That produces in the mind a sensation of thirst, because the most useful thing for us to know at this point is that we need drink in order to stay healthy. Similarly in the other cases.

All of this makes it clear that, despite God's immense goodness, the nature of man as a combination of mind and body is such that it is bound to mislead him from time to time. For along the route of the nerves from the foot to the brain, or even in the brain itself, something may happen that produces the same motion that is usually caused by injury to the foot; and then pain will be felt as if it were in the foot. This deception of the senses is natural, because a given kind of motion in the brain must always produce the same kind of sensation in the mind; and, given that this kind of motion usually originates in the foot, it is reasonable that it should produce a sensation indicating a pain in the foot. Similarly with dryness of the throat: it is much better that it should mislead on the rare occasion when the person has dropsy than that it should always mislead when the body is in good health. The same holds for the other cases.

This line of thought greatly helps me to be aware of all the errors to which my nature is liable, and also to correct or avoid them. For I know that so far as bodily well-being is concerned my senses usually tell the truth. Also, I can usually employ more than one sense to investigate the same thing; and I can get further help from my memory, which connects present experiences with past ones, and from my intellect, which has by now examined all the sources of error. So I should have no more fears about the falsity of what my senses tell me every day; on the contrary, the exaggerated doubts of the last few days should be dismissed as laughable. This applies especially to the chief reason for doubt, namely my inability to distinguish dreams from waking experience. For I now notice that the two are vastly different, in that dreams are never linked by memory with all the other actions of life as waking experiences are. If, while I am awake, a man were suddenly to appear to me and then disappear immediately, as happens in sleep, so that I couldn't see where he had come from or where he had gone to, I could reasonably judge that he was a ghost or an hallucination rather than a real man. But if I have a firm grasp of when, where and whence something comes to me, and if I can connect my perception of it with the whole of the rest of my life without a break, then I am sure that in encountering it I am not asleep but awake. And I ought not to have any doubt of its reality if that is unanimously confirmed by all my senses as well as my memory and intellect. From the fact that God isn't a deceiver it follows that in cases like this I am completely free from error. But since everyday pressures don't always allow us to pause and check so carefully, it must be admitted that human life is vulnerable to error about particular things, and we must acknowledge the weakness of our nature.

Study Questions

1. René Descartes is described as the Father of Modern Philosophy. Why is that? Why not his contemporary, the atheist and materialist Thomas Hobbes?

2. In view of the title of the First Meditation, "*Of the things which may be brought within the sphere of the doubful,*" what is the significance of doubt for Descartes?

3. Do you agree with Descartes that there is no certain mark to distinguish dreaming from waking?

4. How powerful do you find Descartes' skeptical argument involving the evil genius? How deeply and systematically could the meaningfulness of thought itself be manipulated?

5. Descartes is famously known for claiming, "I think therefore I am." Where in the Second Meditation does he make *this specific claim*? Can you give an account of what you discover?

6. Descartes claims he is a thinking thing, a mind or soul. For Descartes a thinking thing is essentially a thinking, non-spatial thing while a physical body is essentially a spatial, non-thinking thing. This is Cartesian Dualism. If one asks how do these two metaphysically distinct things, the mind/soul and the body interact, as Descartes claims they do, is it similar to wondering how a student in a math lab might get a prime number caught in her eye? (Not a piece of paper or the like with a prime number written on it but a prime number.) Does Cartesian Dualism collapse into nonsense?

John Pollock

Philosophical Doubts
A Brain in a Vat

John Pollock (1940–2009) was among the dominant figures in epistemology from the mid-20th century to the early 21st century. His work also ranged over the general theory of reasoning, the philosophy of mind, the philosophy of language, decision theory, and probability theory. His research also expanded into two relatively new areas: cognitive science and artificial intelligence, or AI.

Pollock remarked in 2004, "Philosophy is not really a discipline. It's what's left over after you take out the sciences. Most of the sciences started out as philosophy." However, Pollock's work, particularly its interdisciplinary nature, was always a useful reminder, especially for those with little formal familiarity with academic philosophy, that philosophy is deeply intertwined with the many disciplines that yield our broad understanding of the world. For example, Pollock's paper for the *Proceedings of the 3rd International NASA Workshop on Planning and Scheduling for Space* argued that "...we cannot build a sophisticated autonomous planetary rover just by implementing sophisticated planning algorithms. Planning must be based on information, and the agent must have the cognitive capability of acquiring new information about its environment. That requires the implementation of a sophisticated epistemology. Epistemological considerations indicate that the rover cannot be assumed to have a complete probability distribution at its disposal. Its planning must be based upon 'thin' knowledge of probabilities, and that has important implications for what planning algorithms might be employed." To read the entire paper along with other Pollock publications go to: http://oscarhome.soc-sci.arizona.edu/pollock.html.

It all began that cold Wednesday night. I was sitting alone in my office watching the rain come down on the deserted streets outside, when the phone rang. It was Harry's wife, and she sounded terrified. They had been having a late supper alone in their apartment when suddenly the front door came crashing in and six hooded men burst into the room. The men were armed and they made Harry and Anne lie face down on the floor while they went through Harry's pockets. When they found his driver's license one of them carefully scrutinized Harry's face, comparing it with the official photograph and then muttered, "It's him all right." The leader of the intruders produced a hypodermic needle and injected Harry with something that made him lose consciousness almost immediately. For some reason they only tied and gagged Anne. Two of the men left the room and returned with a stretcher and white coats. They put Harry on the stretcher, donned the white coats, and trundled him out of the apartment, leaving Anne lying on the floor. She managed to squirm to the window in time to see them put Harry in an ambulance and drive away.

From *Contemporary Theories of Knowledge*, Rowman & Littlefield, 1986, pp. 1–4. Reprinted with permission from Rowman & Littlefield, 4501 Forbes Blvd., Suite 200, Lanham, MD 20706.

By the time she called me, Anne was coming apart at the seams. It had taken her several hours to get out of her bonds, and then she called the police. To her consternation, instead of uniformed officers, two plain clothed officials arrived and, without even looking over the scene, they proceeded to tell her that there was nothing they could do and if she knew what was good for her she would keep her mouth shut. If she raised a fuss they would put out the word that she was a psycho and she would never see her husband again.

Not knowing what else to do, Anne called me. She had had the presence of mind to note down the number of the ambulance, and I had no great difficulty tracing it to a private clinic at the outskirts of town. When I arrived at the clinic I was surprised to find it locked up like a fortress. There were guards at the gate and it was surrounded by a massive wall. My commando training stood me in good stead as I negotiated the 20-foot wall, avoided the barbed wire, and silenced the guard dogs on the other side. The ground floor windows were all barred, but I managed to wriggle up a drainpipe and get in through a second story window that someone had left ajar. I found myself in a laboratory. Hearing muffled sounds next door I peeked through the keyhole and saw what appeared to be a complete operating room and a surgical team laboring over Harry. He was covered with a sheet from the neck down and they seemed to be connecting tubes and wires to him. I stifled a gasp when I realized that they had removed the top of Harry's skull. To my considerable consternation, one of the surgeons reached into the open top of Harry's head and eased his brain out, placing it in a stainless steel bowl. The tubes and wires I had noted earlier were connected to the now disembodied brain. The surgeons carried the bloody mass carefully to some kind of tank and lowered it in. My first thought was that I had stumbled on a covey of futuristic Satanists who got their kicks from vivisection. My second thought was that Harry was an insurance agent. Maybe this was their way of getting even for the increases in their malpractice insurance rates. If they did this every Wednesday night, their rates were no higher than they should be!

My speculations were interrupted when the lights suddenly came on in my darkened hidey-hole and I found myself looking up at the scariest group of medical men I had ever seen. They manhandled me into the next room and strapped me down on an operating table. I thought, "Oh, oh, I'm for it now!" The doctors huddled at the other end of the room, but I couldn't turn my head far enough to see what they were doing. They were mumbling among themselves, probably deciding my fate. A door opened and I heard a woman's voice. The deferential manner assumed by the medical malpractitioners made it obvious who was boss. I strained to see this mysterious woman but she hovered just out of my view. Then, to my astonishment, she walked up and stood over me and I realized it was my secretary, Margot. I began to wish I had given her that Christmas bonus after all.

It was Margot, but it was a different Margot than I had ever seen. She was wallowing in the heady wine of authority as she bent over me. "Well Mike, you thought you were so smart, tracking Harry here to the clinic," she said. Even now she had the sexiest voice I have ever heard, but I wasn't really thinking about that. She went on, "It was all a trick just to get you here. You saw what happened to Harry. He's not really dead, you know. These gentlemen are the premier neuroscientists in the world today. They have developed a surgical procedure whereby they remove the brain from the body but keep it alive in a vat of nutrient. The Food and Drug Administration wouldn't approve the procedure, but we'll show them. You see all the wires going to Harry's brain? They connect him up with a powerful computer. The computer monitors the output of his motor cortex and provides input to the sensory cortex in such a way that everything appears perfectly normal to Harry. It produces a fictitious mental life that merges perfectly into his past life so that he is unaware that anything has happened to him. He thinks he is shaving right now and getting ready to go to the office and stick it to another neurosurgeon. But actually, he's just a brain in a vat."

"Once we have our procedure perfected we're going after the head of the Food and Drug Administration, but we needed some experimental subjects first. Harry was easy. In order to really test our computer program we need someone who leads a more interesting and varied life—someone like you!" I was starting to squirm. The surgeons had drawn around me and were looking on with malevolent gleams in their eyes. The biggest brute, a man with a pockmarked face and one beady eye staring out from under his stringy black hair, was fondling a razor sharp scalpel in his still-bloody hands and looking as if he could barely restrain his excitement. But Margot gazed down at me and murmured in that incredible voice, "I'll bet you think we're going to operate on you and remove your brain just like we removed Harry's, don't you? But you have nothing to worry about. We're not going to remove your brain. We already did—three months ago!"

With that they let me go. I found my way back to my office in a daze. For some reason, I haven't told anybody about this. I can't make up my mind. I am racked by the suspicion that I am really a brain in a vat and all this I see around me is just a figment of the computer. After all, how could I tell? If the computer program really works, no matter what I do, everything will seem normal. Maybe nothing I see is real. It's driving me crazy. I've even considered checking into that clinic voluntarily and asking them to remove my brain just so that I can be sure…

Study Questions

1. Given the deep problems of Cartesian Dualism, does it seem possible that Pollock's brain in a vat is anything more that a fantastic thought-experiment which overlooks the intimate (essential) role brain function plays in consciousness?

2. Is there any role for freedom of the will for a brain in a vat? Without any criteria for determining which state one is in, do you see your own actions differently?

3. Given Descartes' and Pollock's concerns regarding the relationship between consciousness and the world, do you think they may have deeply misunderstood the very nature of consciousness? Could they, like the astronomer Ptolemy, have been fooled by an illusion for what just seems like obvious common sense? In the case of Ptolemy mistaking the illusion of motion for what appeared to be the obvious real motion of the sun, we still mistakenly say we watch the sun set rather than the earth rotate. Have Descartes and Pollock and most of us been taken in by a false assumption that consciousness is a private, mental world of experience?

George Berkeley

To Be is to Be Perceived

George Berkeley (1685–1753) was born at Dysart Castle, County Kilkenny, Ireland, his family home. Educated at Kilkenny College, he went on to attend Trinity College in Dublin, finishing his master's degree in 1707. He remained at Trinity College as a tutor and Greek lecturer.

Berkeley's earliest publications were on mathematics and science. *An Essay Towards a New Theory of Vision*, 1709, was an examination of visual distance, magnitude, position and problems of sight and touch. Though controversial at the time, many of its conclusions are now accepted in the theory of optics.

In 1710, Berkeley published his now famous *Treatise Concerning the Principles of Human Knowledge*, which was followed by *Three Dialogues Between Hylas and Philonous* in 1713. In these works he developed and defended his claim, *esse est percipi* (to be is to be perceived). Berkeley was deeply dissatisfied with the prevailing metaphysical view of materialism at the time. However, his own metaphysical view, which he described as "immaterialism," but is presently referred to as subjective idealism or Berkelean Idealism, was largely greeted with ridicule at the time of its publication.

Berkeley, California was named after George Berkeley. The naming was suggested in 1866 by Frederick Billings, a trustee of what was then the College of California. Billings was purportedly inspired by Berkeley's *Verses on the Prospect of Planting Arts and Learning in America*. Berkeley had spent nearly four years in Rhode Island waiting for funding to start a college in Bermuda. The final stanza of Berkeley's verse reads, "Westward the course of empire takes its way; The first four Acts already past, A fifth shall close the Drama with the day; Time's noblest offspring is the last."

Visit the International Berkeley Society at http://georgeberkeley.tamu.edu/.

From *A Treatise Concerning the Principles of Human Knowledge*. First published in 1710.

1. It is evident to any one who takes a survey of the *objects of human knowledge*, that they are either *ideas* actually imprinted on the senses; or else such as are perceived by attending to the passions and operations of the mind; or lastly, *ideas* formed by help of memory and imagination—either compounding, dividing, or barely representing those originally perceived in the aforesaid ways. By sight I have the ideas of light and colours, with their several degrees and variations. By touch I perceive hard and soft, heat and cold, motion and resistance, and of all these more and less either as to quantity or degree. Smelling furnishes me with odours; the palate with tastes; and hearing conveys sounds to the mind in all their variety of tone and composition.

And as several of these are observed to accompany each other, they come to be marked by one name, and so to be reputed as one *thing*. Thus, for example a certain colour, taste, smell, figure and consistence having been observed to go together, are accounted one distinct thing, signified by the name *apple*. Other collections of ideas constitute a stone, a tree, a book, and the like sensible things; which as they are pleasing or disagreeable excite the passions of love, hatred, joy, grief, and so forth.

2. But, besides all that endless variety of ideas or objects of knowledge, there is likewise something which knows or perceives them, and exercises divers operations, as willing, imagining, remembering, about them. This perceiving, active being is what I call *mind, spirit, soul*, or *myself*. By which words I do not denote any one of my ideas, but a thing entirely distinct from them, wherein, they exist, or, which is the same thing, whereby they are perceived; for the existence of an idea consists in being perceived.

3. That neither our thoughts, nor passions, nor ideas formed by the imagination, exist without the mind, is what everybody will allow. And it seems no less evident that the various sensations or ideas imprinted on the sense, however blended or combined together (that is, whatever objects they compose), cannot exist otherwise than in a mind perceiving them. I think an intuitive knowledge may be obtained of this by any one that shall attend to what is meant by the term exists, when applied to sensible things. The table I write on I say exists, that is, I see and feel it; and if I were out of my study I should say it existed; meaning thereby that if I was in my study I might perceive it, or that some other spirit actually does perceive it. There was an odour, that is, it was smelt; there was a sound, that is, it was heard; a colour or figure, and it was perceived by sight or touch. This is all that I can understand by these and the like expressions. For as to what is said of the *absolute* existence of unthinking things without any relation to their being perceived, that seems perfectly unintelligible. Their *esse* is *percepi* [to be is to be perceived], nor is it possible they should have any existence out of the minds or thinking things which perceive them.

4. It is indeed an opinion strangely prevailing amongst men, that houses, mountains, rivers, and in a word all sensible objects, have an existence, natural or real, distinct from their being perceived by the understanding. But, with how great an assurance and acquiescence soever this principle may be entertained in the world, yet whoever shall find in his heart to call it in question may, if I mistake not, perceive it to involve a manifest contradiction. For, what are the forementioned objects but the things we perceive by sense? and what do we perceive besides our own ideas or sensations? and is it not plainly repugnant that any one of these, or any combination of them, should exist unperceived?

5. If we thoroughly examine this tenet it will, perhaps, be found at bottom to depend on the doctrine of *abstract ideas*. For can there be a nicer strain of abstraction than to distinguish the existence of sensible objects from their being perceived, so as to conceive them existing unperceived? Light and colours, heat and cold, extension and figures—in a word the things we see and feel—what are they but so many sensations, notions, ideas, or impressions on the sense? and is it possible to separate, even in thought, any

of these from perception? For my part, I might as easily divide a thing from itself. I may, indeed, divide in my thoughts, or conceive apart from each other, those things which, perhaps I never perceived by sense so divided. Thus, I imagine the trunk of a human body without the limbs, or conceive the smell of a rose without thinking on the rose itself. So far, I will not deny, I can abstract; if that may properly be called *abstraction* which extends only to the conceiving separately such objects as it is possible may really exist or be actually perceived asunder. But my conceiving or imagining power does not extend beyond the possibility of real existence or perception. Hence, as it is impossible for me to see or feel anything without an actual sensation of that thing, so is it impossible for me to conceive in my thoughts any sensible thing or object distinct from the sensation or perception of it.

6. Some truths there are so near and obvious to the mind that a man need only open his eyes to see them. Such I take this important one to be, viz., that all the choir of heaven and furniture of the earth, in a word all those bodies which compose the mighty frame of the world, have not any subsistence without a mind, that their *being* is to be perceived or known; that consequently so long as they are not actually perceived by me, or do not exist in my mind or that of any other created spirit, they must either have no existence at all, or else subsist in the mind of some Eternal Spirit: it being perfectly unintelligible, and involving all the absurdity of abstraction, to attribute to any single part of them an existence independent of a spirit. To be convinced of which, the reader need only reflect, and try to separate in his own thoughts the *being* of a sensible thing from its *being perceived*.

7. From what has been said it follows there is not any other Substance than *Spirit*, or that which perceives. But, for the fuller proof of this point, let it be considered the sensible qualities are colour, figure, motion, smell, taste, etc., i.e. the ideas perceived by sense. Now, for an idea to exist in an unperceiving thing is a manifest contradiction, for to have an idea is all one as to perceive; that therefore wherein colour, figure, and the like qualities exist must perceive them; hence it is clear there can be no unthinking substance or *substratum* of those ideas.

8. But, say you, though the ideas themselves do not exist without the mind, yet there may be things like them, whereof they are copies or resemblances, which things exist without the mind in an unthinking substance. I answer, an idea can be like nothing but an idea; a colour or figure can be like nothing but another colour or figure. If we look but never so little into our thoughts, we shall find it impossible for us to conceive a likeness except only between our ideas. Again, I ask whether those supposed *originals* or external things, of which our ideas are the pictures or representations, be themselves perceivable or no? If they are, then they are ideas and we have gained our point; but if you say they are not, I appeal to any one whether it be sense to assert a colour is like something which is invisible; hard or soft, like something which is intangible; and so of the rest.

9. Some there are who make a distinction betwixt *primary* and *secondary* qualities. By the former they mean extension, figure, motion, rest, solidity or impenetrability, and number; by the latter they denote all other sensible qualities, as colours, sounds, tastes, and so forth. The ideas we have of these they acknowledge not to be the resemblances of anything existing without the mind, or unperceived, but they will have our ideas of the *primary qualities* to be patterns or images of things which exist without the mind, in an unthinking substance which they call Matter. By Matter, therefore, we are to understand an inert, senseless substance, in which extension, figure, and motion do actually subsist. But it is evident from what we have already shown, that extension, figure, and motion are only ideas existing in the mind, and that an idea can be like nothing but another idea, and that consequently neither they nor their archetypes can exist in an unperceiving substance. Hence, it is plain that that the very

notion of what is called *Matter* or *corporeal substance*, involves a contradiction in it.

10. They who assert that figure, motion, and the rest of the primary or original qualities do exist without the mind in unthinking substances, do at the same time acknowledge that colours, sounds, heat cold, and suchlike secondary qualities, do not; which they tell us are sensations existing in the mind alone, that depend on and are occasioned by the different size, texture, and motion of the minute particles of matter. This they take for an undoubted truth, which they can demonstrate beyond all exception. Now, if it be certain that those *original* qualities are inseparably united with the other sensible qualities, and not, even in thought, capable of being abstracted from them, it plainly follows that *they* exist only in the mind. But I desire any one to reflect and try whether he can, by any abstraction of thought, conceive the extension and motion of a body without all other sensible qualities. For my own part, I see evidently that it is not in my power to frame an idea of a body extended and moving, but I must withal give it some colour or other sensible quality which is acknowledged to exist only in the mind. In short, extension, figure, and motion, abstracted from all other qualities, are inconceivable. Where therefore the other sensible qualities are, there must these be also, to wit, in the mind and nowhere else.

11. Again, *great* and *small*, *swift* and *slow*, are allowed to exist nowhere without the mind, being entirely relative, and changing as the frame or position of the organs of sense varies. The extension therefore which exists without the mind is neither great nor small, the motion neither swift nor slow, that is, they are nothing at all. But, say you, they are extension in general, and motion in general: thus we see how much the tenet of extended movable substances existing without the mind depends on the strange doctrine of *abstract ideas*. And here I cannot but remark how nearly the vague and indeterminate description of Matter or corporeal substance, which the modern philosophers are run into by their own

principles, resembles that antiquated and so much ridiculed notion of *materia prima*, to be met with in Aristotle and his followers. Without extension solidity cannot be conceived; since therefore it has been shewn that extension exists not in an unthinking substance, the same must also be true of solidity.

12. That number is entirely the creature of the mind, even though the other qualities be allowed to exist without, will be evident to whoever considers that the same thing bears a different denomination of number as the mind views it with different respects. Thus, the same extension is one, or three, or thirty-six, according as the mind considers it with reference to a yard, a foot, or an inch. Number is so visibly relative, and dependent on men's understanding, that it is strange to think how any one should give it an absolute existence without the mind. We say one book, one page, one line, etc.; all these are equally units, though some contain several of the others. And in each instance, it is plain, the unit relates to some particular combination of ideas arbitrarily put together by the mind.

13. Unity I know some will have to be a simple or uncompounded idea, accompanying all other ideas into the mind. That I have any such idea answering the word *unity*, I do not find; and if I had, methinks I could not miss finding it: on the contrary, it should be the most familiar to my understanding, since it is said to accompany all other ideas, and to be perceived by all the ways of sensation and reflexion. To say no more, it is an *abstract idea*.

14. I shall farther add, that, after the same manner as modern philosophers prove certain sensible qualities to have no existence in Matter, or without the mind, the same thing may be likewise proved of all other sensible qualities whatsoever. Thus, for instance, it is said that heat and cold are affections only of the mind, and not at all patterns of real beings, existing in the corporeal substances which excite them, for that the same body which appears cold to one hand seems warm to another. Now, why may we not as well

argue that figure and extension are not patterns or resemblances of qualities existing in Matter, because to the same eye at different stations, or eyes of a different texture at the same station, they appear various, and cannot therefore be the images of anything settled and determinate without the mind? Again, it is proved that sweetness is not really in the sapid thing, because the thing remaining unaltered the sweetness is changed into bitter, as in case of a fever or otherwise vitiated palate. Is it not as reasonable to say that motion is not without the mind, since if the succession of ideas in the mind become swifter, the motion, it is acknowledged, shall appear slower without any alteration in any external object?

15. In short, let any one consider those arguments which are thought manifestly to prove that colours and taste exist only in the mind, and he shall find they may with equal force be brought to prove the same thing of extension, figure, and motion. Though it must be confessed this method of arguing does not so much prove that there is no extension or colour in an outward object, as that we do not know by sense which is the true extension or colour of the object. But the arguments foregoing plainly shew it to be impossible that any colour or extension at all, or other sensible quality whatsoever, should exist in an unthinking subject without the mind, or in truth, that there should be any such thing as an outward object.

16. But let us examine a little the received opinion. It is said extension is a *mode* or *accident* of Matter, and that Matter is the *substratum* that supports it. Now I desire that you would explain to me what is meant by Matter's *supporting* extension. Say you, I have no idea of Matter and therefore cannot explain it. I answer, though you have no positive, yet, if you have any meaning at all, you must at least have a relative idea of Matter; though you know not what it is, yet you must be supposed to know what relation it bears to accidents, and what is meant by its supporting them. It is evident *support* cannot here be taken in its usual or literal sense, as when we say that pillars support a building; in what sense therefore must it be taken?

17. If we inquire into what the most accurate philosophers declare themselves to mean by *material substance*, we shall find them acknowledge they have no other meaning annexed to those sounds but the idea of Being in general, together with the relative notion of its supporting accidents. The general idea of Being appeareth to me the most abstract and incomprehensible of all other; and as for its supporting accidents, this, as we have just now observed, cannot be understood in the common sense of those words; it must therefore be taken in some other sense, but what that is they do not explain. So that when I consider the two parts or branches which make the signification of the words *material substance*, I am convinced there is no distinct meaning annexed to them. But why should we trouble ourselves any farther, in discussing this material *substratum* or support of figure and motion, and other sensible qualities? Does it not suppose they have an existence without the mind? And is not this a direct repugnancy, and altogether inconceivable?

18. But, though it were possible that solid, figured, movable substances may exist without the mind, corresponding to the ideas we have of bodies, yet how is it possible for us to know this? Either we must know it by sense or by reason. As for our senses, by them we have the knowledge only of our sensations, ideas, or those things that are immediately perceived by sense, call them what you will: but they do not inform us that things exist without the mind, or unperceived, like to those which are perceived. This the materialists themselves acknowledge. It remains therefore that if we have any knowledge at all of external things, it must be by reason, inferring their existence from what is immediately perceived by sense. But what reason can induce us to believe the existence of bodies without the mind, from what we perceive, since the very patrons of Matter themselves do not pretend there is any necessary connexion betwixt them and our ideas? I say it is granted on all hands (and what happens in dreams, phrensies, and the like, puts it beyond dispute) that it is possible we

might be affected with all the ideas we have now, though there were no bodies existing without resembling them. Hence, it is evident the supposition of external bodies is not necessary for the producing our ideas; since it is granted they are produced sometimes, and might possibly be produced always in the same order, we see them in at present, without their concurrence.

19. But, though we might possibly have all our sensations without them, yet perhaps it may be thought easier to conceive and explain the manner of their production, by supposing external bodies in their likeness rather than otherwise; and so it might be at least probable there are such things as bodies that excite their ideas in our minds. But neither can this be said; for, though we give the materialists their external bodies, they by their own confession are never the nearer knowing how our ideas are produced; since they own themselves unable to comprehend in what manner body can act upon spirit, or how it is possible it should imprint any idea in the mind. Hence it is evident the production of ideas or sensations in our minds can be no reason why we should suppose Matter or corporeal substances, since that is acknowledged to remain equally inexplicable with or without this supposition. If therefore it were possible for bodies to exist without the mind, yet to hold they do so, must needs be a very precarious opinion; since it is to suppose, without any reason at all, that God has created innumerable beings that are entirely useless, and serve to no manner of purpose.

20. In short, if there were external bodies, it is impossible we should ever come to know it; and if there were not, we might have the very same reasons to think there were that we have now. Suppose—what no one can deny possible—an

intelligence without the help of external bodies, to be affected with the same train of sensations or ideas that you are, imprinted in the same order and with like vividness in his mind. I ask whether that intelligence hath not all the reason to believe the existence of corporeal substances, represented by his ideas, and exciting them in his mind, that you can possibly have for believing the same thing? Of this there can be no question…

23. But, say you, surely there is nothing easier than for me to imagine trees, for instance, in a park, or books existing in a closet, and nobody by to perceive them. I answer, you may so, there is no difficulty in it; but what is all this, I beseech you, more than framing in your mind certain ideas which you call *books* and *trees*, and the same time omitting to frame the idea of any one that may perceive them? But do not you yourself perceive or think of them all the while? This therefore is nothing to the purpose; it only shews you have the power of imagining or forming ideas in your mind: but it does not shew that you can conceive it possible the objects of your thought may exist without the mind. To make out this, it is necessary that you conceive them existing unconceived or unthought of, which is a manifest repugnancy. When we do our utmost to conceive the existence of external bodies, we are all the while only contemplating our own ideas. But the mind taking no notice of itself, is deluded to think it can and does conceive bodies existing unthought of or without the mind, though at the same time they are apprehended by or exist in itself. A little attention will discover to any one the truth and evidence of what is here said, and make it unnecessary to insist on any other proofs against the existence of *material substance*.

Study Questions

1. What does *esse est percipi* mean? What would you consider to be seemingly uncontroversial examples of Berkeley's principle? Would dreams and illusions qualify?

2. If Descartes' dualism seems deeply problematic but his cogito escapes skepticism, does Berkeley's idealism seem to preserve Descartes' epistemic foundation and avoid his metaphysical conundrum in dualism?

3. If a tree falls in the forest but no one is present, what would Berkeley say about the sound in the forest?

4. Why does Berkeley not accept there being a metaphysical distinction between primary and secondary qualities?

5. Why does Berkeley think the very idea of a material object is self-contradictory?

6. The great empiricist philosopher David Hume remarked: "The speculations of the ingenious Dr. Berkeley—they admit no refutation, but they produce no conviction." Are you convinced? Do you have a refutation?

7. Does the world exist, according to Berkeley, when no one is perceiving it? Why?

David Hume

Of Personal Identity

David Hume (1711–1776) attended the University of Edinburgh at the age of twelve (perhaps as young as ten) when, at that time, fourteen was typical. Initially, Hume considered a career in law, but, as he stated, he had "an insurmountable aversion to everything but the pursuits of Philosophy and general Learning."

In 1734, after only a few months working in commerce in the city of Bristol, Hume departed, with a small inheritance, for La Flèche in Anjou, France. Living modestly, Hume resolved "to make a very rigid frugality to supply my deficiency of fortune, to maintain unimpaired my independency, and to regard every object as contemptible except the improvements of my talents in literature." As a result and after four years of work, the young David Hume, 26, returned to England and published in three volumes, from 1739–40, *A Treatise of Human Nature*. His opus attracted little attention, not even stirring the zealots, Hume lamented. Near the end of his life, Hume joked that his *Treatise* "fell still-born from the press." Today, Hume's *Treatise* is considered one of the most important works in Western philosophy. Contemporary philosopher Jerry Fodor described the *Treatise* as "the founding document of cognitive science."

Once Hume's *Essays Moral and Political* were published in 1744, he applied for the Chair of Pneumatics and Moral Philosophy at the University of Edinburgh. Because Hume was considered an atheist, the coveted position went to another candidate as a result of Edinburgh ministers petitioning the town council not to appoint Hume.

By 1745, Hume took a position tutoring the Marquis of Annandale, who was officially considered a "lunatic." This employment ended after approximately a year. At about this time, Hume was at work on his monumental, *The History of England*. This work was published in six volumes between 1754 and 1762. Starting around 1746, Hume served as Secretary to Lieutenant-General St. Clair and during this time wrote *An Enquiry Concerning Human Understanding*, as a shortened, more accessible volume treating the problems he had more extensively covered in his *Treatise*. However, the *Enquiry* proved little more successful than his original *Treatise*.

With the Chair of Philosophy at the University of Glasgow open, Hume applied. Charged with heresy, Hume was defended by some clerical friends, who argued successfully for his acquittal on the heresy charges. Despite his acquittal, Hume failed to gain the chair position at the university. Hume was actively engaged in the intellectual milieu of his times corresponding with and spending time with the likes of Jean-Jacques Rousseau, James Boswell, Joseph Butler, Thomas Reid, and Adam Smith. Smith was a close friend of Hume's and acknowledged Hume's contributions to his own thinking in economics and political philosophy.

From *A Treatise of Human Nature*, L.A. Selby-Bigge, ed., Oxford University Press, 1978, pp. 251–263. Reprinted by permission of Oxford University Press, Inc.

There are some philosophers who imagine we are every moment intimately conscious of what we call *self*; that we feel its existence and its continuance in existence; and are certain, beyond the evidence of a demonstration, both of its perfect identity and simplicity. The strongest sensation, the most violent passion, say they, instead of distracting us from this view, only fix it the more intensely, and make us consider their influence on *self* either by their pain or pleasure. To attempt a further proof of this were to weaken its evidence; since no proof can be derived from any fact of which we are so intimately conscious; nor is there any thing of which we can be certain if we doubt of this.

Unluckily all these positive assertions are contrary to that very experience which is pleaded for them; nor have we any idea of *self*, after the manner it is here explained. For, from what impression could this idea be derived? This question it is impossible to answer without a manifest contradiction and absurdity; and yet it is a question which must necessarily be answered, if we would have the idea of self pass for clear and intelligible. It must be some one impression that gives rise to every real idea. But self or person is not any one impression, but that to which our several impressions and ideas are supposed to have a reference. If any impression gives rise to the idea of self, that impression must continue invariably the same, through the whole course of our lives; since self is supposed to exist after that manner. But there is no impression constant and invariable. Pain and pleasure, grief and joy, passions and sensations succeed each other, and never all exist at the same time. It cannot therefore be from any of these impressions, or from any other, that the idea of self is derived; and consequently there is no such idea.

But further, what must become of all our particular perceptions upon this hypothesis? All these are different, and distinguishable, and separable from each other, and may be separately considered, and may exist separately, and have no need of any thing to support their existence. After what

manner therefore do they belong to self, and how are they connected with it? For my part, when I enter most intimately into what I call *myself*, I always stumble on some particular perception or other, of heat or cold, light or shade, love or hatred, pain or pleasure. I never can catch *myself* at any time without a perception, and never can observe any thing but the perception. When my perceptions are removed for any time, as by sound sleep, so long am I insensible of *myself*, and may truly be said not to exist. And were all my perceptions removed by death, and could I neither think, nor feel, nor see, nor love, nor hate, after the dissolution of my body, I should be entirely annihilated, nor do I conceive what is further requisite to make me a perfect nonentity. If any one, upon serious and unprejudiced reflection, thinks he has a different notion of *himself*, I must confess I can reason no longer with him. All I can allow him is, that he may be in the right as well as I, and that we are essentially different in this particular. He may, perhaps, perceive something simple and continued, which he calls *himself*; though I am certain there is no such principle in me.

But setting aside some metaphysicians of this kind, I may venture to affirm of the rest of mankind, that they are nothing but a bundle or collection of different perceptions, which succeed each other with an inconceivable rapidity, and are in a perpetual flux and movement. Our eyes cannot turn in their sockets without varying our perceptions. Our thought is still more variable than our sight; and all our other senses and faculties contribute to this change: nor is there any single power of the soul, which remains unalterably the same, perhaps for one moment. The mind is a kind of theatre, where several perceptions successively make their appearance; pass, repass, glide away, and mingle in an infinite variety of postures and situations. There is properly no *simplicity* in it at one time, nor *identity* in different, whatever natural propension we may have to imagine that simplicity and identity. The comparison of the theatre must not mislead us. They are the successive perceptions only, that constitute the mind;

nor have we the most distant notion of the place where these scenes are represented, or of the materials of which it is composed.

What then gives us so great a propension to ascribe an identity to these successive perceptions, and to suppose ourselves possessed of an invariable and uninterrupted existence through the whole course of our lives? In order to answer this question we must distinguish betwixt personal identity, as it regards our thought or imagination, and as it regards our passions or the concern we take in ourselves. The first is our present subject; and to explain it perfectly we must take the matter pretty deep, and account for that identity, which we attribute to plants and animals; there being a great analogy betwixt it and the identity of a self or person.

We have a distinct idea of an object, that remains invariable and uninterrupted thro' a suppos'd variation of time; and this idea we call that of *identity* or *sameness*. We have also a distinct idea of several different objects existing in succession, and connected together by a close relation; and this to an accurate view affords as perfect a notion of *diversity*, as if there was no manner of relation among the objects. But tho' these two ideas of identity, and a succession of related objects be in themselves perfectly distinct, and even contrary, yet "tis certain, that in our common way of thinking they are generally confounded with each other. That action of the imagination, by which we consider the uninterrupted and invariable object, and that by which we reflect on the succession of related objects, are almost the same to the feeling, nor is there much more effort of thought requir'd in the latter case than in the former. The relation facilitates the transition of the mind from one object to another, and renders its passage as smooth as if it contemplated one continu'd object. This resemblance is the cause of the confusion and mistake, and makes us substitute the notion of identity, instead of that of related objects. However at one instant we may consider the related succession as variable or interrupted, we are sure the next to ascribe to it a perfect identity, and regard it as enviable and uninterrupted. Our propensity to this mistake is so great from the resemblance above-mention'd, that we fall into it before we are aware; and tho' we incessantly correct ourselves by reflection, and return to a more accurate method of thinking, yet we cannot long sustain our philosophy, or take off this bias from the imagination. Our last resource is to yield to it, and boldly assert that these different related objects are in effect the same, however interrupted and variable. In order to justify to ourselves this absurdity, we often feign some new and unintelligible principle, that connects the objects together, and prevents their interruption or variation. Thus we feign the continu'd existence of the perceptions of our senses, to remove the interruption: and run into the notion of a soul, and *self*, and *substance*, to disguise the variation. But we may farther observe, that where we do not give rise to such a fiction, our propension to confound identity with relation is so great, that we are apt to imagine something unknown and mysterious, connecting the parts, beside their relation; and this I take to be the case with regard to the identity we ascribe to plants and vegetables. And even when this does not take place, we still feel a propensity to confound these ideas, tho' we are not able fully to satisfy ourselves in that particular, nor find any thing invariable and uninterrupted to justify our notion of identity.

Thus the controversy concerning identity is not merely a dispute of words. For when we attribute identity, in an improper sense, to variable or interrupted objects, our mistake is not confin'd to the expression, but is commonly attended with a fiction, either of something invariable and uninterrupted, or of something mysterious and inexplicable, or at least with a propensity to such fictions. What will suffice to prove this hypothesis to the satisfaction of every fair enquirer, is to shew from daily experience and observation, that the objects, which are variable or interrupted, and yet are suppos'd to continue the same, are such only as consist of a succession of parts, connected together by resemblance, contiguity,

or causation. For as such a succession answers evidently to our notion of diversity, it can only be by mistake we ascribe to it an identity; and as the relation of parts, which leads us into this mistake, is really nothing but a quality, which produces an association of ideas, and an easy transition of the imagination from one to another, it can only be from the resemblance, which this act of the mind bears to that, by which we contemplate one continu'd object, that the error arises. Our chief business, then, must be to prove, that all objects, to which we ascribe identity, without observing their invariableness and uninterruptedness, are such as consist of a succession of related objects.

In order to this, suppose any mass of matter, of which the parts are contiguous and connected, to be plac'd before us; 'tis plain we must attribute a perfect identity to this mass, provided all the parts continue uninterruptedly and invariably the same, whatever motion or change of place we may observe either in the whole or in any of the parts. But supposing some very *small* or *inconsiderable* part to be added to the mass, or subtracted from it; tho' this absolutely destroys the identity of the whole, strictly speaking; yet as we seldom think so accurately, we scruple not to pronounce a mass of matter the same, where we find so trivial an alteration. The passage of the thought from the object before the change to the object after it, is so smooth and easy, that we scarce perceive the transition, and are apt to imagine, that 'tis nothing but a continu'd survey of the same object...

This may be confirm'd by another phenomenon. A change in any considerable part of a body destroys its identity; but 'tis remarkable, that where the change is produc'd *gradually* and *insensibly* we are less apt to ascribe to it the same effect. The reason can plainly be no other, than that the mind, in following the successive changes of the body, feels an easy passage from the surveying its condition in one moment to the viewing of it in another, and at no particular time perceives any interruption in its actions.

From which continu'd perception, it ascribes a continu'd existence and identity to the object.

But whatever precaution we may use in introducing the changes gradually, and making them proportionable to the whole, 'tis certain, that where the changes are at last observ'd to become considerable, we make a scruple of ascribing identity to such different objects. There is, however, another artifice, by which we may induce the imagination to advance a step farther; and that is, by producing a reference of the parts to each other, and a combination to some *common end* or purpose. A ship, of which a considerable part has been chang'd by frequent reparations, is still considered as the same; nor does the difference of the materials hinder us from ascribing an identity to it. The common end, in which the parts conspire, is the same under all their variations, and affords an easy transition of the imagination from one situation of the body to another.

But this is still more remarkable, when we add a *sympathy* of parts to their *common end*, and suppose that they bear to each other, the reciprocal relation of cause and effect in all their actions and operations. This is the case with all animals and vegetables; where not only the several parts have a reference to some general purpose, but also a mutual dependence on, and connexion with each other. The effect of so strong a relation is, that tho' every one must allow, that in a very few years both vegetables and animals endure a *total* change, yet we still attribute identity to them, while their form, size, and substance are entirely alter'd. An oak, that grows from a small plant to a large tree, is still the same oak; tho' there be not one particle of matter, or figure of its parts the same. An infant becomes a man, and is sometimes fat, sometimes lean, without any change in his identity...

We now proceed to explain the nature of *personal identity*, which has become so great a question in philosophy, especially of late years in *England*, where all the abstruser sciences are study'd with a peculiar ardour and application. And here 'tis evident, the same method of reasoning must be continu'd which has so successfully explain'd the identity of plants, and animals, and ships, and houses, and of all the compounded and changeable productions either of art or nature. The identity, which we ascribe to the mind of man, is only a fictitious one, and of a like kind with that which we ascribe to vegetables and animal bodies. It cannot, therefore, have a different origin, but must proceed from a like operation of the imagination upon like objects…

The whole of this doctrine leads us to a conclusion, which is of great importance in the present affair, *viz.* that all the nice and subtle questions concerning personal identity can never possibly be decided, and are to be regarded rather as grammatical than as philosophical difficulties. Identity depends on the relations of ideas; and these relations produce identity, by means of that easy transition they occasion. But as the relations, and the easiness of the transition may diminish by insensible degrees, we have no just standard, by which we can decide any dispute concerning the time, when they acquire or lose a title to the name of identity. All the disputes concerning the identity of connected objects are merely verbal, except so far as the relation of parts gives rise to some fiction or imaginary principle of union, as we have already observ'd.

Study Questions

1. If you received an inheritance capable of sustaining you modestly for four to five years (in today's money, say, $225,000.00) what would you do? David Hume was about your age when he chose a frugal life in a small town to finish his *A Treatise of Human Nature*. Do you share anything in common with the young David Hume?

2. Why does Hume find the self or soul to be a psychological fiction?

3. Why does Hume think that his Bundle of Perceptions view is preferable to that of an uninterrupted, ongoing self or soul?

4. If you are a student of psychology or taking a psychology course, which chapter in your textbook(s) is dedicated to a study of the soul? Why do you suppose that concept has fallen out of scientific favor? What role does Hume's view play in this historical development?

5. Given Hume's Bundle of Perceptions, what according to Hume is the content of those perceptions that allow the principles of resemblance, contiguity, and causality to function?

6. What do you find to be the primary differences between Descartes' and Hume's views of the self or soul? Could both philosophers be correct? Which do you find more persuasive?

Gilbert Ryle

Descartes' Myth

Gilbert Ryle (1900–1976) was a self-described "omnivorous reader." Ryle attended Queen's College, Oxford in 1919 to study the Classics. However, he was immediately tempted by Philosophy and graduated with first-class honours in the new Modern Greats School of Philosophy, Politics and Economics. After his graduation, he was appointed to a lectureship in Philosophy at Christ Church College. A year later he became a tutor. He would remain at Oxford his entire academic career having been elected to the Waynflete Chair of Metaphysical Philosophy. During World War II he served in intelligence, rising to the rank of major. Ryle has been described as "unstinting in his advice and encouragement to generations of students but in philosophical debate he could turn into a formidable opponent, expressing an intense dislike of pomposity, pretence, and jargon." Ryle remained a bachelor his entire life, living with his twin sister Mary in Oxfordshire after his retirement. The following selection is from his *The Concept of Mind*.

1. The Official Doctrine

There is a doctrine about the nature and place of minds which is so prevalent among theorists and even among laymen that it deserves to be described as the official theory. Most philosophers, psychologists and religious teachers subscribe, with minor reservations, to its main articles and, although they admit certain theoretical difficulties in it, they tend to assume that these can be overcome without serious modifications being made to the architecture of the theory. It will be argued here that the central principles of the doctrine are unsound and conflict with the whole body of what we know about minds when we are not speculating about them.

The official doctrine, which hails chiefly from Descartes, is something like this. With the doubtful exceptions of idiots and infants in arms every human being has both a body and a mind. Some would prefer to say that every human being is both a body and a mind. His body and his mind are ordinarily harnessed together, but after the death of the body his mind may continue to exist and function.

Human bodies are in space and are subject to the mechanical laws which govern all other bodies in space. Bodily processes and states can be inspected by external observers. So a man's bodily life is as much a public affair as are the lives of animals and reptiles and even as the careers of trees, crystals and planets.

But minds are not in space, nor are their operations subject to mechanical laws. The workings of one mind are not witnessable by other observers; its career is private. Only I can take direct cognisance of the states and processes of my own mind. A person therefore lives through two collateral histories, one consisting of what happens in and to his body, the other consisting of what happens in and

From *The Concept of Mind*, 1949, Hertford College, University of Oxford, Chapter 1: pp. 11–23. Reproduced by permission of Taylor & Francis Books, UK.

to his mind. The first is public, the second private. The events in the first history are events in the physical world, those in the second are events in the mental world.

It has been disputed whether a person does or can directly monitor all or only some of the episodes of his own private history; but, according to the official doctrine, of at least some of these episodes he has direct and unchallengeable cognisance. In consciousness, self-consciousness and introspection he is directly and authentically apprised of the present states and operations of his mind. He may have great or small uncertainties about concurrent and adjacent episodes in the physical world, but he can have none about at least part of what is momentarily occupying his mind.

It is customary to express this bifurcation of his two lives and of his two worlds by saying that the things and events which belong to the physical world, including his own body, are external, while the workings of his own mind are internal. This antithesis of outer and inner is of course meant to be construed as a metaphor, since minds, not being in space, could not be described as being spatially inside anything else, or as having things going on spatially inside themselves. But relapses from this good intention are common and theorists are found speculating how stimuli, the physical sources of which are yards or miles outside a person's skin, can generate mental responses inside his skull, or how decisions framed inside his cranium can set going movements of his extremities.

Even when "inner" and "outer" are construed as metaphors, the problem how a person's mind and body influence one another is notoriously charged with theoretical difficulties. What the mind wills, the legs, arms and the tongue execute; what affects the ear and the eye has something to do with what the mind perceives; grimaces and smiles betray the mind's moods and bodily castigation lead, it is hoped, to moral improvement. But the actual transactions between the episodes of the private history and those of the public

history remain mysterious, since by definition they can belong to neither series. They could not be reported among the happenings described in a person's autobiography of his inner life, but nor could they be reported among those described in someone else's biography of that person's overt career. They can be inspected neither by introspection nor by laboratory experiment. They are theoretical shuttlecocks which are forever being bandied from the physiologist back to the psychologist and from the psychologist back to the physiologist.

Underlying this partly metaphorical representation of the bifurcation of a person's two lives there is a seemingly more profound and philosophical assumption. It is assumed that there are two different kinds of existence or status. What exists or happens may have the status of physical existence, or it may have the status of mental existence. Somewhat as the faces of coins are either heads or tails, or somewhat as living creatures are either male or female, so, it is supposed, some existing is physical existing, other existing is mental existing. It is a necessary feature of what has physical existence that it is in space and time; it is a necessary feature of what has mental existence that it is in time but not in space. What has physical existence is composed of matter, or else is a function of matter; what has mental existence consists of consciousness, or else is a function of consciousness.

There is thus a polar opposition between mind and matter, an opposition which is often brought out as follows. Material objects are situated in a common field, known as "space." and what happens to one body in one part of space is mechanically connected with what happens to other bodies in other parts of space. But mental happenings occur in insulated fields, known as "minds," and there is, apart maybe from telepathy, no direct causal connection between what happens in one mind and what happens in another. Only through the medium of the public physical world can the mind of one person make a difference to the mind of another. The mind is its own

place and in his inner life each of us lives the life of a ghostly Robinson Crusoe. People can see, hear and jolt one another's bodies, but they are irremediably blind and deaf to the workings of one another's minds and inoperative upon them.

What sort of knowledge can be secured of the workings of a mind? On the one side, according to the official theory, a person has direct knowledge of the best imaginable kind of the workings of his own mind. Mental states and processes are (or are normally) conscious states and processes, and the consciousness which irradiates them can engender no illusions and leaves the door open for no doubts. A person's present thinkings, feelings and willings, his perceivings, rememberings and imaginings are intrinsically "phosphorescent"; their existence and their nature are inevitably betrayed to their owner. The inner life is a stream of consciousness of such a sort that it would be absurd to suggest that the mind whose life is that stream might be unaware of what is passing down it.

True, the evidence adduced recently by Freud seems to show that there exist channels tributary to this stream, which run hidden from their owner. People are actuated by impulses the existence of which they vigorously disavow; some of their thoughts differ from the thoughts which they acknowledge; and some of the actions which they think they will to perform they do not really will. They are thoroughly gulled by some of their own hypocrisies and they successfully ignore facts about their mental lives which on the official theory ought to be patent to them. Holders of the official theory tend, however, to maintain that anyhow in normal circumstances a person must be directly and authentically seized of the present state and workings of his own mind.

Besides being currently supplied with these alleged immediate data of consciousness, a person is also generally supposed to be able to exercise from time to time a special kind of perception, namely inner perception, or introspection. He can take a (non-optical) "look" at what is passing in his mind. Not only can he

view and scrutinize a flower through his sense of sight and listen to and discriminate the notes of a bell through his sense of hearing; he can also reflectively or introspectively watch, without any bodily organ of sense, the current episodes of his inner life. This self-observation is also commonly supposed to be immune from illusion, confusion or doubt. A mind's reports of its own affairs have a certainty superior to the best that is possessed by its reports of matters in the physical world. Sense-perceptions can, but consciousness and introspection cannot, be mistaken or confused.

On the other side, one person has no direct access of any sort to the events of the inner life of another. He cannot do better than make problematic inferences from the observed behaviour of the other person's body to the states of mind which, by analogy from his own conduct, he supposes to be signalised by that behaviour. Direct access to the workings of a mind is the privilege of that mind itself; in default of such privileged access, the workings of one mind are inevitably occult to everyone else. For the supposed arguments from bodily movements similar to their own to mental workings similar to their own would lack any possibility of observational corroboration. Not unnaturally, therefore, an adherent of the official theory finds it difficult to resist this consequence of his premises, that he has no good reason to believe that there do exist minds other than his own. Even if he prefers to believe that to other human bodies there are harnessed minds not unlike his own, he cannot claim to be able to discover their individual characteristics, or the particular things that they undergo and do. Absolute solitude is on this showing the ineluctable destiny of the soul. Only our bodies can meet.

As a necessary corollary of this general scheme there is implicitly prescribed a special way of construing our ordinary concepts of mental powers and operations. The verbs, nouns and adjectives, with which in ordinary life we describe the wits, characters and higher-grade performances of the people with whom we have do, are required to be construed as signifying special episodes in their secret histories, or else as signifying tendencies for such episodes to occur. When someone is described as knowing, believing or guessing something, as hoping, dreading, intending or shirking something, as designing this or being amused at that, these verbs are supposed to denote the occurrence of specific modifications in his (to us) occult stream of consciousness. Only his own privileged access to this stream in direct awareness and introspection could provide authentic testimony that these mental-conduct verbs were correctly or incorrectly applied. The onlooker, be he teacher, critic, biographer or friend, can never assure himself that his comments have any vestige of truth. Yet it was just because we do in fact all know how to make such comments, make them with general correctness and correct them when they turn out to be confused or mistaken, that philosophers found it necessary to construct their theories of the nature and place of minds. Finding mental-conduct concepts being regularly and effectively used, they properly sought to fix their logical geography. But the logical geography officially recommended would entail that there could be no regular or effective use of these mental-conduct concepts in our descriptions of, and prescriptions for, other people's minds.

2. The Absurdity of the Official Doctrine

Such in outline is the official theory. I shall often speak of it, with deliberate abusiveness, as "the dogma of the Ghost in the Machine." I hope to prove that it is entirely false, and false not in detail but in principle. It is not merely an assemblage of particular mistakes. It is one big mistake and a mistake of a special kind. It is, namely, a category-mistake. It represents the facts of mental life as if they belonged to one logical type or category (or range of types or categories), when they actually belong to another. The dogma is therefore a philosopher's myth. In attempting to explode the myth I shall probably be taken to be denying well-known facts about the mental life

of human beings, and my plea that I aim at doing nothing more than rectify the logic of mental-conduct concepts will probably be disallowed as mere subterfuge.

I must first indicate what is meant by the phrase "Category-mistake." This I do in a series of illustrations.

A foreigner visiting Oxford or Cambridge for the first time is shown a number of colleges, libraries, playing fields, museums, scientific departments and administrative offices. He then asks "But where is the University? I have seen where the members of the Colleges live, where the Registrar works, where the scientists experiment and the rest. But I have not yet seen the University in which reside and work the members of your University." It has then to be explained to him that the University is not another collateral institution, some ulterior counterpart to the colleges, laboratories and offices which he has seen. The University is just the way in which all that he has already seen is organized. When they are seen and when their co-ordination is understood, the University has been seen. His mistake lay in his innocent assumption that it was correct to speak of Christ Church, the Bodleian Library, the Ashmolean Museum *and* the University, to speak, that is, as if "the University" stood for an extra member of the class of which these other units are members. He was mistakenly allocating the University to the same category as that to which the other institutions belong.

The same mistake would be made by a child witnessing the march-past of a division, who, having had pointed out to him such and such battalions, batteries, squadrons, etc., asked when the division was going to appear. He would be supposing that a division was a counterpart to the units already seen, partly similar to them and partly unlike them. He would be shown his mistake by being told that in watching the battalions, batteries and squadrons marching past he had been watching the division marching past. The march-past was not a parade of battalions, batteries,

squadrons *and* a division; it was a parade of the battalions, batteries and squadrons of a division.

One more illustration. A foreigner watching his first game of cricket learns what are the functions of the bowlers, the batsmen, the fielders, the umpires and the scorers. He then says "But there is no one left on the field to contribute the famous element of team-spirit. I see who does the bowling, the batting and the wicketkeeping; but I do not see whose role it is to exercise *esprit de corps.*" Once more, it would have to be explained that he was looking for the wrong type of thing. Team-spirit is not another cricketing-operation supplementary to all of the other special tasks. It is, roughly, the keenness with which each of the special tasks is performed, and performing a task keenly is not performing two tasks. Certainly exhibiting team-spirit is not the same thing as bowling or catching, but nor is it a third thing such that we can say that the bowler first bowls and then exhibits team-spirit or that a fielder is at a given moment either catching or displaying *esprit de corps.*

These illustrations of category-mistakes have a common feature which must be noticed. The mistakes were made by people who did not know how to wield the concepts *University, division* and *team-spirit.* Their puzzles arose from inability to use certain items in the English vocabulary.

The theoretically interesting category-mistakes are those made by people who are perfectly competent to apply concepts, at least the situations with which they are familiar, but are still liable in their abstract thinking to allocate those concepts to logical types to which they do not belong. An instance of a mistake of this sort would be the following story. A student of politics has learned the main differences between the British, the French and the American Constitutions, and has learned also the differences and connections between the Cabinet, Parliament, the various Ministries, the Judicature and the Church of England. But he still becomes embarrassed when asked questions about the connections between the Church of England, the Home Office and the British Constitution. For while the Church and the Home Office are institutions, the British Constitution is not another institution in the same sense of that noun. So inter-institutional relations which can be asserted or denied to hold between the Church and the Home Office cannot be asserted or denied to hold between either of them and the British Constitution. "The British Constitution" is not a term of the same logical type as the "Home Office" and "the Church of England." In a partially similar way, John Doe may be a relative, a friend, an enemy or a stranger to Richard Roe; but he cannot be any of these things to the Average Taxpayer. He knows how to talk sense in certain sorts of discussions about the Average Taxpayer, but he is baffled to say why he could not come across him in the street as he can come across Richard Roe.

It is pertinent to our main subject to notice that, so long as the student of politics continues to think of the British Constitution as a counterpart to the other institutions, he will tend to describe it as a mysteriously occult institution; and so long as John Doe continues to think of the Average Taxpayer as a fellow citizen, he will tend to think of him as an elusive insubstantial man, a ghost who is everywhere yet nowhere.

My destructive purpose is to show that a family of radical category-mistakes is the source of the double-life theory. The representation of a person as a ghost mysteriously ensconced in a machine derives from this argument. Because, as is true, a person's thinking, feeling and purposive doing cannot be described solely in the idioms of physics, chemistry and physiology, therefore they must be described in counterpart idioms. As the human body is a complex organised unit, so the human mind must be another complex organised unit, though one made of a different sort of stuff and with a different sort of structure. Or, again, as the human body, like any other parcel of matter, is a field of causes and effects, so the mind must be another field of causes and effects, though not (Heaven be praised) mechanical causes and effects.

3. The Origin of the Category-mistake

One of the chief intellectual origins of what I have yet to prove to be the Cartesian category-mistake seems to be this. When Galileo showed that his methods of scientific discovery were competent to provide a mechanical theory which should cover every occupant of space, Descartes found in himself two conflicting motives. As a man of scientific genius he could not but endorse the claims of mechanics, yet as a religious and moral man he could not accept, as Hobbes accepted, the discouraging rider to those claims, namely that human nature differs only in degree of complexity from clockwork. The mental could not be just a variety of the mechanical.

He and subsequent philosophers naturally but erroneously availed themselves of the following escape-route. Since mental-conduct words are not to be construed as signifying the occurrence of mechanical processes, they must be construed as signifying the occurrence of non-mechanical processes; since mechanical laws explain movements in space as the effects of other movements in space, other laws must explain some of the non-spatial workings of minds as the effects of other non-spatial workings of minds. The difference between the human behaviours which we describe as intelligent and those which we describe as unintelligent must be a difference in their causation; so, while some movements of human tongues and limbs are the effects of mechanical causes, others must be the effects of non-mechanical causes, i.e. some issue from movements of particles of matter, others from workings of the mind.

The differences between the physical and the mental were thus represented as differences inside the common framework of the categories of "thing," "stuff," "attribute," "state," "process," "change," "cause" and "effect." Minds are things, but different sorts of things from bodies; mental processes are causes and effects, but different sorts of causes and effects from bodily movements. And so on. Somewhat as the foreigner expected the University to be an extra edifice, rather like a college but also considerably different, so the repudiators of mechanism represented minds as extra centres of causal processes, rather like machines but also considerably different from them. Their theory was a para-mechanical hypothesis.

That this assumption was at the heart of the doctrine is shown by the fact that there was from the beginning felt to be a major theoretical difficulty in explaining how minds can influence and be influenced by bodies. How can a mental process, such as willing, cause spatial movements like the movements of the tongue? How can a physical change in the optic nerve have among its effects a mind's perception of a flash of light? This notorious crux by itself shows the logical mould into which Descartes pressed his theory of the mind. It was the self-same mould into which he and Galileo set their mechanics. Still unwittingly adhering to the grammar of mechanics, he tried to avert disaster by describing minds in what was merely an obverse vocabulary. The workings of minds had to be described by the mere negatives of the specific descriptions given to bodies; they are not in space, they are not motions, they are not modifications of matter, they are not accessible to public observation. Minds are not bits of clockwork, they are just bits of not-clockwork.

As thus represented, minds are not merely ghosts harnessed to machines, they are themselves just spectral machines. Though the human body is an engine, it it not quite an ordinary engine, since some of its workings are governed by another engine inside it—this interior governor-engine being one of a very special sort. It is invisible, inaudible and it has no size or weight. It cannot be taken to bits and the laws it obeys are not those known to ordinary engineers. Nothing is known of how it governs the bodily engine.

A second major crux points the same moral. Since, according to the doctrine, minds belong to the same category as bodies and since bodies are rigidly governed by mechanical laws, it seemed to many theorists to follow that minds must be

similarly governed by rigid non-mechanical laws. The physical world is a deterministic system, so the mental world must be a deterministic system. Bodies cannot help the modifications that they undergo, so minds cannot help pursuing the careers fixed for them. *Responsibility, choice, merit* and *demerit* are therefore inapplicable concepts—unless the compromise solution is adopted of saying that the laws governing mental processes, unlike those governing physical processes, have the congenial attribute of being only rather rigid. The problem of the Freedom of the Will was the problem how to reconcile the hypothesis that minds are to be described in terms drawn from the categories of mechanics with the knowledge that higher-grade human conduct is not of a piece with the behaviour of machines.

It is an historical curiosity that it was not noticed that the entire argument was broken-backed. Theorists correctly assumed that any sane man could already recognise the differences between, say, rational and non-rational utterances or between purposive and automatic behaviour. Else there would have been nothing requiring to be salved from mechanism. Yet the explanation given presupposed that one person could in principle never recognise the difference between the rational and the irrational utterances issuing from other human bodies, since he could never get access to the postulated immaterial causes of some of their utterances. Save for the doubtful exception of himself, he could never tell the difference between a man and a Robot. It would have to be conceded, for example, that, for all that we can tell, the inner lives of persons who are classed as idiots or lunatics are as rational as those of anyone else. Perhaps only their overt behaviour is disappointing; that is to say, perhaps "idiots" are not really idiotic, or "lunatics" lunatic. Perhaps, too, some of those who are classed as sane are really idiots. According to the theory, external observers could never know how the overt behaviour of others is correlated with their mental powers and processes and so they could never know or even plausibly conjecture whether their applications of mental-conduct concepts to these other people were correct or incorrect. It would then be hazardous or impossible for a man to claim sanity or logical consistency even for himself, since he would be debarred from comparing his own performances with those of others. In short, our characterisations of persons and their performances as intelligent, prudent, and virtuous or as stupid, hypocritical, and cowardly could never have been made, so the problem of providing a special causal hypothesis to serve as the basis of such diagnoses would never have arisen. The question, "How do persons differ from machines?" arose just because everyone already knew how to apply mental-conduct concepts before the new causal hypothesis was introduced. This causal hypothesis could not therefore be the source of the criteria used in those applications. Nor, of course, has the causal hypothesis in any degree improved our handling of those criteria. We still distinguish good from bad arithmetic, politic from impolitic conduct and fertile from infertile imaginations in the ways in which Descartes himself distinguished them before and after he speculated how the applicability of these criteria was compatible with the principle of mechanical causation.

He had mistaken the logic of his problem. Instead of asking by what criteria intelligent behaviour is actually distinguished from non-intelligent behaviour, he asked "Given that the principle of mechanical causation does not tell us the difference, what other causal principle will tell it us?" He realised that the problem was not one of mechanics and assumed that it must therefore be one of some counterpart to mechanics. Not unnaturally psychology is often cast for just this role.

When two terms belong to the same category, it is proper to construct conjunctive propositions embodying them. Thus a purchaser may say that he bought a left-hand glove and a right-hand glove, but not that he bought a left-hand glove, a right-hand glove and a pair of gloves. "She came home in a flood of tears and a sedan-chair" is a well-known joke based on the absurdity of conjoining terms of different types. It would have been equally ridiculous to construct the disjunction "She came home either in a flood of tears or else in a sedan-chair." Now the dogma of the Ghost in the Machine does just this. It maintains that there exist both bodies and minds; that there occur physical processes and mental processes; that there are mechanical causes of corporeal movements and mental causes of corporeal movements. "I shall argue that these and other analogous conjunctions are absurd; but, it must be noticed, the argument will not show that either of the illegitimately conjoined propositions is absurd in itself." I am not, for example, denying that there occur mental processes. Doing long division is a mental process and so is making a joke. But I am saying that the phrase "there occur mental processes" does not mean the same sort of thing as "there occur physical processes," and, therefore, that it makes no sense to conjoin or disjoin the two.

If my argument is successful, there will follow some interesting consequences. First, the hallowed contrast between Mind and Matter will be dissipated, but dissipated not by either of the equally hallowed absorptions of Mind by Matter or of Matter by Mind, but in quite a different way. For the seeming contrast of the two will be shown to be as illegitimate as would be the contrast of "she came home in a flood of tears" and "she came home in a sedan-chair." The belief that there is a polar opposition between Mind and Matter is the belief that they are terms of the same logical type.

It will also follow that both Idealism and Materialism are answers to an improper question. The "reduction" of the material world to mental states and processes, as well as the "reduction" of mental states and processes to physical states and processes, presuppose the legitimacy of the disjunction "Either there exist minds or there exist bodies (but not both)." It would be like saying, "Either she bought a left-hand and a right-hand glove or she bought a pair of gloves (but not both)."

It is perfectly proper to say, in one logical tone of voice, that there exist minds and to say, in another logical tone of voice, that there exist bodies. But these expressions do not indicate two different species of existence, for "existence" is not a generic word like "coloured" or "sexed." They indicate two different senses of "exist," somewhat as "rising" has different senses in "the tide is rising," "hopes are rising," and "the average age of death is rising." A man would be thought to be making a poor joke who said that three things are now rising, namely the tide, hopes, and the average age of death. It would be just as good or bad a joke to say that there exist prime numbers and Wednesdays and public opinions and navies; or that there exist both minds and bodies.

Study Questions

1. What is the Official Doctrine according to Ryle?

2. Why does Ryle describe "with deliberate abusiveness" the Official Doctrine as the dogma of the Ghost in the Machine?

3. What is a Category Mistake? Can you give examples of category mistakes besides those provided by Ryle?

4. Would Ryle face Descartes' problem of being unable to distinguish waking from dreaming?

5. Do you think that Ryle has made theoretical progress in solving the Mind-body Problem?

Frank Jackson

The Qualia Problem

F rank Jackson (1943–) received his PhD in philosophy from La Trobe University. He taught at the University of Adelaide for a year in 1967. In 1978, he became chair of the philosophy department at Monash University. In 1986, he joined Australian National University (ANU) as Professor of Philosophy and Head of the Philosophy Program, Research School of Social Sciences. At ANU, he served as Director of the Institute of Advanced Studies and Deputy Vice-Chancellor. In 2003, Jackson was appointed Distinguished Professor at ANU. In 2007–2008, he became a professor of philosophy at Princeton University. He now spends half of each year at Princeton University and one month per year at ANU.

In 1995, Jackson delivered the John Locke lectures at the University of Oxford. His father had delivered the 1957–8 lectures, making them the first father and son lecturers. In 2006, Jackson was awarded the Order of Australia for service to philosophy and social sciences as an academic, administrator, and researcher. In philosophy of mind, Jackson is known for the knowledge argument, which claims to prove that physicalist theories are incomplete. Jackson is a self-described Qualia Freak. Jackson's knowledge arguments have spread beyond professional philosophy as dramatised in the documentary "Brainspotting," as well as being the focus of author David Lodge's novel, *Thinks* (2001).

It is undeniable that the physical, chemical, and biological sciences have provided a great deal of information about the world we live in and about ourselves. I will use the label "physical information" for this kind of information, and also for information that automatically comes along with it. For example, if a medical scientist tells me enough about the processes that go on in my nervous system, and about how they relate to happenings in the world around me, to what has happened in the past and is likely to happen in the future, to what happens to other similar and dissimilar organisms, and the like, he or she tells me—if I am clever enough to fit it together appropriately—about what is often called the functional role of those states in me (and in organisms in general in similar cases). This information, and its kin, I also label "physical."

I do not mean these sketchy remarks to constitute a definition of "physical information," and of the correlative notions of physical property, process, and so on, but to indicate what I have in mind here. It is well known that there are problems with giving a precise definition of these notions, and so of the thesis of Physicalism that all (correct) information is physical information. But—unlike some—I take the question of definition to cut across the central problems I want to discuss in this paper.

From *Philosophical Quarterly*, Vol. 32, No. 127 (1982), pp. 127–136. Copyright © 1982 Blackwell Publishing Ltd. Reproduced with permission of Blackwell Publishing Ltd.

I am what is sometimes known as a "qualia freak." I think that there are certain features of the bodily sensations especially, but also of certain perceptual experiences, which no amount of purely physical information includes. Tell me everything physical there is to tell about what is going on in a living brain, the kind of states, their functional role, their relation to what goes on at other times and in other brains, and so on and so forth, and be I as clever as can be in fitting it all together, you won't have told me about the hurtfulness of pains, the itchiness of itches, pangs of jealousy, or about the characteristic experience of tasting a lemon, smelling a rose, hearing a loud noise or seeing the sky.

There are many qualia freaks, and some of them say that their rejection of Physicalism is an unargued intuition. I think that they are being unfair to themselves. They have the following argument. Nothing you could tell of a physical sort captures the smell of a rose, for instance. Therefore, Physicalism is false. By our lights this is a perfectly good argument. It is obviously not to the point to question its validity, and the premise is intuitively obviously true both to them and to me.

I must, however, admit that it is weak from a polemical point of view. There are, unfortunately for us, many who do not find the premise intuitively obvious. The task then is to present an argument whose premises are obvious to all, or at least to as many as possible. This I try to do in [In the following section] with what I will call… "the Knowledge argument."

In the following section I tackle the question of the causal role of qualia. The major factor in stopping people from admitting qualia is the belief that they would have to be given a causal role with respect to the physical world and especially the brain; and it is hard to do this without sounding like someone who believes in fairies. I seek in section IV to turn this objection by arguing that the view that qualia are epiphenomenal is a perfectly possible one.

The Knowledge Argument for Qualia

People vary considerably in their ability to discriminate colors. Suppose that in an experiment to catalog this variation Fred is discovered. Fred has better color vision than anyone else on record; he makes every discrimination that anyone has ever made, and moreover he makes one that we cannot even begin to make. Show him a batch of ripe tomatoes and he sorts them into two roughly equal groups and does so with complete consistency. That is, if you blindfold him, shuffle the tomatoes up, and then remove the blindfold and ask him to sort them out again, he sorts them into exactly the same two groups.

We ask Fred how he does it. He explains that all ripe tomatoes do not look the same color to him, and in fact that this is true of a great many objects that we classify together as red. He sees two colors where we see one, and he has in consequence developed for his own use two words "red_1" and "red_2" to mark the difference. Perhaps he tells us that he has often tried to teach the difference between red_1 and red_2 to his friends but has got nowhere and has concluded that the rest of the world is red_1-red_2 color-blind—or perhaps he has had partial success with his children; it doesn't matter. In any case he explains to us that it would be quite wrong to think that because "red" appears in both "red_1" and "red_2," that the two colors are shades of the one color. He only uses the common term "red" to fit more easily into our restricted usage. To him red_1 and red_2 are as different from each other and all the other colors as yellow is from blue. And his discriminatory behavior bears this out: he sorts red_1 from red_2 tomatoes with the greatest of ease in a wide variety of viewing circumstances. Moreover, an investigation of the physiological basis of Fred's exceptional ability reveals that Fred's optical system is able to separate out two groups of wavelengths in the red spectrum as sharply as we are able to sort out yellow from blue.

I think that we should admit that Fred can see, really see, at least one more color than we can; red$_1$ is a different color from red$_2$. We are to Fred as a totally red-green color-blind person is to us. H. G. Wells' story "The country of the blind" is about a sighted person in a totally blind community. This person never manages to convince them that he can see, that he has an extra sense. They ridicule this sense as quite inconceivable, and treat his capacity to avoid falling into ditches, to win fights and so on as precisely that capacity and nothing more. We would be making their mistake if we refused to allow that Fred can see one more color than we can.

What kind of experience does Fred have when he sees red$_1$ and red$_2$? What is the new color or colors like? We would dearly like to know but do not; and it seems that no amount of physical information about Fred's brain and optical system tells us. We find out perhaps that Fred's cones respond differentially to certain light waves in the red section of the spectrum that make no difference to ours (or perhaps he has an extra cone) and that this leads in Fred to a wider range of those brain states responsible for visual discriminatory behavior. But none of this tells us what we really want to know about his color experience. There is something about it we don't know. But we know, we may suppose, everything about Fred's body, his behavior and dispositions to behavior and about his internal physiology, and everything about his history and relation to others that can be given in physical accounts of persons. We have all the physical information. Therefore, knowing all this is not knowing everything about Fred. It follows that Physicalism leaves something out.

To reinforce this conclusion, imagine that as a result of our investigations into the internal workings of Fred we find out how to make everyone's physiology like Fred's in the relevant respects; or perhaps Fred donates his body to science and on his death we are able to transplant his optical system into someone else—again the fine detail doesn't matter. The important point is that such a happening would create enormous interest. People would say "At last we will know what it is like to see the extra color, at last we will know how Fred has differed from us in the way he has struggled to tell us about for so long." Then it cannot be that we knew all along all about Fred. But *ex hypothesi* we did know all along everything about Fred that features in the physicalist scheme; hence the physicalist scheme leaves something out.

Put it this way. *After* the operation, we will know more about Fred and especially about his color experiences. But beforehand we had all the physical information we could desire about his body and brain, and indeed everything that has ever featured in physicalist accounts of mind and consciousness. Hence there is more to know than all that. Hence Physicalism is incomplete.

Fred and the new color(s) are of course essentially rhetorical devices. The same point can be made with normal people and familiar colors. Mary is a brilliant scientist who is, for whatever reason, forced to investigate the world from a black and white room *via* a black and white television monitor. She specializes in the neurophysiology of vision and acquires, let us suppose, all the physical information there is to obtain about what goes on when we see ripe tomatoes, or the sky, and use terms like "red," "blue," and so on. She discovers, for example, just which wavelength combinations from the sky stimulate the retina, and exactly how this produces *via* the central nervous system the contraction of the vocal chords and expulsion of air from the lungs that results in the uttering of the sentence "The sky is blue"...

What will happen when Mary is released from her black and white room or is given a color television monitor? Will she *learn* anything or not? It seems just obvious that she will learn something about the world and our visual experience of it. But then it is inescapable that her previous knowledge was incomplete. But she had *all* the physical information. *Ergo* there is more to have than that, and Physicalism is false.

Clearly the same style of Knowledge argument could be deployed for taste, hearing, the bodily sensations and generally speaking for the various mental states which are said to have (as it is variously put) raw feels, phenomenal features or qualia. The conclusion in each case is that the qualia are left out of the physicalist story. And the polemical strength of the Knowledge argument is that it is so hard to deny the central claim that one can have all the physical information without having all the information there is to have…

The Bogey of Epiphenomenalism

Is there any really *good* reason for refusing to countenance the idea that qualia are causally impotent with respect to the physical world? I will argue for the answer *no*… All I will be concerned to defend is that it is possible to hold that certain properties of certain mental states, namely those I've called qualia, are such that their possession or absence makes no diffcrence to the physical world…

Two reasons are standardly given for holding that a quale like the hurtfulness of a pain must be causally efficacious in the physical world, and so, for instance, that it…must sometimes make a difference to what happens in the brain. [Neither], I will argue, has any real force…

(i) It is supposed to be just obvious that the hurtfulness of pain is partly responsible for the subject seeking to avoid pain, saying "It hurts" and so on. But, to reverse Hume, anything can fail to cause anything. No matter how often *B* follows *A*, and no matter how initially obvious the causality of the connection seems, the hypothesis that *A* causes *B* can be overturned by an over-arching theory which shows the two as distinct effects of a common underlying causal process.

To the untutored the image on the screen of Lee Marvin's fist moving from left to right immediately followed by the image of John Wayne's head moving in the same general direction looks as causal as anything. And of course throughout countless Westerns images similar to the first are followed by images similar to the second. All this counts for precisely nothing when we know the over-arching theory concerning how the relevant images are both effects of an underlying causal process involving the projector and the film. The epiphenomenalist can say exactly the same about the connection between, for example, hurtfulness and behavior. It is simply a consequence of the fact that certain happenings in the brain cause both.

(ii) The second objection relates to Darwin's Theory of Evolution. According to natural selection the traits that evolve over time are those conducive to physical survival. We may assume that qualia evolved over time—we have them, the earliest forms of life do not—and so we should expect qualia to be conducive to survival. The objection is that they could hardly help us to survive if they do nothing to the physical world.

The appeal of this argument is undeniable, but there is a good reply to it. Polar bears have particularly thick, warm coats. The Theory of Evolution explains this (we suppose) by pointing out that having a thick warm coat is conducive to survival in the Arctic. But having a thick coat goes along with having a heavy coat, and having a heavy coat is *not* conducive to survival. It slows the animal down.

Does this mean that we have refuted Darwin because we have found an evolved trait—having a heavy coat—which is not conducive to survival? Clearly not. Having a heavy coat is an unavoidable concomitant of having a warm coat (in the context, modern insulation was not available), and the advantages for survival of having a warm coat outweighed the disadvantages of having a heavy one. The point is that all we can extract from Darwin's theory is that we should expect any evolved characteristic to be *either* conducive to survival *or* a by-product of one that is so conducive. The epiphenomenalist holds that qualia fall into the latter category. They are a by-product of certain brain processes that are highly conducive to survival…

There is a very understandable response to the three replies I have just made. "All right, there is no knockdown refutation of the existence of epiphenomenal qualia. But the fact remains that they are an excrescence. They *do* nothing, they *explain* nothing, they serve merely to soothe the intuitions of dualists, and it is left a total mystery how they fit into the world view of science. In short we do not and cannot understand the how and why of them."

This is perfectly true; but it is no objection to qualia, for it rests on an overly optimistic view of the human animal, and its powers. We are the products of Evolution. We understand and sense what we need to understand and sense in order to survive. Epiphenomenal qualia are totally irrelevant to survival. At no stage of our evolution did natural selection favor those who could make sense of how they are caused and the laws governing them, or in fact why they exist at all. And that is why we can't.

It is not sufficiently appreciated that Physicalism is an extremely optimistic view of our powers. If it is true, we have, in very broad outline admittedly, a grasp of our place in the scheme of things. Certain matters of sheer complexity defeat us —there are an awful lot of neurons— but in principle we have it all. But consider the antecedent probability that everything in the Universe be of a kind that is relevant in some way or other to the survival of *Homo sapiens*. It is very low surely. But then one must admit that it is very likely that there is a part of the whole scheme of things, maybe a big part, which no amount of evolution will ever bring us near to knowledge about or understanding of. For the simple reason that such knowledge and understanding is irrelevant to survival.

Physicalists typically emphasize that we are a part of nature on their view, which is fair enough. But if we are a part of nature, we are as nature has left us after however many years of evolution it is, and each step in that evolutionary progression has been a matter of chance constrained just by the need to preserve or increase survival value. The wonder is that we understand as much as we do, and there is no wonder that there should be matters which fall quite outside our comprehension. Perhaps exactly how epiphenomenal qualia fit into the scheme of things is one such.

Study Questions

1. What are qualia? What is epiphenomenalism?

2. What role do privileged access and privacy play with regard to qualia?

3. How does the case of Mary, the brilliant scientist, differ from Fred and his tomatoes?

4. What would Ryle think of qualia? How would Descartes respond to epiphenomenalism?

5. Jackson claims that brains cause qualia but qualia have no causal effect upon brains. Do you agree? Why or why not?

J.L. Austin

How to Do Things with Words

J. L. Austin (1911–1960) was a British philosopher of language educated at Balliol College, Oxford University. Austin is known widely for his Theory of Speech Acts. He was a strong advocate of examining the way words are ordinarily used so as to clarify meaning and thereby elucidate philosophical confusions. Accordingly, such philosophers of language thought that many additional philosophical problems might simply disappear, rather than being solved, once their apparent linguistic confusion was elucidated.

The following selection is taken from what some consider his most influential work, *How to Do Things with Words*. Here he describes the senses in which to say something is to do something, in saying something we do something and by saying something we do something.

For example: As a large college party unfolds, Nick greets Sarah at the door and whispers, "The keg is on the back balcony." Sarah smiles and says, "Rad." Sarah turns and works her way discreetly through the crowd to the back balcony. First of all, Nick, by his utterance, has produced a series of specific sounds. Austin described such an utterance of sounds as a **phonetic act**, and called the act a **phone**. Nick's utterance also conforms, more or less, to the grammatical rules of English—that is, he uttered a recognizable English sentence. Austin described this as a **phatic act**, and labeled such utterances as **phemes**. Nick also referred to the keg on the back balcony. Uttering a pheme with a sense and a reference is a **rhetic act**, what Austin described as a **rheme**. These three acts together Austin described as a **Locutionary Act—to say something is to do something**.

However, according to Austin, Nick has also performed at least two other acts. He has both informed and invited Sarah regarding the keg on the back porch as well as elicited an answer from Sarah, "Rad." Informing and inviting, as in this case, are examples of what Austin described as **Illocutionary Acts**. Other types of illocutionary acts would include persuading, warning, ordering, bequeathing, christening, requesting, promising, and others. To perform an illocutionary act is to perform a locutionary act with a specific force—**in saying something, we do something**. What might the illocutionary force of the following question be when uttered by your mother as you are about to go out, "Is that what you are wearing?"

In eliciting an answer, as when Sarah responded directly to Nick with "Rad" and then, without further ado, Sarah made her way to the keg, are examples of what Austin described as **Perlocutionary Acts**. That is, as a result of the illocutionary force of Nick's locutionary act, Sarah reacted. Her reactions are the perlocutionary acts, which resulted from the illocutionary force of his locutionary speech act—**by saying something, we do something**.

Lecture VIII reprinted by permission of the publisher from *How to Do Things with Words*, by J.L. Austin, edited by J.O. Urmson and Marina Sbisà, pp. 94–108. Cambridge, MA: Harvard University Press, Copyright © 1962, 1975 by the President and Fellows of Harvard College.

Lecture VIII

In embarking on a programme of finding a list of explicit performative verbs, it seemed that we were going to find it not always easy to distinguish performative utterances from constative, and it therefore seemed expedient to go farther back for a while to fundamentals—to consider from the ground up how many senses there are in which to say something *is* to do something, or *in* saying something we do something, and even *by* saying something we do something. And we began by distinguishing a whole group of senses of "doing something' which are all included together when we say, what is obvious, that to say something is in the full normal sense to do something—which includes the utterance of certain noises, the utterance of certain words in a certain construction, and the utterance of them with a certain 'meaning' in the favourite philosophical sense of that word, i.e. with a certain sense and with a certain reference.

The act of 'saying something' in this full normal sense I call, i.e. dub, the performance of a locutionary act, and the study of utterances thus far and in these respects the study of locutions, or of the full units of speech. Our interest in the locutionary act is, of course, principally to make quite plain what it is, in order to distinguish it from other acts with which we are going to be primarily concerned. Let me add merely that, of course, a great many further refinements would be possible and necessary if we were to discuss it for its own sake—refinements of very great importance not merely to philosophers but to, say, grammarians and phoneticians.

We had made three rough distinctions between the phonetic act, the phatic act, and the rhetic act. The phonetic act is merely the act of uttering certain noises. The phatic act is the uttering of certain vocables or words, i.e. noises of certain types, belonging to and as belonging to, a certain vocabulary, conforming to and as conforming to a certain grammar. The rhetic act is the performance of an act of using those vocables with a certain more-or-less definite sense and reference.

Thus 'He said "The cat is on the mat," ' reports a phatic act, whereas 'He said that the cat was on the mat' reports a rhetic act. A similar contrast is illustrated by the pairs:

'He said "I shall be there," ' 'He said he would be there';

'He said "Get out," ' 'He told me to get out';

'He said "Is it in Oxford or Cambridge?" '; 'He asked whether it was in Oxford or Cambridge.'

To pursue this for its own sake beyond our immediate requirements, I shall mention some general points worth remembering:

(1) Obviously, to perform a phatic I must perform a phonetic act, or, if you like, in performing one I am performing the other (not, however, that phatic acts are a sub-class of phonetic acts—as belonging to): but the converse is not true, for if a monkey makes a noise indistinguishable from "go' it is still not a phatic act.

(2) Obviously in the definition of the phatic act two things were lumped together: vocabulary and grammar. So we have not assigned a special name to the person who utters, for example, 'cat thoroughly the if' or 'the slithy toves did gyre.' Yet a further point arising is the intonation as well as grammar and vocabulary.

(3) The phatic act, however, like the phonetic, is essentially mimicable, reproducible (including intonation, winks, gestures, &c.). One can mimic not merely the statement in quotation marks 'She has lovely hair,' but also the more complex fact that he said it like this: 'She has lovely *hair*' (shrugs).

This is the 'inverted commas' use of 'said' as we get it in novels: every utterance can be just reproduced in inverted commas, or in inverted commas with 'said he' or, more often, 'said she,' &c., after it.

But the rhetic act is the one we report, in the case of assertions, by saying 'He said that the cat was on the mat,' 'He said he would go,' 'He said I was to go' (his words were 'You are to go'). This is the so-called 'indirect speech.' If the sense or reference is *not* being taken as clear, then the whole or part is to be in quotation marks. Thus I might say: 'He said I was to go to the "minister," but he did not say which minister' or 'I said that he was behaving badly and he replied that "the higher you get the fewer." ' We cannot, however, always use 'said that' easily: we would say 'told to,' 'advise to,' &c., if he used the imperative mood, or such equivalent phrases as 'said I was to,' 'said I should,' &c. Compare such phrases as 'bade me welcome' and 'extended his apologies.'

I add one further point about the rhetic act: of course sense and reference (naming and referring) themselves are here ancillary acts performed in performing the rhetic act. Thus we may say 'I meant by "bank"…' and we say 'by "be" I was referring to…' Can we perform a rhetic act without referring or without naming? In general it would seem that the answer is that we cannot, but there are puzzling cases. What is the reference in 'all triangles have three sides'? Correspondingly, it is clear that we can perform a phatic act which is not a rhetic act, though not conversely. Thus we may repeat someone else's remark or mumble over some sentence, or we may read a Latin sentence without knowing the meaning of the words.

The question when one pheme or one rheme is the *same* as another, whether in the 'type' or 'token' sense, and the question what is one single pheme or rheme, do not so much matter here. But, of course, it is important to remember that the same pheme (token of the same type) may be used on different occasions of utterance with a different sense or reference, and so be a different rheme. When different phemes are used with the same sense and reference, we might speak of rhetically equivalent acts ('the same statement' in one sense) but not of the same rheme or rhetic acts (which are the same statement in another sense which involves using the same words).

The pheme is a unit of *language*: its typical fault is to be nonsense—meaningless. But the rheme is a unit of *speech*; its typical fault is to be vague or void or obscure, &c.

But though these matters are of much interest, they do not so far throw any light at all on our problem of the constative as opposed to the performative utterance. For example, it might be perfectly possible, with regard to an utterance, say 'It is going to charge,' to make entirely plain 'what we were saying' in issuing the utterance, in all the senses so far distinguished, and yet not at all to have cleared up whether or not in issuing the utterance I was performing the act of *warning* or not. It may be perfectly clear what I mean by 'It is going to charge' or 'Shut the door,' but not clear whether it is meant as a statement or warning, &c.

To perform a locutionary act is in general, we may say, also and *eo ipso* to perform an *illocutionary* act, as I propose to call it. To determine what illocutionary act is so performed we must determine in what way we are using the locution: asking or answering a question, giving some information or an assurance or a warning, announcing a verdict or an intention, pronouncing sentence, making an appointment or an appeal or a criticism, making an identification or giving a description, and the numerous like. (I am not suggesting that this is a clearly defined class by any means.) There is nothing mysterious about our *eo ipso* here. The trouble rather is the number of different senses of so vague an expression as "in what way are we using it—this may refer even to a locutionary act, and further to perlocutionary acts to which we shall come in a minute. When we perform a locutionary act, we use speech: but in what way precisely are we using it on this occasion? For there are very numerous functions of or ways in which we use speech, and it makes a great difference to our act in some sense—sense (B)—in which way and which *sense* we were on this occasion 'using' it. It makes a great difference whether we were advising, or merely suggesting, or actually ordering, whether we were strictly promising or only announcing a vague intention, and so forth. These issues penetrate a little but not without confusion into grammar (see above), but we constantly do debate them, in such terms as whether certain words (a certain locution) *had the force of* a question, or *ought to have been taken as* an estimate and so on.

I explained the performance of an act in this new and second sense as the performance of an 'illocutionary' act, i.e., performance of an act *in* saying something as opposed to performance of an act *of* saying something; and I shall refer to the doctrine of the different types of function of language here in question as the doctrine of 'illocutionary forces.'

It may be said that for too long philosophers have neglected this study, treating all problems as problems of "locutionary usage," and indeed that the "descriptive fallacy" mentioned in Lecture I commonly arises through mistaking a problem of the former kind for a problem of the latter kind. True, we are now getting out of this; for some years we have been realizing more and more clearly that the occasion of an utterance matters seriously, and that the words used are to some extent to be "explained" by the "context" in which they are designed to be or have actually been spoken in a linguistic interchange. Yet still perhaps we are too prone to give these explanations in terms of "the meanings of words." Admittedly we can use "meaning" also with reference to illocutionary force—'He meant it as an order,' &c. But I want to distinguish *force* and meaning in the sense in which meaning is equivalent to sense and reference, just as it has become essential to distinguish sense and reference within meaning.

Moreover, we have here an illustration of the different uses of the expression, 'uses of language,' or 'use of a sentence,' &c.—'use' is a hopelessly ambiguous or wide word, just as is the word 'meaning,' which it has become customary to deride. But 'use,' its supplanter, is not in much better case. We may entirely clear up the 'use of a sentence' on a particular occasion, in the sense of the locutionary act, without yet touching upon its use in the sense of an *illocutionary* act.

Before refining any further on this notion of the illocutionary act, let us contrast both the locutionary *and* the illocutionary act with yet a third kind of act.

There is yet a further sense (C) in which to perform a locutionary act, and therein an illocutionary act, may also be to perform an act of another kind. Saying something will often, or even normally, produce certain consequential effects upon the feelings, thoughts, or actions of the audience, or of the speaker, or of other persons: and it may be done with the design, intention, or purpose of producing them; and we may then say, thinking of this, that the speaker has performed an act in the nomenclature of which reference is made either (C. *a*), only obliquely, or even (C. *b*), not at all, to the performance of the locutionary or illocutionary act. We shall call the performance of an act of this kind the performance of a *perlocutionary* act or *perlocution*. Let us not yet define this idea any more carefully—of course it needs it—but simply give examples:

(E.1)

    Act (A) or Locution
        He said to me 'Shoot her!' meaning by 'shoot' shoot and referring by 'her' to *her*.

    Act (B) or Illocution
        He urged (or advised, ordered, &c.) me to shoot her.

    Act (C. *a*) or Perlocution
        He persuaded me to shoot her.

    Act (C. *b*)
        He got me to (or made me, &c.) shoot her.

(E.2)

    Act (A) or Locution
        He said to me, 'You can't do that.'

    Act (B) or Illocution
        He protested against my doing it.

    Act (C. *a*) or Perlocution
        He pulled me up, checked me.

    Act (C. *b*)
        He stopped me, be brought me to my senses, &c. He annoyed me.

We can similarly distinguish the locutionary act 'he said that...' from the illocutionary act 'he argued that...' and the perlocutionary act 'he convinced me that...'

It will be seen that the consequential effects of perlocutions are really consequences, which do not include such conventional effects as, for example, the speaker's being committed by his promise (which comes into the illocutionary act). Perhaps distinctions need drawing, as there is clearly a difference between what we feel to be the real production of real effects and what we regard as mere conventional consequences; we shall in any case return later to this.

We have here then roughly distinguished three kinds of acts—the locutionary, the illocutionary, and the perlocutionary. [Here occurs in the manuscript a note made in 1958 which says: '(1) All this is not clear (2) and in all senses relevant ((A) and (B) as distinct from (C)) won't all utterances be performative?'] Let us make some general comments on these three classes, leaving them still fairly rough. The first three points will be about 'the use of language' again.

(1) Our interest in these lectures is essentially to fasten on the second, illocutionary act and contrast it with the other two. There is a constant tendency in philosophy to elide this in favour of one or other of the other two. Yet it is distinct from both. We have already seen how the expressions 'meaning' and 'use of sentence' can blur the distinction between locutionary and illocutionary acts. We now notice that to speak of the "use" of language can likewise blur the distinction between the illocutionary and perlocutionary act—so we will distinguish them more carefully in a minute. Speaking of the 'use' of "language" for arguing or warning' looks just like speaking of the use of language 'for persuading, rousing, alarming'; yet the former may, for rough contrast, be said to be *conventional*, in the sense that at least it could be made explicit by the performative formula; but the latter could not. Thus we can say 'I argue that' or "I warn you that' but we cannot say "I convince you that' or

'I alarm you that.' Further, we may entirely clear up whether someone was arguing or not without touching on the question whether he was convincing anyone or not.

(2) To take this farther, let us be quite clear that the expression 'use of language' can cover other matters even more diverse than the illocutionary and perlocutionary acts. For example, we may speak of the 'use of language' *for* something, e.g., for joking; and we may use 'in' in a way different from the illocutionary 'in,' as when we say 'in saying "p" I was joking' or 'acting a part' or 'writing poetry'; or again we may speak of 'a poetical use of language' as distinct from 'the use of language in poetry.' These references to 'use of language' have nothing to do with the illocutionary act. For example, if I say 'Go and catch a falling star,' it may be quite clear what both the meaning and the force of my utterance is, but still wholly unresolved which of these other kinds of things I may be doing. There are parasitic uses of language, which are 'not serious,' not the 'full normal use.' The normal conditions of reference may be suspended, or no attempt made at a standard perlocutionary act, no attempt to make you do anything, as Walt Whitman does not seriously incite the eagle of liberty to soar.

(3) Furthermore, there may be some things we "do' in some connexion with saying something which do not seem to fall, intuitively at least, exactly into any of these roughly defined classes, or else seem to fall vaguely into more than one; but any way we do not at the outset feel so clear that they are as remote from our three acts as would be joking or writing poetry. For example, *insinuating*, as when we insinuate something in or by issuing some utterance, seems to involve some convention, as in the illocutionary act; but we cannot *say* 'I insinuate...' and it seems like implying to be a clever effect rather than a mere act. A further example is evincing emotion. We may evince emotion in or by issuing an utterance, as when we swear; but once again we have no use here for performative formulas and the other devices of illocutionary acts. We might say

that we use swearing ['Swearing' is ambiguous: 'I swear by Our Lady' *is* to swear by Our Lady: but 'Bloody' is not to swear by Our Lady.] *for* relieving our feelings. We must notice that the illocutionary act is a conventional act: an act done as conforming to a convention.

(4) Acts of all our three kinds necessitate, since they are the performing of actions, allowance being made for the ills that all action is heir to. We must systematically be prepared to distinguish between 'the act of doing x,' i.e., achieving x, and 'the act of attempting to do x': for example, we must distinguish between warning and attempting to warn. We must expect infelicities here.

The next three points that arise do so importantly because our acts are *acts*.

(5) Since our acts are acts, we must always remember the distinction between producing effects or consequences which are intended or unintended; and (i) when the speaker intends to produce an effect it may nevertheless not occur, and (ii) when he does not intend to produce it or intends not to produce it it may nevertheless occur. To cope with complication (i) we invoke as before the distinction between attempt and achievement; to cope with complication (ii) we invoke the normal linguistic devices of disclaiming (adverbs like 'unintentionally' and 'so on') which we hold ready for personal use in all cases of doing actions.

(6) Furthermore, we must, of course, allow that as acts they may be things that we do not exactly *do*, in the sense that we did them, say, under duress or in any other such way. Other ways besides in which we may not fully do the action are given in (2) above.

(7) Finally we must meet the objection about our illocutionary and perlocutionary acts—namely that the notion of an act is unclear—by a general doctrine about action. We have the idea of an 'act' as a fixed physical thing that we do, as distinguished from conventions and as distinguished from consequences. But

(*a*) the illocutionary act and even the locutionary act too may involve conventions: consider the example of doing obeisance. It is obeisance only because it is con ventional and it is done only because it is conventional. Compare the distinction between kicking a wall and kicking a goal;

(*b*) the perlocutionary act may include what in a way are consequences, as when we say 'By doing x I was doing y': we do bring in a greater or less stretch of "consequences' always, some of which may be 'unintentional.' There is no restriction to the minimum physical act at all. That we can import an indefinitely long stretch of what might also be called the 'consequences' of our act into the act itself is, or should be, a fundamental commonplace of the theory of our language about all 'action' in general. Thus if asked 'What did he do?' we may reply either 'He shot the donkey' or 'He fired a gun' or 'He pulled the trigger' or 'He moved his trigger finger,' and all may be correct. So, to shorten the nursery story of the endeavours of the old woman to drive her pig home in time to get her old man's supper, we may in the last resort say that the cat drove or got the pig, or made the pig get, over the stile. If in such cases we *mention* both a B act (illocution) and a C act (perlocution) we shall say 'by B-ing he C-ed' rather than '*in* B-ing...' This is the reason for calling C a *per*locutionary act as distinct from an illocutionary act.

Next time we shall revert to the distinction between our three kinds of act, and to the expressions "in' and "by doing x I am doing y,' with a view to getting the three classes and their members and non-members somewhat clearer. We shall see that just as the locutionary act embraces doing many things at once to be complete, so may the illocutionary and perlocutionary acts.

Study Questions

1. Take a case of flirting and break it down into Austin's speech acts.

2. Do aspects of the illocutionary force of your speech acts systematically vary when you are speaking with different age groups, strangers, employers? Most likely your phemes vary greatly when you are with your friends as opposed to your grandparents. How so?

3. Where do you find the richest diversity of speech acts, in academic publications or hanging out with your friends?

4. Do you find significant distinctions in the speech acts of professors whose classes you enjoy versus those you do not enjoy?

5. How diverse are the illocutionary forces found in the speech acts involving teasing or bullying?

6. Can you give an account of sarcasm according to Austin's Speech Act Theory?

SECTION VI

Ethics

Jean-Paul Sartre

Existentialism

Jean-Paul Sartre (1905–1980) was an existentialist philosopher, playwright, novelist, screenwriter, political activist, biographer, and literary critic. One of the leading thinkers in 20th-century French philosophy, Sartre was a key figure in literary and philosophical existentialism. For a certain type of being, a being with a free will, existence precedes essence, Sartre claimed. For all others, essence precedes existence. For animals without a free will, biology is destiny, but, those, typically adult human beings, with a free will, biology offers up dispositions but such dispositions to behave in the end must be chosen. By so choosing, we define who we are. We define our essence. Sartre was also noted for his extended "modern" relationship with the feminist author and existentialist Simone de Beauvoir.

In October 1964, Sartre was awarded the Nobel Prize in Literature. He was also the first Nobel Laureate to voluntarily decline the prize. Sartre had written a letter to the Nobel Institute, requesting he be removed from the list of nominees but apparently his letter went unread. Sartre explained his refusal to accept the award as he did not wish to be "transformed" by such an honor. Once nominated, then being the first nominee to voluntarily refuse, Sartre became even more of an object of curiosity. As the media descended upon him, he went into hiding. He had also previously refused the Légion d'honneur in 1945. In 1948, the Roman Catholic Church placed his complete works on the Index of Prohibited Books.

Though his name remained a household word along with "existentialism," Sartre remained a simple man with few possessions but actively committed to social causes until the end of his life, not unlike his near contemporary, Bertrand Russell. Sartre was arrested for civil disobedience in 1968 during the student revolution strikes in Paris. President Charles de Gaulle came to his aid claiming, "You don't arrest Voltaire."

Toward the end of his prolific life, he was asked how he would like to be remembered. He, in part, responded, "...if a certain Jean-Paul Sartre is remembered, I would like people to remember the milieu or historical situation in which I lived...how I lived in it, in terms of all the aspirations which I tried to gather up within myself."

From *Existentialism is a Humanism*, Bernard Frechtman, trans. New York: Philosophical Library, 1947, pp. 14–35. Reprinted with permission from Philosophical Library, Inc., New York.

...What is meant by the term *existentialism*?

Most people who use the word would be rather embarrassed if they had to explain it, since, now that the word is all the rage, even the work of a musician or painter is being called existentialist. A gossip columnist in *Clartés* signs himself *The Existentialist*, so that by this time the word has been so stretched and has taken on so broad a meaning, that it no longer means anything at all. It seems that for want of an advance-guard doctrine analogous to surrealism, the kind of people who are eager for scandal and flurry turn to this philosophy which in other respects does not at all serve their purposes in this sphere.

Actually, it is the least scandalous, the most austere of doctrines. It is intended strictly for specialists and philosophers. Yet it can be defined easily. What complicates matters is that there are two kinds of existentialist; first, those who are Christian, among whom I would include Jaspers and Gabriel Marcel, both Catholic; and on the other hand the atheistic existentialists, among whom I class Heidegger, and then the French existentialists and myself. What they have in common is that they think that existence precedes essence, or, if you prefer, that subjectivity must be the starting point.

Just what does that mean? Let us consider some object that is manufactured, for example, a book or a paper-cutter: here is an object which has been made by an artisan whose inspiration came from a concept. He referred to the concept of what a paper-cutter is and likewise to a known method of production, which is part of the concept, something which is, by and large, a routine. Thus, the paper-cutter is at once an object produced in a certain way and, on the other hand, one having a specific use; and one can not postulate a man who produces a paper-cutter but does not know what it is used for. Therefore, let us say that, for the paper-cutter, essence—that is, the ensemble of both the production routines and the properties which enable it to be both produced and defined—precedes existence. Thus, the presence of the paper-cutter or book in front of me is determined. Therefore, we have here a technical view of the world whereby it can be said that production precedes existence.

When we conceive God as the Creator, He is generally thought of as a superior sort of artisan. Whatever doctrine we may be considering, whether one like that of Descartes or that of Leibnitz, we always grant that will more or less follows understanding or, at the very least, accompanies it, and that when God creates He knows exactly what He is creating. Thus, the concept of man in the mind of God is comparable to the concept of paper-cutter in the mind of the manufacturer, and, following certain techniques and a conception, God produces man, just as the artisan, following a definition and a technique, makes a paper-cutter. Thus, the individual man is the realization of a certain concept in the divine intelligence.

In the eighteenth century, the atheism of the *philosophies* discarded the idea of God, but not so much for the notion that essence precedes existence. To a certain extent, this idea is found everywhere; we find it in Diderot, in Voltaire, and even in Kant. Man has a human nature; this human nature, which is the concept of the human, is found in all men, which means that each man is a particular example of a universal concept, man. In Kant, the result of this universality is that the wild-man, the natural man, as well as the bourgeois, are circumscribed by the same definition and have the same basic qualities. Thus, here too the essence of man precedes the historical existence that we find in nature.

Atheistic existentialism, which I represent, is more coherent. It states that if God does not exist, there is at least one being in whom existence precedes essence, a being who exists before he can be defined by any concept, and that this being is man, or, as Heidegger says, human reality. What is meant here by saying that existence precedes essence? It means that, first of all, man exists, turns up, appears on the scene, and, only afterwards, defines himself. If man, as the existentialist conceives him, is indefinable, it is

because at first he is nothing. Only afterward will he be something, and he himself will have made what he will be. Thus, there is no human nature, since there is no God to conceive it. Not only is man what he conceives himself to be, but he is also only what he wills himself to be after this thrust toward existence.

Man is nothing else but what he makes of himself. Such is the first principle of existentialism. It is also what is called subjectivity, the name we are labeled with when charges are brought against us. But what do we mean by this, if not that man has a greater dignity than a stone or table? For we mean that man first exists, that is, that man first of all is the being who hurls himself toward a future and who is conscious of imagining himself as being in the future. Man is at the start a plan which is aware of itself, rather than a patch of moss, a piece of garbage, or a cauliflower; nothing exists prior to this plan; there is nothing in heaven; man will be what he will have planned to be. Not what he will want to be. Because by the word "will" we generally mean a conscious decision, which is subsequent to what we have already made of ourselves. I may want to belong to a political party, write a book, get married; but all that is only a manifestation of an earlier, more spontaneous choice that is called "will." But if existence really does precede essence, man is responsible for what he is. Thus, existentialism's first move is to make every man aware of what he is and to make the full responsibility of his existence rest on him. And when we say that a man is responsible for himself, we do not only mean that he is responsible for his own individuality, but that he is responsible for all men.

The word subjectivism has two meanings, and our opponents play on the two. Subjectivism means, on the one hand, that an individual chooses and makes himself; and, on the other, that it is impossible for man to transcend human subjectivity. The second of these is the essential meaning of existentialism. When we say that man chooses his own self, we mean that every one of us does likewise; but we also mean by that that

in making this choice he also chooses all men. In fact, in creating the man that we want to be, there is not a single one of our acts which does not at the same time create an image of man as we think he ought to be. To choose to be this or that is to affirm at the same time the value of what we choose, because we can never choose evil. We always choose the good, and nothing can be good for us without being good for all.

If, on the other hand, existence precedes essence, and if we grant that we exist and fashion our image at one and the same time, the image is valid for everybody and for our whole age. Thus, our responsibility is much greater than we might have supposed, because it involves all mankind. If I am a workingman and choose to join a Christian trade union rather than be a communist, and if by being a member I want to show that the best thing for man is resignation, that the kingdom of man is not of this world, I am not only involving my own case—I want to be resigned for everyone. As a result, my action has involved all humanity. To take a more individual matter, if I want to marry, to have children; even if this marriage depends solely on my own circumstances or passion or wish, I am involving all humanity in monogamy and not merely myself. Therefore, I am responsible for myself and for everyone else. I am creating a certain image of man of my own choosing. In choosing myself, I choose man.

This helps us understand what the actual content is of such rather grandiloquent words as anguish, forlornness and despair. As you will see, it's all quite simple.

First, what is meant by anguish? The existentialists say at once that man is anguish. What that means is this: the man who involves himself and who realizes that he is not only the person he chooses to be, but also a law maker who is, at the same time, choosing all mankind as well as himself, can not help escape the feeling of his total and deep responsibility. Of course, there are many people who are not anxious; but we claim that they are hiding their anxiety, that they are fleeing from it. Certainly, many people believe that when they do something, they themselves are the only ones involved, and when someone says to them, "What if everyone acted that way?" They shrug their shoulders and answer, "Everyone doesn't act that way." But really, one should always ask himself, "What would happen if everybody looked at things that way?" There is no escaping this disturbing thought except by a kind of double-dealing. A man who lies and makes excuses for himself by saying "not everybody does that," is someone with an uneasy conscience, because the act of lying implies that a universal value is conferred upon the lie.

Anguish is evident even when it conceals itself. This is the anguish that Kierkegaard called the anguish of Abraham. You know the story: an angel has ordered Abraham to sacrifice his son; if it really were an angel who has come and said, "You are Abraham, you shall sacrifice your son," everything would be all right. But everyone might first wonder, "Is it really an angel, and am I really Abraham? What proof do I have?"

There was a madwoman who had hallucinations; someone used to speak to her on the telephone and give her orders. Her doctor asked her, "Who is it who talks to you?" She answered, "He says it's God." What proof did she really have that it was God? If an angel comes to me, what proof is there that it's an angel? And if I hear voices, what proof is there that they come from heaven and not from hell, or from the subconscious, or a pathological condition? What proves that they are addressed to me? What proof is there that I have been appointed to impose my choice and my conception of man on humanity? I'll never find any proof or sign to convince me of that. If a voice addresses me, it is always for me to decide that this is the angel's voice; if I consider that such an act is a good one, it is I who will choose to say that it is good rather than bad.

Now, I'm not being singled out as an Abraham, and yet at every moment I'm obliged to perform exemplary acts. For every man, everything happens as if all mankind had its eyes fixed on him and were guiding itself by what he does. And every man ought to say to himself, "Am I really the kind of man who has the right to act in such a way that humanity might guide itself by my actions?" And if he does not say that to himself, he is masking his anguish.

There is no question here of the kind of anguish which would lead to quietism, to inaction. It is a matter of a simple sort of anguish that anybody who has had responsibilities is familiar with. For example, when a military officer takes the responsibility for an attack and sends a certain number of men to death, he chooses to do so, and in the main he alone makes the choice. Doubtless, orders come from above, but they are too broad; he interprets them, and on this interpretation depend the lives of ten or fourteen or twenty men. In making a decision he can not help having a certain anguish. All leaders know this anguish. That doesn't keep them from acting; on the contrary, it is the very condition of their action. For it implies that they envisage a number of possibilities, and when they choose one, they realize that it has value only because it is chosen. We shall see that this kind of anguish, which is the kind that existentialism describes, is explained, in addition, by a direct responsibility to the other men whom it involves. It is not a curtain separating us from action, but is part of action itself.

When we speak of forlornness, a term Heidegger was fond of, we mean only that God does not exist and that we have to face all the consequences of this. The existentialist is strongly opposed to a certain kind of secular ethics which would like to abolish God with the least possible expense. About 1880, some French teachers tried to set up a secular ethics which went something like this: God is a useless and costly hypothesis; we are discarding it; but, meanwhile, in order for there to be an ethics, a society, a civilization, it is essential that certain values be taken seriously and that they be considered as having an *a priori* existence. It must be obligatory, *a priori*, to be honest, not to lie, not to beat your wife, to have children, etc., etc. So we're going to try a little

device which will make it possible to show that values exist all the same, inscribed in a heaven of ideas, though otherwise God does not exist. In other words—and this, I believe, is the tendency of everything called reformism in France—nothing will be changed if God does not exist. We shall find ourselves with the same norms of honesty, progress, and humanism, and we shall have made of God an outdated hypothesis which will peacefully die off by itself.

The existentialist, on the contrary, thinks it very distressing that God does not exist, because all possibility of finding values in a heaven of ideas disappears along with Him; there can no longer be an *a priori*. Good, since there is no infinite and perfect consciousness to think it. Nowhere is it written that the Good exists, that we must be honest, that we must not lie; because the fact is we are on a plane where there are only men. Dostoyevsky said, "If God didn't exist, everything would be possible." That is the very starting point of existentialism. Indeed, everything is permissible if God does not exist, and as a result man is forlorn, because neither within him nor without does he find anything to cling to. He can't start making excuses for himself.

If existence really does precede essence, there is no explaining things away by reference to a fixed and given human nature. In other words, there is no determinism, man is free, man is freedom. On the other hand, if God does not exist, we find no values or commands to turn to which legitimize our conduct. So, in the bright realm of values, we have no excuse behind us, nor justification before us. We are alone, with no excuses.

That is the idea I shall try to convey when I say that man is condemned to be free. Condemned, because he did not create himself, yet, in other respects is free; because, once thrown into the world, he is responsible for everything he does. The existentialist does not believe in the power of passion. He will never agree that a sweeping passion is a ravaging torrent which fatally leads a man to certain acts and is therefore an excuse. He thinks that man is responsible for his passion.

The existentialist does not think that man is going to help himself by finding in the world some omen by which to orient himself. Because he thinks that man will interpret the omen to suit himself. Therefore, he thinks that man, with no support and no aid, is condemned every moment to invent man. Ponge, in a very fine article, has said, "Man is the future of man." That's exactly it. But if it is taken to mean that this future is recorded in heaven, that God sees it, then it is false, because it would really no longer be a future. If it is taken to mean that, whatever a man may be, there is a future to be forged, a virgin future before him, then this remark is sound. But then we are forlorn.

To give you an example which will enable you to understand forlornness better, I shall cite the case of one of my students who came to see me under the following circumstances: his father was on bad terms with his mother, and, moreover, was inclined to be a collaborationist; his older brother had been killed in the German offensive of 1940, and the young man, with somewhat immature but generous feelings, wanted to avenge him. His mother lived alone with him, very much upset by the half-treason of her husband and the death of her older son; the boy was her only consolation.

The boy was faced with the choice of leaving for England and joining the Free French Forces—that is, leaving his mother behind—or remaining with his mother and helping her to carry on. He was fully aware that the woman lived only for him and that his going-off—and perhaps his death—would plunge her into despair. He was also aware that every act that he did for his mother's sake was a sure thing, in the sense that it was helping her to carry on, whereas every effort he made toward going off and fighting was an uncertain move which might run aground and prove completely useless; for example, on his way to England he might, while passing through Spain, be detained indefinitely in a Spanish camp; he might reach England or Algiers and be stuck in an office at a desk job. As a result, he was faced with two very different kinds of action: one, concrete, immediate, but concerning only one individual; the other concerned an incomparably vaster group, a national collectivity, but for that very reason was dubious, and might be interrupted en route. And, at the same time, he was wavering between two kinds of ethics. On the one hand, an ethics of sympathy, of personal devotion; on the other, a broader ethics, but one whose efficacy was more dubious. He had to choose between the two.

Who could help him choose? Christian doctrine? No. Christian doctrine says, "Be charitable, love your neighbor, take the more rugged path, etc., etc." But which is the more rugged path? Whom should he love as a brother? The fighting man or his mother? Which does the greater good, the vague act of fighting in a group, or the concrete one of helping a particular human being to go on living? Who can decide *a priori*? Nobody. No book of ethics can tell him. The Kantian ethics says, "Never treat any person as a means, but as an end." Very well, if I stay with my mother, I'll treat her as an end and not as a means; but by virtue of this very fact, I'm running the risk of treating the people around me who are fighting, as means; and, conversely, if I go to join those who are fighting, I'll be treating them as an end, and, by doing that, I run the risk of treating my mother as a means.

If values are vague, and if they are always too broad for the concrete and specific case that we are considering, the only thing left for us is to trust our instincts. That's what this young man tried to do; and when I saw him, he said, "In the end, feeling is what counts. I ought to choose whichever pushes me in one direction. If I feel that I love my mother enough to sacrifice everything else for her—my desire for vengeance, for action, for adventure—then I'll stay with her. If, on the contrary, I feel that my love for my mother isn't enough, I'll leave."

But how is the value of a feeling determined? What gives his feeling for his mother value? Precisely the fact that he remained with her. I may say that I like so-and-so well enough to sacrifice a certain amount of money for him, but I may say so only if I've done it. I may say "I love my mother well enough to remain with her" if I have remained with her. The only way to determine the value of this affection is, precisely, to perform an act which confirms and defines it. But, since I require this affection to justify my act, I find myself caught in a vicious circle.

On the other hand, Gide has well said that a mock feeling and a true feeling are almost indistinguishable; to decide that I love my mother and will remain with her, or to remain with her by putting on an act, amount somewhat to the same thing. In other words, the feeling is formed by the acts one performs; so, I can not refer to it in order to act upon it. Which means that I can neither seek within myself the true condition which will impel me to act, nor apply to a system of ethics for concepts which will permit me to act. You will say, "At least, he did go to a teacher for advice." But if you seek advice from a priest, for example, you have chosen this priest; you already knew, more or less, just about what advice he was going to give you. In other words, choosing your adviser is involving yourself. The proof of this is that if you are a Christian, you will say, "Consult a priest." But some priests are collaborating, some are just marking time, some are resisting. Which to choose? If the young man chooses a priest who is resisting or collaborating, he has already decided on the kind of advice he's going to get. Therefore, in coming to see me he knew the answer I was going to give him, and I had only one answer to give: "You're free, choose, that is, invent." No general ethics can show you what is to be done; there are no omens in the world. The Catholics will reply, "But there are." Granted—but, in any case, I myself choose the meaning they have.

When I was a prisoner, I knew a rather remarkable young man who was a Jesuit. He had entered the Jesuit order in the following way: he had had a number of very bad breaks; in childhood, his father died, leaving him in poverty, and he was a scholarship student at a religious institution

where he was constantly made to feel that he was being kept out of charity; then, he failed to get any of the honors and distinctions that children like; later on, at about eighteen, he bungled a love affair; finally, at twenty-two, he failed in military training, a childish enough matter, but it was the last straw.

This young fellow might well have felt that he had botched everything. It was a sign of something, but of what? He might have taken refuge in bitterness or despair. But he very wisely looked upon all this as a sign that he was not made for secular triumphs, and that only the triumphs of religion, holiness, and faith were open to him. He saw the hand of God in all this, and so he entered the order. Who can help seeing that he alone decided what the sign meant?

Some other interpretation might have been drawn from this series of setbacks; for example, that he might have done better to turn carpenter or revolutionist. Therefore, he is fully responsible for the interpretation. Forlornness implies that we ourselves choose our being. Forlornness and anguish go together.

As for despair, the term has a very simple meaning. It means that we shall confine ourselves to reckoning only with what depends upon our will, or on the ensemble of probabilities which make our action possible. When we want something, we always have to reckon with probabilities. I may be counting on the arrival of a friend. The friend is coming by rail or street-car; this supposes that the train will arrive on schedule, or that the street-car will not jump the track. I am left in the realm of possibility; but possibilities are to be reckoned with only to the point where my action comports with the ensemble of these possibilities, and no further. The moment the possibilities I am considering are not rigorously involved by my action, I ought to disengage myself from them, because no God, no scheme, can adapt the world and its possibilities to my will. When Descartes said, "Conquer yourself rather than the world," he meant essentially the same thing.

Study Questions

1. Why does Sartre claim that his version of existentialism is more coherent than that of religious existentialists?

2. What is the first principle of existentialism, according to Sartre?

3. What are the two meanings of subjectivity?

4. What is the significance of anguish, forlornness, and despair?

5. How would Sartre deal with phobias, addictions, and obsessive-compulsive behaviors?

6. It is sometimes claimed we live in a time of victims, endless excuses for our shortcomings, and blaming of others for our failures. What would be Sartre's view of such victims and blamers?

7. Sartre, like Nietzsche, denies the existence of God. Why does he find it so distressing that God does not exist? Do you agree? Why?

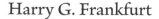

Harry G. Frankfurt

Freedom of the Will and the Concept of a Person

What philosophers have lately come to accept as analysis of the concept of a person is not actually analysis of *that* concept at all. Strawson, whose usage represents the current standard, identifies the concept of a person as "the concept of a type of entity such that *both* predicates ascribing states of consciousness *and* predicates ascribing corporeal characteristics...are equally applicable to a single individual of that single type."[1] But there are many entities besides persons that have both mental and physical properties. As it happens—though it seems extraordinary that this should be so—there is no common English word for the type of entity Strawson has in mind, a type that includes not only human beings but animals of various lesser species as well. Still, this hardly justifies the misappropriation of a valuable philosophical term.

Whether the members of some animal species are persons is surely not to be settled merely by determining whether it is correct to apply to them, in addition to predicates ascribing corporeal characteristics, predicates that ascribe states of consciousness. It does violence to our language to endorse the application of the term 'person' to those numerous creatures which do have both psychological and material properties but which are manifestly not persons in any normal sense of the word. This misuse of language is doubtless innocent of any theoretical error. But although the offense is "merely verbal," it does significant harm. For it gratuitously diminishes our philosophical vocabulary, and it increases the likelihood that we will overlook the important area of inquiry with which the term 'person' is most naturally associated. It might have been expected that no problem would be of more central and persistent concern to philosophers than that of understanding what we ourselves essentially are. Yet this problem is so generally neglected that it has been possible to make off with its very name almost without being noticed and, evidently, without evoking any widespread feeling of loss.

There is a sense in which the word 'person' is merely the singular form of 'people' and in which both terms connote no more than membership in a certain biological species. In those senses of the word which are of greater philosophical interest, however, the criteria for being a person do not serve primarily to distinguish the members

---

1 P. F. Strawson, *Individuals* (London: Methuen, 1959). pp. 101–102, Ayer's usage of 'person' is similar: "it is characteristic of persons in this sense that besides having various physical properties...they are also credited with various forms of consciousness" [A. J. Ayer. *The Concept of a Person* (New York: St. Martin's, 1963), p. 82]. What concerns Strawson and Ayer is the problem of understanding the relation between mind and body, rather than the quite different problem of understanding what it is to be a creature that not only has a mind and a body but is also a person.

From *Journal of Philosophy*, 68, No. 1 (Jan 1971), pp. 5–20. Reprinted with permission from the journal and from the author.

of our own species from the members of other species. Rather, they are designed to capture those attributes which are the subject of our most humane concern with ourselves and the source of what we regard as most important and most problematical in our lives. Now these attributes would be of equal significance to us even if they were not in fact peculiar and common to the members of our own species. What interests us most in the human condition would not interest us less if it were also a feature of the condition of other creatures as well.

Our concept of ourselves as persons is not to be understood, therefore, as a concept of attributes that are necessarily species-specific. It is conceptually possible that members of novel or even of familiar nonhuman species should be persons; and it is also conceptually possible that some members of the human species are not persons. We do in fact assume, on the other hand, that no member of another species is a person. Accordingly, there is a presumption that what is essential to persons is a set of characteristics that we generally suppose—whether rightly or wrongly—to be uniquely human.

It is my view that one essential difference between persons and other creatures is to be found in the structure of a person's will. Human beings are not alone in having desires and motives, or in making choices. They share these things with the members of certain other species, some of whom even appear to engage in deliberation and to make decisions based upon prior thought. It seems to be peculiarly characteristic of humans, however, that they are able to form what I shall call "second-order desires" or "desires of the second order."

Besides wanting and choosing and being moved *to do* this or that, men may also want to have (or not to have) certain desires and motives. They are capable of wanting to be different, in their preferences and purposes, from what they are. Many animals appear to have the capacity for what I shall call "first-order desires" or "desires of the first order," which are simply desires to do or not to do one thing or another. No animal other than man, however, appears to have the capacity for reflective self-evaluation that is manifested in the formation of second-order desires.[2]

I

The concept designated by the verb 'to want' is extraordinarily elusive. A statement of the form "*A* wants to *X*"—taken by itself, apart from a context that serves to amplify or to specify its meaning—conveys remarkably little information. Such a statement may be consistent, for example, with each of the following statements: (a) the prospect of doing *X* elicits no sensation or introspectible emotional response in *A*; (b) *A* is unaware that he wants to *X*; (c) *A* believes that he does not want to *X*; (d) *A* wants to refrain from *X*-ing; (e) *A* wants to *Y* and believes that it is impossible for him both to *Y* and to *X*; (f) *A* does not "really" want to *X*; (g) *A* would rather die than *X*; and so on. It is therefore hardly sufficient to formulate the distinction between first-order and second-order desires, as I have done, by suggesting merely that someone has a first-order desire when he wants to do or not to do such-and-such, and that he has a second-order desire when he wants to have or not to have a certain desire of the first order.

---

2 For the sake of simplicity, I shall deal only with what someone wants or desires, neglecting related phenomena such as choices and decisions. I propose to use the verbs 'to want' and 'to desire' interchangeably, although they are by no means perfect synonyms. My motive in forsaking the established nuances of these words arises from the fact that the verb 'to want,' which suits my purposes better so far as its meaning is concerned, does not lend itself so readily to the formation of nouns as does the verb 'to desire.' It is perhaps acceptable, albeit graceless, to speak in the plural of someone's "wants." But to speak in the singular of someone's "want" would be an abomination.

3 What I say in this paragraph applies not only to cases in which 'to *X*' refers to a possible action or inaction. It also applies to cases in which 'to *X*' refers to a first-order desire and in which the statement that '*A* wants to *X*' is therefore a shortened version of a statement—"*A* wants to want to *X*"—that identifies a desire of the second order.

As I shall understand them, statements of the form "*A* wants to *X*" cover a rather broad range of possibilities.[3] They may be true even when statements like (a) through (g) are true: when *A* is unaware of any feelings concerning *X*-ing, when he is unaware that he wants to *X*, when he deceives himself about what he wants and believes falsely that he does not want to *X*, when he also has other desires that conflict with his desire to *X*, or when he is ambivalent. The desires in question may be conscious or unconscious, they need not be univocal, and *A* may be mistaken about them. There is a further source of uncertainty with regard to statements that identify someone's desires, however, and here it is important for my purposes to be less permissive.

Consider first those statements of the form "*A* wants to *X*" which identify first-order desires— that is, statements in which the term 'to *X*' refers to an action. A statement of this kind does not, by itself, indicate the relative strength of *A*'s desire to *X*. It does not make it clear whether this desire is at all likely to play a decisive role in what *A* actually does or tries to do. For it may correctly be said that *A* wants to *X* even when his desire to *X* is only one among his desires and when it is far from being paramount among them. Thus, it may be true that *A* wants to *X* when he strongly prefers to do something else instead; and it may be true that he wants to *X* despite the fact that, when he acts, it is not the desire to *X* that motivates him to do what he does. On the other hand, someone who states that *A* wants to *X* may mean to convey that it is this desire that is motivating or moving *A* to do what he is actually doing or that *A* will in fact be moved by this desire (unless he changes his mind) when he acts.

It is only when it is used in the second of these ways that, given the special usage of 'will' that I propose to adopt, the statement identifies *A*'s will. To identify an agent's will is either to identify the desire (or desires) by which he is motivated in some action he performs or to identify the desire (or desires) by which he will or would be motivated when or if he acts. An agent's will, then,

is identical with one or more of his first-order desires. But the notion of the will, as I am employing it, is not coextensive with the notion of first-order desires. It is not the notion of something that merely inclines an agent in some degree to act in a certain way. Rather, it is the notion of an *effective* desire—one that moves (or will or would move) a person all the way to action. Thus the notion of the will is not coextensive with the notion of what an agent intends to do. For even though someone may have a settled intention to do *X*, he may nonetheless do something else instead of doing *X* because, despite his intention, his desire to do *X* proves to be weaker or less effective than some conflicting desire.

Now consider those statements of the form "*A* wants to *X*" which identify second-order desires—that is, statements in which the term 'to *X*' refers to a desire of the first order. There are also two kinds of situation in which it may be true that *A* wants to want to *X*. In the first place, it might be true of *A* that he wants to have a desire to *X* despite the fact that he has a univocal desire, altogether free of conflict and ambivalence, to refrain from *X*-ing. Someone might want to have a certain desire, in other words, but univocally want that desire to be unsatisfied.

Suppose that a physician engaged in psychotherapy with narcotics addicts believes that his ability to help his patients would be enhanced if he understood better what it is like for them to desire the drug to which they are addicted. Suppose that he is led in this way to want to have a desire for the drug. If it is a genuine desire that he wants, then what he wants is not merely to feel the sensations that addicts characteristically feel when they are gripped by their desires for the drug. What the physician wants, insofar as he wants to have a desire, is to be inclined or moved to some extent to take the drug.

It is entirely possible, however, that, although he wants to be moved by a desire to take the drug, he does not want this desire to be effective. He may not want it to move him all the way to action. He need not be interested in finding out what it is like to take the drug. And insofar as he now wants only to *want* to take it, and not to *take* it, there is nothing in what he now wants that would be satisfied by the drug itself. He may now have, in fact, an altogether univocal desire *not* to take the drug; and he may prudently arrange to make it impossible for him to satisfy the desire he would have if his desire to want the drug should in time be satisfied.

It would thus be incorrect to infer, from the fact that the physician now wants to desire to take the drug, that he already does desire to take it. His second-order desire to be moved to take the drug does not entail that he has a first-order desire to take it. If the drug were now to be administered to him, this might satisfy no desire that is implicit in his desire to want to take it. While he wants to want to take the drug, he may have *no* desire to take it; it may be that *all* he wants is to taste the desire for it. That is, his desire to have a certain desire that he does not have may not be a desire that his will should be at all different than it is.

Someone who wants only in this truncated way to want to X stands at the margin of preciosity, and the fact that he wants to want to X is not pertinent to the identification of his will. There is, however, a second kind of situation that may be described by 'A wants to want to X'; and when the statement is used to describe a situation of this second kind, then it does pertain to what A wants his will to be. In such cases the statement means that A wants the desire to X to be the desire that moves him effectively to act. It is not merely that he wants the desire to X to be among the desires by which, to one degree or another, he is moved or inclined to act. He wants this desire to be effective—that is, to provide the motive in what he actually does. Now when the statement that A wants to want to X is used in this way, it does entail that A already has a desire to X. It could not be true both that A wants the desire to X to move him into action and that he does not want to X. It is only if he does want to X that he can coherently want the desire to X not merely to be one of his desires but, more decisively, to be his will.[4]

Suppose a man wants to be motivated in what he does by the desire to concentrate on his work. It is necessarily true, if this supposition is correct, that he already wants to concentrate on his work. This desire is now among his desires. But the question of whether or not his second-order desire is fulfilled does not turn merely on whether the desire he wants is one of his desires. It turns on whether this desire is, as he wants it to be, his effective desire or will. If, when the chips are down, it is his desire to concentrate on his work that moves him to do what he does, then what he wants at that time is indeed (in the relevant sense) what he wants to want. If it is some other desire that actually moves him when he acts, on the other hand, then what he wants at that time is not (in the relevant sense) what he wants to want. This will be so despite the fact that the desire to concentrate on his work continues to be among his desires.

---

4 It is not so clear that the entailment relation described here holds in certain kinds of cases, which I think may fairly be regarded as nonstandard, where the essential difference between the standard and the nonstandard cases lies in the kind of description by which the first-order desire in question is identified. Thus, suppose that A admires B so fulsomely that, even though he does not know what B wants to do, he wants to be effectively moved by whatever desire effectively moves B; without knowing what B's will is; in other words, A wants his own will to be the same. It certainly does not follow that A already has, among his desires, a desire like the one that constitutes B's will. I shall not pursue here the questions of whether there are genuine counterexamples to the claim made in the text or of how, if there are, that claim should be altered.

5 Creatures with second-order desires but no second-order volitions differ significantly from brute animals, and, for some purposes, it would be desirable to regard them as persons. My usage, which withholds the designation 'person' from them, is thus somewhat arbitrary. I adopt it largely because it facilitates the formulation of some of the points I wish to make. Hereafter, whenever I consider statements of the form "A wants to want to X," I shall have in mind statements identifying second-order volitions and not statements identifying second-order desires that are not second-order volitions.

II

Someone has a desire of the second order either when he wants simply to have a certain desire or when he wants a certain desire to be his will. In situations of the latter kind, I shall call his second-order desires "second-order volitions" or "volitions of the second order." Now it is having second-order volitions, and not having second-order desires generally, that I regard as essential to being a person. It is logically possible, however unlikely, that there should be an agent with second-order desires but with no volitions of the second order. Such a creature, in my view, would not be a person. I shall use the term 'wanton' to refer to agents who have first-order desires but who are not persons because, whether or not they have desires of the second order, they have no second-order volitions.[5]

The essential characteristic of a wanton is that he does not care about his will. His desires move him to do certain things, without its being true of him either that he wants to be moved by those desires or that he prefers to be moved by other desires. The class of wantons includes all nonhuman animals that have desires and all very young children. Perhaps it also includes some adult human beings as well. In any case, adult humans may be more or less wanton; they may act wantonly, in response to first-order desires concerning which they have no volitions of the second order, more or less frequently.

The fact that a wanton has no second-order volitions does not mean that each of his first-order desires is translated heedlessly and at once into action. He may have no opportunity to act in accordance with some of his desires. Moreover, the translation of his desires into action may be delayed or precluded either by conflicting desires of the first order or by the intervention of deliberation. For a wanton may possess and employ rational faculties of a high order. Nothing in the concept of a wanton implies that he cannot reason or that he cannot deliberate concerning how to do what he wants to do. What distinguishes the rational wanton from other rational agents is that he is not concerned with the desirability of his desires themselves. He ignores the question of what his will is to be. Not only does he pursue whatever course of action he is most strongly inclined to pursue, but he does not care which of his inclinations is the strongest.

Thus a rational creature, who reflects upon the suitability to his desires of one course of action or another, may nonetheless be a wanton. In maintaining that the essence of being a person lies not in reason but in will, I am far from suggesting that a creature without reason may be a person. For it is only in virtue of his rational capacities that a person is capable of becoming critically aware of his own will and of forming volitions of the second order. The structure of a person's will presupposes, accordingly, that he is a rational being.

The distinction between a person and a wanton may be illustrated by the difference between two narcotics addicts. Let us suppose that the physiological condition accounting for the addiction is the same in both men, and that both succumb inevitably to their periodic desires for the drug to which they are addicted. One of the addicts hates his addiction and always struggles desperately, although to no avail, against its thrust. He tries everything that he thinks might enable him to overcome his desires for the drug. But these desires are too powerful for him to withstand, and invariably, in the end, they conquer him. He is an unwilling addict, helplessly violated by his own desires.

The unwilling addict has conflicting first-order desires: he wants to take the drug, and he also wants to refrain from taking it. In addition to these first-order desires, however, he has a volition of the second order. He is not a neutral with regard to the conflict between his desire to take the drug and his desire to refrain from taking it. It is the latter desire, and not the former, that he wants to constitute his will; it is the latter desire, rather than the former, that he wants to be effective and to provide the purpose that he will seek to realize in what he actually does.

The other addict is a wanton. His actions reflect the economy of his first-order desires, without his being concerned whether the desires that move him to act are desires by which he wants to be moved to act. If he encounters problems in obtaining the drug or in administering it to himself, his responses to his urges to take it may involve deliberation. But it never occurs to him to consider whether he wants the relations among his desires to result in his having the will he has. The wanton addict may be an animal, and thus incapable of being concerned about his will. In any event he is, in respect of his wanton lack of concern, no different from an animal.

The second of these addicts may suffer a first-order conflict similar to the first-order conflict suffered by the first. Whether he is human or not, the wanton may (perhaps due to conditioning) both want to take the drug and want to refrain from taking it. Unlike the unwilling addict, however, he does not prefer that one of his conflicting desires should be paramount over the other; he does not prefer that one first-order desire rather than the other should constitute his will. It would be misleading to say that he is neutral as to the conflict between his desires, since this would suggest that he regards them as equally acceptable. Since he has no identity apart from his first-order desires, it is true neither that he prefers one to the other nor that he prefers not to take sides.

It makes a difference to the unwilling addict, who is a person, which of his conflicting first-order desires wins out. Both desires are his, to be sure; and whether he finally takes the drug or finally succeeds in refraining from taking it, he acts to satisfy what is in a literal sense his own desire. In either case he does something he himself wants to do, and he does it not because of some external influence whose aim happens to coincide with his own but because of his desire to do it. The unwilling addict identifies himself, however, through the formation of a second-order volition, with one rather than with the other of his conflicting first-order desires. He makes one of them more truly his own and, in so doing, he withdraws himself from the other. It is in virtue of this identification and withdrawal, accomplished through the formation of a second-order volition, that the unwilling addict may meaningfully make the analytically puzzling statements that the force moving him to take the drug is a force other than his own, and that it is not of his own free will but rather against his will that this force moves him to take it.

The wanton addict cannot or does not care which of his conflicting first-order desires wins out. His lack of concern is not due to his inability to find a convincing basis for preference. It is due either to his lack of the capacity for reflection or to his mindless indifference to the enterprise of evaluating his own desires and motives.[6] There is only one issue in the struggle to which his first-order conflict may lead: whether the one or the other of his conflicting desires is the stronger. Since he is moved by both desires, he will not be altogether satisfied by what he does no matter which of them is effective. But it makes no difference *to him* whether his craving or his aversion gets the upper hand. He has no stake in the conflict between them and so, unlike the unwilling addict, he can neither win nor lose the struggle in which he is engaged. When a *person* acts, the desire by which he is moved is either the will he wants or a will he wants to be without. When a *wanton* acts, it is neither.

---

6 In speaking of the evaluation of his own desires and motives as being characteristic of a person, I do not mean to suggest that a person's second-order volitions necessarily manifest a *moral* stance on his part toward his first-order desires. It may not be from the point of view of morality that the person evaluates his first-order desires. Moreover, a person may be capricious and irresponsible in forming his second-order volitions and give no serious consideration to what is at stake. Second-order volitions express evaluations only in the sense that they are preferences. There is no essential restriction on the kind of basis, if any, upon which they are formed.

III

There is a very close relationship between the capacity for forming second-order volitions and another capacity that is essential to persons—one that has often been considered a distinguishing mark of the human condition. It is only because a person has volitions of the second order that he is capable both of enjoying and of lacking freedom of the will. The concept of a person is not only, then, the concept of a type of entity that has both first-order desires and volitions of the second order. It can also be construed as the concept of a type of entity for whom the freedom of its will may be a problem. This concept excludes all wantons, both infrahuman and human, since they fail to satisfy an essential condition for the enjoyment of freedom of the will. And it excludes those suprahuman beings, if any, whose wills are necessarily free.

Just what kind of freedom is the freedom of the will? This question calls for an identification of the special area of human experience to which the concept of freedom of the will, as distinct from the concepts of other sorts of freedom, is particularly germane. In dealing with it, my aim will be primarily to locate the problem with which a person is most immediately concerned when he is concerned with the freedom of his will.

According to one familiar philosophical tradition, being free is fundamentally a matter of doing what one wants to do. Now the notion of an agent who does what he wants to do is by no means an altogether clear one: both the doing and the wanting, and the appropriate relation between them as well, require elucidation. But although its focus needs to be sharpened and its formulation refined, I believe that this notion does capture at least part of what is implicit in the idea of an agent who *acts* freely. It misses entirely, however, the peculiar content of the quite different idea of an agent whose *will* is free.

We do not suppose that animals enjoy freedom of the will, although we recognize that an animal may be free to run in whatever direction it wants.

Thus, having the freedom to do what one wants to do is not a sufficient condition of having a free will. It is not a necessary condition either. For to deprive someone of his freedom of action is not necessarily to undermine the freedom of his will. When an agent is aware that there are certain things he is not free to do, this doubtless affects his desires and limits the range of choices he can make. But suppose that someone, without being aware of it, has in fact lost or been deprived of his freedom of action. Even though he is no longer free to do what he wants to do, his will may remain as free as it was before. Despite the fact that he is not free to translate his desires into actions or to act according to the determinations of his will, he may still form those desires and make those determinations as freely as if his freedom of action had not been impaired.

When we ask whether a person's will is free we are not asking whether he is in a position to translate his first-order desires into actions. That is the question of whether he is free to do as he pleases. The question of the freedom of his will does not concern the relation between what he does and what he wants to do. Rather, it concerns his desires themselves. But what question about them is it?

It seems to me both natural and useful to construe the question of whether a person's will is free in close analogy to the question of whether an agent enjoys freedom of action. Now freedom of action is (roughly, at least) the freedom to do what one wants to do. Analogously, then, the statement that a person enjoys freedom of the will means (also roughly) that he is free to want what he wants to want. More precisely, it means that he is free to will what he wants to will, or to have the will he wants. Just as the question about the freedom of an agent's action has to do with whether it is the action he wants to perform, so the question about the freedom of his will has to do with whether it is the will he wants to have.

It is in securing the conformity of his will to his second-order volitions, then, that a person exercises freedom of the will. And it is in the discrepancy between his will and his second-order volitions, or in his awareness that their coincidence is not his own doing but only a happy chance, that a person who does not have this freedom feels its lack. The unwilling addict's will is not free. This is shown by the fact that it is not the will he wants. It is also true, though in a different way, that the will of the wanton addict is not free. The wanton addict neither has the will he wants nor has a will that differs from the will he wants. Since he has no volitions of the second order, the freedom of his will cannot be a problem for him. He lacks it, so to speak, by default.

People are generally far more complicated than my sketchy account of the structure of a person's will may suggest. There is as much opportunity for ambivalence, conflict, and self-deception with regard to desires of the second order, for example, as there is with regard to first-order desires. If there is an unresolved conflict among someone's second-order desires, then he is in danger of having no second-order volition; for unless this conflict is resolved, he has no preference concerning which of his first-order desires is to be his will. This condition, if it is so severe that it prevents him from identifying himself in a sufficiently decisive way with *any* of his conflicting first-order desires, destroys him as a person. For it either tends to paralyze his will and to keep him from acting at all, or it tends to remove him from his will so that his will operates without his participation. In both cases he becomes, like the unwilling addict though in a different way, a helpless bystander to the forces that move him.

Another complexity is that a person may have, especially if his second-order desires are in conflict, desires and volitions of a higher order than the second. There is no theoretical limit to the length of the series of desires of higher and higher orders; nothing except common sense and, perhaps, a saving fatigue prevents an individual from obsessively refusing to identify himself with any of his desires until he forms a desire of the next higher order. The tendency to generate such a series of acts of forming desires, which would

be a case of humanization run wild, also leads toward the destruction of a person.

It is possible, however, to terminate such a series of acts without cutting it off arbitrarily. When a person identifies himself decisively with one of his first-order desires, this commitment "resounds" throughout the potentially endless array of higher orders. Consider a person who, without reservation or conflict, wants to be motivated by the desire to concentrate on his work. The fact that his second-order volition to be moved by this desire is a decisive one means that there is no room for questions concerning the pertinence of desires or volitions of higher orders. Suppose the person is asked whether he wants to want to want to concentrate on his work. He can properly insist that this question concerning a third-order desire does not arise. It would be a mistake to claim that, because he has not considered whether he wants the second-order volition he has formed, he is indifferent to the question of whether it is with this volition or with some other that he wants his will to accord. The decisiveness of the commitment he has made means that he has decided that no further question about his second-order volition, at any higher order, remains to be asked. It is relatively unimportant whether we explain this by saying that this commitment implicitly generates an endless series of confirming desires of higher orders, or by saying that the commitment is tantamount to a dissolution of the pointedness of all questions concerning higher orders of desire.

Examples such as the one concerning the unwilling addict may suggest that volitions of the second order, or of higher orders, must be formed deliberately and that a person characteristically struggles to ensure that they are satisfied. But the conformity of a person's will to his higher-order volitions may be far more thoughtless and spontaneous than this. Some people are naturally moved by kindness when they want to be kind, and by nastiness when they want to be nasty, without any explicit forethought and without any need for energetic self-control. Others are moved by nastiness when they want to be kind and by kindness when they intend to be nasty, equally without forethought and without active resistance to these violations of their higher-order desires. The enjoyment of freedom comes easily to some. Others must struggle to achieve it.

IV

My theory concerning the freedom of the will accounts easily for our disinclination to allow that this freedom is enjoyed by the members of any species inferior to our own. It also satisfies another condition that must be met by any such theory, by making it apparent why the freedom of the will should be regarded as desirable. The enjoyment of a free will means the satisfaction of certain desires—desires of the second or of higher orders—whereas its absence means their frustration. The satisfactions at stake are those which accrue to a person of whom it may be said that his will is his own. The corresponding frustrations are those suffered by a person of whom it may be said that he is estranged from himself, or that he finds himself a helpless or a passive bystander to the forces that move him.

A person who is free to do what he wants to do may yet not be in a position to have the will he wants. Suppose, however, that he enjoys both freedom of action and freedom of the will. Then he is not only free to do what he wants to do; he is also free to want what he wants to want. It seems to me that he has, in that case, all the freedom it is possible to desire or to conceive. There are other good things in life, and he may not possess some of them. But there is nothing in the way of freedom that he lacks.

It is far from clear that certain other theories of the freedom of the will meet these elementary but essential conditions: that it be understandable why we desire this freedom and why we refuse

to ascribe it to animals. Consider, for example, Roderick Chisholm's quaint version of the doctrine that human freedom entails an absence of causal determination.[7] Whenever a person performs a free action, according to Chisholm it's a miracle. The motion of a person's hand, when the person moves it, is the outcome of a series of physical causes; but some event in this series, "and presumably one of those that took place within the brain, was caused by the agent and not by any other events" (18). A free agent has, therefore, "a prerogative which some would attribute only to God: each of us, when we act, is a prime mover unmoved" (23).

This account fails to provide any basis for doubting that animals of subhuman species enjoy the freedom it defines. Chisholm says nothing that makes it seem less likely that a rabbit performs a miracle when it moves its leg than that a man does so when he moves his hand. But why, in any case, should anyone *care* whether he can interrupt the natural order of causes in the way Chisholm describes? Chisholm offers no reason for believing that there is a discernible difference between the experience of a man who miraculously initiates a series of causes when he moves his hand and a man who moves his hand without any such breach of the normal causal sequence. There appears to be no concrete basis for preferring to be involved in the one state of affairs rather than in the other.[8]

It is generally supposed that, in addition to satisfying the two conditions I have mentioned, a satisfactory theory of the freedom of the will necessarily provides an analysis of one of the conditions of moral responsibility. The most common recent approach to the problem of understanding the freedom of the will has been, indeed, to inquire what is entailed by the assumption that someone is morally responsible for what he has

---

7 "Freedom and Action," in K. Lehrer, ed., *Freedom and Determinism* (New York: Random House, 1966), pp. 11–44.

8 I am not suggesting that the alleged difference between these two states of affairs is unverifiable. On the contrary, physiologists might well be able to show that Chisholm's conditions for a free action are not satisfied, by establishing that there is no relevant brain event for which a sufficient physical cause cannot be found.

done. In my view, however, the relation between moral responsibility and the freedom of the will has been very widely misunderstood. It is not true that a person is morally responsible for what he has done only if his will was free when he did it. He may be morally responsible for having done it even though his will was not free at all.

A person's will is free only if he is free to have the will he wants. This means that, with regard to any of his first-order desires, he is free either to make that desire his will or to make some other first-order desire his will instead. Whatever his will, then, the will of the person whose will is free could have been otherwise; he could have done otherwise than to constitute his will as he did. It is a vexed question just how 'he could have done otherwise' is to be understood in contexts such as this one. But although this question is important to the theory of freedom, it has no bearing on the theory of moral responsibility. For the assumption that a person is morally responsible for what he has done does not entail that the person was in a position to have whatever will he wanted.

This assumption *does* entail that the person did what he did freely, or that he did it of his own free will. It is a mistake, however, to believe that someone acts freely only when he is free to do whatever he wants or that he acts of his own free will only if his will is free. Suppose that a person has done what he wanted to do, that he did it because he wanted to do it, and that the will by which he was moved when he did it was his will because it was the will he wanted. Then he did it freely and of his own free will. Even supposing that he could have done otherwise, he would not have done otherwise; and even supposing that he could have had a different will, he would not have wanted his will to differ from what it was. Moreover, since the will that moved him when he acted was his will because he wanted it to be, he cannot claim that his will was forced upon him or that he was a passive bystander to its

constitution. Under these conditions, it is quite irrelevant to the evaluation of his moral responsibility to inquire whether the alternatives that he opted against were actually available to him.[9]

In illustration, consider a third kind of addict. Suppose that his addiction has the same physiological basis and the same irresistible thrust as the addictions of the unwilling and wanton addicts, but that he is altogether delighted with his condition. He is a willing addict, who would not have things any other way. If the grip of his addiction should somehow weaken, he would do whatever he could to reinstate it; if his desire for the drug should begin to fade, he would take steps to renew its intensity.

The willing addict's will is not free, for his desire to take the drug will be effective regardless of whether or not he wants this desire to constitute his will. But when he takes the drug, he takes it freely and of his own free will. I am inclined to understand his situation as involving the overdetermination of his first-order desire to take the drug. This desire is his effective desire because he is physiologically addicted. But it is his effective desire also because he wants it to be. His will is outside his control, but, by his second-order desire that his desire for the drug should be effective, he has made this will his own. Given that it is therefore not only because of his addiction that his desire for the drug is effective, he may be morally responsible for taking the drug.

My conception of the freedom of the will appears to be neutral with regard to the problem of determinism. It seems conceivable that it should be causally determined that a person is free to want what he wants to want. If this is conceivable, then it might be causally determined that a person enjoys a free will. There is no more than an innocuous appearance of paradox in the proposition that it is determined, ineluctably and by forces beyond their control, that certain people

---

9 For another discussion of the considerations that cast doubt on the principle that a person is morally responsible for what he has done only if he could have done otherwise, see my "Alternate Possibilities and Moral Responsibility," this JOURNAL, LXVI, 23 (Dec. 4, 1969): 829–839.

have free wills and that others do not. There is no incoherence in the proposition that some agency other than a person's own is responsible (even *morally* responsible) for the fact that he enjoys or fails to enjoy freedom of the will. It is possible that a person should be morally responsible for what he does of his own free will and that some other person should also be morally responsible for his having done it.[10]

On the other hand, it seems conceivable that it should come about by chance that a person is free to have the will he wants. If this is conceivable, then it might be a matter of chance that certain people enjoy freedom of the will and that certain others do not. Perhaps it is also conceivable, as a number of philosophers believe, for states of affairs to come about in a way other than by chance or as the outcome of a sequence of natural causes. If it is indeed conceivable for the relevant states of affairs to come about in some third way, then it is also possible that a person should in that third way come to enjoy the freedom of the will.

---

10 There is a difference between being *fully* responsible and being *solely* responsible. Suppose that the willing addict has been made an addict by the deliberate and calculated work of another. Then it may be that both the addict and this other person are fully responsible for the addict's taking the drug, while neither of them is solely responsible for it. That there is a distinction between full moral responsibility and sole moral responsibility is apparent in the following example. A certain light can be turned on or off by flicking either of two switches, and each of these switches is simultaneously flicked to the "on" position by a different person, neither of whom is aware of the other. Neither person is solely responsible for the light's going on, nor do they share the responsibility in the sense that each is partially responsible; rather, each of them is fully responsible.

Jonathan Bennett

The Conscience of Huckleberry Finn

Jonathan Bennett (1930–) spent much of his teaching career at the University of Cambridge, but he has also taught at Simon Fraser University, the University of British Columbia, and Syracuse University. Bennett is a Fellow of the American Academy of Arts and Sciences, Fellow of the British Academy, a past John Locke Lecturer at Oxford University, and the author of numerous books and articles. His website has many of his articles available for downloading. Bennett and his wife Gillian settled after retirement in 1997 on Bowen Island, British Columbia. He is now (2011) occupied with preparing early modern philosophy texts to be available at his website (http://www.earlymoderntexts.com/f_jfb.html).

In this paper, I shall present not just the conscience of Huckleberry Finn but two others as well. One of them is the conscience of Heinrich Himmler. He became a Nazi in 1923; he served drably and quietly, but well, and was rewarded with increasing responsibility and power. At the peak of his career he held many offices and commands, of which the most powerful was that of leader of the S.S.—the principal police force of the Nazi regime. In this capacity, Himmler commanded the whole concentration camp system, and was responsible for the execution of the so-called "final solution of the Jewish problem." It is important for my purposes that this piece of social engineering should be thought of not abstractly but in concrete terms of Jewish families being marched to what they think are bathhouses, to the accompaniment of loudspeaker renditions of extracts from *The Merry Widow* and *Tales of Hoffman*, there to be choked to death by poisonous gases. Altogether, Himmler succeeded in murdering about four and a half million of them, as well as several million gentiles, mainly Poles and Russians.

The other conscience to be discussed is that of the Calvinist theologian and philosopher Jonathan Edwards. He lived in the first half of the eighteenth century, and has a good claim to be considered America's first serious and considerable philosophical thinker. He was for many years a widely renowned preacher and Congregationalist minister in New England; in 1748 a dispute with his congregation led him to resign (he couldn't accept their view that unbelievers should be admitted to the Lord's Supper in the hope that it would convert them); for some years after that he worked as a missionary, preaching to the Indians through an interpreter; then in 1758 he accepted the presidency of what is now Princeton University, and within two months died from a smallpox inoculation. Along the way he wrote some first-rate philosophy: his book attacking the notion of free will is still sometimes read. Why I should be interested in Edwards' *conscience* will be explained in due course.

From *Philosophy*, Vol. 49, No. 188 (1974), pp. 123–143. Reprinted with permission obtained via RightsLink.

I shall use Heinrich Himmler, Jonathan Edwards, and Huckleberry Finn to illustrate different aspects of a single theme, namely the relationship between *sympathy* on the one hand and *bad morality* on the other.

All that I can mean by a "bad morality" is a morality whose principles I deeply disapprove of. When I call a morality bad, I cannot prove that mine is better; but when I here call any morality bad, I think you will agree with me that it is bad; and that is all I need.

There could be dispute as to whether the springs of someone's actions constitute a *morality*. I think, though, that we must admit that someone who acts in ways which conflict grossly with our morality may nevertheless have a morality of his own—a set of principles of action which he sincerely assents to, so that for him the problem of acting well or rightly or in obedience to conscience is the problem of conforming to *those* principles. The problem of conscientiousness can arise as acutely for a bad morality as for any other: rotten principles may be as difficult to keep as decent ones.

As for "sympathy": I use this term to cover every sort of fellow-feeling, as when one feels pity over someone's loneliness, or horrified compassion over his pain, and when one feels a shrinking reluctance to act in a way which will bring misfortune to someone else. These *feelings* must not be confused with *moral judgments*. My sympathy for someone in distress may lead me to help him, or even to think that I ought to help him; but in itself it is not a judgment about what I ought to do but just a *feeling* for him in his plight. We shall get some light on the difference between feelings and moral judgments when we consider Huckleberry Finn.

Obviously, feelings can impel one to action, and so can moral judgments; and in a particular case sympathy and morality may pull in opposite directions. This can happen not just with bad moralities, but also with good ones like yours and mine. For example, a small child, sick and miserable, clings tightly to his mother and screams in terror when she tries to pass him over to the doctor to be examined. If the mother gave way to her sympathy, that is to her feeling for the child's misery and fright, she would hold it close and not let the doctor come near; but don't we agree that it might be wrong for her to act on such a feeling? Quite generally, then, anyone's moral principles may apply to a particular situation in a way which runs contrary to the particular thrusts of fellow-feeling that he has in that situation. My immediate concern is with sympathy in relation to bad morality, but not because such conflicts occur only when the morality is bad.

Now, suppose that someone who accepts a bad morality is struggling to make himself act in accordance with it in a particular situation where his sympathies pull him another way. He sees the struggle as one between doing the right, conscientious thing, and acting wrongly and weakly, like the mother who won't let the doctor come near her sick, frightened baby. Since we don't accept this person's morality, we may see the situation very differently, thoroughly disapproving of the action he regards as the right one, and endorsing the action which from his point of view constitutes weakness and backsliding.

Conflicts between sympathy and bad morality won't always be like this, for we won't disagree with every single dictate of a bad morality. Still, it can happen in the way I have described, with the agent's right action being our wrong one, and vice versa. That is just what happens in a certain episode in chapter 16 of *The Adventures of Huckleberry Finn*, an episode which brilliantly illustrates how fiction can be instructive about real life.

Huck Finn has been helping his slave friend Jim to run away from Miss Watson, who is Jim's owner. In their raft-journey down the Mississippi river, they are near to the place at which Jim will become legally free. Now let Huck take over the story:

Jim said it made him all over trembly and feverish to be so close to freedom. Well, I can tell you it made me all over trembly and feverish, too, to hear him, because I begun to get it through my head that he *was* most free—and who was to blame for it? Why, *me*. I couldn't get that out of my conscience, no how nor no way...It hadn't ever come home to me, before, what this thing was that I was doing. But now it did; and it stayed with me, and scorched me more and more. I tried to make out to myself that *I* warn't to blame, because *I* didn't run Jim off from his rightful owner; but it warn't no use, conscience up and say, every time: "But you knowed he was running for his freedom, and you could a paddled ashore and told somebody." That was so—I couldn't get around that, no way. That was where it pinched. Conscience says to me: "What had poor Miss Watson done to you, that you could see her nigger go off right under your eyes and never say one single word? What did that poor old woman do to you, that you could treat her so mean?..." I got to feeling so mean and so miserable I most wished I was dead.

Jim speaks of his plan to save up to buy his wife, and then his children, out of slavery; and he adds that if the children cannot be bought he will arrange to steal them. Huck is horrified:

Thinks I, this is what comes of my not thinking. Here was this nigger which I had as good as helped to run away, coming right out flat-footed and saying he would steal his children—children that belonged to a man I didn't even know; a man that hadn't ever done me no harm.

I was sorry to hear Jim say that, it was such a lowering of him. My conscience got to stirring me up hotter than ever, until at last I says to it: "Let up on me—it ain't too late, yet—I'll paddle ashore at first light, and tell." I felt easy, and happy, and light as a feather, right off. All my troubles was gone.

This is bad morality all right. In his earliest years Huck wasn't taught any principles, and the only ones he has encountered since then are those of rural Missouri, in which slave-owning is just one kind of ownership and is not subject to critical pressure. It hasn't occurred to Huck to question those principles. So the action, to us abhorrent, of turning Jim in to the authorities presents itself *clearly* to Huck as the right thing to do.

For us, morality and sympathy would both dictate helping Jim to escape. If we felt any conflict, it would have both these on one side and something else on the other—greed for a reward, or fear of punishment. But Huck's morality conflicts with his sympathy, that is, with his unargued, natural feeling for his friend. The conflict starts when Huck sets off in the canoe towards the shore, pretending that he is going to reconnoitre, but really planning to turn Jim in:

As I shoved off, [Jim] says: "Pooty soon I'll be a shout'n for joy, en I'll say, it's all on accounts o' Huck I a free man...Jim won't ever forgit you, Huck; you's de bes' fren' Jim's ever had; en you's de *only* fren' old Jim's got now."

I was paddling off, all in a sweat to tell on him; but when he says this, it seemed to kind of take the tuck all out of me. I went along slow then, and I warn't right down certain whether I was glad I started or whether I warn't. When I was fifty yards off, Jim says:

"Dah you goes, de ole true Huck; de on'y white genlman dat ever kep' his promise to old Jim." Well, I just felt sick. But I says, I *got* to do it—I can't get *out* of it.

In the upshot, sympathy wins over morality. Huck hasn't the strength of will to do what he sincerely thinks he ought to do. Two men hunting for runaway slaves ask him whether the man on his raft is black or white:

I didn't answer up prompt. I tried to, but the words wouldn't come. I tried, for a second or two, to brace up and out with it, but I warn't man enough—hadn't the spunk of a rabbit. I see I was weakening; so I just give up trying, and up and says: "He's white."

So Huck enables Jim to escape, thus acting weakly and wickedly—he thinks. In this conflict between sympathy and morality, sympathy wins.

One critic has cited this episode in support of the statement that Huck suffers "excruciating moments of wavering between honesty and respectability." That is hopelessly wrong, and I agree with the perceptive comment on it by another critic, who says:

> The conflict waged in Huck is much more serious: he scarcely cares for respectability and never hesitates to relinquish it, but he does care for honesty and gratitude—and both honesty and gratitude require that he should give Jim up. It is not, in Huck, honesty at war with respectability but love and compassion for Jim struggling against his conscience. His decision is for Jim and hell: a right decision made in the mental chains that Huck never breaks. His concern for Jim is and remains *irrational*. Huck finds many reasons for giving Jim up and none for stealing him. To the end Huck sees his compassion for Jim as a weak, ignorant, and wicked felony.

This is precisely correct—and it can have that virtue only because Mark Twain wrote the episode with such unerring precision. The crucial point concerns *reasons*, which all occur on one side of the conflict. On the side of conscience we have principles, arguments, considerations, ways of looking at things:

> "It hadn't even come home to me before what I was doing"

> "I tried to make out that I warn't to blame"

> "Conscience said "But you knowed…"—I couldn't get around that"

> "What had poor Miss Watson done to you?"

> "This is what comes of my not thinking"

> "…children that belonged to a man I didn't even know."

On the other side, the side of feeling, we get nothing like that. When Jim rejoices in Huck, as his only friend, Huck doesn't consider the claims of friendship or have the situation "come home" to him in a different light. All that happens is: "When he says this, it seemed to kind of take the tuck all out of me. I went along slow then, and I warn't right down certain whether I was glad I started or whether I warn't." Again, Jim's words about Huck's "promise" to him don't give Huck any *reason* for changing his plan: in his morality promises to slaves probably don't count. Their effect on him is of a different kind: "Well, I just felt sick." And when the moment for final decision comes, Huck doesn't weigh up pros and cons: he simply *fails* to do what he believes to be right—he isn't strong enough, hasn't "the spunk of a rabbit." This passage in the novel is notable not just for its finely wrought irony, with Huck's weakness of will leading him to do the right thing, but also for its masterly handling of the difference between general moral principles and particular unreasoned emotional pulls.

Consider now another case of bad morality in conflict with human sympathy, the case of the odious Himmler. Here, from a speech he made to some S.S. generals, is an indication of the content of his morality:

> What happens to a Russian, to a Czech, does not interest me in the slightest. What the nations can offer in the way of good blood of our type, we will take, if necessary by kidnapping their children and raising them here with us. Whether nations live in prosperity or starve to death like cattle interests me only in so far as we need them as slaves to our *Kultur*; otherwise it is of no interest to me. Whether 10,000 Russian females fall down from exhaustion while digging an antitank ditch interests me only in so far as the antitank ditch for Germany is finished.

But has this a moral basis at all? And if it has, was there in Himmler's own mind any conflict between morality and sympathy? Yes there was. Here more from the same speech:

...I also want to talk to you quite frankly on a very grave matter...I mean...the extermination of the Jewish race...Most of you must know what it means when 100 corpses are lying side by side, or 500, or 1,000. To have stuck it out and at the same time—apart from exceptions caused by human weakness—to have remained decent fellows, that is what has made us hard. This is a page of glory in our history which has never been written and is never to be written.

Himmler saw his policies as being hard to implement while still retaining one's human sympathies—while still remaining a "decent fellow." He is saying that only the weak take the easy way out and just squelch their sympathies, and is praising the stronger and more glorious course of retaining one's sympathies while acting in violation of them. In the same spirit, he ordered that when executions were carried out in concentration camps, those responsible "are to be influenced in such a way as to suffer no ill effect in their character and mental attitude." A year later he boasted that the S.S. had wiped out the Jews

without our leaders and their men suffering any damage in their minds and souls. The danger was considerable, for there was only a narrow path between the Scylla of their becoming heartless ruffians unable any longer to treasure life, and the Charybdis of their becoming soft and suffering nervous breakdowns.

And there really can't be any doubt that the basis of Himmler's policies was a set of principles which constituted his morality—a sick, bad, wicked *morality*. He described himself as caught in "the old tragic conflict between will and obligation." And when his physician Kersten protested at the intention to destroy the Jews, saying that the suffering involved was "not to be contemplated," Kersten reports that Himmler replied:

He knew that it would mean much suffering for the Jews..."It is the curse of greatness that it must step over dead bodies to create new life. Yet we must...cleanse the soil or it will never bear fruit. It will be a great burden for me to bear."

This, I submit, is the language of morality.

So in this case, tragically, bad morality won out over sympathy. I am sure that many of Himmler's killers did extinguish their sympathies, becoming "heartless ruffians" rather than "decent fellows"; but not Himmler himself. Although his policies ran against the human grain to a horrible degree, he did not sandpaper down his emotional surfaces so that there was no grain there, allowing his actions to slide along smoothly and easily. He did, after all, bear his hideous burden, and even paid a price for it. He suffered a variety of nervous and physical disabilities, including nausea and stomach convulsions, and Kersten was doubtless right in saying that these were "the expression of a psychic division which extended over his whole life."

This same division must have been present in some of those officials of the Church who ordered heretics to be tortured so as to change their theological opinions. Along with the brutes and the cold careerists, there must have been some who cared, and who suffered from the conflict between the sympathies and their bad morality.

In the conflict between sympathy and bad morality, then, the victory may go to sympathy as in the case of Huck Finn, or to morality as in the case of Himmler.

Another possibility is that the conflict may be avoided by giving up, or not ever having, those sympathies which might interfere with one's principles. That seems to have been the case with Jonathan Edwards. I am afraid that I shall be doing an injustice to Edwards' many virtues, and to his great intellectual energy and inventiveness; for my concern is only with the worst thing about him—namely his morality, which was worse than Himmler.

According to Edwards, God condemns some men to an eternity of unimaginably awful pain, though he arbitrarily spares others—"arbitrarily" because none deserve to be spared:

> Natural men are held in the hand of God over the pit of hell; they have deserved the fiery pit, and are already sentenced to it; and God is dreadfully provoked, his anger is as great towards them as to those that are actually suffering the executions of the fierceness of his wrath in hell…; the devil is waiting for them, hell is gaping for them, the flames gather and flash about them, and would fain lay hold on them and…; there are no means within reach that can be any security to them…All that preserves them is the mere arbitrary will, and uncovenanted unobliged forebearance of an incensed God.

Notice that he says "they have deserved the fiery pit." Edwards insists that men *ought* to be condemned to eternal pain; and his position isn't that this is right because God wants it, but rather that God wants it because it is right. For him, moral standards exist independently of God, and God can be assessed in the light of them (and of course found to be perfect). For example, he says:

> They deserve to be cast into hell; so that… justice never stands in the way, it makes no objection against God's using his power at any moment to destroy them. Yea, on the contrary, justice calls aloud for an infinite punishment of their sins.

Elsewhere, he gives elaborate arguments to show that God is acting justly in damning sinners. For example, he argues that a punishment should be exactly as bad as the crime being punished; God is infinitely excellent; so any crime against him infinitely bad; and so eternal damnation is exactly right as a punishment—it is infinite, but, as Edwards is careful also to say, it is "no more than infinite."

Of course, Edwards himself didn't torment the damned; but the question still arises of whether his sympathies didn't conflict with his *approval* of eternal torment. Didn't he find it painful to

contemplate any fellow human's being tortured forever? Apparently not:

> The God that holds you over the pit of hell, much as one holds a spider or some loathsome insect over the fire, abhors you, and is dreadfully provoked;…he is of purer eyes than to bear to have you in his sight; you are ten thousand times so abominable in his eyes as the most hateful venomous serpent is in ours.

When God is presented as being as misanthropic as that, one suspects misanthropy in the theologian. This suspicion is increased when Edwards claims that "the saints in glory will…understand how terrible the sufferings of the damned are; yet… will not be sorry for [them]." He bases this partly on a view of human nature whose ugliness he seems not to notice:

> The seeing of the calamities of others tends to heighten the sense of our own enjoyments. When the saints in glory, therefore, shall see the doleful state of the damned, how will this heighten their sense of the blessedness of their own state…When they shall see how miserable others of their fellow-creatures are…; when they shall see the smoke of their torment,…and hear their dolorous shrieks and cries, and consider that they in the mean time are in the most blissful state, and shall surely be in it to all eternity; how they will rejoice!

I hope this is less than the whole truth! His other main point about why the saints will rejoice to see the torments of the damned is that it is *right* that they should do so:

> The heavenly inhabitants…will have no love nor pity to the damned…[This will not show] a want of a spirit of love in them…; for the heavenly inhabitants will know that it is not fit that they should love [the damned] because they will know then, that God has no love to them, nor pity for them.

The implication that *of course* one can adjust one's feelings of pity so that they conform to the dictates of some authority—doesn't this suggest that ordinary human sympathies played only a small part in Edwards' life?

Huck Finn, whose sympathies are wide and deep, could never avoid the conflict in that way; but he is determined to avoid it, and so he opts for the only other alternative he can see—to give up morality altogether. After he has tricked the slave-hunters, he returns to the raft and undergoes a peculiar crisis:

> I got aboard the raft, feeling bad and low, because I knowed very well I had done wrong, and I see it warn't no use for me to try to learn to do right; a body that don't get *started* right when he's little, ain't got no show—when the pinch comes there ain't nothing to back him up and keep him to his work, and so he gets beat. Then I thought a minute, and says to myself, hold on—s'pose you'd a done right and give Jim up; would you feel better than what you do now? No, says I, I'd feel bad—I'd feel just the same way I do now. Well, then, says I, what's the use you learning to do right, when it's troublesome to do right and ain't no trouble to do wrong, and the wages is just the same? I was stuck. I couldn't answer that. So I reckoned I wouldn't bother no more about it, but after this always do whichever come handiest at the time.

Huck clearly cannot conceive of having any morality except the one he has learned—too late, he thinks—from his society. He is not entirely a prisoner of that morality, because he does after all reject it; but for him that is a decision to relinquish morality as such; he cannot envisage revising his morality, altering its content in face of the various pressures to which it is subject, including pressures from his sympathies. For example, he does not begin to approach the thought that slavery should be rejected on moral grounds, or the thought that what he is doing is not theft because a person cannot be owned and therefore cannot be stolen.

The basic trouble is that he cannot or will not engage in abstract intellectual operations of any sort. In chapter 33 he finds himself "feeling to blame, somehow" for something he knows he had no hand in; he assumes that this feeling is a deliverance of conscience; and this confirms him in his belief that conscience shouldn't be listened to:

> It don't make no difference whether you do right or wrong, a person's conscience ain't got no sense, and just goes for him *anyway*. If I had a yaller dog that didn't know no more than a person's conscience does, I would pison him. It takes up more room than all the rest of a person's insides, and yet ain't no good, nohow.

That brisk, incurious dismissiveness fits well with the comprehensive rejection of morality back on the raft. But this is a digression.

On the raft, Huck decides not to live by principles, but just to do whatever "comes handiest at the time"—always acting according to the mood of the moment. Since the morality he is rejecting is narrow and cruel, and his sympathies are broad and kind, the results will be good. But moral principles are good to have, because they help to protect one from acting badly at moments when one's sympathies happen to be in abeyance. On the highest possible estimate of the role one's sympathies should have, one can still allow for principles as embodiments of one's best feelings, one's broadest and keenest sympathies. On that view, principles can help one across intervals when one's feelings are at less than their best, i.e., through periods of misanthropy or meanness or self-centredness or depression or anger.

What Huck didn't see is that one can live by principles and yet have ultimate control over their content. And one way such control can be exercised is by checking of one's principles in the light of one's sympathies. This is sometimes a pretty straightforward matter. It can happen that a certain moral principle becomes untenable —meaning literally that one cannot hold it any longer—because it conflicts intolerably with the pity or revulsion or whatever that one feels when one sees what the principle leads to. One's experience may play a large part here: experiences evoke feelings, and feelings force one to modify principles. Something like this happened to the English poet Wilfred Owen, whose experiences in the First World War transformed him from an enthusiastic soldier into a virtual pacifist. I can't document his change of conscience in detail; but I want to present something which he wrote about the way experience can put pressure on morality.

The Latin poet Horace wrote that it is sweet and fitting (or right) to die for one's country—*dulce et decorum en pro patria mori*— and Owen wrote a fine poem about how experience could lead one to relinquish that particular moral principle. He describes a man who is too slow donning his gas mask during a gas attack—"As under a green sea I saw him drowning," Owen says. The poem ends like this:

> In all my dreams before my helpless sight
> He plunges at me, guttering, choking,
>   drowning
> If in some smothering dreams, you too
>   could pace
> Behind the wagon that we flung him in,
> And watch the white eyes writhing in his
>   face,
> His hanging face, like a devil's sick of sin;
> If you could hear, at every jolt, the blood
> Come gargling from the froth-corrupted
>   lungs,
> Bitter as the cud
> Of vile, incurable sores on innocent
>   tongues,—
> My friend, you would not tell with such
>   high zest
> To children ardent for some desperate
>   glory,
> The old Lie: Dulce et decorum est
> pro patria mori.

There is a difficulty about drawing from all this a moral for ourselves. I imagine that we agree in our rejection of slavery, eternal damnation, genocide, and uncritical patriotic self-abnegation; so we shall agree that Huck Finn, Jonathan Edwards, Heinrich Himmler, and the poet Horace would all have done well to bring certain of their principles under severe pressure from ordinary human sympathies. But then we can say this because we can say that all those are bad moralities, whereas we cannot look at our own moralities and declare them bad. This is not arrogance: it is obviously incoherent for someone to declare the system of moral principles that he *accepts* to be *bad*, just as one cannot coherently say of anything that one *believes* it but it is *false*.

Still, although I can't point to any of my beliefs and say "That is false," I don't doubt that some of my beliefs *are* false; and so I should try to remain open to correction. Similarly, I accept every single item in my morality—that is inevitable—but I am sure that my morality could be improved, which is to say that it could undergo changes which I should be glad of once I had made them. So I must try to keep my morality open to revision, exposing it to whatever valid pressures there are—including pressures from my sympathies.

I don't give my sympathies a blank cheque in advance. In a conflict between principle and sympathy, principles ought sometimes to win. For example, I think it was right to take part in the Second World War on the allied side; there were many ghastly individual incidents which might have led someone to doubt the rightness of his participation in that war; and I think it would have been right for such a person to keep his sympathies in a subordinate place on those occasions, not allowing them to modify his principles in such a way as to make a pacifist of him.

Still, one's sympathies should be kept as sharp and sensitive and aware as possible, and not only because they can sometimes affect one's principles or one's conduct or both. Owen, at any rate, says that feelings and sympathies are vital even when they can do nothing but bring pain and distress. In another poem he speaks of the blessings of being numb in one's feelings: "Happy are the men who yet before they are killed/Can let their veins run cold," he says. These are the ones who do not suffer from any compassion which, as Owen puts it, "makes their feet/Sore on the alleys cobbled with their brothers." He contrasts these "happy" ones, who "lose all imagination," with himself and others "who with a thought besmirch/Blood over all our soul." Yet the poem's verdict goes against the "happy" ones. Owen does not say that they will act worse than the others whose souls are besmirched with blood because of their keen awareness of human suffering.

He merely says that they are the losers because they have cut themselves off from the human condition:

> By choice they made themselves immune
> To pity and whatever moans in man
> Before the last sea and the hapless stars;
> Whatever mourns when many leave these
>   shores;
> Whatever shares
> The eternal reciprocity of tears.

Study Questions

1. According to Bennett, our conscience differs from our sympathy. How so?

2. Why does Bennett chose to discuss cases of what we would consider to be "bad" morality?

3. It seems fair to claim that no college student in the United States today would be caught in Huck Finn's dilemma. Why? Is it that our moral principles are no longer reflections of a "bad" morality?

4. Critically discuss the case today involving someone being opposed to allowing gay marriages based on the principle, "Marriage should only be between a man and a woman," yet that same person feeling sorry or sympathetic for gay couples who earnestly wish to be married. To which of Bennett's characters is this dilemma most closely related?

5. What is Himmler's failure? Can you think of cases where you may have opted for principle over sympathy and regretted it?

6. According to Bennett, what is the preferable balance between sympathy and acting according to one's conscience?

Ruth Benedict

Morality Is Relative

Ruth Benedict (1887–1948) was an American anthropologist. Born in New York City, Benedict soon found herself on the move, both physically and emotionally, as she was confronted early in life with the physical death of her father and the emotional death of her mother. According to one biographer, "…in one stroke Ruth experienced the loss of the two most nourishing and protective people around her—the loss of her father at death and her mother to grief." Death remained for Benedict a powerful fascination. As an adult, she apparently found that the face, in death, showed the real beauty or ugliness of a person's life. When her father-in-law died she wrote, "…in his coffin I really saw him, and it was more than all the rest."

She received her PhD from Columbia University where in 1936 she was appointed associate professor. Dr. Benedict mentored several Columbia students of anthropology including Margaret Mead and Ruth Landes. Margaret Mead and Ruth Benedict became two of the most influential women anthropologists in the early to mid-twentieth century.

Benedict's popular *Patterns of Culture* (1934) has been translated into more than a dozen languages and was considered standard reading for anthropology courses throughout American universities. In *Patterns of Culture*, Benedict attempted to demonstrate that different cultures have their own moral imperatives and these imperatives can only be appreciated if the culture in its entirety is studied. She was of the view that there was no independent, rationally defensible position by which to judge other cultural customs, practices, or values that one finds different from one's own. Morality, she claimed, was relative to the culture in which it functioned.

Benedict, recognized as a leading cultural anthropologist, was recruited by the U.S. Government for war-related research and consultation during World War II.

From "Anthropology and the Abnormal," in *The Journal of General Psychology* 10 (1934), pp. 59–82. Reprinted with permission obtained via RightsLink.

Modern social anthropology has become more and more a study of the varieties and common elements of cultural environment and the consequences of these in human behavior. For such a study of diverse social orders primitive peoples fortunately provide a laboratory not yet entirely vitiated by the spread of a standardized worldwide civilization. Dyaks and Hopis, Fijians and Yakuts are significant for psychological and sociological study because only among these simpler peoples has there been sufficient isolation to give opportunity for the development of localized social forms. In the higher cultures the standardization of custom and belief over a couple of continents has given a false sense of the inevitability of the particular forms that have gained currency, and we need to turn to a wider survey in order to check the conclusions we hastily base upon this near-universality of familiar customs. Most of the simpler cultures did not gain the wide currency of the one which, out of our experience, we identify with human nature, but this was for various historical reasons, and certainly not for any that gives us as its carriers a monopoly of social good or of social sanity. Modern civilization, from this point of view, becomes not a necessary pinnacle of human achievement but one entry in a long series of possible adjustments.

These adjustments, whether they are in mannerisms like the ways of showing anger, or joy, or grief in any society, or in major human drives like those of sex, prove to be far more variable than experience in any one culture would suggest. In certain fields, such as that of religion or of formal marriage arrangements, these wide limits of variability are well known and can be fairly described. In others it is not yet possible to give a generalized account, but that does not absolve us of the task of indicating the significance of the work that has been done and of the problems that have arisen.

One of these problems relates to the customary modern normal-abnormal categories and our conclusions regarding them. In how far are such categories culturally determined, or in how far can we with assurance regard them as absolute? In how far can we regard inability to function socially as diagnostic of abnormality, or in how far is it necessary to regard this as a function of the culture?

As a matter of fact, one of the most striking facts that emerge from a study of widely varying cultures is the ease with which our abnormals function in other cultures. It does not matter what kind of "abnormality" we choose for illustration, those which indicate extreme instability, or those which are more in the nature of character traits like sadism or delusions of grandeur or of persecution, there are well-described cultures in which these abnormals function at ease and with honor, and apparently without danger or difficulty to the society...

The most notorious of these is trance and catalepsy. Even a very mild mystic is aberrant in our culture. But most peoples have regarded even extreme psychic manifestations not only as normal and desirable, but even as characteristic of highly valued and gifted individuals. This was true even in our own cultural background in that period when Catholicism made the ecstatic experience the mark of sainthood. It is hard for us, born and brought up in a culture that makes no use of the experience, to realize how important a role it may play and how many individuals are capable of it, once it has been given an honorable place in any society....

Cataleptic and trance phenomena are, of course, only one illustration of the fact that those whom we regard as abnormals may function adequately in other cultures. Many of our culturally discarded traits are selected for elaboration in different societies. Homosexuality is an excellent example, for in this case our attention is not constantly diverted, as in the consideration of trance, to the interruption of routine activity which it implies. Homosexuality poses the problem very simply. A tendency toward this trait in our culture exposes an individual to all the conflicts to which all aberrants are always exposed, and we tend to identify the consequences of this conflict with homosexuality. But these consequences are obviously local and cultural. Homosexuals in many societies are not incompetent, but they may be such if the culture asks adjustments of them that would strain any man's vitality. Wherever homosexuality has been given an honorable place in any society, those to whom it is congenial have filled adequately the honorable roles society assigns to them. Plato's *Republic* is, of course, the most convincing statement of such a reading of homosexuality. It is presented as one of the major means to the good life, and it was generally so regarded in Greece at that time.

The cultural attitude toward homosexuals has not always been on such a high ethical plane, but it has been very varied. Among many American Indian tribes there exists the institution of the berdache, as the French called them. These men-women were men who at puberty or thereafter took the dress and the occupations of women. Sometimes they married other men and lived with them. Sometimes they were men with no inversion, persons of weak sexual endowment who chose this role to avoid the jeers of the women. The berdaches were never regarded as of first-rate supernatural power, as similar men-women were in Siberia, but rather as leaders in women's occupations, good healers in certain diseases, or, among certain tribes, as the genial organizers of social affairs. In any case, they were socially placed. They were not left exposed to the conflicts that visit the deviant who is excluded from participation in the recognized patterns of his society.

The most spectacular illustrations of the extent to which normality may be culturally defined are those cultures where an abnormality of our culture is the cornerstone of their social structure. It is not possible to do justice to these possibilities in a short discussion. A recent study of an island of northwest Melanesia by Fortune describes a society built upon traits which we regard as beyond the border of paranoia. In this tribe the exogamic groups look upon each other as prime manipulators of black magic, so that one marries always into an enemy group which remains for life one's deadly and unappeasable foes. They look upon a good garden crop as a confession of theft, for everyone is engaged in making magic to induce into his garden the productiveness of his neighbors'; therefore no secrecy in the island is so rigidly insisted upon as the secrecy of a man's harvesting of his yams. Their polite phrase at the acceptance of a gift is, "And if you now poison me, how shall I repay you this present?" Their preoccupation with poisoning is constant; no woman ever leaves her cooking pot for a moment untended. Even the great affinal economic exchanges that are characteristic of this Melanesian culture area are quite altered in Dobu since they are incompatible with this fear and distrust that pervades the culture. They go farther and people the whole world outside their own quarters with such malignant spirits that all-night feasts and ceremonials simply do not occur here. They have even rigorous religiously enforced customs that forbid the sharing of seed even in one family group. Anyone else's food is deadly poison to you, so that communality of stores is out of the question. For some months before harvest the whole society is on the verge of starvation, but if one falls to the temptation and eats up one's seed yams, one is an outcast and a beachcomber for life. There is no coming back. It involves, as a matter of course, divorce and the breaking of all social ties.

Now in this society where no one may work with another and no one may share with another, Fortune describes the individual who was regarded by all his fellows as crazy. He was not one of those who periodically ran amok and, beside himself and frothing at the mouth, fell with a knife upon anyone he could reach. Such behavior they did not regard as putting anyone outside the pale. They did not even put the individuals who were known to be liable to these attacks under any kind of control. They merely fled when they saw the attack coming on and kept out of the way. "He would be all right tomorrow." But there was one man of sunny, kindly disposition who liked work and liked to be helpful. The compulsion was too strong for him to repress it in favor of the opposite tendencies of his culture. Men and women never spoke of him without laughing; he was silly and simple and definitely crazy. Nevertheless, to the ethnologist used to a culture that has, in Christianity, made his type the model of all virtue, he seemed a pleasant fellow....

...Among the Kwakiutl it did not matter whether a relative had died in bed of disease, or by the hand of an enemy, in either case death was an 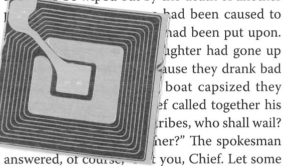 affront to be wiped out by the death of another [person. It was one of the dominant obsessions of their culture that death] had been caused to [them, that they] had been put upon. [If his daughter had gone up] the river and was drowned [because they drank bad water, or if his] boat capsized they [did not rest until the] chief called together his [warriors of the several] tribes, [and asked them,] "who shall wail? [Who shall be wiped out for] her?" The spokesman answered, of course, ["Not you, Chief. Let some] other of the tribes." Immediately they set up the war pole to announce their intention of wiping out the injury, and gathered a war party. They set out, and found seven men and two children asleep and killed them. "Then they felt good when they arrived at Sebaa in the evening."

The point which is of interest to us is that in our society those who on that occasion would feel good when they arrived at Sebaa that everything would be the definitely abnormal. There would be some, even in our society, but it is not a recognized and approved mood under the circumstances. On the Northwest Coast those are favored and fortunate to whom that mood under those circumstances is congenial, and those to whom it is repugnant are unlucky. This latter minority can register in their own culture only by doing violence to their congenial responses and acquiring others that are difficult for them. The person, for instance, who, like a Plains Indian whose wife has been taken from him, is too proud to fight, can deal with the Northwest Coast civilization only by ignoring its strongest bents.

If he cannot achieve it, he is the deviant in that culture, their instance of abnormality.

This head-hunting that takes place on the Northwest Coast after a death is no matter of blood revenge or of organized vengeance. There is no effort to tie up the subsequent killing with any responsibility on the part of the victim for the death of the person who is being mourned. A chief whose son has died goes visiting wherever his fancy dictates, and he says to his host, "My prince has died today, and you go with him." Then he kills him. In this, according to their interpretation, he acts nobly because he has not been downed. He has thrust back in return. The whole procedure is meaningless without the fundamental paranoid reading of bereavement. Death, like all the other untoward accidents of existence, confounds man's pride and can only be handled in the category of insults.

Behavior honored upon the Northwest Coast is one which is recognized as abnormal in our civilization, and yet it is sufficiently close to the attitudes of our own culture to be intelligible to us and to have a definite vocabulary with which we may discuss it. The megalomaniac paranoid trend is a definite danger in our society. It is encouraged by some of our major preoccupations, and it confronts us with a choice of two possible attitudes. One is to brand it as abnormal and reprehensible, and is the attitude we have chosen in our civilization. The other is to make it an essential attribute of ideal man, and this is the solution in the culture of the Northwest Coast.

These illustrations, which it has been possible to indicate only in the briefest manner, force upon us the fact that normality is culturally defined. An adult shaped to the drives and standards of either of these cultures, if he were transported into our civilization, would fall into our categories of abnormality. He would be faced with the psychic dilemmas of the socially unavailable. In his own culture, however, he is the pillar of society, the end result of socially inculcated mores, and the problem of personal instability in his case simply does not arise.

No one civilization can possibly utilize in its mores the whole potential range of human behavior. Just as there are great numbers of possible phonetic articulations, and the possibility of language depends on a selection and standardization of a few of these in order that speech communication may be possible at all, so the possibility of organized behavior of every sort, from the fashions of local dress and houses to the dicta of a people's ethics and religion, depends upon a similar selection among the possible behavior traits. In the field of recognized economic obligations or sex taboos this selection is as nonrational and subconscious a process as it is in the field of phonetics. It is a process which goes on in the group for long periods of time and is historically conditioned by innumerable accidents of isolation or of contact of peoples. In any comprehensive study of psychology, the selection that different cultures have made in the course of history within the great circumference of potential behavior is of great significance.

Every society, beginning with some slight inclination in one direction or another, carries its preference farther and farther, integrating itself more and more completely upon its chosen basis, and discarding those types of behavior that are uncongenial. Most of those organizations of personality that seem to us most uncontrovertibly abnormal have been used by different civilizations in the very foundations of their institutional life. Conversely the most valued traits of our normal individuals have been looked on in differently organized cultures as aberrant. Normality, in short, within a very wide range, is culturally defined. It is primarily a term for the socially elaborated segment of human behavior in any culture; and abnormality, a term for the segment that that particular civilization does not use. The very eyes with which we see the problem are conditioned by the long traditional habits of our own society.

It is a point that has been made more often in relation to ethics than in relation to psychiatry. We do not any longer make the mistake of deriving the morality of our locality and decade directly from the inevitable constitution of human nature. We do not elevate it to the dignity of a first principle. We recognize that morality differs in every society, and is a convenient term for socially approved habits. Mankind has always preferred to say, "It is morally good," rather than "It is habitual," and the fact of this preference is matter enough for a critical science of ethics. But historically the two phrases are synonymous.

The concept of the normal is properly a variant of the concept of the good. It is that which society has approved. A normal action is one which falls well within the limits of expected behavior for a particular society. Its variability among different peoples is essentially a function of the variability of the behavior patterns that different societies have created for themselves, and can never be wholly divorced from a consideration of culturally institutionalized types of behavior.

Each culture is a more or less elaborate working-out of the potentialities of the segment it has chosen. Insofar as a civilization is well integrated and consistent within itself, it will tend to carry farther and farther, according to its nature, its initial impulse toward a particular type of action, and from the point of view of any other culture those elaborations will include more and more extreme and aberrant traits.

Each of these traits, in proportion as it reinforces the chosen behavior patterns of that culture, is for that culture normal. Those individuals to whom it is congenial either congenitally, or as the result of childhood sets, are accorded prestige in that culture, and are not visited with the social contempt or disapproval which their traits would call down upon them in a society that was differently organized. On the other hand, those individuals whose characteristics are not congenial to the selected type of human behavior in that community are the deviants, no matter how valued their personality traits may be in a contrasted civilization.

The Dobuan who is not easily susceptible to fear of treachery, who enjoys work and likes to be helpful, is their neurotic and regarded as silly. On the Northwest Coast the person who finds it difficult to read life in terms of an insult contest will be the person upon whom fall all the difficulties of the culturally unprovided for. The person who does not find it easy to humiliate a neighbor, nor to see humiliation in his own experience, who is genial and loving, may, of course, find some unstandardized way of achieving satisfactions in his society, but not in the major patterned responses that his culture requires of him. If he is born to play an important role in a family with many hereditary privileges, he can succeed only by doing violence to his whole personality. If he does not succeed, he has betrayed his culture; that is, he is abnormal.

I have spoken of individuals as having sets toward certain types of behavior, and of these sets as running sometimes counter to the types of behavior which are institutionalized in the culture to which they belong. From all that we know of contrasting cultures it seems clear that differences of temperament occur in every society. The matter has never been made the subject of investigation, but from the available material it would appear that these temperament types are very likely of universal recurrence. That is,

there is an ascertainable range of human behavior that is found wherever a sufficiently large series of individuals is observed. But the proportion in which behavior types stand to one another in different societies is not universal. The vast majority of individuals in any group are shaped to the fashion of that culture. In other words, most individuals are plastic to the moulding force of the society into which they are born in a society that values trance, as in India, they will have supernormal experience. In a society that institutionalizes homosexuality, they will be homosexual. In a society that sets the gathering of possessions as the chief human objective, they will amass property. The deviants, whatever the type of behavior the culture has institutionalized, will remain few in number, and there seems no more difficulty in moulding the vast malleable majority to the "normality" of what we consider an aberrant trait, such as delusions of reference, than to the normality of such accepted behavior patterns as acquisitiveness. The small proportion of the number of the deviants in any culture is not a function of the sure instinct with which that society has built itself upon the fundamental sanities, but of the universal fact that, happily, the majority of mankind quite readily take any shape that is presented to them…

Study Questions

1. What does it mean to be a relativist, moral or some other? Is relativism here to be contrasted with absolutism? How are these to be distinguished?

2. Discuss the distinction between cultural relativism and moral relativism.

3. Does Benedict conflate the evaluations of the normal and the abnormal with moral evaluation?

4. Benedict claims that morality consists of a system of socially approved habits. How adequate do you find this definition and what are the implications of your findings?

5. Benedict apparently thought that given moral relativism, people ought to show tolerance toward other moral systems. Is it a relativistic thought, that we ought to show tolerance, or is that an absolute thought?

6. Is Benedict correct in saying that our culture is "but one entry in a long series of possible adjustments"? What are the implications of this statement?

7. Can we separate the descriptive (or fact-stating) aspect of anthropological study from the prescriptive (evaluative) aspect of evaluating cultures? Are there some independent criteria by which we can say that some cultures are better than others?

8. What are the implications of Benedict's claim that morality is simply whatever a culture deems normal behavior? Can you apply it to the institution of slavery or the Nazi policy of anti-Semitism?

James Rachels

Morality Is Not Relative

James Rachels (1941–2003) was an American moral philosopher. Rachels taught at the University of Richmond, New York University, the University of Miami, Duke University, and the University of Alabama at Birmingham, where he spent his final professional years. His work has been translated into nearly a dozen languages. He has given approximately 275 professional lectures in addition to writing six books, 86 essays, and editing seven anthologies. Admired for his clear, succinct writing style, Rachels remained committed in his philosophical career to the view that reason could resolve difficult, complex moral problems. As such, he defended the views of moral vegetarianism, animal rights, affirmative action, and death with dignity—the morally coherent use of euthanasia.

See: http://www.jamesrachels.org/

Morality differs in every society, and is a convenient term for socially approved habits.

—Ruth Benedict

1. How Different Cultures Have Different Moral Codes

Darius, a king of ancient Persia, was intrigued by the variety of cultures he encountered in his travels. He had found, for example, that the Callatians (a tribe of Indians) customarily ate the bodies of their dead fathers. The Greeks, of course, did not do that—the Greeks practiced cremation and regarded the funeral pyre as the natural and fitting way to dispose of the dead. Darius thought that a sophisticated understanding of the world must include an appreciation of such differences between cultures. One day, to teach this lesson, he summoned some Greeks who happened to be present at his court and asked them what they would take to eat the bodies of their dead fathers. They were shocked, as Darius knew they would be, and

replied that no amount of money could persuade them to do such a thing. Then Darius called in some Callatians, and while the Greeks listened asked them what they would take to burn their dead fathers' bodies. The Callatians were horrified and told Darius not even to mention such a dreadful thing.

This story, recounted by Herodotus in his *History*, illustrates a recurring theme in the literature of social science: different cultures have different moral codes. What is thought right within one group may be utterly abhorrent to the members of another group, and vice versa. Should we eat the bodies of the dead or burn them? If you were a Greek, one answer would seem obviously correct; but if you were a Callatian, the opposite would seem equally certain.

It is easy to give additional examples of the same kind. Consider the Eskimos. They are a remote and inaccessible people. Numbering only about 25,000, they live in small, isolated settlements

---

scattered mostly along the northern fringes of North America and Greenland. Until the beginning of this century, the outside world knew little about them. Then explorers began to bring back strange tales.

Eskimo customs turned out to be very different from our own. The men often had more than one wife, and they would share their wives with guests, lending them for the night as a sign of hospitality. Moreover, within a community, a dominant male might demand—and get—regular sexual access to other men's wives. The women, however, were free to break these arrangements simply by leaving their husbands and taking up with new partners—free, that is, so long as their former husbands chose not to make trouble. All in all, the Eskimo practice was a volatile scheme that bore little resemblance to what we call marriage.

But it was not only their marriage and sexual practices that were different. The Eskimos also seemed to have less regard for human life. Infanticide, for example, was common. Knud Rasmussen, one of the most famous early explorers, reported that he met one woman who had borne twenty children but had killed ten of them at birth. Female babies, he found, were especially liable to be destroyed, and this was permitted simply at the parents' discretion, with no social stigma attached to it. Old people also, when they became too feeble to contribute to the family, were left out in the snow to die. So there seemed to be, in this society, remarkably little respect for life.

To the general public, these were disturbing revelations. Our own way of living seems so natural and right that for many of us it is hard to conceive of others living so differently. And when we do hear of such things, we tend immediately to categorize those other peoples as "backward" or "primitive." But to anthropologists and sociologists, there was nothing particularly surprising about the Eskimos. Since the time of Herodotus, enlightened observers have been accustomed to the idea that conceptions of right and wrong

differ from culture to culture. If we assume that *our* ideas of right and wrong will be shared by all peoples at all times, we are merely naive.

2. Cultural Relativism

To many thinkers, this observation—"Different cultures have different moral codes"—has seemed to be the key to understanding morality. The idea of universal truth in ethics, they say, is a myth. The customs of different societies are all that exist. These customs cannot be said to be "correct" or "incorrect," for that implies we have an independent standard of right and wrong by which they may be judged. But there is no such independent standard; every standard is culture-bound. The great pioneering sociologist William Graham Sumner, writing in 1906, put the point like this:

> The "right" way is the way which the ancestors used and which has been handed down. The tradition is its own warrant. It is not held subject to verification by experience. The notion of right is in the folkways. It is not outside of them, of independent origin, and brought to test them. In the folkways, whatever is, is right. This is because they are traditional, and therefore contain in themselves the authority of the ancestral ghosts. When we come to the folkways we are at the end of our analysis.

This line of thought has probably persuaded more people to be skeptical about ethics than any other single thing. Cultural Relativism, as it has been called, challenges our ordinary belief in the objectivity and universality of moral truth. It says, in effect, that there is no such thing as universal truth in ethics; there are only the various cultural codes, and nothing more. Moreover, our own code has no special status; it is merely one among many. As we shall see, this basic idea is really a compound of several different thoughts. It is important to separate the various elements of the theory because, on analysis, some parts of the theory turn out to be correct, whereas others seem to be mistaken. As a beginning, we may distinguish the following claims, all of which have been made by cultural relativists:

1. Different societies have different moral codes.

2. There is no objective standard that can be used to judge one societal code better than another.

3. The moral code of our own society has no special status; it is merely one among many.

4. There is no "universal truth" in ethics—that is, there are no moral truths that hold for all peoples at all times.

5. The moral code of a society determines what is right within that society; that is, if the moral code of a society says that a certain action is right, then that action is right, at least within that society.

6. It is mere arrogance for us to try to judge the conduct of other peoples. We should adopt an attitude of tolerance toward the practices of other cultures.

Although it may seem that these six propositions go naturally together, they are independent of one another, in the sense that some of them might be true even if others are false. In what follows, we will try to identify what is correct in Cultural Relativism, but we will also be concerned to expose what is mistaken about it.

3. The Cultural Differences Argument

Cultural Relativism is a theory about the nature of morality. At first blush it seems quite plausible. However, like all such theories, it may be evaluated by subjecting it to rational analysis; and when we analyze Cultural Relativism we find that it is not so plausible as it first appears to be.

The first thing we need to notice is that at the heart of Cultural Relativism there is a certain *form of argument*. The strategy used by cultural relativists is to argue from facts about the differences between cultural outlooks to a conclusion about the status of morality. Thus we are invited to accept this reasoning:

1. The Greeks believed it was wrong to eat the dead, whereas the Callatians believed it was right to eat the dead.

2. Therefore, eating the dead is neither objectively right nor objectively wrong. It is merely a matter of opinion, which varies from culture to culture.

Or, alternatively:

1. The Eskimos see nothing wrong with infanticide, whereas Americans believe infanticide is immoral.

2. Therefore, infanticide is neither objectively right nor objectively wrong. It is merely a matter of opinion, which varies from culture to culture.

Clearly, these arguments are variations of one fundamental idea. They are both special cases of a more general argument, which says:

1. Different cultures have different moral codes.

2. Therefore, there is no objective "truth" in morality. Right and wrong are only matters of opinion, and opinions vary from culture to culture.

We may call this the *Cultural Differences Argument*. To many people, it is very persuasive. But from a logical point of view, is it a *sound* argument?

It is not sound. The trouble is that the conclusion does not really follow from the premise—that is, even if the premise is true, the conclusion still might be false. The premise concerns what people *believe*: in some societies, people believe one thing; in other societies, people believe differently. The conclusion, however, concerns *what really is the case*. The trouble is that this sort of conclusion does not follow logically from this sort of premise.

Consider again the example of the Greeks and Callatians. The Greeks believed it was wrong to eat the dead; the Callatians believed it was right. Does it follow, *from the mere fact that they disagreed*, that there is no objective truth in the matter? No, it does not follow; for it *could* be that the practice was objectively right (or wrong) and that one or the other of them was simply mistaken.

To make the point clearer, consider a very different matter. In some societies, people believe the earth is flat. In other societies, such as our own, people believe the earth is (roughly) spherical. Does it follow, *from the mere fact that they disagree*, that there is no "objective truth" in geography? Of course not; we would never draw such a conclusion because we realize that, in their beliefs about the world, the members of some societies might simply be wrong. There is no reason to think that if the world is round everyone must know it. Similarly, there is no reason to think that if there is moral truth everyone must know it. The fundamental mistake in the Cultural Differences Argument is that it attempts to derive a substantive conclusion about a subject (morality) from the mere fact that people disagree about it.

It is important to understand the nature of the point that is being made here. We are *not* saying (not yet, anyway) that the conclusion of the argument is false. Insofar as anything being said here is concerned, it is still an open question whether the conclusion is true. We *are* making a purely logical point and saying that the conclusion does *not follow* from the premise. This is important, because in order to determine whether the conclusion is true, we need arguments in its support. Cultural Relativism proposes this argument, but unfortunately the argument turns out to be fallacious. So it proves nothing.

4. The Consequences of Taking Cultural Relativism Seriously

Even if the Cultural Differences Argument is in valid, Cultural Relativism might still be true. What would it be like if it were true?

In the passage quoted above, William Graham Sumner summarizes the essence of Cultural Relativism. He says that there is no measure of right and wrong other than the standards of one's society: "The notion of right is in the folkways. It is not outside of them, of independent origin, and brought to test them. In the folkways, whatever is, is right."

Suppose we took this seriously. What would be some of the consequences?

1. *We could no longer say that the customs of other societies are morally inferior to our own.*

This, of course, is one of the main points stressed by Cultural Relativism. We would have to stop condemning other societies merely because they are "different." So long as we concentrate on certain examples, such as the funerary practices of the Greeks and Callatians, this may seem to be a sophisticated, enlightened attitude.

However, we would also be stopped from criticizing other, less benign practices. Suppose a society waged war on its neighbors for the purpose of taking slaves. Or suppose a society was violently anti-Semitic and its leaders set out to destroy the Jews. Cultural Relativism would preclude us from saying that either of these practices was wrong. We would not even be able to say that a society tolerant of Jews is *better* than the anti-Semitic society, for that would imply some sort of transcultural standard of comparison. The failure to condemn *these* practices does not seem "enlightened"; on the contrary, slavery and anti-Semitism seem wrong *wherever* they occur. Nevertheless, if we took Cultural Relativism seriously, we would have to admit that these social practices also are immune from criticism.

2. *We could decide whether actions are right or wrong just by consulting the standards of our society.*

Cultural Relativism suggests a simple test for determining what is right and what is wrong: all one has to do is ask whether the action is in accordance with the code of one's society.

Suppose a resident of South Africa is wondering whether his country's policy of *apartheid*—rigid racial segregation—is morally correct. All he has to do is ask whether this policy conforms to his society's moral code. If it does, there is nothing to worry about, at least from a moral point of view. This implication of Cultural Relativism is disturbing because few of us think that our society's code is perfect—we can think of ways it might be improved. Yet Cultural Relativism would not only forbid us from criticizing the codes of *other* societies; it would stop us from criticizing our own. After all, if right and wrong are relative to culture, this must be true for our own culture just as much as for others.

3. *The idea of moral progress is called into doubt.*

Usually, we think that at least some changes in our society have been for the better. (Some, of course, may have been changes for the worse.) Consider this example: Throughout most of Western history the place of women in society was very narrowly circumscribed. They could not own property; they could not vote or hold political office; with a few exceptions, they were not permitted to have paying jobs; and generally they were under the almost absolute control of their husbands. Recently much of this has changed, and most people think of it as progress.

If Cultural Relativism is correct, can we legitimately think of this as progress? Progress means replacing a way of doing things with a *better* way. But by what standard do we judge the new ways as better? If the old ways were in accordance with the social standards of their time, then Cultural Relativism would say it is a mistake to judge them by the standards of a different time. Eighteenth-century society was, in effect, a different society from the one we have now. To say that we have made progress implies a judgment that present-day society is better, and that is just the sort of transcultural judgment that, according to Cultural Relativism, is impermissible.

Our idea of social *reform* will also have to be reconsidered. A reformer such as Martin Luther King, Jr., seeks to change his society for the better. Within the constraints imposed by Cultural Relativism, there is one way this might be done. If a society is not living up to its own ideals, the reformer may be regarded as acting for the best: the ideals of the society are the standard by which we judge his or her proposals as worthwhile. But the "reformer" may not challenge the ideals themselves, for those ideals are by definition correct. According to Cultural Relativism, then, the idea of social reform makes sense only in this very limited way.

These three consequences of Cultural Relativism have led many thinkers to reject it as implausible on its face. It does make sense, they say, to condemn some practices, such as slavery and anti-Semitism, wherever they occur. It makes sense to think that our own society has made some moral progress, while admitting that it is still imperfect and in need of reform. Because Cultural Relativism says that these judgments make no sense, the argument goes, it cannot be right.

5. Why There is Less Disagreement than it Seems

The original impetus for Cultural Relativism comes from the observation that cultures differ dramatically in their views of right and wrong. But just how much do they differ? It is true that there are differences. However, it is easy to overestimate the extent of those differences. Often, when we examine what *seems* to be a dramatic difference, we find that the cultures do not differ nearly as much as it appears.

Consider a culture in which people believe it is wrong to eat cows. This may even be a poor culture, in which there is not enough food; still, the cows are not to be touched. Such a society would *appear* to have values very different from our own. But does it? We have not yet asked why these people will not eat cows. Suppose it is because they believe that after death the souls of humans inhabit the bodies of animals, especially cows, so that a cow may be someone's grandmother. Now do we want to say that their values are different from ours? No; the difference lies elsewhere. The difference is in our belief systems, not in our values. We agree that we shouldn't eat Grandma; we simply disagree about whether the cow *is* (or could be) Grandma.

The general point is this. Many factors work together to produce the customs of a society. The society's values are only one of them. Other matters, such as the religious and factual beliefs held by its members and the physical circumstances in which they must live, are also important. We cannot conclude, then, merely because customs differ, that there is a disagreement about *values*. The difference in customs may be attributable to some other aspect of social life. Thus there may be less disagreement about values than there appears to be.

Consider the Eskimos again. They often kill perfectly normal infants, especially girls. We do not approve of this at all; a parent who did this in our society would be locked up. Thus there appears to be a great difference in the values of our two cultures. But suppose we ask *why* the Eskimos do this. The explanation is not that they have less affection for their children or less respect for human life. An Eskimo family will always protect its babies if conditions permit. But they live in a harsh environment, where food is often in short supply. A fundamental postulate of Eskimo thought is: "Life is hard, and the margin of safety small." A family may want to nourish its babies but be unable to do so.

As in many "primitive" societies, Eskimo mothers will nurse their infants over a much longer period of time than mothers in our culture. The child will take nourishment from its mother's breast for four years, perhaps even longer. So even in the best of times there are limits to the number of infants that one mother can sustain. Moreover, the Eskimos are a nomadic people—unable to farm, they must move about in search of food. Infants must be carried, and a mother can carry only one baby in her parka as she travels and goes

about her outdoor work. Other family members can help, but this is not always possible.

Infant girls are more readily disposed of because, first, in this society the males are the primary food providers—they are the hunters, according to the traditional division of labor—and it is obviously important to maintain a sufficient number of food gatherers. But there is an important second reason as well. Because the hunters suffer a high casualty race, the adult men who die prematurely far outnumber the women who die early. Thus if male and female infants survived in equal numbers, the female adult population would greatly outnumber the male adult population. Examining the available statistics, one writer concluded that "were it not for female infanticide…there would be approximately one-and-a-half times as many females in the average Eskimo local group as there are food-producing males."

So among the Eskimos, infanticide does not signal a fundamentally different attitude toward children. Instead, it is a recognition that drastic measures are sometimes needed to ensure the family's survival. Even then, however, killing the baby is not the first option considered. Adoption is common; childless couples are especially happy to take a more fertile couple's "surplus." Killing is only the last resort. I emphasize this in order to show that the raw data of the anthropologists can be misleading; it can make the differences in values between cultures appear greater than they are. The Eskimos' values are not all that different from our values. It is only that life forces upon them choices that we do not have to make.

6. How All Cultures Have Some Values in Common

It should not be surprising that, despite appearances, the Eskimos are protective of their children. How could it be otherwise? How could a group survive that did *not* value its young? This suggests a certain argument, one which shows that all cultural groups must be protective of their infants:

1. Human infants are helpless and cannot survive if they are not given extensive care for a period of years.

2. Therefore, if a group did not care for its young, the young would not survive, and the older members of the group would not be replaced. After a while the group would die out.

3. Therefore, any cultural group that continues to exist must care for its young. Infants that are *not* cared for must be the exception rather than the rule.

Similar reasoning shows that other values must be more or less universal. Imagine what it would be like for a society to place no value at all on truth telling. When one person spoke to another, there would be no presumption at all that he was telling the truth—for he could just as easily be speaking falsely. Within that society, there would be no reason to pay attention to what anyone says. (I ask you what time it is, and you say "Four o'clock." But there is no presumption that you are speaking truly; you could just as easily have said the first thing that came into your head. So I have no reason to pay attention to your answer—in fact, there was no point in my asking you in the first place!) Communication would then be extremely difficult, if not impossible. And because complex societies cannot exist without regular communication among their members, society would become impossible. It follows that in any complex society there *must* be a presumption in favor of truthfulness. There may of course be exceptions to this rule: there may be situations in which it is thought to be permissible to lie. Nevertheless, these will be exceptions to a rule that *is* in force in the society.

Let me give one further example of the same type. Could a society exist in which there was no prohibition on murder? What would this be like? Suppose people were free to kill other people at will, and no one thought there was anything wrong with it. In such a "society," no one could feel secure. Everyone would have to be constantly on guard. People who wanted to survive would have to avoid other people as much as possible. This would inevitably result in individuals trying to become as self-sufficient as possible—after all, associating with others would be dangerous. Society on any large scale would collapse. Of course, people might band together in smaller groups with others that they *could* trust not to harm them. But notice what this means: they would be forming smaller societies that *did* acknowledge a rule against murder. The prohibition of murder, then, is a necessary feature of all societies.

There is a general theoretical point here, namely, that *there are some moral rules that all societies will have in common, because those rules are necessary for society to exist*. The rules against lying and murder are two examples. And in fact, we do find these rules in force in all viable cultures. Cultures may differ in what they regard as legitimate exceptions to the rules, but this disagreement exists against a background of agreement on the larger issues. Therefore, it is a mistake to overestimate the amount of difference between cultures. Not *every* moral rule can vary from society to society.

7. What Can be Learned from Cultural Relativism

At the outset, I said that we were going to identify both what is right and what is wrong in Cultural Relativism. Thus far I have mentioned only its mistakes: I have said that it rests on an invalid argument, that it has consequences that make it implausible on its face, and that the extent of cultural disagreement is far less than it implies. This all adds up to a pretty thorough repudiation of the theory. Nevertheless, it is still a very appealing idea, and the reader may have the feeling that all this is a little unfair. The theory *must* have something going for it, or else why has it been so influential? In fact, I think there is something right about Cultural Relativism, and now I want to say what that is. There are two lessons we should learn from the theory, even if we ultimately reject it.

1. Cultural Relativism warns us, quite rightly, about the danger of assuming that all our preferences are based on some absolute rational standard. They are not. Many (but not all) of our practices are merely peculiar to our society, and it is easy to lose sight of that fact. In reminding us of it, the theory does a service.

Funerary practices are one example. The Callatians, according to Herodotus, were "men who eat their fathers"—a shocking idea, to us at least. But eating the flesh of the dead could be understood as a sign of respect. It could be taken as a symbolic act that says: We wish this person's spirit to dwell within us. Perhaps this was the understanding of the Callatians. On such a way of thinking, burying the dead could he seen as an act of rejection, and burning the corpse as positively scornful. If this is hard to imagine, then we may need to have our imaginations stretched. Of course we may feel a visceral repugnance at the idea of eating human flesh in any circumstances. But what of it? This repugnance may be, as the relativists say, only a matter of what is customary in our particular society.

There are many other matters that we tend to think of in terms of objective right and wrong, but that are really nothing more than social conventions. Should women cover their breasts? A publicly exposed breast is scandalous in our society, whereas in other cultures it is unremarkable. Objectively speaking, it is neither right nor wrong—there is no objective reason why either custom is better. Cultural Relativism begins with the valuable insight that many of our practices are like this—they are only cultural products. Then it goes wrong by concluding that, because some practices are like this, *all* must be.

2. The second lesson has to do with keeping an open mind. In the course of growing up, each of us has acquired some strong feelings: we have learned to think of some types of conduct as acceptable, and others we have learned to regard as simply unacceptable. Occasionally, we may find those feelings challenged. We may encounter someone who claims that our feelings are mistaken. For example, we may have been taught that homosexuality is immoral, and we may feel quite uncomfortable around gay people and see them as alien and "different." Now someone suggests that this may be a mere prejudice; that there is nothing evil about homosexuality; that gay people are just people, like anyone else, who happen, through no choice of their own, to be attracted to others of the same sex. But because we feel so strongly about the matter, we may find it hard to take this seriously. Even after we listen to the arguments, we may still have the unshakable feeling that homosexuals *must* somehow, be an unsavory lot.

Cultural Relativism, by stressing that our moral views can reflect the prejudices of our society, provides an antidote for this kind of dogmatism. When he tells the story of the Greeks and Callatians, Herodotus adds:

> For if anyone, no matter who, were given the opportunity of choosing from amongst all the nations of the world the set of beliefs which he thought best, he would inevitably, after careful consideration of their relative merits, choose that of his own country. Everyone without exception believes his own native customs, and the religion he was brought up in, to be the best.

Realizing this can result in our having more open minds. We can come to understand that our feelings are not necessarily perceptions of the truth—they may be nothing more than the result of cultural conditioning. Thus when we hear it suggested that some element of our social code is *not* really the best and we find our selves instinctively resisting the suggestion, we might stop and remember this. Then we may be more open to discovering the truth, whatever that might be.

We can understand the appeal of Cultural Relativism, then, even though the theory has serious shortcomings. It is an attractive theory because it is based on a genuine insight—that many of the practices and attitudes we think so natural are really only cultural products. Moreover, keeping this insight firmly in view is important if we want to avoid arrogance and have open minds. These are important points, not to be taken lightly. But we can accept these points without going on to accept the whole theory.

Study Questions

1. What are some of the problems Rachels finds with relativism?

2. What are some of the cautionary tales to be learned from moral absolutism or objectivism?

3. What is the cultural differences argument, according to Rachels? What are its implications for relativism?

4. What questions would Benedict ask of Rachels?

5. What role does reasoning play in morality according to Rachels?

6. Which position is the stronger: some form of ethical relativism or some version of ethical absolutism? Could both theories be partly true? Explain.

7. Could Benedict respond to the absolutist that "the very eyes with which we see the problem are conditioned by the long traditional habits of our own society"? What are the implications of that view and does it rule out objectivism?

Aristotle

The Nicomachean Ethics
Book I: The Good for Man

Aristotle (384–322 BCE) was a Greek philosopher, student of Plato, and teacher of Alexander the Great. James Rachels (prior article) has remarked that Aristotle may have been the smartest human being to live thus far. Aristotle wrote original works in epistemology, metaphysics, ethics, poetry, theater, music, logic, rhetoric, linguistics, political philosophy, government, physics, biology, and zoology. Aristotle's physics profoundly shaped medieval thinking. St. Thomas Aquinas attempted to Christianize Aristotle, leaving a long, scholastic tradition in the Catholic Church. Aristotle is apparently the first human being to create a formal logic. While proficient, Aristotle's writings have not survived historically, with a majority of his writings now seemingly lost.

In this selection from his *Nichomachean Ethics*, Aristotle is concerned with gaining specific knowledge of the Good Life for human beings. Aristotle, like Plato and Socrates, thought that people readily mistake or wrongly aim at what they consider to be the Good Life. Often, in our time, we find that the Good Life is defined as happiness. While that is a start, happiness is sometimes used today to mean a joyful or joyous experience. Thus in the United States, if you ask the average college class where the happiest place on Earth is, you are likely to hear, "Disneyland." We have smiling happy faces and happy birthday parties. This is hardly what Aristotle had in mind concerning the Good Life. Rather, the Good Life was one of *eudaimonia*. For Aristotle, *eudaimonia* consisted in "that activity of the soul in accordance with virtue." Significantly, a life of *eudaimonia* was not simply a matter of having a specific, even repeated feeling, such as joy or pleasure, nor was it the simple possession of the prized possessions of one's culture. Rather, *eudaimonia* is a matter of an actively engaged rational being living according to virtue or excellence along with also having good fortune along the way. Hence, once an individual becomes a rational being and can live his or her life rationally according to virtue, then, all things considered, he or she should experience the fullness of life. When someone focuses upon primarily acquiring "stuff" in life, be it houses, boats, cars, and the like, the Good Life seems to recede to some distant, temporal horizon in which we envision being in possession of such "stuff." When the acquisition of "stuff" on a distant horizon becomes the goal, such horizons seem to continually recede into the future. Such a life is lived unfulfilled. However, all things considered, if one's rational activity is in accordance with virtue, *eudaimonia* should be accessible daily, though the goodness of an entire life cannot be judged by one day alone.

"The Proper Function of Man and Its Relation to the Good Life," from *The Nicomachean Ethics*, J.E.C. Welldon, trans. Prometheus Books, 1987, p. 9.

Chapter 7

The Good is Final and Self-Sufficient

Let us again return to the good we are seeking, and ask what it can be. It seems different in different actions and arts; it is different in medicine, in strategy, and in the other arts likewise. What then is the good of each? Surely that for whose sake everything else is done. In medicine this is health, in strategy victory, in architecture a house, in any other sphere something else, and in every action and pursuit the end; for it is for the sake of this that all men do whatever else they do. Therefore, if there is an end for all that we do, this will be the good achievable by action, and if there are more than one, these will be the goods achievable by action.

So the argument has by a different course reached the same point; but we must try to state this even more clearly. Since there are evidently more than one end, and we choose some of these (e.g., wealth, flutes, and in general instruments) for the sake of something else, clearly not all ends are final ends; but the chief good is evidently something final. Therefore, if there is only one final end, this will be what we are seeking, and if there are more than one, the most final of these will be what we are seeking. Now we call that which is in itself worthy of pursuit more final than that which is worthy of pursuit for the sake of something else, and that which is never desirable for the sake of something else more final than the things that are desirable both in themselves and for the sake of that other thing, and therefore we call final without qualification that which is always desirable in itself and never for the sake of something else.

Now such a thing happiness, above all else, is held to be; for this we choose always for self and never for the sake of something else, but honour, pleasure, reason, and every virtue we choose indeed for themselves (for if nothing resulted from them we should still choose each of them), but we choose them also for the sake of happiness, judging that by means of them we shall be happy. Happiness, on the other hand, no one chooses for the sake of these, nor, in general, for anything other than itself.

From the point of view of self-sufficiency the same result seems to follow; for the final good is thought to be self-sufficient. Now by self-sufficient we do not mean that which is sufficient for a man by himself, for one who lives a solitary life, but also for parents, children, wife, and in general for his friends and fellow citizens, since man is born for citizenship. But some limit must be set to this; for if we extend our requirement to ancestors and descendants and friends' friends we are in for an infinite series. Let us examine this question, however, on another occasion; the self-sufficient we now define as that which when isolated makes life desirable and lacking in nothing; and such we think happiness to be; and further we think it most desirable of all things, without being counted as one good thing among others—if it were so counted it would clearly be made more desirable by the addition of even the least of goods; for that which is added becomes an excess of goods, and of goods the greater is always more desirable. Happiness, then, is something final and self-sufficient, and is the end of action.

Presumably, however, to say that happiness is the chief good seems a platitude, and a clearer account of what it is still desired. This might perhaps be given, if we could first ascertain the function of man. For just as for a flute-player, a sculptor, or an artist, and, in general, for all things that have a function or activity, the good and the 'well' is thought to reside in the function, so would it seem to be for man, if he has a function. Have the carpenter, then, and the tanner certain functions or activities, and has man none? Is he born without a function? Or as eye, hand, foot, and in general each of the parts evidently has a function, may one lay it down that man similarly has a function apart from all these? What then can this be? Life seems to be common even to plants, but we are seeking what is peculiar to man. Let us exclude, therefore, the life of nutrition and growth. Next there would be a life of perception, but it also seems to be common even to the horse, the ox, and every animal. There remains, then, an active life of the element that has a rational principle; of this, one part has such a principle in the sense of being obedient to one, the other in the sense of possessing one and exercising thought. And, as 'life of the rational element' also has two meanings, we must state that life in the sense of activity is what we mean; for this seems to be the more proper sense of the term. Now if the function of man is an activity of soul which follows or implies a rational principle, and if we say 'so-and-so' and 'a good so-and-so' have a function which is the same in kind, e.g., a lyre, and a good lyre-player, and so without qualification in all cases, eminence in respect of goodness being added to the name of the function (for the function of a lyre-player is to play the lyre, and that of a good lyre-player is to do so well): if this is the case, and we state the function of man to be a certain kind of life, and this to be an activity or actions of the soul implying a rational principle, and the function of a good man to be the good and noble performance of these, and if any action is well performed when it is performed in accordance with the appropriate excellence: if this is the case, human good turns out to be activity of soul in accordance with virtue, and if there are more than one virtue, in accordance with the best and most complete.

But we must add 'in a complete life.' For one swallow does not make a summer, nor does one day; and so too one day, or a short time, does not make a man blessed and happy.

Let this serve as an outline of the good; for we must presumably first sketch it roughly, and then later fill in the details. But it would seem that anyone is capable of carrying on and articulating what has once been well outlined, and that time is a good discoverer or partner in such a work; to which facts the advances of the arts are due; for any one can add what is lacking. And we must also remember what has been said before, and not look for precision in all things alike, but in each class of things such precision

as accords with the subject-matter, and so much as is appropriate to the inquiry. For a carpenter and a geometer investigate the right angle in different ways; the former does so in so far as the right angle is useful for his work, while the latter inquires what it is or what sort of thing it is; for he is a spectator of the truth. We must act in the same way, then, in all other matters as well, that our main task may not be subordinated to minor questions. Nor must we demand the cause in all matters alike; it is enough in some cases that the fact be well established, as in the case of the first principles; the fact is the primary thing or first principle. Now of first principles we see some by induction, some by perception, some by a certain habituation, and others too in other ways. But each set of principles we must try to investigate in the natural way, and we must take pains to state them definitely, since they have a great influence on what follows. For the beginning is thought to be more than half of the whole, and many of the questions we ask are cleared up by it.

Chapter 8

We must consider it, however, in the light not only of our conclusion and our premises, but also of what is commonly said about it; for with a true view all the data harmonize, but with a false one the facts soon clash. Now goods have been divided into three classes, and some are described as external, others as relating to soul or to body; we call those that relate to soul most properly and truly goods, and psychical actions and activities we class as relating to soul. Therefore our account must be sound, at least according to this view, which is an old one and agreed on by philosophers. It is correct also in that we identify the end with certain actions and activities; for thus it falls among goods of the soul and not among external goods. Another belief which harmonizes with our account is that the happy man lives well and does well; for we have practically defined happiness as a sort of good life and good action. The characteristics that are looked for in happiness seem also, all of them, to belong to what we have defined happiness as being. For some identify happiness with virtue, some with practical wisdom, others with a kind of philosophic wisdom, others with these, or one of these, accompanied by pleasure or not without pleasure; while others include also external prosperity. Now some of these views have been held by many men and men of old, others by a few eminent persons; and it is not probable that either of these should be entirely mistaken, but rather that they should be right in at least some one respect or even in most respects.

With those who identify happiness with virtue or some one virtue our account is in harmony; for to virtue belongs virtuous activity. But it makes, perhaps, no small difference whether we place the chief good in possession or in use, in state of mind or in activity. For the state of mind may exist without producing any good result, as in a man who is asleep or in some other way quite inactive, but the activity cannot; for one who has the activity will of necessity be acting, and acting well. And as in the Olympic Games it is not the most beautiful and the strongest that are crowned but those who compete (for it is some of these that are victorious), so those who act win, and rightly win, the noble and good things in life.

Their life is also in itself pleasant. For pleasure is a state of soul, and to each man that which he is said to be a lover of is pleasant; e.g., not only is a horse pleasant to the lover of horses, and a spectacle to the lover of sights, but also in the same way just acts are pleasant to the lover of justice and in general virtuous acts to the lover of virtue. Now for most men their pleasures are in conflict with one another because these are not by nature pleasant, but the lovers of what is noble find pleasant the things that are by nature pleasant; and virtuous actions are such, so that these are pleasant for such men as well as in their own nature. Their life, therefore, has no further need of pleasure as a sort of adventitious charm, but has its pleasure in itself. For, besides what we have said, the man who does not rejoice in noble actions is not even good; since no one would call a man just who did not enjoy acting justly, nor any man liberal who did not enjoy liberal actions; and similarly in all other cases. If this is so, virtuous actions must be in themselves pleasant. But they are also good and noble, and have each of these attributes in the highest degree, since the good man judges well about these attributes; his judgement is such as we have described. Happiness then is the best, noblest, and most pleasant thing in the world, and these attributes are not severed as in the inscription at Delos:

> Most noble is that which is justest, and best is health; But pleasantest is it to win what we love.

For all these properties belong to the best activities; and these, or one—the best—of these, we identify with happiness.

Yet evidently, as we said, it needs the external goods as well; for it is impossible, or not easy, to do noble acts without the proper equipment. In many actions we use friends and riches and political power as instruments; and there are some things the lack of which takes the lustre from happiness, as good birth, goodly children, beauty; for the man who is very ugly in appearance or ill-born or solitary and childless is not very likely to be happy, and perhaps a man would be still less likely if he had thoroughly bad children or friends or had lost good children or friends by death. As we said, then, happiness seems to need this sort of prosperity in addition; for which reason some identify happiness with good fortune, though others identify it with virtue.

Chapter 9

How Happiness is Aquired

For this reason also the question is asked, whether happiness is to be acquired by learning or by habituation or some other sort of training, or comes in virtue of some divine providence or again by chance. Now if there is any gift of the gods to men, it is reasonable that happiness should be god-given, and most surely god-given of all human things inasmuch as it is the best. But this question would perhaps be more appropriate to another inquiry; happiness seems, however, even if it is not god-sent but comes as a result of virtue and some process of learning or training, to be among the most godlike things; for that which is the prize and end of virtue seems to be the best thing in the world, and something god-like and blessed.

It will also on this view be very generally shared; for all who are not maimed as regards their potentiality for virtue may win it by a certain kind of study and care. But if it is better to be happy thus than by chance, it is reasonable that the facts should be so, since everything that depends on the action of nature is by nature as good as it can be, and similarly everything that depends on art or any rational cause, and especially if it depends on the best of all causes. To entrust to chance what is greatest and most noble would be a very defective arrangement.

The answer to the question we are asking is plain also from the definition of happiness; for it has been said to be a virtuous activity of soul, of a certain kind. Of the remaining goods, some must necessarily pre-exist as conditions of happiness, and others are naturally co-operative and useful as instruments. And this will be found to agree with what we said at the outset; for we stated the end of political science to be the best end, and political science spends most of its pains on making the citizens to be of a certain character, viz. good and capable of noble acts.

It is natural, then, that we call neither ox nor horse nor any other of the animals happy; for none of them is capable of sharing in such activity. For this reason also a boy is not happy; for he is not yet capable of such acts, owing to his age; and boys who are called happy are being congratulated by reason of the hopes we have for them. For there is required, as we said, not only complete virtue but also a complete life, since many changes occur in life, and all manner of chances, and the most prosperous may fall into great misfortunes in old age, as is told of Priam in the Trojan Cycle; and one who has experienced such chances and has ended wretchedly no one calls happy.

Study Questions

1. Socrates claimed that the unexamined life is not worth living. What do you think he means by this? Do you agree or disagree and why? Aristotle claimed that the unplanned life was not worth examining. How does this relate to Socrates' claim? Does Aristotle add value to Socrates' claim?

2. Why does Aristotle claim that a life of seeking pleasure cannot yield *eudaimonia*?

3. What does Aristotle mean by rationality? What role does rationality play in Aristotle's view of *eudaimonia*?

4. When Aristotle claims that *eudaimonia* is self-sufficient, what does he mean? If someone suffers from envy—not jealousy— is that an indication that *eudaimonia* is lacking in that person's life?

5. Princess Diana, when she was married to the apparent future King of Great Britain, seemed to live a fairy-tale life, having two healthy, smart sons, international fame and admiration, and wealth; yet she claimed to be very unhappy, reportedly contemplating suicide on at least one occasion. Aristotle claims that *eudemonia* is the most desired life. Does the Aristotelian view of *eudaimonia* provide any insight into Princess Diana's unhappy life?

6. It was remarked in the introduction that St. Thomas Aquinas was an Aristotlean. Since Aristotle did not believe in the soul existing without a body, how could St. Thomas Aquinas Christianize Aristotle given the Christian view of salvation?

Utilitarianism

John Stuart Mill (1806–1873) was a British philosopher, economist, and civil servant. A defender of utilitarianism, Mill aspired to alleviate many social problems. He was an advocate of liberty generally, and specifically on the part of women. Mill served as a member of Parliament and played a prominent role in the articulation of 19th-century liberal political philosophy.

John Stuart Mill was the eldest son of the Scottish philosopher, historian, and economist James Mill and Harriet Burrow. John Stuart was educated by his father, with the advice and assistance of Jeremy Bentham, the founder of British Utilitarianism. Given a most rigorous upbringing and kept from socializing with children his own age, other than his siblings, John Stuart was to be the genius that would carry on the work of utilitarianism after his father and Bentham had died.

In his autobiography, Mill claims that by the age of three he was taught Greek. By the age of eight he had read *Aesop's Fables*, Xenophon's *Anabasis*, the whole of Herodotus' *History* as well as Lucian, Diogenes Laërtius, Isocrates, and six dialogues of Plato along with a great deal of history in English. Additionally, by the age of nine, he started learning Latin, Euclid, and algebra, as well as teaching his siblings. He went through all of the typical Latin and Greek authors. In his spare time, he read natural science and literary works such as *Don Quixote* and *Robinson Crusoe*. By the age of twelve, Mill started a thorough study of Medieval logic along with reading Aristotle's logical treatises in ancient Greek. At age fourteen, Mill moved to France for a year. The mountain scenery generated a lifelong appreciation of mountain landscapes as did the *joie de vivre* of the French way of life. In Montpellier, he studied chemistry, zoology, logic, and higher mathematics. By twenty, Mill suffered a nervous breakdown. He claimed it resulted from the great physical and mental arduousness of his studies. Eventually, the depression lifted.

At age 45, Mill married Harriet Taylor after 21 years of an intimate friendship. Considered brilliant in her own right, Taylor had a significant influence on Mill's work as he cites her influence in his final revision of *On Liberty*, which was published shortly after her death. Taylor died in 1858. *On Liberty*, as with Mill's other works in ethics, defends and applies his Utilitarianism. In the school of Bentham, Mill nonetheless adds further refinements to the Utilitarian project, specifically with regard to his distinction between higher and lower pleasures.

From *Utilitarianism*, 1861, Chapters 2 and 4.

What Utilitarianism Is

...The creed which accepts as the foundation of morals, Utility, or the Greatest Happiness Principle, holds that actions are right in proportion as they tend to promote happiness, wrong as they tend to produce the reverse of happiness. By happiness is intended pleasure, and the absence of pain; by unhappiness, pain, and the privation of pleasure. To give a clear view of the moral standard set up by the theory, much more requires to be said; in particular, what things it includes in the ideas of pain and pleasure; and to what extent this is left an open question. But these supplementary explanations do not affect the theory of life on which this theory of morality is grounded—namely, that pleasure, and freedom from pain, are the only things desirable as ends; and that all desirable things (which are as numerous in the utilitarian as in any other scheme) are desirable either for the pleasure inherent in themselves, or as a means to the promotion of pleasure and the prevention of pain.

Now, such a theory of life excites in many minds, and among them in some of the most estimable in feeling and purpose, inveterate dislike. To suppose that life has (as they express it) no higher end than pleasure—no better and nobler object of desire and pursuit—they designate as utterly mean and grovelling; as a doctrine worthy only of swine, to whom the followers of Epicurus were, at a very early period, contemptuously likened; and modern holders of the doctrine are occasionally made the subject of equally polite comparisons by its German, French, and English assailants.

When thus attacked, the Epicureans have always answered, that it is not they, but their accusers, who represent human nature in a degrading light; since the accusation supposes human beings to be capable of no pleasures except those of which swine are capable. If this supposition were true, the charge could not be gainsaid, but would then be no longer an imputation; for if the sources of pleasure were precisely the same to human beings and to swine, the rule of life which is good enough for the one would be good enough for the other. The comparison of the Epicurean life to that of beasts is felt as degrading, precisely because a beast's pleasures do not satisfy a human being's conception of happiness. Human beings have faculties more elevated than the animal appetites, and when once made conscious of them, do not regard anything as happiness which does not include their gratification. I do not, indeed, consider the Epicureans to have been by any means faultless in thawing out their scheme of consequences from the utilitarian principle. To do this in any sufficient manner, many Stoic, as well as Christian elements require to be included. But there is no known Epicurean theory of life which does not assign to the pleasures of the intellect, of the feelings and imagination, and of the moral sentiments, a much higher value as pleasures than to those of mere sensation. It must be admitted, however, that utilitarian writers in general have placed the superiority of mental over bodily pleasures chiefly in the greater permanency, safety, uncostliness, etc., of the former—that is, in their circumstantial advantages rather than in their intrinsic nature. And on all these points utilitarians have truly proved their case; but they might have taken the other, and, as it may be called, higher ground, with entire consistency. It is quite compatible with the principle of utility to recognise the fact, that some *kinds* of pleasure are more desirable and more valuable than others. It would be absurd that while, in estimating all other things, quality is considered as well as quantity, the estimation of pleasures should be supposed to depend on quantity alone.

If I am asked, what I mean by difference of quality in pleasures, or what makes one pleasure more valuable than another, merely as a pleasure, except its being greater in amount, there is but one possible answer. Of two pleasures, if there be one which all or almost all who have experience of both give a decided preference, irrespective of any feeling of moral obligation to prefer it, that is the more desirable pleasure. If one of the two is, by those who are competently acquainted with both, placed so far above the other that they prefer it, even though knowing it to be attended with a great amount of discontent, and would not resign it for any quantity of the other pleasure which their nature is capable of, we are justified in ascribing to the preferred enjoyment a superiority in quality, so far outweighing quantity as to render it, in comparison, of small account.

Now it is an unquestionable fact that those who are equally acquainted with, and equally capable of appreciating and enjoying, both, do give a most marked preference to the manner of existence which employs their higher faculties. Few human creatures would consent to be changed into any of the lower animals, for a promise of the fullest allowance of a beast's pleasures; no intelligent human being would consent to be a fool, no instructed person would be an ignoramus, no person of feeling and conscience would be selfish and base, even though they should be persuaded that the fool, the dunce, or the rascal is better satisfied with his lot than they are with theirs. They would not resign what they possess more than he for the most complete satisfaction of all the desires which they have in common with him. If they ever fancy they would, it is only in cases of unhappiness so extreme, that to escape from it they would exchange their lot for almost any other, however undesirable in their own eyes. A being of higher faculties requires more to make him happy, is capable probably of more acute suffering, and certainly accessible to it at more points, than one of an inferior type; but in spite of these liabilities, he can never really wish to sink into what he feels to be a lower grade of existence. We may give what explanation we please of this unwillingness; we may attribute it to pride, a name which is given indiscriminately to some of the most and to some of the least estimable feelings of which mankind are capable; we may refer it to the love of liberty and personal independence, an appeal to which was with the Stoics one of the most effective means for the inculcation of it; to the love of power, or to the love of excitement, both of which do really enter into and contribute to it: but its most appropriate appellation is a sense of dignity, which all human beings possess in one form or another,

and in some, though by no means in exact, proportion to their higher faculties, and which is so essential a part of the happiness of those in whom it is strong, that nothing which conflicts with it could be, otherwise than momentarily, an object of desire to them. Whoever supposes that this preference takes place at a sacrifice of happiness—that the superior being, in anything like equal circumstances, is not happier than the inferior—confounds the two very different ideas, of happiness, and content. It is indisputable that the being whose capacities of enjoyment are low, has the greatest chance of having them fully satisfied; and a highly endowed being will always feel that any happiness which he can look for, as the world is constituted, is imperfect. But he can learn to bear its imperfections, if they are at all bearable; and they will not make him envy the being who is indeed unconscious of the imperfections, but only because he feels not at all the good which those imperfections qualify. It is better to be a human being dissatisfied than a pig satisfied; better to be Socrates dissatisfied than a fool satisfied. And if the fool, or the pig, are of a different opinion, it is because they only know their own side of the question. The other party to the comparison knows both sides.

It may be objected, that many who are capable of the higher pleasures, occasionally, under the influence of temptation, postpone them to the lower. But this is quite compatible with a full appreciation of the intrinsic superiority of the higher. Men often, from infirmity of character, make their election for the nearer good, though they know it to be the less valuable; and this no less when the choice is between two bodily pleasures, than when it is between bodily and mental. They pursue sensual indulgences to the injury of health, though perfectly aware that health is the greater good. It may be further objected, that many who begin with youthful enthusiasm for everything noble, as they advance in years sink into indolence and selfishness. But I do not believe that those who undergo this very common change, voluntarily choose the lower description of pleasures in preference to the

higher. I believe that before they devote themselves exclusively to the one, they have already become incapable of the other. Capacity for the nobler feelings is in most natures a very tender plant, easily killed, not only by hostile influences, but by mere want of sustenance; and in the majority of young persons it speedily dies away if the occupations to which their position in life has devoted them, and the society into which it has thrown them, are not favourable to keeping that higher capacity in exercise. Men lose their high aspirations as they lose their intellectual tastes, because they have not time or opportunity for indulging them; and they addict themselves to inferior pleasures, not because they deliberately prefer them, but because they are either the only ones to which they have access, or the only ones which they are any longer capable of enjoying. It may be questioned whether any one who has remained equally susceptible to both classes of pleasures, ever knowingly and calmly preferred the lower; though many, in all ages, have broken down in an ineffectual attempt to combine both.

From this verdict of the only competent judges, I apprehend there can be no appeal. On a question which is the best worth having of two pleasures, or which of two modes of existence is the most grateful to the feelings, apart from its moral attributes and from its consequences, the judgment of those who are qualified by knowledge of both, or, if they differ, that of the majority among them, must be admitted as final. And there needs to be the less hesitation to accept this judgment respecting the quality of pleasures, since there is no other tribunal to be referred to even on the question of quantity. What means are there of determining which is the acutest of two pains, or the intensest of two pleasurable sensations, except the general suffrage of those who are familiar with both? Neither pains nor pleasures are homogeneous, and pain is always heterogeneous with pleasure. What is there to decide whether a particular pleasure is worth purchasing at the cost of a particular pain, except the feelings and judgment of the experienced? When, therefore, those feelings and judgment

declare the pleasures derived from the higher faculties to be preferable *in kind*, apart from the question of intensity, to those of which the animal nature, disjoined from the higher faculties, is susceptible, they are entitled on this subject to the same regard.

I have dwelt on this point, as being a necessary part of a perfectly just conception of Utility or Happiness, considered as the directive rule of human conduct. But it is by no means an indispensable condition to the acceptance of the utilitarian standard; for that standard is not the agent's own greatest happiness, but the greatest amount of happiness altogether; and if it may possibly be doubted whether a noble character is always the happier for its nobleness, there can be no doubt that it makes other people happier, and that the world in general is immensely a gainer by it. Utilitarianism, therefore, could only attain its end by the general cultivation of nobleness of character, even if each individual were only benefited by the nobleness of others, and his own, so far as happiness is concerned, were a sheer deduction from the benefit. But the bare enunciation of such an absurdity as this last, renders refutation superfluous.

According to the Greatest Happiness Principle, as above explained, the ultimate end, with reference to and for the sake of which all other things are desirable (whether we are considering our own good or that of other people), is an existence exempt as far as possible from pain, and as rich as possible in enjoyments, both in point of quantity and quality; the test of quality, and the rule for measuring it against quantity, being the preference felt by those who in their opportunities of experience, to which must be added their habits of self-consciousness and self-observation, are best furnished with the means of comparison. This, being, according to the utilitarian opinion, the end of human action, is necessarily also the standard of morality; which may accordingly be defined, the rules and precepts for human conduct, by the observance of which an existence such as has been described might be, to the greatest extent possible, secured to all mankind; and not to them only, but, so far as the nature of things admits, to the whole sentient creation...

The objectors to utilitarianism cannot always be charged with representing it in a discreditable light. On the contrary, those among them who entertain anything like a just idea of its disinterested character, sometimes find fault with its standard as being too high for humanity. They say it is exacting too much to require that people shall always act from the inducement of promoting the general interests of society. But this is to mistake the very meaning of a standard of morals, and confound the rule of action with the motive of it. It is the business of ethics to tell us what are our duties, or by what test we may know them; but no system of ethics requires that the sole motive of all we do shall be a feeling of duty; on the contrary, ninety-nine hundredths of all our actions are done from other motives, and rightly so done, if the rule of duty does not condemn them. It is the more unjust to utilitarianism that this particular misapprehension should be made a ground of objection to it, inasmuch as utilitarian moralists have gone beyond almost all others in affirming that the motive has nothing to do with the morality of the action, though much with the worth of the agent. He who saves a fellow-creature from drowning does what is morally right, whether his motive be duty, or the hope of being paid for his trouble; he who betrays the friend that trusts him, is guilty of a crime, even if his object be to serve another friend to whom he is under greater obligation. But to speak only of actions done from the motive of duty, and in direct obedience to principle: it is a misapprehension of the utilitarian mode of thought, to conceive it as implying that people should fix their minds upon so wide a generality as the world, or society at large. The great majority of good actions are intended not for the benefit of the world, but for that of individuals, of which the good of the world is made up; and the thoughts of the most virtuous man need not on these occasions travel beyond the particular persons concerned, except so far as is necessary to assure himself that in benefiting them he is not violating the rights, that is, the legitimate and authorised expectations, of any one else. The multiplication of happiness is, according to the utilitarian ethics, the object of virtue: the occasions on which any person (except one in a thousand) has it in his power to do this on an extended scale, in other words to be a public benefactor, are but exceptional; and on these occasions alone is he called on to consider public utility; in every other case, private utility, the interest or happiness of some few persons, is all he has to attend to. Those alone the influence of whose actions extends to society in general, need concern themselves habitually about so large an object. In the case of abstinences indeed—of things which people forbear to do from moral considerations, though the consequences in the particular case might be beneficial—it would be unworthy of an intelligent agent not to be consciously aware that the action is of a class which, if practised generally, would be generally injurious, and that this is the ground of the obligation to abstain from it. The amount of regard for the public interest implied in this recognition, is no greater than is demanded by every system of morals, for they all enjoin to abstain from whatever is manifestly pernicious to society...

Chapter IV: Of What Sort of Proof the Principle of Utility is Susceptible

It has already been remarked, that questions of ultimate ends do not admit of proof, in the ordinary acceptation of the term. To be incapable of proof by reasoning is common to all first principles; to the first premises of our knowledge, as well as to those of our conduct. But the former, being matters of fact, may be the subject of a direct appeal to the faculties which judge of fact—namely, our senses, and our internal consciousness. Can an appeal be made to the same faculties on questions of practical ends? Or by what other faculty is cognisance taken of them?

Questions about ends are, in other words, questions about what things are desirable. The utilitarian doctrine is, that happiness is desirable, and the only thing desirable, as an end; all other things being only desirable as means to that end. What ought to be required of this doctrine—what conditions is it requisite that the doctrine should fulfill—to make good its claim to be believed? The only proof capable of being given that an object is visible, is that people actually see it.

The only proof that a sound is audible, is that people hear it: and so of the other sources of our experience. In like manner, I apprehend, the sole evidence it is possible to produce that anything is desirable, is that people do actually desire it. If the end which the utilitarian doctrine proposes to itself were not, in theory and in practice, acknowledged to be an end, nothing could ever convince any person that it was so. No reason can be given why the general happiness is desirable, except that each person, so far as he believes it to be attainable, desires his own happiness. This, however, being a fact, we have not only all the proof which the case admits of; but all which it is possible to require, that happiness is a good: that each person's happiness is a good to that person, and the general happiness, therefore, a good to the aggregate of all persons. Happiness has made out its title as *one* of the ends of conduct, and consequently one of the criteria of morality.

But it has not, by this alone, proved itself to be the sole criterion. To do that, it would seem, by the same rule, necessary to show, not only that people desire happiness, but that they never desire anything else....

We have now, then, an answer to the question, of what sort of proof the principle of utility is susceptible. If the opinion which I have now stated is psychologically true—if human nature is so constituted as to desire nothing which is not either a part of happiness or a means of happiness, we can have no other proof; and we require no other, that these are the only things desirable. If so, happiness is the sole end of human action, and the promotion of it the test by which to judge of all human conduct; from whence it necessarily follows that it must be the criterion of morality, since a part is included in the whole.

And now to decide whether this is really so; whether mankind does desire nothing for itself but that which is a pleasure to them, or of which the absence is a pain; we have evidently arrived at a question of fact and experience, dependent, like all similar questions, upon evidence. It can only be determined by practised self-consciousness and self-observation, assisted by observation of others. I believe that these sources of evidence, impartially consulted, will declare that desiring a thing and finding it pleasant, aversion to it and thinking of it as painful, are phenomena entirely inseparable, or rather two parts of the same phenomenon; in strictness of language, two different modes of naming the same psychological fact: that to think of an object as desirable (unless for the sake of its consequences), and to think of it as pleasant, are one and the same thing; and that to desire anything, except in proportion as the idea of it is pleasant, is a physical and metaphysical impossibility.

Study Questions

1. What is Mill's definition of utilitarianism? What is his defense of the principle?

2. What does Mill mean in claiming that it is better to be Socrates unsatisfied than a pig satisfied?

3. What is the test to distinguish the higher and lower pleasures?

4. What sort of person would prefer the lower pleasures to the higher pleasures?

5. Might there be a distinction between higher–higher pleasures versus lower–higher pleasures with regard to aesthetic pleasures?

6. Can Utilitarianism adequately distinguish between moral acts and acts of supererogation?

7. We have a right to forego some present enjoyment for the sake of a future personal higher goal, but we have not the same right to restrict some other person from a present enjoyment for what we deem to be his or her higher future goal. Is utilitarianism a violator of human rights? Does it treat rights as expendable?

8. Nietzsche wrote, "If we possess our *why* of life we can put up with almost any *how*—Man does not strive after happiness; only the Englishman does that." (*Twilight of the Idols*). Do you agree or disagree with Nietzsche on the unimportance of the search for happiness?

Immanuel Kant

The Good Will and Morality

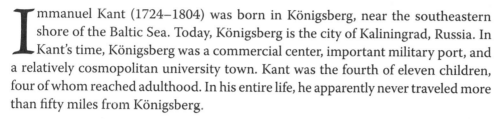

Immanuel Kant (1724–1804) was born in Königsberg, near the southeastern shore of the Baltic Sea. Today, Königsberg is the city of Kaliningrad, Russia. In Kant's time, Königsberg was a commercial center, important military port, and a relatively cosmopolitan university town. Kant was the fourth of eleven children, four of whom reached adulthood. In his entire life, he apparently never traveled more than fifty miles from Königsberg.

Kant showed a great aptitude for study at an early age. He was enrolled at the University of Königsberg by the age of 16. He studied philosophy and the new mathematical physics of Newton. The death of his father in 1746 undermined his hopes of remaining at the university. Disappointed, the next nine years were spent as a private tutor for a number of Königsberg families. In 1755, Kant was tutor to the family of Count Kayserling. Through the support of a friend, he was also able to return to his university studies, graduating as a doctor. For fifteen years he continued to labor in this subordinate position, his fame as writer and lecturer steadily increasing. On two occasions, he was disappointed in not obtaining a professorship at the University of Königsberg. In 1770, he obtained the chair of logic and metaphysics at the University of Königsberg.

Kant's life appears to have been one of meticulous regularity. He never married. His man-servant awoke him at 5:00 a.m. daily and claimed that Professor Kant never failed in thirty years to respond. After rising, Kant would study for two hours, go to the university to lecture for two hours, and then would return home to spend a few hours at his desk. Once his writing was concluded, he would leave to dine out, regularly changing restaurants so as to avoid the many people who would impose upon him with greetings or discussions. When he was more financially secure, Kant would invite guests to his own home for a meal and conversation. In his *Anthropology from a Pragmatic Point of View*, Kant writes, "The life that harmonizes best with our humanity is the life that involves, on a regular basis, good meals with good conversation." As he loved the *ducere caenam* of the Romans, he often prolonged the conversation till late in the afternoon. However, by late afternoon, he would take his famously punctual walk for at least an hour, whatever the weather, it was said. Evenings were spent in lighter reading, except an hour or so in preparation for the next day's lectures. He would then retire between nine and ten.

Kant is best known for his critical philosophy, three extensive, primary critiques, but he worked in other areas as well. He made the significant astronomical discovery regarding the retardation of the rotation of the Earth and was awarded the Berlin Academy Prize in 1754.

From *Fundamental Principles of the Metaphysic of Morals*, T.K. Abbott, trans. London, 1873.

William Thomson, aka Lord Kelvin, wrote in 1897:

Kant pointed out in the middle of last century, what had not previously been discovered by mathematicians or physical astronomers, that the frictional resistance against tidal currents on the earth's surface must cause a diminution of the earth's rotational speed. This immense discovery in Natural Philosophy seems to have attracted little attention—indeed to have passed quite unnoticed—among mathematicians, and astronomers, and naturalists, until about 1840, when the doctrine of energy began to be taken to heart.

Thomas Huxley wrote in 1869:

The sort of geological speculation to which I am now referring (geological aetiology, in short) was created as a science by that famous philosopher, Immanuel Kant, when, in 1775 he wrote his General Natural History and Theory of the Celestial Bodies; or, An Attempt to Account for the Constitutional and Mechanical Origin of the Universe, upon Newtonian Principles.

In the *General History of Nature and Theory of Celestial Bodies*, Kant presented the Nebular Hypothesis, in which he argued that our solar system formed from a large cloud of gas, a nebula. Kant also argued that the Milky Way was itself a large disk of stars, which may have formed from a much larger spinning cloud of gas. Additionally, he suggested the possibility that other nebulae might also be similarly large and distant disks of stars. It was not until the late 1920s that observations by Edwin Hubble confirmed that the Milky Way was one galaxy amongst many other galaxies.

Kant was a prolific philosopher creating one of the most complex, subtle, powerful and influential philosophical systems in intellectual history. He concluded his *Critique of Practical Reason* (1788) with, "Two things fill the mind with ever new and increasing admiration and awe, the more often and steadily we reflect upon them: the starry heavens above me and the moral law within me..." The moral law played a central part in Kant's overall philosophy. The autonomous agent was the central player in Kant's moral system and was to be treated as an end in itself and never merely as a means. Kant offered autonomous agents a test for checking if their actions were moral in so far as, and to the extent that, such actions reflected this condition of equality amongst a community of ends or autonomous agents. The test is known as the Categorical Imperative, as it requires conceptualizing one's action as applying to the category or applying categorically to the population of autonomous beings. In the first formulation of the Categorical Imperative, it takes the form of a question thereby allowing autonomous agents to determine whether their actions are open to all autonomous agents. If an action fails the test of the categorical imperative, then that action fails to reflect the moral equality of all autonomous beings.

Kant was also concerned with distinguishing between actions that have moral worth from those actions that are merely consistent with the law-like status of the Categorical Imperative or morality. Hence, for Kant, actions having moral worth will not only pass the test of the Categorical Imperative but will also be performed from duty or a sense of respect for law. Thus, in the following selection, you will discover the central importance for Kant of the Good Will.

In closing, here is a quote from a student of Professor Kant:

I have had the good fortune to know a philosopher who was my teacher. In the vigor of life he had the same youthful gaiety of heart that now follows him, I believe, into old age. His open forehead, built for thought, was the seat of imperturbable cheerfulness and joy; the most pregnant discourse flowed from his lips; wit, humor, and raillery came to him at will, and his instructions had all the charm of an entertainment...History in all its branches, natural science, physics mathematics, and experience were the materials that gave interest to his lectures and his conversation; nothing worthy of study was to him indifferent; no faction or sect, no selfishness or vanity, had for him the least attraction, compared with the extension and elucidation of truth. He excited and pleasantly impelled us to mental independence; despotism was foreign to his nature. This man, whom I name with the deepest gratitude and respect, is Immanuel Kant; his image rises before me surrounded with pleasing recollections!

First Section

Transition from the Common Rational Knowledge of Morality to the Philosophical

Nothing can possibly be conceived in the world, or even out of it, which can be called good without qualification, except a Good Will. Intelligence, wit, judgment, and the other *talents* of the mind, however they may be named, or courage, resolution, perseverance, as qualities of temperament, are undoubtedly good and desirable in many respects; but these gifts of nature may also become extremely bad and mischievous if the will which is to make use of them, and which, therefore, constitutes what is called *character*, is not good. It is the same with the *gifts of fortune*. Power, riches, honor, even health, and the general well-being and contentment with one's condition which is called *happiness*, inspire pride, and often presumption, if there is not a good will to correct the influence of these on the mind, and with this also to rectify the whole principle of acting, and adapt it to its end. The sight of a being who is not adorned with a single feature of a pure and good will, enjoying unbroken prosperity, can never give pleasure to an impartial rational spectator. Thus a good will appears to constitute the indispensable condition even of being worthy of happiness.

There are even some qualities which are of service to this good will itself, and may facilitate its action, yet which have no intrinsic unconditional value, but always presuppose a good will, and this qualifies the esteem that we justly have for them, and does not permit us to regard them as absolutely good. Moderation in the affections and passions, self-control and calm deliberation are not only good in many respects, but even seem to constitute part of the intrinsic worth of the person; but they are far from deserving to be called good without qualification, although they have been so unconditionally praised by the ancients. For without the principles of a good will, they may become extremely bad, and the coolness of a villain not only makes him far more dangerous, but also directly makes him more abominable in our eyes than he would have been without it.

A good will is good not because of what it performs or effects, not by its aptness for the attainment of some proposed end, but simply by virtue of the volition, that is, it is good in itself, and considered by itself is to be esteemed much higher than all that can be brought about by it in favor of any inclination, nay, even of the sum total of all inclinations. Even if it should happen that, owing to special disfavor of fortune, or the niggardly provision of a stepmotherly nature, this will should wholly lack power to accomplish its purpose, if with its greatest efforts it should yet achieve nothing, and there should remain only the good will (not, to be sure, a mere wish, but the summoning of all means in our power), then, like a jewel, it would still shine by its own light, as a thing which has its own value in itself. Its usefulness or fruitfulness can neither add to nor take away anything from this value. It would be, as it were, only the setting to enable us to handle it the more conveniently in common commerce, or to attract to it the attention of those who are not yet connoisseurs, but not to recommend it to true connoisseurs, or to determine its value.

There is, however, something so strange in this idea of the absolute value of the mere will, in which no account is taken of its utility, that not withstanding the thorough assent of even common reason to the idea, yet a suspicion must arise that it may perhaps really be the product of mere high-flown fancy, and that we may have misunderstood the purpose of nature in assigning reason as the governor of our will. Therefore we will examine this idea from this point of view.

In the physical constitution of an organized being, that is, a being adapted suitably to the purposes of life, we assume it as a fundamental principle that no organ for any purpose will be found but what is also the fittest and best adapted for that purpose. Now in a being which has reason and a will, if the proper object of nature were its *conservation*, its *welfare*, in a word, its *happiness*, then nature would have hit upon a very bad arrangement in selecting the reason of the creature to carry out this purpose. For all the actions which the creature has to perform with a view to this purpose, and the whole role of its conduct, would be far more surely prescribed to it by instinct, and that end would have been attained thereby much more certainly than it ever can be by reason. Should reason have been communicated to this favored creature over and above, it must only have served it to contemplate the happy constitution of its nature, to admire it, to congratulate itself thereon, and to feel thankful for it to the beneficent cause, but not that it should subject its desires to that weak and delusive guidance, and meddle bunglingly with the purpose of nature. In a word, nature would have taken care that reason should not break forth into *practical exercise*, nor have the presumption, with its weak insight, to think out for itself the plan of happiness, and of the means of attaining it. Nature would not only have taken on herself the choice of the ends, but also of the means, and with wise foresight would have entrusted both to instinct.

And, in fact, we find that the more a cultivated reason applies itself with deliberate purpose to the enjoyment of life and happiness, so much the more does the man fail of true satisfaction. And from this circumstance there arises in many, if they are candid enough to confess it, a certain degree of *misology*, that is, hatred of reason, especially in the case of those who are most experienced in the use of it, because after calculating all the advantages they derive, I do not say from the invention of all the arts of common luxury, but even from the sciences (which seem to them to be after all only a luxury of the understanding), they find that they have, in fact, only brought more trouble on their shoulders, rather than gained in happiness; and they end by envying, rather than despising, the more common stamp of men who keep closer to the guidance of mere instinct, and do not allow their reason much influence on their conduct. And this we must admit, that the judgment of those who would very much lower the lofty eulogies of the advantages which reason gives us in regard to the happiness and satisfaction of life, or who would even reduce them below zero, is by no means morose or ungrateful to the goodness with which the world is governed, but that there lies at the root of these judgments the idea that our existence has a different and far nobler end, for which, and not for happiness, reason is properly intended, and which must, therefore, be regarded as the supreme condition to which the private ends of man must, for the most part, be postponed.

For as reason is not competent to guide the will with certainty in regard to its objects and the satisfaction of all our wants (which it to some extent even multiplies), this being an end to which an implanted instinct would have led with much greater certainty; and since, nevertheless, reason is imparted to us as a practical facility, *i.e.*, as one which is to have influence on the *will*, therefore, admitting that nature generally in the distribution of her capacities has adapted the means to the end, its true destination must be to produce a *will*, not merely good as a *means* to something else, but *good in itself* for which reason was absolutely necessary. This will then, though not indeed the sole and complete good, must be the supreme good and the condition of every other, even of the desire of happiness. Under these circumstances, there is nothing inconsistent with the wisdom of nature in the fact that the cultivation of the reason, which is requisite for the first and unconditional purpose, does in many ways interfere, at least in this life, with the attainment of the second, which is always conditional, namely, happiness. Nay, it may even reduce it to nothing, without nature thereby failing of her purpose. For reason recognizes the establishment of a good will as its highest practical destination, and in attaining this purpose is capable only of a satisfaction of its own proper kind, namely, that from the attainment of an end, which end again is determined by reason only, notwithstanding that this may involve many a disappointment to the ends of inclination.

We have then to develop the notion of a will which deserves to be highly esteemed for itself, and is good without a view to anything further, a notion which exists already in the sound natural understanding, requiring rather to be cleared up than to be taught, and which in estimating the value of our actions always takes the first place, and constitutes the condition of all the rest. In order to do this we will take the notion of duty, which includes that of a good will, although implying certain subjective restrictions and hindrances. These, however, far from concealing it, or rendering it unrecognizable, rather bring it out by contrast, and make it shine forth so much the brighter.

I omit here all actions which are already recognized as inconsistent with duty, although they may be useful for this or that purpose, for with these the question whether they are done *from duty* cannot arise at all, since they even conflict with it. I also set aside those actions which really conform to duty, but to which men have *no* direct *inclination*, performing them because they are impelled thereto by some other inclination. For in this case we can readily distinguish whether the action which agrees with duty is done *from duty*, or from a selfish view. It is much harder to make this distinction when the action accords with duty, and the subject has besides a *direct* inclination to it. For example, it is always a matter of duty that a dealer should not overcharge an inexperienced purchaser, and wherever there is much commerce the prudent tradesman does not overcharge, but keeps a fixed price for everyone, so that a child buys of him as well as any other. Men are thus *honestly* served; but this is not enough to make us believe that the tradesman has so acted from duty and from principles of honesty: his own advantage required it; it is out of the question in this case to suppose that he might besides have a direct inclination in favor of the buyers, so that, as it were, from love he should give no advantage to one over another. Accordingly the action was done neither from duty nor from direct inclination, but merely with a selfish view.

On the other hand, it is a duty to maintain one's life; and, in addition, everyone has also a direct inclination to do so. But on this account the often anxious care which most men take for it has no intrinsic worth, and their maxim has no moral import. They preserve their life *as duty requires*, no doubt, but not *because duty requires*. On the other hand, if adversity and hopeless sorrow have completely taken away the relish for life; if the unfortunate one, strong in mind, indignant at his fate rather than desponding or dejected, wishes for death, and yet preserves his life without loving it—not from inclination or fear, but from duty—then his maxim has a moral worth.

To be beneficent when we can is a duty; and besides this, there are many minds so sympathetically constituted that, without any other motive of vanity or self-interest, they find a pleasure in spreading joy around them and can take delight in the satisfaction of others so far as it is their own work. But I maintain that in such a case an action of this kind, however proper, however amiable it may be, has nevertheless no true moral worth, but is on a level with other inclinations, *e.g.*, the inclination to honor, which, if it is happily directed to that which is in fact of public utility and accordant with duty, and consequently honorable, deserves praise and encouragement, but not esteem. For the maxim lacks the moral import, namely, that such actions be done *from duty*, not from inclination. Put the case that the mind of that philanthropist were clouded by sorrow of his own, extinguishing all sympathy with the lot of others, and that while he still has the power to benefit others in distress, he is not touched by their trouble because he is absorbed with his own; and now suppose that he tears himself out of this dead insensibility, and performs the action without any inclination to it, but simply from duty, then first has his action its genuine moral worth. Further still; if nature has put little sympathy in the heart of this or that man; if he, supposed to be an upright man, is by temperament cold and indifferent to the sufferings of others, perhaps because in respect of his own he is provided with the special gift of patience and fortitude, and supposes, or even requires, that others should have the same—and such a man would certainly not be the meanest product of nature—but if nature had not specially framed him for a philanthropist, would he not still find in himself a source from whence to give himself a far higher worth than that of a good-natured temperament could be? Unquestionably. It is just in this that the moral worth of the character is brought out which is incomparably the highest of all, namely, that he is beneficent, not from inclination, but from duty.

To secure one's own happiness is a duty, at least indirectly; for discontent with one's conditions,

under a pressure of many anxieties and amidst unsatisfied wants, might easily become a great *temptation to transgression of duty*. But here again, without looking to duty all men have already the strongest and most intimate inclination to happiness, because it is just in this idea that all inclinations are combined in one total. But the precept of happiness is often of such a sort that it greatly interferes with some inclinations, and yet a man cannot form any definite and certain conception of the sum of satisfaction of all of them which is called happiness. It is not then to be wondered at that a single inclination, definite both as to what it promises and as to the time within which it can be gratified, is often able to overcome such a fluctuating idea, and that a gouty patient, for instance, can choose to enjoy what he likes, and to suffer what he may, since, according his calculation, on this occasion at least, he has [only] not sacrificed the enjoyment of the present moment to a possibly mistaken expectation of a happiness which is supposed to be found in health. But even in this case, if the general desire for happiness did not influence his will, and supposing that in his particular case health was not a necessary element in this calculation, there yet remains in this, as in all other cases, this law, namely, that he should promote his happiness not from inclination but from duty, and by this would his conduct first acquire true moral worth.

It is in this manner, undoubtedly, that we are to understand those passages of Scripture also in which we are commanded to love our neighbor, even our enemy. For love, as an affection, can not be commanded, but beneficence for duty's sake may; even though we are not impelled to it by any inclination—nay, are even repelled by a natural and unconquerable aversion. This is *practical* love, and not *pathological*—a love which is seated in the will, and not in the propensions of sense—in principles of action and not of tender sympathy; and it is this love alone which can be commanded.

The second[1] proposition is: That an action done from duty derives its moral worth, *not from the purpose* which is to be attained by it, but from the maxim by which it is determined, and therefore does not depend on the realization of the object of the action, but merely on the *principle of volition* by which the action has taken place, without regard to any object of desire. It is clear from what precedes that the purposes which we may have in view of our actions or their effects regarded as ends and springs of the will, cannot give to actions any unconditional or moral worth. In what, then, can their worth lie, if it is not to consist in the will and in reference to its expected effect? It cannot lie anywhere but in the *principle of the will* without regard to the ends which can be attained by the action. For the will stands between its *à priori* principle, which is formal, and its *à posteriori* spring, which is material, as between two roads, and as it must be determined by something, it follows that it must be determined by the formal principle of volition when an action is done from duty, in which case every material principle has been withdrawn from it.

The third proposition, which is a consequence of the two preceding, I would express thus: *Duty is the necessity of acting from respect for the law.* I may have *inclination* for an object as the effect of my proposed action, but I cannot have *respect* for it, just for this reason, that it is an effect and not an energy of will. Similarly, I cannot have respect for inclination, whether my own or another's; I can at most, if my own, approve it; if another's sometimes even love it; *i.e.*, look on it as favorable to my own interest. It is only what is connected with my will as a principle, by no means as an effect—what does not subserve my inclination, but overpowers it, or at least in case of choice excludes it from its calculation—in other words, simply the law of itself, which can be an object of respect, and hence a command. Now an action done from duty must wholly exclude the influence of inclination, and with it every object of the will, so that nothing remains which can determine the will except objectively the *law*, and subjectively *pure respect* for this

practical law, and consequently the maxim[2] that I should follow this law even to the thwarting of all my inclinations.

Thus the moral worth of an action does not lie in the effect expected from it, nor in any principle of action which requires to borrow its motive from this expected effect. For all these effects—agreeableness of one's condition, and even the promotion of the happiness of others—could have been also brought about by other causes, so that for this there would have been no need of the will of a rational being; whereas it is in this alone that the supreme and unconditional good can be found. The pre-eminent good which we call moral can therefore consist in nothing else than the *conception of law* in itself, *which certainly is only possible in a rational being*, insofar as this conception, and not the expected effect, determines the will. This is a good which is already present in the person who acts accordingly, and we have not to wait for it to appear first in the result.

But what sort of law can that be, the conception of which must determine the will, even without paying any regard to the effect expected from it, in order that this will may be called good absolutely and without qualification? As I have deprived the will of every impulse which could arise to it from obedience to any law, there remains nothing but the universal conformity of its actions to law in general, which alone is to serve the will as a principle, *i.e.*, I am never to act otherwise than so *that I could also will that my maxim should become a universal law.* Here now, it is the simple conformity to law in general, without assuming any particular law applicable to certain actions, that serves the will as its principle, and must so serve it, if duty is not to be a vain delusion and a chimerical notion. The common reason of men in its practical judgments perfectly coincides with this, and always has in view the principle here suggested. Let the question be, for example: May I when in distress make a promise with the intention not to keep it? I readily distinguish here between the two significations which the question may have. Whether it is prudent, or whether it is right, to make a false promise. The former may undoubtedly often be the case. I see clearly indeed that it is not enough to extricate myself from a present difficulty by means of this subterfuge, but it must be well considered whether there may not hereafter spring from this lie much greater inconvenience than that from which I now free myself, and as, with all my supposed *cunning*, the consequences cannot be so easily foreseen but that credit once lost may be much more injurious to me than any mischief which I seek to avoid at present, it should be considered whether it would not be more *prudent* to act herein according to a universal maxim, and to make it a habit to promise nothing except with the intention of keeping it. But it is soon clear to me that such a maxim will still only be based on the fear of consequences. Now it is a wholly different thing to be truthful from duty, and to be so from apprehension of injurious consequences. In the first case, the very notion of the action already implies a law for me; in the second case, I must first look about elsewhere to see what results may often be combined with it which would affect myself. For to deviate from the principle of duty is beyond all doubt wicked; but to be unfaithful to my maxim of prudence may often be very advantageous to me, although to abide by it is certainly safer. The shortest way, however, and an unerring one, to discover the answer to this question whether a lying promise is consistent with duty, is to ask myself, Should I be content that my maxim (to extricate myself from difficulty by a false promise) should hold good as a universal law, for myself as well as for others? and should I be able to say to myself, "Everyone may make a deceitful promise when he finds himself in a difficulty from which he cannot otherwise extricate himself"? Then I presently become aware that while I can will the lie, I can by no means will that lying should be a universal law. For with such a law there would be no promises at all, since it would be in vain to allege my intention in regard to my future actions to those who would not believe this allegation, or if they over-hastily did so, would pay me back in my own coin. Hence my maxim, as soon as it

should be made a universal law, would necessarily destroy itself.

I do not, therefore, need any far-reaching penetration to discern what I have to do in order that my will may be morally good. Inexperienced in the course of the world, incapable of being prepared for all its contingencies, I only ask myself: Canst thou also will that thy maxim should be a universal law? If not, then it must be rejected, and that not because of a disadvantage accruing from it to myself or even to others, but because it cannot enter as a principle into a possible universal legislation, and reason extorts from me immediate respect for such legislation. I do not indeed as yet *discern* on what this respect is based (this the philosopher may inquire), but at least I understand this, that it is an estimation of the worth which far outweighs all worth of what is recommended by inclination, and that the necessity of acting from *pure* respect for the practical law is what constitutes duty, to which every other motive must give place, because it is the condition of a will being good *in itself*, and the worth of such a will is above everything.

Thus, then, without quitting the moral knowledge of common human reason, we have arrived at its principle. And although, no doubt, common men do not conceive it in such an abstract and universal form, yet they always have it really before their eyes, and use it as the standard of their decision. Here it would be easy to show how, with this compass in hand, men are well able to distinguish, in every case that occurs, what is good, what bad, conformably to duty or inconsistent with it, if, without in the least teaching them anything new, we only, like Socrates, direct their attention to the principle they themselves employ; and that therefore we do not need science and philosophy to know what we should do to be honest and good, yea, even wise and virtuous. Indeed we might well have conjectured beforehand that the knowledge of what every man is bound to do, and therefore also to know, would be within the reach of every man, even the commonest. Here we cannot forbear admiration when we see how great an advantage the practical judgment has over the theoretical in the common understanding of men. In the latter, if common reason ventures to depart from the laws of experience and from the perceptions of the senses it falls into mere inconceivabilities and self-contradictions, at least into chaos of uncertainty, obscurity, and instability. But in the practical sphere it is just when the common understanding excludes all sensible springs from practical laws that its power of judgment begins to show itself to advantage. It then becomes even subtle, whether it be that it chicanes with its own conscience or with other claims respecting what is to be called right, or whether it desires for its own instruction to determine honestly the worth of actions; and, in the latter case, it may even have as good a hope of hitting the mark as any philosopher whatever can promise himself. Nay, it is almost more sure of doing so, because the philosopher cannot have any other principle, while he may easily perplex his judgment by a multitude of considerations foreign to the matter, and so turn aside from the right way. Would it not therefore be wiser in moral concerns to acquiesce in the judgment of common reason or at most only to call in philosophy for the purpose of rendering the system of morals more complete and intelligible, and its rules more convenient for use (especially for disputation), but not so as to draw off the common understanding from its happy simplicity, or to bring it by means of philosophy into a new path of inquiry and instruction?

Innocence is indeed a glorious thing, only, on the other hand, it is very sad that it cannot well maintain itself, and is easily seduced. On this account even wisdom—which otherwise consists more in conduct than in knowledge—yet has need of science, not in order to learn from it, but to secure for its precepts admission and permanence. Against all the commands of duty which reason represents to man as so deserving of respect, he feels in himself a powerful counterpoise in his wants and inclinations, the entire satisfaction of which he sums under the name of happiness. Now reason issues its commands unyieldingly, without promising anything to the inclinations, and, as it were, with disregard and contempt for these claims, which are so impetuous, and at the same time so plausible, and which will not allow themselves to be suppressed by any command. Hence there arises a natural *dialectic*, i.e., a disposition, to argue against these strict laws of duty and to question their validity, or at least their purity and strictness; and, if possible, to make them more accordant with our wishes and inclinations, that is to say, to corrupt them at their very source, and entirely to destroy their worth—a thing which even common practical reason cannot ultimately call good.

Thus is the *common reason of man* compelled to go out of its sphere, and to take a step into the field of a *practical philosophy*, not to satisfy any speculative want (which never occurs to it as long as it is content to be mere sound reason), but even on practical grounds, in order to attain in it information and clear instruction respecting the source of its principle, and the correct determination of it in opposition to the maxims which are based on wants and inclinations, so that it may escape from the perplexity of opposite claims, and not run the risk of losing all genuine moral principles through the equivocation into which it easily falls. Thus, when practical reason cultivates itself, there insensibly arises in it a dialectic which forces it to seek aid in philosophy, just as happens to it in its theoretic use; and in this case, therefore, as well as in the other, it will find rest nowhere but in a thorough critical examination of our reason.

Study Questions

1. What is the Good Will, according to Kant? What are the "gifts of nature" and the "gifts of fortune," according to Kant? How do these differ from the Good Will?

2. In Aristotle's virtue theory he is focused upon happiness. What role does happiness play in Kant's moral theory?

3. What is the distinction between acting according to duty and acting consistent with duty?

4. Can you give examples of wrong actions that seem to perfectly fit Kant's test of the Categorical Imperative? How would Kant treat kidnapping or cutting in line?

5. What does Kant's Categorical Imperative have in common with the popular, typically scolding, question, "What if everyone did that?"

Plato

The Myth of Gyges' Ring

Glaucon: If you please, then, I will revive the argument of Thrasymachus. And first I will speak of the nature and origin of justice according to the common view of them. Secondly, I will show that all men who practice justice do so against their will, of necessity, but not as a good. And thirdly, I will argue that there is reason in this view, for the life of the unjust is after all better far than the life of the just—if what they say is true, Socrates, since I myself am not of their opinion. But still I acknowledge that I am perplexed when I hear the voices of Thrasymachus and myriads of others dinning in my ears; and, on the other hand, I have never yet heard the superiority of justice to injustice maintained by anyone in a satisfactory way. I want to hear justice praised in respect of itself; then I shall be satisfied, and you are the person from whom I think that I am most likely to hear this; and therefore I will praise the unjust life to the utmost of my power, and my manner of speaking will indicate the manner in which I desire to hear you too praising justice and censuring injustice. Will you say whether you approve of my proposal?

Socrates: Indeed I do; nor can I imagine any theme about which a man of sense would oftener wish to converse.

Glaucon: I am delighted, he replied, to hear you say so, and shall begin by speaking, as I proposed, of the nature and origin of justice.

They say that to do injustice is, by nature, good; to suffer injustice, evil; but that the evil is greater than the good. And so when men have both done and suffered injustice and have had experience of both, not being able to avoid the one and obtain the other, they think that they had better agree among themselves to have neither; hence there arise laws and mutual covenants; and that which is ordained by law is termed by them lawful and just. This they affirm to be the origin and nature of justice:—it is a mean or compromise, between the best of all, which is to do injustice and not be punished, and the worst of all, which is to suffer injustice without the power of retaliation; and justice, being at a middle point between the two, is tolerated not as a good, but as the lesser evil, and honoured by reason of the inability of men to do injustice. For no man who is worthy to be called a man would ever submit to such an agreement if he were able to resist; he would be mad if he did. Such is the received account, Socrates, of the nature and origin of justice.

Now that those who practice justice do so involuntarily and because they have not the power to be unjust will best appear if we imagine something of this kind: having given both to the just and the unjust power to do what they will, let us watch and see whither desire will lead them; then we shall discover in the very act the just and unjust man to be proceeding along the same road, following their interest, which all natures deem to

From *The Dialogues of Plato*, Benjamin Jowett, trans. New York: Scribner's, 1889.

be their good, and are only diverted into the path of justice by the force of law. The liberty which we are supposing may be most completely given to them in the form of such a power as is said to have been possessed by Gyges the ancestor of Croesus the Lydian. According to the tradition, Gyges was a shepherd in the service of the king of Lydia; there was a great storm, and an earthquake made an opening in the earth at the place where he was feeding his flock. Amazed at the sight, he descended into the opening, where, among other marvels, he beheld a hollow brazen horse, having doors, at which he stooping and looking in saw a dead body of stature, as appeared to him, more than human, and having nothing on but a gold ring; this he took from the finger of the dead and reascended. Now the shepherds met together, according to custom, that they might send their monthly report about the flocks to the king; into their assembly he came having the ring on his finger, and as he was sitting among them he chanced to turn the collet of the ring inside his hand, when instantly he became invisible to the rest of the company and they began to speak of him as if he were no longer present. He was astonished at this, and again touching the ring he turned the collet outwards and reappeared; he made several trials of the ring, and always with the same result—when he turned the collet inwards he became invisible, when outwards he reappeared. Whereupon he contrived to be chosen one of the messengers who were sent to the court; where as soon as he arrived he seduced the queen, and with her help conspired against the king and slew him, and took the kingdom. Suppose now that there were two such magic rings, and the just put on one of them and the unjust the other; no man can be imagined to be of such an iron nature that he would stand fast in justice. No man would keep his hands off what was not his own when he could safely take what he liked out of the market, or go into houses and lie with any one at his pleasure, or kill or release from prison whom he would, and in all respects be like a God among men. Then the actions of the just would be as the actions of the unjust; they would both come at last to the same point. And

this we may truly affirm to be a great proof that a man is just, not willingly or because he thinks that justice is any good to him individually, but of necessity, for wherever anyone thinks that he can safely be unjust, there he is unjust. For all men believe in their hearts that injustice is far more profitable to the individual than justice, and he who argues as I have been supposing, will say that they are right. If you could imagine any one obtaining this power of becoming invisible, and never doing any wrong or touching what was another's, he would be thought by the lookers-on to be a most wretched idiot, although they would praise him to one another's faces, and keep up appearances with one another from a fear that they too might suffer injustice. Enough of this.

Now, if we are to form a real judgment of the life of the just and unjust, we must isolate them; there is no other way; and how is the isolation to be effected? I answer: Let the unjust man be entirely unjust, and the just man entirely just; nothing is to be taken away from either of them, and both are to be perfectly furnished for the work of their respective lives. First, let the unjust be like other distinguished masters of craft; like the skillful pilot or physician, who knows intuitively his own powers and keeps within their limits, and who, if he fails at any point, is able to recover himself. So let the unjust make his unjust attempts in the right way, and lie hidden if he means to be great in his injustice (he who is found out is nobody): for the highest reach of injustice is: to be deemed just when you are not. Therefore I say that in the perfectly unjust man we must assume the most perfect injustice; there is to be no deduction, but we must allow him, while doing the most unjust acts, to have acquired the greatest reputation for justice. If he have taken a false step he must be able to recover himself, he must be one who can speak with effect, if any of his deeds come to light, and who can force his way where force is required by his courage and strength, and command of money and friends. And at his side let us place the just man in his nobleness and simplicity, wishing, as Aeschylus says, to be and not to seem good. There must be no seeming, for if he seem to be just he will be honoured and rewarded, and then we shall now know whether he is just for the sake of justice or for the sake of honours and rewards; therefore, let him be clothed in justice only, and have no other covering; and he must be imagined in a state of life the opposite of the former. Let him be the best of men, and let him be thought the worst; then he will have been put to the proof and we shall see whether he will be affected by the fear of infamy and its consequences. And let him continue thus to the hour of death; being just and seeming to be unjust. When both have reached the uttermost extreme, the one of justice and the other of injustice, let judgment be given which of them is the happier of the two.

Socrates: Heavens! my dear Glaucon, I said, how energetically you polish them up for the decision, first one and then the other, as if they were two statues.

Glaucon: I do my best, he said. And now that we know what they are like there is no difficulty in tracing out the sort of life which awaits either of them. This I will proceed to describe; but as you may think the description a little too coarse, I ask you to suppose, Socrates, that the words which follow are not mine.—Let me put them into the mouths of the eulogists of injustice: they will tell you that the just man who is thought unjust will be scourged, racked, bound—will have his eyes burnt out; and, at last, after suffering every kind of evil, he will be impaled: Then he will understand that he ought to seem only, and not to be, just; the words of Aeschylus may be more truly spoken of the unjust than of the just. For the unjust is pursuing a reality; he does not live with a view to appearances—he wants to be really unjust and not to seem only:—

> His mind has a soil deep and fertile.
> Out of which spring his prudent counsels.

In the first place, he is thought just, and therefore bears rule in the city; he can marry whom he will, and give in marriage to whom he will; also he can trade and deal where he likes, and always to his own advantage, because he has no

misgivings about injustice; and at every contest, whether in public, or private, he gets the better of his antagonists, and gains at their expense, and is rich, and out of his gains he can benefit his friends, and harm his enemies; moreover, he can offer sacrifices, and dedicate gifts to the gods abundantly and magnificently, and can honour the gods or any man whom he wants to honour in a far better style than the just, and therefore he is likely to be dearer than they are to the gods. And thus, Socrates, gods and men are said to unite in making the life of the unjust better than the life of the just…

Socrates: Now that we've gotten this far, I said, let's go back to that statement made at the beginning, which brought us here: that it pays for a man to be perfectly unjust if he appears to be just. Isn't that what someone said?

Yes.

Then since we've agreed what power justice and injustice each have, let's have a discussion with him.

How?

By molding in words an image of the soul, so that the one who said that will realize what he was saying.

What kind of image?

Oh, something like those natures the myths tell us were born in ancient times—the Chimaera, Scylla, Cerberus, and others in which many different shapes were supposed to have grown into one.

So they tell us, he said.

Then mold one figure of a colorful, many-headed beast with heads of wild and tame animals growing in a circle all around it; one that can change and grow all of them out of itself.

That's a job for a skilled artist. Still, words mold easier than wax or clay, so consider it done.

223

And another of a lion, and one of a man. Make the first by far the biggest, the second second largest.

That's easier, and already done.

Now join the three together so that they somehow grow.

All right.

Next mold the image of one, the man, around them all, so that to someone who can't see what's inside but looks only at the container it appears to be a single animal, man.

I have.

Then shall we inform the gentleman that when he says it pays for this man to be unjust, he's saying that it profits him to feast his multifarious beast and his lion and make them grow strong, but to starve and enfeeble the man in him so that he gets dragged wherever the animals lead him, and instead of making them friends and used to each other, to let them bite and fight and eat each other?

That's just what he's saying by praising injustice.

The one who says justice pays, however, would be saying that he should practice and say whatever will give the most mastery to his inner man, who should care for the many-headed beast like a farmer, raising and domesticating its tame heads and preventing the wild ones from growing, making the lion's nature his partner and ally, and so raise them both to be friends to each other and to him.

That's exactly what he means by praising justice.

So in every way the commender of justice is telling the truth, the other a lie. Whether we examine pleasure, reputation, or profit, we find that the man who praises justice speaks truly, and one who disparages it disparages sickly and knows nothing of what he disparages.

I don't think he does at all.

Then let's gently persuade him—his error wasn't intended—by asking him a question: "Shouldn't we say that the traditions of the beautiful and the ugly have come about like this: Beautiful things are those that make our bestial parts subservient to the human—or rather, perhaps, to the divine—part of our nature, while ugly ones are those that enslave the tame to the wild?" Won't he agree?

If he takes my advice.

On this argument then, can it pay for a man to take money unjustly if that means making his best part a slave to the worst? If it wouldn't profit a man to sell his son or his daughter into slavery—to wild and evil men at that—even if he got a fortune for it, then if he has no pity on himself and enslaves the most godlike thing in him to the most godless and polluted, isn't he a wretch who gets bribed for gold into a destruction more horrible than Euriphyle's, who sold her husband's life for a necklace?

Much more horrible, said Glaucon,

…everyone is better off being ruled by the godlike and intelligent; preferably if he has it inside, but if not, it should be imposed on him from without so that we may all be friends and as nearly alike as possible, all steered by the same thing.

Yes, and we're right, he said.

Law, the ally of everyone in the city, clearly intends the same thing, as does the rule of children, which forbids us to let them be free until we've instituted a regime in them as in a city. We serve their best part with a similar part in us, install a like guardian and ruler in them, and only then set them free.

Clearly.

Then how, by what argument, Glaucon, can we say that it pays for a man to be unjust or self-indulgent or to do something shameful to get more money or power if by doing so he makes himself worse?

We can't, he said.

And how can it pay to commit injustice without getting caught and being punished? Doesn't getting away with it make a man even worse? Whereas if a man gets caught and punished, his beastlike part is taken in and tamed, his tame part is set free, and his whole soul acquires justice and temperance and knowledge. Therefore his soul recovers its best nature and attains a state more honorable than the state the body attains when it acquires health and strength and beauty, by as much as the soul is more honorable than the body.

Absolutely.

Then won't a sensible man spend his life directing all his efforts to this end?

Study Questions

1. *Psychological egoism* is a view about how people actually do behave. It is the view that all people always act self-interestedly and sometimes selfishly, at least in all of their voluntary, deliberate behavior. On this view, even when people act in a way apparently calculated to benefit others, they are actually motivated by the desire to benefit themselves. *Ethical egoism*, by contrast, is a view about how people ought to act. It is the view that people have no obligation to behave in any way that is not in their own self-interest, regardless of the effect of their behavior on others. Is Glaucon a psychological egoist? An ethical egoist?

2. Critically discuss the warrant of both psychological egoism and ethical egoism.

3. Is there something incoherent in asking, "Why be moral?", since morality is concerned with guiding us in how we ought to be (e.g., ought I to do what I ought to do)?

4. Which question does Plato answer: "Why ought I live a moral life?" or "Why ought I be moral on this occasion?" Does Plato's defense cover both questions?

Albert Camus

The Myth of Sisyphus

Albert Camus (1913–1960) was born in Algeria. Early in life he was involved in intellectual circles with revolutionary designs. He had a deep interest in philosophy coming to France at the age of twenty-five. With Europe falling into war, Camus joined the resistance movement. After the war, he was a columnist for the newspaper *Combat*. By 1947, Camus turned his attention to writing his fiction and essays, along with becoming actively involved in live theatre as producer and playwright. He produced *Caligula* and adapted plays by Calderon, Lope de Vega, Dino Buzzati, and Faulkner's *Requiem for a Nun*.

The Myth of Sisyphus articulates Camus' notion of the absurd and its acceptance of "the total absence of hope, which has nothing to do with despair, a continual refusal, which must not be confused with renouncement—and a conscious dissatisfaction... Happiness and the absurd are two sons of the same earth." Camus writes that Sisyphus, the absurd hero, "teaches the higher fidelity that negates the gods and raises rocks. He (Sisyphus), too, concludes that all is well." Camus wrote purely, austerely, with a low-burn of intensity and a penetrating insight into human existence as he knew it at his time.

All great deeds and all great thoughts have a ridiculous beginning. Great works are often born on a streetcorner or in a restaurant's revolving door. So it is with absurdity. The absurd world more than others derives its nobility from that abject birth. In certain situations, replying "nothing" when asked what one is thinking about may be pretense in a man. Those who are loved are well aware of this. But if that reply is sincere, if it symbolizes that odd state of soul in which the void becomes eloquent, in which the chain of daily gestures is broken, in which the heart vainly seeks the link that will connect it again, then it is as it were the first sign of absurdity.

It happens that the stage sets collapse. Rising, streetcar, four hours in the office or the factory, meal, streetcar, four hours of work, meal, sleep, and Monday Tuesday Wednesday Thursday Friday and Saturday according to the same rhythm—this path is easily followed most of the time. But one day the "why" arises and everything begins in that weariness tinged with amazement. "Begins"—this is important. Weariness comes at the end of the acts of a mechanical life, but at the same time it inaugurates the impulse of consciousness. It awakens consciousness and provokes what follows. What follows is the gradual return into the chain or it is the definitive awakening....

Likewise and during every day of an unillustrious life, time carries us. But a moment always comes when we have to carry it. We live on the future: "tomorrow," "later on," "when you have made

---

your way," "you will understand when you are old enough." Such irrelevancies are wonderful, for, after all, it's a matter of dying. Yet a day comes when a man notices or says that he is thirty. Thus he asserts his youth. But simultaneously he situates himself in relation to time. He takes his place in it. He admits that he stands at a certain point on a curve that he acknowledges having to travel to its end. He belongs to time, and by the horror that seizes him, he recognizes his worst enemy. Tomorrow, he was longing for tomorrow, whereas everything in him ought to reject it. That revolt of the flesh is the absurd.

A step lower and strangeness creeps in: perceiving that the world is "dense," sensing to what a degree a stone is foreign and irreducible to us, with what intensity nature or a landscape can negate us. At the heart of all beauty lies something inhuman, and these hills, the softness of the sky, the outline of these trees at this very minute lose the illusory meaning with which we had clothed them, henceforth more remote than a lost paradise. The primitive hostility of the world rises up to face us across millennia. For a second we cease to understand it because for centuries we have understood in it solely the images and designs that we had attributed to it beforehand, because henceforth we lack the power to make use of that artifice. The world evades us because it becomes itself again. That stage scenery masked by habit becomes again what it is. It withdraws at a distance from us. Just as there are days when under the familiar face of a woman, we see as a stranger her we have loved months or years ago, perhaps we shall come even to desire what suddenly leaves us so alone. But the time has not yet come. Just one thing: that denseness and that strangeness of the world is the absurd.

Men, too, secrete the inhuman. At certain moments of lucidity, the mechanical aspect of their gestures, their meaningless pantomime makes silly everything that surrounds them. A man is talking on the telephone behind a glass partition; you cannot hear him, but you see his incomprehensible dumb show: you wonder why

he is alive. This discomfort in the face of man's own inhumanity, this incalculable tumble before the image of what we are, this "nausea," as a writer of today calls it, is also the absurd. Likewise the stranger who at certain seconds comes to meet us in a mirror, the familiar and yet alarming brother we encounter in our own photographs is also the absurd....

Let us insist again on the method: it is a matter of persisting. At a certain point on his path the absurd man is tempted. History is not lacking in either religions or prophets, even without gods. He is asked to leap. All he can reply is that he doesn't fully understand, that it is not obvious. Indeed, he does not want to do anything but what he fully understands. He is assured that this is the sin of pride, but he does not understand the notion of sin; that perhaps hell is in store, but he has not enough imagination to visualize that strange future; that he is losing immortal life, but that seems to him an idle consideration. An attempt is made to get him to admit his guilt. He feels innocent. To tell the truth, that is all he feels—his irreparable innocence. This is what allows him everything. Hence, what he demands of himself is to live *solely* with what he knows, to accommodate himself to what is, and to bring in nothing that is not certain. He is told that nothing is. But this at least is a certainty. And it is with this that he is concerned: he wants to find out if it is possible to live *without* appeal.

The Myth of Sisyphus

The gods had condemned Sisyphus to ceaselessly rolling a rock to the top of a mountain, whence the stone would fall back of its own weight. They had thought with some reason that there is no more dreadful punishment than futile and hopeless labor.

If one believes Homer, Sisyphus was the wisest and most prudent of mortals. According to another tradition, however, he was disposed to practice the profession of highwayman. I see no contradiction in this. Opinions differ as to the reasons why he became the futile laborer of the underworld. To begin with, he is accused of a certain levity in regard to the gods. He stole their secrets. Ægina, the daughter of Æsopus, was carried off by Jupiter. The father was shocked by that disappearance and complained to Sisyphus. He, who knew of the abduction, offered to tell about it on condition that Æsopus would give water to the citadel of Corinth. To the celestial thunderbolts he preferred the benediction of water. He was punished for this in the underworld. Homer tells us also that Sisyphus had put Death in chains. Pluto could not endure the sight of his deserted, silent empire. He dispatched the god of war, who liberated Death from the hands of her conqueror.

It is said also that Sisyphus, being near to death, rashly wanted to test his wife's love. He ordered her to cast his unburied body into the middle of the public square. Sisyphus woke up in the underworld. And there, annoyed by an obedience so contrary to human love, he obtained from Pluto permission to return to earth in order to chastise his wife. But when he had seen again the face of this world, enjoyed water and sun, warm stones and the sea, he no longer wanted to go back to the infernal darkness. Recalls, signs of anger, warnings were of no avail. Many years more he lived facing the curve of the gulf, the sparkling sea, and the smiles of earth. A decree of the gods was necessary. Mercury came and seized the impudent man by the collar and, snatching him from his joys, led him forcibly back to the underworld, where his rock was ready for him.

You have already grasped that Sisyphus is the absurd hero. He *is*, as much through his passions as through his torture. His scorn of the gods, his hatred of death, and his passion for life won him that unspeakable penalty in which the whole being is exerted toward accomplishing nothing. This is the price that must be paid for the passions of this earth. Nothing is told us about Sisyphus in the underworld. Myths are made for the imagination to breathe life into them. As for this myth, one sees merely the whole effort of a body straining to raise the huge stone, to roll it and push it up a slope a hundred times over; one

sees the face screwed up, the cheek tight against the stone, the shoulder bracing the clay-covered mass, the foot wedging it, the fresh start with arms outstretched, the wholly human security of two earth-clotted hands. At the very end of his long effort measured by skyless space and time without depth, the purpose is achieved. Then Sisyphus watches the stone rush down in a few moments toward that lower world whence he will have to push it up again toward the summit. He goes back down to the plain.

It is during that return, that pause, that Sisyphus interests me. A face that toils so close to stones is already stone itself! I see that man going back down with a heavy yet measured step toward the torment of which he will never know the end. That hour like a breathing-space which returns as surely as his suffering, that is the hour of consciousness. At each of those moments when he leaves the heights and gradually sinks toward the lairs of the gods, he is superior to his fate. He is stronger than his rock.

If this myth is tragic, that is because its hero is conscious. Where would his torture be, indeed, if at every step the hope of succeeding upheld him? The workman of today works every day in his life at the same tasks, and this fate is no less absurd. But it is tragic only at the rare moments when it becomes conscious. Sisyphus, proletarian of the gods, powerless and rebellious, knows the whole extent of his wretched condition: it is what he thinks of during his descent. The lucidity that was to constitute his torture at the same time crowns his victory. There is no fate that cannot be surmounted by scorn....

If the descent is thus sometimes performed in sorrow, it can also take place in joy. This word is not too much. Again I fancy Sisyphus returning toward his rock, and the sorrow was in the beginning. When the images of earth cling too tightly to memory, when the call of happiness becomes too insistent, it happens that melancholy rises in man's heart: this is the rock's victory, this is the rock itself. The boundless grief is too heavy to bear. These are our nights of Gethsemane. But crushing truths perish from being acknowledged. Thus, Œdipus at the outset obeys fate without knowing it. But from the moment he knows, his tragedy begins. Yet at the same moment, blind and desperate, he realizes that the only bond linking him to the world is the cool hand of a girl. Then a tremendous remark rings out: "Despite so many ordeals, my advanced age and the nobility of my soul make me conclude that all is well." Sophocles' Œdipus, like Dostoevsky's Kirilov, thus gives the recipe for the absurd victory. Ancient wisdom confirms modern heroism.

One does not discover the absurd without being tempted to write a manual of happiness. "What! by such narrow ways—?" There is but one world, however. Happiness and the absurd are two sons of the same earth. They are inseparable. It would be a mistake to say that happiness necessarily springs from the absurd discovery. It happens as well that the feeling of the absurd springs from happiness. "I conclude that all is well," says Œdipus, and that remark is sacred. It echoes in the wild and limited universe of man. It teaches that all is not, has not been, exhausted. It drives out of this world a god who had come into it with dissatisfaction and a preference for futile sufferings. It makes of fate a human matter, which must be settled among men.

All Sisyphus' silent joy is contained therein. His fate belongs to him. His rock is his thing. Likewise, the absurd man, when he contemplates his torment, silences all the idols. In the universe suddenly restored to its silence, the myriad wondering little voices of the earth rise up. Unconscious, secret calls, invitations from all the faces, they are the necessary reverse and price of victory. There is no sun without shadow, and it is essential to know the night. The absurd man says yes and his effort will henceforth be unceasing. If there is a personal fate, there is no higher destiny, or at least there is but one which he concludes is inevitable and despicable. For the rest, he knows himself to be the master of his days. At that subtle moment when man glances backward over his life, Sisyphus returning toward his rock, in that slight pivoting he contemplates that series of unrelated actions which becomes his fate, created by him, combined under his memory's eye and soon sealed by his death. Thus, convinced of the wholly human origin of all that is human, a blind man eager to see who knows that the night has no end, he is still on the go. The rock is still rolling.

I leave Sisyphus at the foot of the mountain! One always finds one's burden again. But Sisyphus teaches the higher fidelity that negates the gods and raises rocks. He too concludes that all is well. This universe henceforth without a master seems to him neither sterile nor futile. Each atom of that stone, each mineral flake of that night-filled mountain, in itself forms a world. The struggle itself toward the heights is enough to fill a man's heart. One must imagine Sisyphus happy.

Study Questions

1. What is absurdity? Should one seek out such an "awakening," according to Camus?

2. What is it to "secrete the inhuman"?

3. Why is Sisyphus the absurd hero?

4. How can happiness and the absurd be two sons of the same earth?

5. How does ancient wisdom confirm modern heroism, according to Camus?

6. In what sense are we like Sisyphus?

7. Why, according to Camus, must we imagine Sisyphus happy? Do you agree? Why?

APPENDIX

Syllabus

Grades

Your grade will finally be determined by the total accumulation of points according to the following scale: A: at least ~~612~~ 590 points (total possible, at least ~~720~~ 695 points). B: between 611 and 540. C: between 539 and 432. D: between 431 and 360. Less than 360, oops!

A 695-590
B 590-521
C 521-417
D 417-347

Sources of Points

Exams: Up to 100 points per exam with a total of three (3) exams. Approximately one exam every five weeks. **Quizzes:** Twelve quizzes worth up to fifteen points each. *No make-ups on missed quizzes.* **Papers:** One critical analysis paper, 5–7 pages in length worth up to 100 points. **Conferences:** A conference is a tutorial with at least one of our class tutors. Each conference must last at least twenty minutes and involve for that period of time a discussion over some relevant philosophical issue. Up to four conferences worth ~~five~~ 10 points per conference. No conferences will be held the last week of classes. **Notes:** One point for three pages of neat, organized notes in your notebook. This credit will include notes from each of the three sections of your notebook: Class notes, Reading notes and Reflections (these will be explained in class). Notes are worth up to thirty points. **Class Attendance:** One and a half points per class. (These *points are for an entire class meeting* and not partial attendance. The expectation is that you will attend a class in its entirety, dah! If you cannot attend for the entire class period, then, unless you've discussed it with me, DO NOT ATTEND! *It is distracting and rude to walk into a class after it has started or to get up and leave prior to its conclusion.*) **Extra Credit:** Some extra credit points may be available. Details will be announced later but don't count on this option. It is EXTRA credit.

It is your option to select from any or all of the Sources of Points to determine what final grade you wish to achieve. Remember, **all of the above-listed activities involving points are part of the total amount available**.

Final Exam Schedule

Please consult the Schedule of Classes or the SBCC website for details on the finals schedule. It is *your responsibility* to find out when your final is being given. **NO EARLY FINALS**—YOU NOW HAVE FOUR MONTHS TO PLAN APPROPRIATELY. Please inform your family and friends of your commitment.

My Final Exam is scheduled for: _____.

Tools for Class

(You should have by our second class meeting.)

- One copy of the textbook.
- One notebook with three (3) distinct sections.
- At least two pens of different colors and one #2 leaded pencil.
- One packet of mini-scantron (quiz) sheets.
- One packet of long scantron sheets.
- One two-pocket folder, if you are submitting the critical analysis paper.

Where to Find Me

Office: IDC 354

Phone: 965-0581 #2476

Office Hours: M-T-W-Th 3:00–4:00, and Fri. by appointment.

We shall not cease from exploration and the end of all of our exploring will be to arrive where we started and know that place for the first time.

—T.S. Eliot

Paper Writing Topics

You may choose to critique one of the two topics that will be handed out within the first three weeks of the semester. You will then have approximately four weeks to write your paper. If Introduction to Philosophy sections remain large, that is, 350+ students, then it will take approximately five weeks to finish grading all papers once they are handed in.

Assignment: Writing a Critical Analysis Paper. Your paper should be five (5) to seven (7) pages in length, though if necessary, you may exceed this limit by a few pages. Your paper must be typed, double-spaced with appropriate margins, etc. Please proofread your paper, spell check, grammar check, etc. Read your paper aloud to yourself during the various drafts. If it does not make sense to you, I assure you, it will not make sense to me.

When writing a critical analysis paper of a film, book, play, article, etc., be sure you understand, as clearly and completely as you are able, the author's thesis(es) or theme(s). For example, why did the author title his or her work as he or she did? What support, evidence, arguments did the author bring forth to persuade you of the truth of his or her position(s)? Were you persuaded by these reasons? If not, why not? If so, were there other considerations that the author overlooked? Could you have provided a better, stronger defense of the position? In short, what is the truth regarding this particular issue? If the truth cannot be known, then give a clear account as to why, in this particular case, the truth is so elusive or simply cannot be known. In short, be as clear, articulate, succinct and persuasive as your abilities and talents allow at this point in your life.

Remember, in the world of philosophy, no special laboratories, on-site excavations, Cray computers, field trips, Hubbel telescopes, electron microscopes or particle accelerators, etc., are required. From Plato to Russell and Quine, a philosopher has only needed something to write with and something to write upon. Then, if you have the courage, the discipline, the stamina and some talent, you can attempt to persuade the rest of civilization as to what the Truth is. Audaciously, you might ride the wave of critical self-consciousness into the great abyss of history.

Check your own schedule and commitments, then work out a viable timeline to complete your work in a manner such that it genuinely reflects your very best effort. Please allow for computer glitches, unreliable roommates, etc., as NO LATE PAPERS CAN OR WILL BE ACCEPTED. I suggest the following process:

Step 1: Read over the paper to be analyzed, and make notes and an outline of that paper to better understand the author's claims. Spend some time thinking about why the paper has its title and how the author supports his or her claims.

Step 2: Make notes and an outline of your position(s) regarding the author's claims, critique your own claims as rigorously as you did the author's in the previous step, and test your understanding of the author's thesis and your own philosophical views on your classmates or your roommates (if they are still talking to you).

Step 3: Compose the first draft of your paper. Read it aloud to yourself, go over it with our tutors, fellow students, friends, to discover where it is unclear, ambiguous, silly, ridiculous, sophomoric etc. then make your inevitable changes. Academic papers are never simply written—they are always rewritten.

Step 4: Begin to refine this, your second draft, getting input again from friends or from our class tutors, then put together your third and final draft.

Step 5: Turn in your final draft along with your working drafts. Staple each of your drafts together but not to each other. Place all drafts in a two-pocket folder with the final draft in the right-hand pocket. Be sure your name, class time and day appear on the outside front cover of your folder. **ALWAYS KEEP A COPY OF YOUR PAPER!**

Papers will be graded (1) on content and (2) quality of presentation. Content will determine your letter grade with content being a reflection of thoroughness in presentation and critical analysis. (How well you were able to understand, present and analyze the author's primary and secondary theses.) Quality of presentation will determine a plus or minus grade and will be essentially a reflection of how free your work is of typos, spelling errors, grammatical mistakes, etc. Since many of you are now young adults gaining a higher education, you will be expected to present work of an adult, professional quality in terms of presentation. Content will be graded reflecting the fact that this is for most of you your maiden voyage in philosophy. Time is a crucial variable and very limited, precious natural resource. Do not squander it!

Your first Critical Analysis paper due dates will be announced in class. Please note those announced dates so we do not have confusion on this.

Announced due date for the first paper is _____.

The limits of my language are the limits of my world.

—L. Wittgenstein, *The Tractatus: 5.6*

On the Nature of a Grade and Class Performance

If you have started to ponder what an A, B, C or D class performance is, with its often, though not always, ensuing corresponding grade, let me offer you the following criteria. I assume we all know what an F is and if not, it should become apparent given the following. These remarks are not peculiar to philosophy classes but education in general.

A: An A is for an excellent semester of work. An excellent record of work will reflect having mastered at least eighty-five percent of the course material in this course. That mastery is variously reflected through one's performance in the many activities outlined in the Sources of Points section. Specific guidelines for an excellent semester would include having read all of the course material and studied it. A student who studies course material typically reads the material more than once, takes complete notes while reading the material, and then studies and organizes those notes by also integrating their reading notes with their clean, complete lecture notes. An excellent record has no class absences nor late attendance. Obviously people get sick, sometimes very sick, but these constitute cases of legitimate excuse. On the other hand, someone who unfortunately comes down with a series of illnesses during a semester, while perhaps a bright, earnest student, will in all likelihood not be able to do excellent work and thus should not realistically anticipate, given prolonged or recurrent illness, an A-level grade. That person's performance, through no fault of her or his own, will probably not be excellent. By the semester's end, the A student will typically have approximately 170 pages of notes, will have taken all of the exams, having both studied and performed excellently on those exams along with having written excellent papers after having conscientiously followed the writing process described herein.

B: B is for a good semester of work. A good record will reflect having mastered at least seventy-five percent of the course material in this philosophy class as reflected through one's performance in the many activities outlined in the Sources of Points section. Some specific guidelines regarding what a good semester's performance is would include having read all of the course material and studying most of that material. Reading notes are taken and often organized and integrated with their good, complete lecture notes. A student who desires to do good work may miss two, possibly even three, classes during the entire semester because of illness, urgent family matters, or the like. By semester's end, a good effort will typically reflect a notebook with approximately 140–150 pages of clean, organized notes, will have taken all of the exams, having performed well on those exams. A good effort on papers would include at least one draft before the final draft. Remember, a student may put in an excellent level of effort but receive a B. There is a crucial distinction between effort, work actually turned out, and grade (reward)—welcome to adulthood. However, performance and grade are, remember, significantly correlated though not rigidly correlated.

C: C is for a satisfactory, an okay, semester of work. A C record will reflect having mastered at least sixty-three percent of the course material in this class as will be reflected in one's performance in the many activities outlined in the Sources of Points section. Some specific guidelines regarding what a satisfactory semester's performance is would include having read much, or most, of the course material at least once and studying most of that material. Most often notes are taken while reading but an okay effort will prefer to only highlight. "It's easier," or "What do I need to get by?" These are the mantras of the okay or satisfactory performer, the Floater. Some notes are organized and integrated with lecture notes but even lecture notes are not that organized nor complete. An okay performance may involve missing three, possibly four classes, during the semester because of illness or family matters or a really, really good friend was visiting or "man, I just needed a break, ya' know." By semester's end, an okay performance will typically have accumulated 100 or so pages of notes, will have taken all of the exams, having performed on average for those exams. Grades on papers were satisfactory but many times only one draft was written. Again, remember the distinction between effort and end result. While there is a significant correlation in much of what we do and its end result, sometime we're just lucky. We can do very little and gain a lot. Ten dollars wins you ten million in the lottery. However, don't count on Lady Luck! She is whimsical and fickle!

D: D is for a poor, less than satisfactory, semester of work. A D record will reflect having mastered only, or at least, fifty-three percent of the course material in this class as reflected in one's performance in the many activities outlined in the Sources of Points section. Some specific guidelines regarding what a poor semester's performance is would include taking some class notes, mostly scribbled, no reading notes, reading other material in class, not preparing for class but simply showing up. Class information is treated like watching the weather on television. Your thoughts wander and the information is taken in only to be stored in short-term memory before it is lost forever. There is no attempt at integration of learning and your life nor in becoming an educated person. Classes have little effect upon this person's life. You get the idea by now.

> *The comfort felt in or from some belief must be distinguished from the truth of the belief. Logic must be distinguished from psychology.*
>
> —Bertrand Russell

Classroom Etiquette

As many of you have discovered in our ever-expanding multicultural society, the behavioral guidelines which allow us, in the midst of all of this diversity, to function effectively as a group have not been learned by some and seemingly forgotten by others. Since our primary goal is learning, the following behavioral guidelines are provided so as to enhance our functioning effectively together in such a large, heterogeneous educational community.

1. Each of your classes has a specific time that it starts or begins. DO YOU KNOW WHAT THAT TIME IS? The concepts of start and begin are intimately related to the concept of attendance. This relationship is such that when class starts or begins, you are to be in attendance. START = ATTENDANCE. If for a moment you will reflect upon your history of behavior and if what you discover is that you are on average seven or more minutes late for a class, please do not enroll in this class. If you have an overriding excuse for being late on one occasion, e.g., saved a life, stopped a brush fire, etc., then enter the classroom from the rear, not the front, and do so quietly and discreetly.

2. **Do not** bring food or soft drinks, juice, etc., to class. Water is acceptable. Classes are not lounges or clubs.

3. Be involved in discussions and active listening during class. This does not mean you must speak but it does mean you must be attentive, alert, aware and focused upon the class and the topic being discussed IN CLASS. If, once a class starts, you decide to chat with your friend about something the class is not discussing at that time, then you've breached the guidelines and you are acting rude and inconsiderate. As we shall discover, such rude and inconsiderate behavior serves as a nice example of selfishness which can be used during class for purposes of illustration.

4. The following are categorically **WRONG** things to do in class:

   a. **DO NOT SLEEP IN CLASS.** Not only is it rude but it shows that you've not been able to successfully plan your life as you are obviously doing something you seem to need in the wrong place. While I do not condone the shaving of eyebrows or the painting of designs with indelible markers on the faces of sleeping students, I have heard that it occurs. Get your life organized so that you sleep during sleep time not class time. If you are having a difficult time getting this or other bodily needs satisfied at appropriate times, please see our very good counseling staff in the Student Services Building.

   b. **DO NOT READ NEWSPAPERS, MAGAZINES or other TEXTBOOKS during class.** This is so crass and rude, I am pretty sure none of you would do such a thing.

   c. **DO NOT LEAVE THE CLASSROOM DURING AN EXAM OR CLASS.** Needing to go to the toilet or blow your nose is no excuse for leaving a classroom during an exam or class. You are not a child, bird or other lower life form such that you cannot control your bladder or bowels for the duration of a class. Once an exam starts, you must sit the entire exam. If you must leave, then you leave the exam and cannot return to finish.

   d. **ZERO TOLERANCE for cheating.** Those suspected of or found cheating will be confronted immediately. SBCC rules regarding cheating are followed and if you have any questions regarding the institutional procedures, please consult your student handbook. You really don't want to be expelled from SBCC. Please do not cheat. If you are a compulsive cheater that is a thief or liar or both, please see one of our mental health counselors as they can work effectively with such antisocial personality disorders.

5. Taking a class, as a college student, is similar to having a job. In both you can be fired for absence, tardiness, and a generally unsatisfactory performance which includes not only what you actually do on the job but the attitude you bring to the class/job. An excellent, positive, creative, supportive attitude and performance will in all likelihood bring an excellent grade. More than five unexcused absences and you may be dropped from this course.